THROUGH HER EYES

THROUGH HER EYES

MAHEEN MAZHAR

atmosphere press

Published by Atmosphere Press

Cover design by Zain Naqvi

atmospherepress.com

To my parents.

Dear Mom and Dad,

Thank you for being the air beneath my wings,
pushing me to fly higher.

Love, your Mahu

CHAPTER ONE

June 15th, 1997, the month in which Lahore became hotter than hell and the time of the year where load shedding was always at its peak: the government shut out electricity every three to five hours as an effort to conserve electricity, as certain areas in the country had a very limited water supply. Thank God that hospitals had generators that ran twenty-four-seven, or else God knows what would happen to the patients. The red brick hospital building was humongous, with black gates on each side. It was a private hospital complex, located within the residential suburb of Garden Town. The front side of the hospital building faced the highway while the backside of the hospital blended in with privately owned houses. Although Dr. Bokhari technically wasn't allowed to create three privately owned hospital buildings in the middle of an entirely residential area, money and power spoke louder than law and order in Pakistan. A piece of paper with Mohammad Ali Jinnah's face *the man who created Pakistan* spoke louder than everything in this country. One could quickly get away with anything if one had money. Laws for rich differed vastly from laws for the poor and underprivileged.

I sat there on the old rusty wooden bench and turned my gaze up; staring at the rectangular-shaped portrait of a newborn baby sleeping with his eyes closed, gently resting his hands by his face on a pillow; then at the awards and certifications of Dr. Bokhari's that were hung on the white wall in front of me. Dr. Bokhari's accomplishments were caged in identical-looking black wooden frames. One recognition after another. The number of breakthroughs Dr. Bokhari had made in the field of gynecology were never-ending. Dr. Bokhari was among the top three gynecologists in all of Pakistan and the first doctor in the entire country to establish an IVF center in Pakistan and the first one to successfully deliver a test tube baby in the country. Dr. Bokhari was a professor of gynecology as well the founder of Farid Hammad Hospital and Farid Hammad Medical College, one of the most well-respected medical colleges in the country. Dr. Bokhari also had affiliations with King's College, UK, and King's College Hospital, where he was associated with Assistant Conception Research. Amongst various other accomplishments, Dr. Bokhari happened to be the chairman of the World Congress Academic Session.

The waiting room formed an L right in between the nursery and maternity ward with the nurse's station on my left, separated from the waiting area by a clear glass window. Two nurses in green uniforms and scarves on their heads sat at the desk behind the glass window, while the other nurses walked back and forth from between the nurse's station and the maternity ward. The black leather seats in the middle of the waiting area were joint, placed in rows of three, and against the wall were wooden benches entirely occupied by my relatives. I looked at all my family members around me. About half of the waiting room was full of mine and Ahsan's family.

The rest of the room was filled with families of other patients who had come in after us, and some of them had even left before us. People were going in and out of the clear glass doors, screaming names, trying to call each other's relatives from a distance. Men and women, as well as parents all, dressed up. Women in bright-colored Shalwar kameez (traditional outfit) with smiles across their faces; some wore scarves on their heads while others wore scarves around their necks. Men wore kurtas (long shirts) or just T's and pants as they sat around, chatting, laughing, while others eagerly waited. Children ran around yelling; their parents unbothered by anything, continued talking. The chemist from the third floor kept coming back to hand over medications the nurses ordered every fifteen to twenty minutes or so. Or at least that's what I had noticed sitting in the room for what felt like forever.

My sister was sitting right across from me with Nishat and Shafqat, her son Farooq chatting with my son Farooq, teasing him on how he's about to become a father. Their names were purely coincidental, my son Farooq was younger, and the other Farooq was older, so we called him "Babu." In front of Babu sat Aamir, Nadeem and Salman all in a straight row talking to each other. On the bench next to mine sat Faiza's younger brother Shahrukh, fiddling his fingers through his hair. To the left of Shahrukh sat his eleven-year-old sister Mano wearing an A-line purple dress, whispering something in Shahrukh's ear. Behind them sat Faiza's cousin Maria staring at aunt Samina and aunt Saima arguing, "It's going to be a boy."

Samina said, "No, it's going to be a girl."

Saima cut her off in the middle. "No, it's going to be a boy," Samina insisted again.

"Stop you guys" Maria interfered in-between. "Girl or boy,

let's just hope everything happens smoothly Inshallah (God willing)." On the right side of me sat Ahayaudin, my best friend and batch-mate from when I was in the army. Ahayaudin and I met while I was training in the Pakistani Military Academy. We were roommates; we both gave our saluting test together. He and I both failed the first time, but I passed the second time and went to Abbottabad on our holidays to take a break from training while Ahaya had to stay back at the academy and wasn't allowed to leave academy premises till passing the saluting test. He failed three times before our platoon commander passed Ahaya.

He kept pushing back his glasses that sat awkwardly on the broader edge of his nose. On the other side sat Ahsan, Faiza's dad and Farooq's father-in-law. Ahsan was a self-made Businessman. He had two carpet factories that ran under the name of Bisco Carpets and two garment factories in the region of Punjab. One of his garment factories was exclusively for international imports; it imported clothes to US-based brands like JC Penney's and Sears. I had only visited one of his textiles factories, which was near the city of Multan, about a five-hour drive from the city of Lahore. In front of Ahsan sat Javed; another friend of mine and batchmate from the army. I left the army as Major Mir Mazhar Qayyum about ten years ago and then joined the police force. While in the army, my family and I moved from city-to-city countless times because my postings as an officer kept changing. Other times I used to be away for long periods because of war. In the days when my children were young, Nishat used to easily handle everything while I used to be away. However, as our children got older, she wanted us to settle down and have a stable life like a typical family. So, I joined the police and made my way up to the DIG level (Deputy Inspector General).

The table in front of me was packed with gifts and giant baskets of all kinds of sweets wrapped up in shiny bright yellow plastic wraps and closed with a bow shaped ribbon around it. On one side of the table were red and gold boxes of "mithai" (Traditional sweets) and on the other side of the table were two giant wooden baskets of chocolate truffles that Faiza's elder brother Tariq had brought from Dubai. The ambiance of the fresh flowers took over the strong smell of antiseptics. Thank God for that, or else when we had just arrived, the hospital smelled like rotten bodies. The white tile floors were regularly wiped and sparkled. The furniture was clean. There were two ladies dressed in a simple all grey shalwar kameez who regularly came back every hour and wiped off the floor with a brittle mop.

The nurses on duty were the same as when we had come in late last night. By now they had recognized each one of my family members because of the number of times each one of us had gone up to them to ask about Faiza's progress. Yet the answer was always "Nothing yet, only the doctor can tell you." Yet Dr. Bokhari was nowhere to be seen. Ahsan sat alongside me the entire night. We discussed baby names, politics, cricket, and business while sipping chai and eating biscuits to keep us awake. Meanwhile, Shahrukh and Aamir fell asleep, but Farooq restlessly walked from one corner of the room to the other. He would come to sit down for a few minutes, chat with Salman and start walking again. We were all praying under our breath for everything to happen successfully.

Farooq and Salman already had names in mind planned out for a baby girl. Salman had even bought baby name books, and he kept himself busy reading them as all of us waited all night. We were all hoping for a girl, but when it came to names our choices didn't match. Salman had something else in mind, while I had something else in my mind, and Farooq had something else in his mind. We wouldn't love a boy any less, but Nishat and I were desperately hoping for a girl. In a country where most of the population prays to have a boy as their firstborn or first grandkid, I wanted my first grandchild to be a girl. I always wanted a girl in the family. Nishat and I had hoped for one every time, but God had something else in mind. We had four boys, Nadeem being the eldest, then Farooq, Salman and last but not the least, Aamir. Out of the four, Farooq was the first one to get married just last year. He was only twenty years old and Faiza was eighteen. They had met in college.

This was the beginning of the seventeenth hour of waiting in the hospital room. The tea man was walking back and forth asking people if they wanted anything. I called him over again, "Hey excuse me." He walked towards me. "Can I get another cup of tea please," I asked him kindly. This was my seventh cup of tea of the day, not including the three cups I had last night to keep me awake. Yet still, there was no news. I could sense it, something just didn't feel right. Faiza was already seven days above her original due date on the eighth of June and her labor pains had only started last night. However, they weren't strong enough, so Farooq told me the nurses had induced Faiza with fake pains. The case was being handled by Dr. Rashid Bokhari himself. Being in the police, I had many great connections around the city and had known Dr. Bokhari for many years and trusted him to handle Faiza's case. Dr. Bokhari and I were very well connected with each other. Dr. Bokhari never used to charge me money if I ever had to come to Farid Hamad Hospital for any reason. In return if he ever needed any favor from me, I would be there to help always. In Pakistan, who you know is extremely important because you never know what connection might be useful to you where and how. Dr. Bokhari was somewhat egoistic but nonetheless a very qualified professional and a good acquaintance.

At this point, I was getting anxious. I kept thinking to myself, "Why is it taking so long, it's been so many damn hours. Is it even normal to stay in labor for that long?" Ahaya looked at me as I leaned my head back on the wall behind me, my left foot still relentlessly tapping on the floor and my gaze up in the air. "It's going to be okay, don't stress out so much."

Ahaya's large hands landed on my shoulders. "Why has it been so long? I am telling you there's something not right." I looked at him as he tried calming me down again.

"It's ok, you are just overthinking it. Sometimes in such situations it takes a bit longer. Don't panic." He put his hand on my shoulder again, and I shrugged his hand off. "God is there, just don't stress. He won't let anything bad happen," Ahaya tried assuring me again. With my voice raised at him, "No. I am telling you, something is not right." I thundered.

Ahaya and I have argued several times, but never had I ever spoken to him in the manner I did in the spur of the moment. My voice was so loud that everyone in the room suddenly became silent and started looking at Ahaya and I. I ignored them and continued. "Look at that family over there," I said pointing, straight in front of me towards the white door that was completely open. There stood a man with whitish-grey hair and glasses holding his newly born grandson whose cries echoed in the entire waiting area. Alongside the man stood his wife adoring the tiny hands and feet of the baby as they wrapped him in a blue blanket. The son brought his wife out of the room in a wheelchair. They looked like they were almost about to leave until the grandpa decided that he wanted to cut the giant cake one of their relatives had brought. "They came in after us," I said.

"Relax, it's going to be okay Mazhar," I heard my sister's voice in the distance.

Nishat got up and went over towards the double doors of the maternity ward to stand next to Shafqat. Another woman was standing there near the doors of the ward in a pink shalwar suit with silver sequins on it. Her daughter in law was also inside waiting to give birth. The woman walked towards Nishat and started talking to her. "Is your daughter having a kid? " the lady asked. "No, my son is having a kid. My daughter-in-law has been in labor for a while now," Nishat answered. The lady nodded her head. "*Mashalla*h (Praise is to god), so since it's your first grandchild. You must want a grandson, right?" she asked.

"No, actually I want a granddaughter," Nishat said to her.

The expression on the lady's face began to change.

"You really want a granddaughter? Wouldn't you prefer having a grandson first and then having whatever?" the woman said. Nishat looked compelled by the lady's response. "No, we actually want a granddaughter. Do you not want a granddaughter?" Nishat asked her.

"No, not at all." The lady shook her head left then right and adjusted her scarf. "I already have a granddaughter," she added very unenthusiastically, "and I want a grandson for sure this time."

Nishat stared at her in shock before responding. "We don't decide such things, girl, or boy. Both are blessings of God, but I hope you get what you want," Nishat said to her.

In the meanwhile, a nurse came out from the labor ward and went up to the lady in the pink, who Nishat was talking to. "Congratulations, it's a boy," the nurse said.

The lady couldn't stop smiling. "See, I told you," she said to Nishat. Nishat congratulated her as she ran inside to see her daughter in law.

Shafqat stopped the nurse. "Can you please tell us if Faiza's okay? Is it a girl or a boy?"

"I am sorry, ma'am. I can't tell you anything. You will have to wait for the doctor to tell you," the nurse said to as she walked back into the delivery room, carrying the medicine tray in her hands.

Upon hearing the nurse's response, Nishat walked closer to Shafqat. "It's a girl; that's why they aren't telling us," Nishat said to Shafqat smilingly. I didn't know, maybe it could be a girl or was there something else going on?

I looked at Farooq, strolling from one corner to the other, continually picking at his fingernails. Then I glanced at Ahsan who stood in the corner against the other wall tapping his hand on his white kurta. Every passing minute in that waiting area felt like an hour at this point. Farooq picked up the bottle of water from the table and poured some in his palm and splashed it on to his face in order to resist falling asleep. Farooq got up and walked towards the main desk in front of the maternity ward and asked about Faiza again. This was the tenth time they had said the same thing: "Only the doctor can come and tell you exactly what's happening."

"My wife has been in labor for the past several hours, and why isn't anyone telling me what's going on?" His voice raised. The men and women sitting alongside us turned around to gaze at him.

"Sir, the doctor is inside. We don't have any other information. Please take a seat and wait for him to come out," the nurse said to him. As he walked back and sat on the seat next to me, I put my hand on his shoulder and tried my best to comfort him. That's all I could really do. "If only I knew what was actually going on," I thought to myself. There were so many thoughts that occupied my mind at that moment about Faiza and the baby. Was everything okay?

Ahsan came over and sat right next to Farooq and me. His eyebrows drew in closer as he bit his bottom lip. Ahsan never said it, but I could tell he was as worried as I was. He wasn't as chatty as he usually was, and Faiza was his most beloved daughter. Everyone knew he was super sensitive about her in every way. I still remember the story Faiza had told me about when she was younger and had once burned her hand by accident while ironing her dad's clothes even after the servants in her house had told her they would do it for her, but she did it anyway because she wanted to. Since that day, Ahsan never let her touch the iron again. He never even allowed her to go close to the kitchen either for the same reason. Or all the stories that I have heard about her childhood when Faiza did something mischievous with her brothers, like prank calling people, the moment they would all get caught

Faiza never got in trouble with Ahsan. Her brothers always did. Faiza wasn't spoiled, rather the most caring and down to earth person I had ever met. However, Faiza was Ahsan's life, and he loved her more than anything else.

Two more hours had passed sitting there in the waiting area. I could feel my heartbeat rising at this point. An eerie silence almost took over the entire room. The chit chatter had stopped and everyone impatiently waited. I sat there with my face squished inside my hands as my fingers pushed away my glasses from my forehead and my right foot continually tapped on the floor again. The same nurse who I had spoken to earlier came back walking towards us from the maternity ward. I lifted my hands away from my face, and Ahsan put his arm over my shoulder telling me it will all be okay.

Finally, after another twenty-some minutes, I saw Dr. Bokhari walking towards us from the other side of the maternity ward. His green gown was still on, the sides of his grey hair hanging out from the dome-shaped green cap that covered his head. His walk was slow with his gaze down and an unnerved expression on his face. The kind one gets when they barely escape something horrendous. Farooq hustled over towards him and stopped him in the middle of the waiting area. I stood up. Everyone in the room started looking towards Farooq and Dr. Bokhari. "How's Faiza? How's the baby? Is everything ok?" Farooq asked.

Dr. Bokhari stood there with his left-hand folded over his right, holding on to the side of his palms. I could see his grip tightening up as he clenched his fists. "Congratulations. It's a baby girl and both the mother and daughter are fine now," he said. Farooq sighed and began smiling as he shook Dr. Bokhari's hand and walked towards me. I hugged him with all the force I had. "Congratulations Mashallah," I said to him. I was ecstatic. God had finally heard my prayers and given me the daughter I had always wished and prayed for in the form of my granddaughter. It didn't matter that she came a generation late, but she was the first girl in the family. Everyone hugged each other. "Mubarak, Nishat, your wish of having a granddaughter came true," my sister said to Nishat. Nishat's smile spread from one corner of her face to the other as everyone congratulated her.

"See, I told you, you were panicking for no reason," Ahaya said to me as he hugged me.

Everyone was cheering and laughing so loudly that the only noises that could be heard across the entire hospital floor were all my family and relatives. Everyone was moving around the entire room giving each other hugs. Sounds of "Mubarak ho (Congratulations)" echoed throughout the entire floor. Salman ripped open all the sweet baskets, and everyone picked up a piece of mithai and started feeding it to each other.

Ahsan came over and hugged me. "Congratulations" I said.

"Congratulations" Ahsan said.

Nishat picked up one of the most enormous sweet baskets on the table and walked over to the nurse's station. "Here this is for all of you guys. We just had a granddaughter, and we want you guys to keep these sweets and distribute them amongst all the staff you have here right now," Nishat said. The nurse's jaw dropped as she took the basket from Nishat's hand and stared at the perfectly round *ladoos* (Traditional sweet).

"You guys are this happy on a birth of a baby girl?" the nurse asked. Her jaw remained dropped with surprise.

"Yes, any doubts?" Nishat answered.

"In our hospital, I have only seen families be this happy about a birth of a baby boy, never a baby girl," the nurse said to Nishat.

"There is no difference between a daughter and a son, and this is the first girl in our family, so anything for her," Nishat said.

"May God give your granddaughter a healthy life," the nurse said as she took the sweets. Soon all the nurses, the cleaning ladies, and the hospital janitors all gathered up in a crowd and thanked Nishat and me for feeding them. Ahsan took one of the chocolate baskets that Tariq had brought and handed all the chocolate truffles out to the nurses. All the nurses took the offerings with bright smiles and much gratitude.

I reached into the right pocket of my white kurta (long shirt) for my wallet and pulled out the cash I had and walked up to the corner of the room where the workers were standing and distributed it amongst the two cleaning ladies, the two custodians standing in the corner and the tea boy who had brought me tea countless times in the past twenty-four hours and all the staff members present in the hospital at the time. "Your granddaughter is lucky to be born in your family. God bless you" the custodian said to me, folding his hands in front of me. "Thank you," I told him. This was such a special day for every single person in my family.

There had always been a preference for a male child in a country like Pakistan, and girls were always seen as being inferior to boys because one day girls have to get married and leave, whereas a boy never has to leave his family and carries the family's name forward. Usually when a girl child is born in smallest parts of the country like Quetta, people frown and look down upon her because a girl is not seen as an heir of the family but as a liability that has to be taken care of till a certain age, and when she comes of age, she's married off and sent to what's seen as her "real home" according to our so-called society. When I was posted in Quetta as an officer, I saw many girls be denied the right to education not only because of the socioeconomic background of their families but because they were expected to stay at home and fit inside gender roles that our society has created for them. However, for both my family and Ahsan's family, the birth of a baby girl was no less than

Eid. Most of my friends and colleagues were wealthy landowners and landlords in Lahore, who belonged to very respectful families. Some of them were richer than us because of all the wealth they had acquired from their parents and so forth. Yet, most of them had a mindset that a boy is somehow more valuable than a girl. I never weighed my happiness of a grandchild on its gender, but I was a bit more excited about having a girl, perhaps because I never had one of my own.

A nurse with a clipboard in her hand called Farooq's name. "Are you Farooq Mazhar?"

"Yes," he answered.

"Your wife has been moved to room 604 now. You can go and see her," the nurse said.

Farooq smiled. "What about my baby? Is she in the room yet?" he asked.

"No not yet " the nurse said. " Dr. Bokhari will bring her in soon," she concluded. Farooq followed the nurse through to the room Faiza was in.

Before we were all allowed to go in the room, I saw Dr. Bokhari passing by, and I rushed to stop him. "Thank you so much, Dr. Bokhari." I shook his hand. At first, he wasn't making eye contact with me, and then when I shook his hand, he gave me a brittle smile.

"I just wanted to ask you, was everything okay?" I paused as he stared at me with a blank face and then continued. "I was just a bit worried because the delivery took a really long time," I said to him. He paused and wiped the sweat off his forehead with his left hand. "Don't you trust me, Mazhar? Your daughter in law and granddaughter are both fine. Nothing unusual happened. The delivery just took a while, that's all. I am sorry, I am busy I have to go," Dr. Bokhari said as he moved along the hallway. I ignored Bokhari's arrogant behavior and chose to focus on his words.

Everyone got up from our seats and turned left into the hallway towards the private rooms. Private rooms were a luxury not available to every patient. We had paid ten thousand rupees per day for Faiza to get her own private room post-delivery. Usually, post-delivery patients are moved to a general ward which is half the rate, where there are several beds placed in line, each covered by a curtain and very few nurses taking care of a tremendous amount of patients. This was still decent because private hospitals have more facilities and more delicate equipment than government hospitals. However, these luxuries in this country are only available to those who can afford them.

Others have to go to government hospitals, where, God forbid, they put four or five people on the same stretcher and sheets are never washed. There is no care of hygiene or sanitation at all. It's not even that we as a nation don't have the money to make living better for the masses of Pakistan; it's that the leaders we have sitting in power are so corrupted that all the money that should be used to improve the lives of the poor turns into black money and goes directly into the Swiss Bank accounts of our politicians. Once the money goes outside of Pakistan, no one can track it down; that's how all our political leaders get so rich, and our lower class has nothing to survive off of. I have always said one thing. "Either you have the money to live in this country and then you are a king, or you don't, and life is a constant struggle every day."

When the fruit vendor takes his cart out on the street and pushes it by hand as he screams "*sabji sabziwala* (fruit vendor)" to let people know he's here to sell vegetables. He doesn't know how much he will earn in a day or what he will take back home for his kids to eat for dinner. A little four by four square-shaped cart with fruits on it is all he has. It's his bread and butter.

I walked down the hallway to room 604. "It's over, why are you still scared?" I heard Farooq's voice as soon as I opened the door to the room. Farooq sat leaned forward on the wooden chair to the left side of the bed. The nurse standing on the right side was draining Paracetamol into the clear IV bag that was hanging above the right side of Faiza's head. She was lying on the bed with her head tilted towards the left and her hands resting on top of her stomach.

"Are you okay beta? What happened?" I asked her and waved my hand across her head.

"Hmm," she answered in a heavy drowsy voice.

Ahsan leaned towards her and kissed her on the forehead. "Congratulations." Shafqat held her hand and sat alongside the long edge of the bed.

Shahrukh and Aamir came inside with a large bouquet of flowers and a pink balloon that they placed on the table underneath the tv on the wall right in front of the bed. The line of people waiting to meet Faiza spread from the corner of the door all the way to the back end of the hallway. One by one all my relatives kept coming in till there was no more space in the room to even stand peacefully. One by one everyone congratulated Faiza and now even the hospital room was filled with bouquets and sweet baskets. Faiza's gaze shifted from left to right, scanning the room. "Do you want to eat anything? Water?" Nishat asked her. She shook her head left and turned towards Farooq.

"Did the nurses tell you how long it's going to be before they bring her in to the room? I want her in the room." Faiza looked at Farooq with her glassy green eyes.

Tariq gently hugged Faiza, then Shahrukh, and finally Mano excitedly came to hug her sister. "Where's the baby?" Mano asked as her voice lowered and her smiled began to fade away. "She's com..." before Farooq could even finish his sentence, the door knob turned and the nurse walked through the door carrying another IV bag hung on a large steel stand. Following her was another nurse whose hands formed tightly around the edges of the infant bassinet that she was wheeling into the room and asked me to move back a few steps so she could place the bassinet alongside Faiza's bed. This was the first time I ever saw my granddaughter. Precious little life laying right in the middle of the white sheets that covered the bassinet pad. Her head was turned the other way but her tiny little body was covered in a blue striped blanket and her head covered with a plain white hat. I held Nishat's hand tightly, admiring the beautiful gift of God that had just entered our lives. The entire room became silent for a second as all eyes were on our baby girl. The nurse untangled her IV cord from the corner of the bassinet and cautiously while holding the drip, placed the baby in Faiza's arms. Faiza kissed her forehead and snuggled her against her chest. Her tears steadily dripped down her cheeks.

Everyone stepped a little closer to Faiza's bed. "Mashallah," Faiza's aunt called out. "Such a beautiful daughter just like her mom," she added. Everyone was eager to pick the baby but Farooq got up from his chair and leaned in closer to pick the baby up first.

"Her neck, her neck. Is my grip, right?" Farooq said as he was making efforts to hold his daughter in his hands for the first time. Tears burst from Farooq's eyes as he smiled and gently kissed the baby on the forehead. Strolling as Farooq looked at her with warm eyes, Farooq brought the baby towards me. My hands trembled as I took my granddaughter in my hands. Her tiny little body was all wrapped up in a pink blanket. The only thing visible was the baby's face, part of which was covered by the white cotton hat on her head. She was breathtakingly gorgeous. The most perfect, most beautiful baby I had ever seen in my life. Her skin was as soft and white as milk.

Her cheeks were big, puffy, and red, making her face look rounder and her chin smaller, forming the perfect shape of a heart. The baby's nose was shaped just right—not too big nor too small. Just right. It looked so cute sticking out just a bit from her tiny little face. Her lower lip was a bit thicker than her upper lip but they were the perfect shade of rosy pink. Her fair complexion made her features even more prominent. The innocence of my granddaughter's face was priceless. Her tiny eyelids closed. Her lips gently pressed together.

"Come here, she's opened her eyes," Ahsan's voice echoed through the room.

"Mashallah, her eyes are just like Faiza's," Tariq's voice spread across the entire room. She was still in Ahsan's lap but we all gathered up close just to see her eyes. Her eyes were blue and transparent like the ocean. They were big, like giant marbles placed underneath the sun. So light one could almost see their own reflection in them. My granddaughter's eyes had this beautiful sparkle in them as if they were trying to convey something. She had gotten her eyes from Faiza.

"She couldn't have been any more perfect than this," Farooq said as he took the baby in his arms.

"Is she smiling?" Nishat said as the corners of her mouth began to lift.

We all just couldn't stop admiring her.

Ahaya smiled at me, "Mazhar, when are you throwing us a celebration party?"

"Of course, I am going to throw a party as soon as the baby and Faiza come home," I said, looking back at Ahaya.

"Inshallah," Ahsan added. "We are going to welcome our granddaughter in her house in the grandest manner possible." Salman moved away from the corner of the room and came closer to see the baby.

"I am so happy I have someone to play with now when I come home from college," Salman said joyfully as he took her in his arms and cradled her.

"So do I," Shahrukh said. "I am going to spoil her so much and play with her and teach her how to play with cars when she gets older and teach her how to drive."

"Let her grow up first, then you can teach her to drive." Ahsan said laughing.

"Yes, not everyone is like you Shahrukh, that at the age of

twelve you ran away with your brother's sports car without a license," Tariq said as he put his hand around Shahrukh's shoulder and rolled his eyes.

"Why did you have to put me on the spot like that?" Shahrukh said laughingly. Ahsan stared at both his sons talking and then smiled.

"This isn't fair. Why won't anyone let me see the baby?" Mano complained as she went towards the chair near the door and sat down, turning her face away from everyone else in the room.

"Don't be sad," Farooq said to her as he took the baby in his arms and walked towards her chair. Farooq lowered the baby on to her lap, yet he didn't let go of his grip around the baby. Farooq lowered down with his knees on the ground as he supported the baby with his hand.

"Be careful, Farooq," I called out towards him.

"Don't worry, I am dad," he said. The tiny pink hat from her head fell off.

"Her forehead is just like abu's (dad's). She's so pretty I can't wait to take her home and play with her," Mano said enthusiastically. Suddenly something caught my eye.

On the upper right side of the baby's forehead, there was a round patch of blue discoloration the size of a tangerine. The patch of skin from her forehead to the top of her head was all blue and looked somewhat like a big round bruise. I walked over toward Farooq who had been staring at the mark on the baby's forehead.

"What's this over here?" I said, pointing at the patch of discoloration on the top of her forehead.

"I was looking at that too," Farooq said.

"Maybe it's a birthmark? Or it will go away eventually?" I said, leaning down closer to her head as she started crying.

"We should still get it checked once Dr. Bokhari comes in to check on her," Farooq said. I agreed with him. Nonetheless, my princess was still the most beautiful baby I had ever seen.

Seconds later, I heard a massive noise amongst all the chitter-chatter. The baby was wheezing; her breath would start and stop again. "We need a nurse, get a nurse," Farooq screamed. Tariq ran outside to find a nurse. Everyone in the room began panicking. The nurse came in and checked the baby's pulse. The entire room became silent. The only sound in the room was of the heart rate monitor going "beep" and the sound of the baby crying.

"Her oxygen levels are getting low," the nurse said as she called over another nurse who walked in the room carrying an oxygen mask in her hand. The nurse put the oxygen mask over the baby's head and tightened the green string in the back. I could hear my granddaughter's breathy cries through the clear oval-shaped masked that covered almost her entire face from under her eye to her neck.

"You are the father, right?" the nurse said, looking at Farooq who was standing with his hands on Faiza's shoulders.

"Yes, I am the father," he said, stepping forward.

"Will you keep holding the pump at the end of the mask, so the baby's oxygen doesn't stop?"

There was a wire that kept on sliding down the mask from her face. The mask was too big for the baby. Farooq stood behind her bassinet and wrapped his fingers around the end of the pump near the baby's chin, as the edges of the mask pressed into her cheeks.

Nishat dug her nails into my skin, tightly grabbing on to my arm. "Why isn't she breathing?" she asked.

"Don't panic. Let the nurse check," I answered, as I had no idea what was going on. The room had become silent. Salman, Shahrukh, Tariq and Aamir all stood in front of the nurse staring at the baby. Mano left the bag of chips she was munching on, on the corner table and came and stood by Ahsan. Shafqat shifted her dupatta (scarf) from her shoulders to her head, folded her hands in prayer in front of her face and started praying.

"Nurse, where can I find Dr. Bokhari right now? What's happening? Why is she unable to breathe? I need to know now," Farooq's voice trembled.

"I am sorry, he's currently in the operation theater," the nurse tried explaining to me.

"Is there any other doctor or child specialist in the hospital that we can call right away?" he asked the nurse as she fixed the IV needle on the baby's hand.

"Dr. Ghazanfar Ali sits in the pediatrics department on the third floor; I can call him for you."

"Please do," I told her as she walked out the door.

Faiza couldn't stop crying at this point. "It's going to be ok. The baby is going to be fine," Shafqat assured her, putting her hand over her head. Suddenly all the laughter, chitter chatter and party planning died out again, and here we were back to worrying about what was to happen next. I stood there by Farooq's side looking right at the baby crying, pushing her hands and feet in all directions.

Momentarily, a man in brown trousers, a yellow shirt and a white coat and grey hair walked into the room. Alongside the doctor on duty was a nurse. "Hi I am Dr. Ali, " he mumbled as he put on his blue latex gloves and began examining the baby.

"Doctor, she was fine momentarily, and then she started having difficulty breathing," Salman said as he stepped forward towards the baby bassinet. The doctor checked her heart rate and the looked over at the neon green waves on the white box-like monitor. Dr. Ali turned away from the monitor looking at us.

"She's too weak. Her body seems like it's in stress," he paused and fixed his mustache.

"Your daughter can't support her lungs by herself. We will have to put her in an incubator until she can breathe on her own," Dr. Ali added.

"But doctor, why this all of a sudden? She was fine a few minutes ago," Farooq asked. Faiza grabbed on to Farooq's hand and squeezed it tightly in between her fingers as she tried hard to hold back her tears.

"It happens," Dr. Ali said as he was writing notes on the file in his hands. He continued, "Sometimes this happens when the umbilical cord is cut off in an obstructive way. It causes a shock to the baby's natural body and therefore the baby's body becomes stressed out after birth. She will be fine," he said.

"How long will she have to be in the incubator?" Ahsan asked.

Dr. Ali shrugged his shoulders. "It could be a day, two days, or just a night. Depends on how fast she's able to sustain her oxygen levels," he said. Dr. Ali looked at all of us in the room and then at the nurse standing beside him and said, "Let's take the baby into the Neonatal Intensive Care Unit."

"Uh, what?" Farooq asked.

"We are going to put her in an incubator," Dr. Ali answered.

The nurse untangled the baby's IV cord from the corner of Faiza's bed. "Can I just hug her once before she goes away?" Faiza asked. Her voice was shaking as she reached her arms out to hold her baby, but Faiza wasn't allowed to pick her up because of all the machinery that was attached to the baby. Faiza looked at her from the glass edge of her bassinet, and we all watched as the nurse pulled the baby out of the room. We followed the baby to the door.

"The NICU is located three doors down from the operation theatre. Only one family member may visit the baby at a time," the nurse said as she shut the door behind her and took the baby. I followed the nurse out the door. I watched my granddaughter's bassinet being driven away from me till the nurse took a left turn, and I couldn't see the bassinet anymore. I came back into the room.

At this point, there were only close family members that were left in the room. Everyone else had gone outside to give us some space. Faiza began sobbing loudly. We all tried consoling her, but she wouldn't stop.

"I thought she was dead," Faiza's voice barely made out. "She wasn't making her way out naturally. The doctor decided to use forceps to pull her head out and when she came out she was as still as a stone." Faiza's voice shook as she wept. "I saw Dr. Bokhari and the nurses tapping on her bare body, but not a single muscle in her body was responsive. One of the nurses had her lifted upright in front of my eyes, her body was all blue as if she had been bruised. The doctor kept on tapping her back harder each time. I stared at the nurses with helplessness, praying that somehow my baby would survive, but the look in the nurses' eyes only convinced me more that she wasn't going to make it. Those two minutes felt like someone had taken the life out of me. As soon as I heard her cry for the first time I could breathe again."

CHAPTER TWO

That night Farooq stayed in the hospital with Faiza. The next day I reached the hospital in my black Police jeep. Upon my arrival, the security guard at the gate noticed the police jeep, gave me a salute, and let me in without asking a single question. The hospital was empty at that time of the morning, just a few sweepers and janitors walking around from one corner to the other. When Nishat and I reached the hospital room, Faiza was deep asleep and Farooq by her side wide awake, trying to pass time changing channels on the tv screen with the volume off. I went over to Farooq and hugged him.

"Did you eat anything after last night?" I asked.

"No, I didn't," Farooq said in a throaty voice. There was an alertness in his eyes behind the glasses that sat on his long nose.

"How's the baby? Did you see her?" I asked Farooq as I took a seat on the bench in the corner.

Farooq rubbed his eyes and started speaking, "She wasn't with the rest of the kids. Her incubator was in a special corner all by itself. My baby was all covered with a glass dome placed underneath a bright blue light. There were three tiny wires attached to her delicate little body. Her tiny white fingers held on tightly to the transparent wire. The oxygen mask hugged the baby's cheeks tightly, covering her face. I could only see her eyes and the upper half of her nose. Her bright blue marble-like eyes stared at me through the glass dome in which she was placed. The baby wasn't crying, but I spotted a single drop of tear in the corner of her right eye making its way down her cheek. Her eyes looked right at me. She was right there in front of me, within my reach but I could not touch her. It felt like as if she wanted me to save her from this misery. As if she was telling me, "Dad take me out of this stupid machine to a safer place where I would be free from all of this." As if she was telling me to get her out of this cage. Standing there in that corner of the nursery being able to do nothing but cry, I felt like the most helpless father in the world. My daughter was asking me to help her, and I couldn't even do that much for her." Farooq completely broke down. He constantly tried hiding his tears with his hands in front of his face then took off his glasses and rubbed his eyes.

Nishat sat there crying. I put my hand on her shoulder. "Everything will be fine," I said. I got up and began walking around restlessly. The door opened. I thought maybe the nurses were bringing the baby back, but Salman and Aamir walked through the door with breakfast. Shortly after, Ahsan and Shafqat walked into the room. Shafqat hugged Nishat then walked over towards Faiza's bed and kissed her on the forehead as she was still under the influence of painkillers.

Faiza opened her eyes, and the first thing she asked was "Where's my baby?" in a low voice.

"She's still in the NICU," Farooq answered.

Ahsan's breathing was loud, and there was sweat on his forehead that he wiped off with his forearm. "Dr. Bokhari," he said with a breathy voice. "He doesn't answer anything,"

Ahsan continued as Shahrukh passed him the cup of water from the table. "I saw Dr. Bokhari outside, he told me they will be bringing the baby in shortly," Ahsan said. He paused and then spoke again. "I asked him what's going on with my granddaughter, but Dr. Bokhari didn't give me a legitimate answer. It's like he doesn't even care," Ahsan said as he sat down on the chair.

In the meantime, a nurse came in to change the drip attached to Faiza's IV. Another woman dressed in a dull grey shalwar suit and a broom in her hand came in the room to clean the bathroom. When she finished cleaning, the woman walked up to Nishat. "Ma'am I heard you had a granddaughter, and you gave money to all the hospital employees," she said smilingly in an attempt to ask for money.

"Of course, I will give to you too," Nishat said as she reached into her bag and pulled out some money from the back zip. "Take the sweets as well and pray for our granddaughter," Nishat added.

"May God give her a long life," the woman said as she folded her hands together in front of Nishat and thanked her before walking out the door.

It was about 2 pm when the door opened and Dr. Bokhari walked in, fixing the stethoscope around his neck. Behind him a nurse carried a vanilla-colored file and behind her another nurse pushed in a bassinet in which my granddaughter was laying all curled up in white sheets, deep asleep. "I am sorry to keep you guys waiting for so long," Dr. Bokhari said then paused as he took the folder from the nurse's hands and started flipping through the papers in it. "There were a few complications at birth due to which she was having trouble breathing, but now she's stable." He smiled. "Other than that, she's a healthy baby weighing seven and a half pounds, and her heart rate and oxygen levels have returned to normal," Dr. Bokhari concluded.

"Are you sure everything is, okay? There's nothing more to worry about?" I asked Dr. Bokhari curiously.

"No Mazhar Saab, everything is under control now," he assured me. Faiza's smile went from one ear to the other upon hearing that. Farooq and her were ecstatic as they played with their new baby girl. "You can take her home now. We must do a final check-up for Faiza, and then the mother and baby may go," Dr. Bokhari concluded.

"Thank you so much, Dr. Bokhari," I said as Dr. Bokhari began checking Faiza's heart rate and blood pressure and taking off the IV from her hand. "Doctor what about the mark on her forehead?" Farooq asked, leaning over the baby bassinet looking at the blue bruise-like mark on the baby's forehead.

"It will go away with time," Dr. Bokhari said.

After all the formalities for the hospital discharge were finished, I gave Farooq my wallet and told him to go to the cashier counter on the first floor of the hospital building and clear the bill. I knew Dr. Bokhari wouldn't take money from me because of the connection I had with him, but I wouldn't leave without paying the bill. Ahsan waited with me in the hallway outside the rooms and Shahrukh, Aamir, and Salman left the hospital early as they had to decorate the house for the arrival of the new baby. Tariq went to go pick up Mano from school and was going to come straight to our house. Meanwhile, I called my driver to bring the jeep outside towards the main entrance. I had also called up Sattar, my other driver to bring the other car from home because all of us family members had to go back together. Fifteen minutes later we all gathered in the main lobby downstairs near the double entrance gates of the hospital. Farooq had gone back upstairs to get Faiza. Ahsan and I waited in the lobby. Salman and Aamir had already left the hospital so they could go home and decorate the entrance a bit. When Faiza, Farooq, Nishat, and Shafqat came down to the lobby with the baby we left. We all divided up and started heading home.

When I first moved to Defence about ten years ago, there was nothing around. It was all acres of land filled with luscious green grass and empty plots. You could only hear the chirping of birds. Traffic was never too bad because the area wasn't super populated. When Nishat and I sold Nishat's Haveli (mansion) in Hyderabad and used that money to make our house in Phase One ten years ago, there was only one other house miles away from us, and that was my elder brother's. Around our house was all empty land that people often used for growing crops or just buying property and waiting for the area to develop. Business and houses developed in the area right in front of my eyes which grew the population of Defence like never before. When my kids were growing up, there wasn't even a single bakery near our house. I remember when Nishat's nephew was born she drove an hour to Walton Street on the other side of the city to buy sweets. Now there were hundreds of houses around us and a giant market in H block which had everything from food stores, pharmacies, home stores to clothing stores. Everything could be delivered right to our doorstep with just a phone call, even KFC, which my children were crazy about even now.

What used to be an empty road extremely feasible to drive on had now become a havoc of noise. Cars honked at each other nonstop. The fruit wagons, rickshaws, horse carriages, trucks, buses, and cars all crowded against each other fighting to get in the same lane. The lane system didn't even really exist; anyone shoved their truck or car or rickshaw anywhere they wanted, and they honked as if there was no tomorrow. A Rickshaw is Lahore's form of a taxi. Even though we do have taxi services that one could call when needed, a rickshaw is the iconic and desi way of traveling. It has an engine and the handles of a motorbike with one wheel in the front and two wheels and a seating area for passengers in the back. The sides and the back of the rikshaw are covered with plastic cloth which is often decorated and painted in all sorts of bright colors. When my kids were younger, taking a ride around Defence on a rickshaw was their favorite thing to do. Nadeem, Farooq, and Aamir used to go to the local market in a rickshaw to buy chocolate, and when they got back home I always used to ask, "How shaky was the ride? Did you feel all the bumps on the main road?"

Nadeem and Farooq loved it, but Aamir used to always say, "It's too bumpy for me." And I always used to say if you hadn't travelled in a rickshaw, you weren't truly from Lahore.

Everyone drives on the left side of the road and uses right-hand side cars where the steering wheel is on the right, but sometimes it's common to see someone driving a left-hand side car because they want to show off how they have imported their car from abroad. Not everyone in Lahore lives by a certain standard. Most people in Pakistan are poor, live in slums and work at people's houses to earn their bread and butter. On the road, when I see people on bikes, it's not just one or two people sitting on a bike. More often it's entire families of four or five squished together on a single motorcycle with no helmet or belt or any form of safety precautions. Often, I saw women carrying their newborn babies in their laps as they went around the city on the bike, and it scared me because what if something were to happen suddenly. But what can one do? This is how people live and what they can afford.

We passed the National Hospital and the H block market area and turned left by the blue "Sector M" sign into the lane of our house. Passing the M block park, the car stopped right in front of the tall black steel gates of our house, "104 M."

Every house in Lahore had a gate and a nameplate on the left or right pillars of the entrance of each house. Mine was to the left. It said "104 M," and underneath it said "House of DIG Mir Mazhar Qayyum." My driver honked, and the guard on duty inside opened the gate with big bright smiles and then gathered around our cars.

"Mubarak sir," he said as he opened the car door for me.

"She's beautiful Mash Allah," the other guard said, looking at the baby as Farooq and Faiza got out the car.

Azeem Saab hustled from the main door over to the car in his black shalwar kameez, bright orange hair and a thick white mustache. He congratulated me, then Farooq and then Faiza. Azeem took the baby in his hands. "Mashallah, she's so beautiful," he said, cradling the baby in his arms. Azeem Saab had been with me since even before Aamir was born. He wasn't just the caretaker of the house but more like our own family. I trusted him more than anything. Whether it be anything to do with the house or my finances, Azeem handled everything. He was more like my right hand than house help. At night, I usually slept with a gun near my bedside for safety reasons. You never know what you might need or what might happen in this country, just in case. But when Azeem was at home, I was at peace. He would sleep in the lobby with the gun, and I would sleep in peace knowing that he was there. Nothing was going to happen anyway, but one must always be careful in this country.

All of us went inside the house and into the living room. To the left of the entrance was the antique phone table with an attached maroon chair and behind the maroon printed couch was the wooden spiral staircase leading up to the second floor. The maroon door in front of the steps was my room, and the room next to my room was Aamir and Salman's. Behind the stairs was a little corner which used to be empty but now was about to be filled with toys. Upstairs we had Nadeem's room and then Farooq's and an extra guest bedroom. On the other side of the staircase was the main lobby with maroon flower printed sofas. The wooden floor in the lobby was covered with things Nishat had ordered for the baby. There were diaper boxes, a brand-new sleeping cot that I had gotten from England, even her diapers were from England because the ones that were in the local market here were awful. A baby potty seat that she would use when she would be a little older and a bunch of playpens. Everything was unopened. I told Azeem to take everything and store it behind the stairs for now, except for the white and green monkey playpen that Ahsan had brought for the baby. Even before she was born, Ahsan had sent a truck full of toys for her that had playpens, stuffed animals, a huge Barbie dollhouse and a dressing table, all the things that she wouldn't even need until she got older.

We all sat in the lobby talking when Salman popped the question: "What are we going to name her?" he said. The baby name book had never left his hands. The cook came from the kitchen and put Mithai and chai on the rectangle-shaped glass table in the middle of the room.

"How about Sana?" Farooq said.

"That's too common," Tariq disappointingly said.

"How about Anaya?" Shahrukh added.

"No, no way," Salman said putting the baby name book aside for a second. "Anaya was the name of my high school crush whose boyfriend punched me in the face when I give her roses on Valentine's Day," he said with a mournful face.

Everyone in the room started laughing. "I still remember that day when Salman came back from school with a black eye and he told everyone that he got hit by the ball while playing cricket," Aamir started teasing Salman in front of everyone.

"Alright enough pulling each other's leg, now let's decide on a name for the baby," I said. Farooq asked each one of us for a name but nothing appealed to him.

Salman dug his face back into the baby book. "Ahh, I found

it," he said.

"What is it? "Faiza asked.

"Maheen," he smiled, turning is head to look at Faiza.

"What does it mean?" Farooq asked him as he took a sip of his tea.

"Maheen's an Arabic name. It means moonlike," Salman said.

That was a beautiful name. She was as beautiful as the moon, and just like how the moon lights up the night sky, she had become the light in all of our lives. "I love it," I said putting my tea on the table right next to me.

"How about Pari?" Tariq screamed from across room, sitting on the maroon floor with his legs straight out, one on top of the other, and leaning over towards his right shoulder buried in the pillow.

"But every other girl's name is Pari, and not to mention that was also the name of Salman's other ex-girlfriend," Aamir said as he finished the piece of mango he was still chewing on. Salman stared right at Aamir.

"What?" Aamir said, chewing his mango.

"I will get back at you for this later," Salman whispered into Aamir's ear.

"Alright, Maheen it is," Farooq said leaning forward into his seat and resting, clasping his hands together on his knees.

"Dad, do you or Uncle Ahsan want to do the gurthi ceremony?" The Gurthi was a tradition in which an elder member of the family gives a taste of honey to the newly born baby. Farooq looked at me and then at Ahsan.

"Mazhar Saab, I think you should be the one to do it," Ahsan said.

I got up and quickly rushed to the bathroom to wash my hands and came back. I walked over to pick up the jar of honey from the table. I opened the bottle and poured just a pea-size amount on to the spoon in my hand. As I walked across the living room to the other sofa, Azeem, Isaac, Malik, and Sakina the cleaning lady all left their work and stood in the corner in a line, gazing at the baby. I barely touched my right index fingers to my palm to get just a tiny amount of honey on to it and lowered down to reach the baby. As I got close to her, she started crying, and Faiza kept cradling her. I put my finger over her tongue gently. “There we go,” I said, pulling my finger back.

The sound of claps echoed in the entire house. “Yay, now she’s going to turn out just like you, dad,” Salman said smilingly.

“Strong-willed and full of anger,” Nishat said laughingly as she tapped me on the shoulder, standing right behind me.

“I am not angry all the time? Or maybe yes, “I laughed as I turned around and hugged her.

“At least she’ll turn out strongheaded” Nadeem said in a soft-spoken way.

The next few days went by in the blink of an eye with all my friends and guests rushing in and out of the house to meet Maheen. And then there were all of Farooq’s friends from Lahore University of Management Sciences (LUMS). They all came to meet Maheen, and nobody in our house knew if anything else existed or not. Maheen had become the center of our world. Mano came every day after school, and Faiza taught her how to wrap a diaper properly around Maheen’s waist. Every time I heard the sound of Maheen crying in the house, I would immediately come out of my room, stand by the spiral staircase and yell, “Is she okay?” and Faiza’s voice would echo back, “Yes, Abu, don’t worry; she’s fine.” I still got worried each time. I didn’t like it when she cried. I wanted to fix whatever it was that bothered her right that second.

The weekend went by completely fine. All of us were busy with our lives revolving around Maheen. The hours that she was up all of us fought to hold her in our arms. The hours she slept one of us was always sitting by her side watching over our princess sleeping.

Everything was perfect until Friday rolled around and Maheen's milk like white skin began turning yellow. Maheen developed a severe case of jaundice. For the longest time, we tried treating her at home. Farooq and Faiza tried every home remedy to treat her. They fed her regularly, but Maheen would vomit everything out. Nishat used to sit in the sun all day long with Maheen protecting her from direct sunlight with an umbrella. We tried everything we could at home to get her jaundice under control but it led to her getting a high fever. By the third day, Maheen's face, arms, and legs had turned all yellow. We took her to the hospital once again. On the day that Faiza and Farooq were taking Maheen back to the Hospital, Nishat couldn't stop crying. She kept on saying "Don't take Maheen to the hospital, I will treat her at home, I will sit in the sun all day long with her in my lap." Nishat cried. Salman and Aamir consoled Nishat that jaundice in children is very common, to let her go to the hospital and she would be fine. Farid Hammad Hospital was a bit of a distance, so we took Maheen to National Hospital, which was right around the corner.

For the next three days, Maheen was kept in the hospital. Faiza and Farooq would visit the hospital day and night. Maheen was kept underneath a neon blue light wrapped up in wires. We were allowed to see her from the outside, but no one was allowed to go into the intensive care unit where she was kept. Nishat and I visited the hospital every day, but we wouldn't stay long. Nishat would start crying every time she saw Maheen wrapped up in wires again breathing through a clear tube that was attached to her nose and to all the computer monitors that sat beside her bassinet. I looked at her, but if I stayed there too long, I would start crying too. We spent a couple of hours a day in the hospital, and as soon as Shafqat and Ahsan were there to look after Faiza and Farooq, Nishat and I used to come home. Finally, after a week of staying in the hospital, Maheen came back home happy and healthy.

The following months were the happiest times of my life; all was well. The sun shone bright and the afternoons were pleasant during the spring of 1998. When Maheen was around seven months old. I had gotten the wooden floor in the house changed to all carpet just so when she would crawl around the house I didn't want her to get hurt. Anything that could even possibly harm Maheen, I didn't want in my house. Maheen loved attention. If I ever put her down on the ground so she could play with her toys, she cried until I picked her back up. Every time I held her in my arms, she would point at my shiny bald head and try pulling on the hair I had left, which wasn't much anyway. I couldn't resist the temptation to pull on her chubby white cheeks. Her cheeks were always rosy pink and her eyes had changed color. They were bright green, like the color of summer grass. In the sun her eyes would become so transparent that I could see the reflection of the sun in them. Her fair complexion, shiny brown hair, puffy cheeks, and sparkly eyes made her look like one of those model babies found in magazines.

She loved trying to pick up the phone, which was heavier than her in size. I had one of those old antique telephones on the table in the lobby near the front entrance. Attached to the table was an antique style chair. Whenever Mano was in the house, Maheen always made Mano sit on the chair attached to the telephone table. Sitting on Mano's lap, Maheen always tried to pick up the phone set or play around with the phone wire. The black telephone was one of those retro telephones that had a huge ear peace and a typical circular dialing pad where one would slide to dial numbers and a circular nob on top that made noise. Maheen's favorite thing to do was listen to the beeping sound that came out of the phone when the headset was placed off its holder. Azeem had to disconnect the wire of the phone, so Maheen didn't accidentally call people. But whenever Maheen couldn't hear the ringing sound from the phone, Maheen got mad and would throw the phone away. Other times she loved sitting in the play tents that Tariq had brought for her from Italy. The blue, red and yellow triangle-shaped tent made from fabric and white steel sticks was huge; it could fit about three to four adults in it comfortably. Faiza and Farooq always set the tent up in the lobby in the effort that maybe Maheen might crawl one day by just playing in the tent but instead Maheen would sit in the tent with Mano for hours and refused to move at all. If Mano ever wanted to come out of the tent, Maheen started crying; Mano had no choice but to listen to Maheen. Everyone enjoyed playing with her so much. Every second of the day a family member was always playing with Maheen. Faiza used to get so mad sometimes because she would never get time with her daughter alone. Despite spending hours in the tent with ample space, Maheen still never learned how to crawl.

Every kid falls a million times before they get up and finally learn how to walk. We gave Maheen time, thinking she was probably just a late bloomer and would eventually stop falling, gain proper balance, but the fact that she was about to turn one and still wouldn't walk worried all of us. Sure, every kid takes their time, but something was alarming. Faiza was the one who always made Maheen stand up on purpose so she would at least try to walk, but Maheen would never try. Every time Faiza tried, Maheen always lost her balance and would go back to sitting in Faiza's lap.

As each day passed, Faiza's worry towards Maheen increased. When anyone asked her why Maheen wasn't walking by now, Faiza didn't know how to answer that question. People never asked out of concern, they always asked out of sympathy, and Faiza couldn't stand that. Even being overweight in our society is a huge problem, so of course, people were going to make their own assumptions about this too. Faiza worked hard to try to get Maheen to start walking. Faiza spent twenty-four hours a day revolving around Maheen. Faiza began to think that maybe all of this was due to the trauma that Maheen and Faiza faced in the delivery room. It could have been; I still remember the bad vibes I was having that day in Farid Hammad Hospital. Farooq was getting concerned too. Therefore, the three of us decided to take Maheen to Sikandar Hayat Hospital for an MRI scan to make sure that everything was okay.

Sikandar Hayat Hospital was Pakistan's most advanced hospital when it came to medical technology and proper medical treatment. The hospital was initially made for cancer research by Iman Khan; Pakistan's current Prime Minister and former world class sportsman. After Khan's mother passed away due to cancer; he created a hospital that would give free treatment to those who couldn't afford treatment for cancer or any other medical issue. The hospital ran on donations and loans to provide free medical treatment to the underprivileged, but those who could afford to do so paid out of pocket. The hospital had qualified doctors from all over the world working there. In a country where only the rich can afford to pay for private hospitals and the average person living in the village must go to the government hospital where he doesn't even know if the equipment used on him is sterile or not,

Sikandar Hayat helped eliminate that difference by bringing together everyone under the same roof and by giving everyone the same quality of treatment, whether one had money or not. SKH at that time was the only hospital that had MRI scanning technology in Lahore, so Farooq, Faiza and I decided to take Maheen there.

The technicians on duty put Maheen asleep to complete the scan so she wouldn't move inside the MRI machine. Faiza held Maheen tightly in her arms as she distracted her with toy keys while the nurse injected anesthesia into Maheen's hand. Faiza was crying, Farooq was a little panicked, and Maheen's screams echoed in the entire hospital, and minutes later she was knocked out in Faiza's lap. The nurse took Maheen from Faiza's lap and took her inside the MRI room. All of us stood outside watching. Till the time the door of the MRI was open I saw the nurse settling Maheen in the machine for the scan. Above Maheen's head was a round dome-like machine that came over her and once her face was covered and we couldn't see what was happening on the other side, the nurse shut the door behind her and Farooq, Faiza and I took a seat in the lobby. Farooq put his hand around Faiza's shoulder, hugging her in a little closer.

After fifteen minutes, the exam was done, and Faiza went to get Maheen from the exam room. The lady with the dupatta over her head sitting at the reception desk told Farooq that the reports would be available within the next two days. Maheen was still deeply asleep when we took her home. Faiza was extremely concerned for Maheen and wanted to go to a child specialist, regardless of what the MRI results were going to be. Dr. Gunzafar Ali seemed like the best bet we had now. We had met him once in Farid Hammad Hospital, but he had his own practice in Johar Town. I made a few phone calls and immediately got Maheen scheduled for a check-up. Dr. Ghazanfar was the most sought-after child specialist, and his waiting time was about a month for any new patient, but I used my connections and got Maheen on his schedule within days.

The MRI reports came in a day later, and according to the doctors at Sikandar Hayat, the scans of Maheen's brain were completely normal. The report showed no signs of damage or anything dangerous. That news gave Faiza, Farooq and I mental relief, but Farooq still thought that we should go see Dr. Ali and get his opinion about the MRI report. His clinic was located right behind Wapda Hospital. The clinic was built within a complex that resembled a house from the outside. Upon entering inside, to one side of the driveway was Dr. Ali's house, and the other side was the entrance to his clinic. Sattar parked the car near the sidewall, and Faiza, Farooq and I took Maheen inside. We waited about twenty minutes before the nurse took us inside and sat us down on the wooden chairs in front of the reception desk. Maheen kept pulling my glasses off my face, and I very gently kept removing her hand off them as she sat on my lap. When Maheen's name was called, we all went inside.

The check-up room was unclean and smelly. It smelled like rotten eggs, and the walls had dust piled up around the corners right behind the doctor's chair. I sat Maheen down on the bed in the corner, and Faiza stood next to her as I sat next to Farooq in front of the desk waiting for the doctor. The glass door opened and in came Dr. Ali. He walked over and stood right in front of his chair as he reached out his right hand towards me. "Hello, Mir Saab," he said, shaking my hand.

Farooq handed him the file with the MRI results. "Doctor, Maheen's been falling a lot lately, and we are getting concerned at this point," Farooq said, looking at the doctor.

"And doctor, she never learned how to crawl either, and she falls down every time she sits up," Faiza added.

Dr. Ali picked up the big brown paper envelope with the MRI scans and tore it open. As he was taking the tape off the envelope, his fingers paused in the middle, and he took a good look at Farooq and Faiza for a second then started talking.

"Aren't you guys the same family who called me to check your daughter at Farid Hammad Hospital because your daughter was having difficulty breathing?" Dr. Ali said, pointing at Maheen.

"Yes, doctor," Farooq answered. Dr. Ali put on his glasses and took a close look at the MRI report. He paused for a second as he read the report and spoke again.

"The MRI report looks completely fine, her brain is completely healthy," he said, flipping through the scans in the file and then reading the report to himself. "Maybe she's just slow." He said in an assuring tone.

"But doctor, can you at least take a look at her?" Faiza asked. Dr. Ali half-heartedly checked Maheen's reflexes, but because the MRI scan was fine, he wasn't that interested in checking Maheen.

The doctors never found a clear diagnosis for Maheen, all of them said the same thing: "There's nothing to be treated." When a few more months passed and Maheen still made no efforts to walk, people started telling us that maybe she had black magic done on her and that we should sacrifice goats to take evil eyes of off Maheen. The whole rumor about black magic made Farooq and Faiza even more furious. Without further ado, Farooq and Faiza decided to start Maheen's physical therapy with the intention that it would help Maheen stand up on her own two feet faster. That was all the two of them wanted, their daughter to stand on her own two feet.

Within a matter of days, Farooq found two well-known therapists at National hospital, Dr. Haider Khan and his wife Dr. Asmara Khan, who also specialized in physical therapy for children. National Hospital was and still is probably the fanciest private hospital in all of Lahore. It looks more like a five-star hotel than a hospital. The entrance has revolving doors made from glass, and even the receptionists at the front desk are dressed up in suits as if they work at a hotel. Faiza used to take Maheen for her therapy sessions, and I used to go with her. The physical therapy department on the fourth floor had a desk and a few chairs lined up for the patient's family. The office was separated from the physical therapy area by a plain white curtain made from silk fabric. The area on the other side of the curtain consisted of numerous beds each separated by a white curtain, like there would be in any hospital ward. During therapy sessions, Haider used to turn on the Electric Stimulation Monitor. As it was warming up, he applied a jelly substance to the spongy squares that were attached on the wires. Then he used to make Maheen lie down and apply the pads to her legs. Maheen hated it. Haider turned the machine on and it made almost like a vibrating "woooooz" sound. Each time it beeped, Maheen's entire body would quiver from head to toe. She kept screaming louder and louder each time the monitor beeped and she felt the shock in her body. Maheen hated therapy more than anything, and I couldn't bear watching Maheen cry, but this was necessary.

My granddaughter was my pride, the most precious gift that I had ever received from God after prayers and prayers for a daughter. Even if Maheen sneezed I used to make Azeem Saab turn all the ACs off in the house and wrap Maheen in a blanket, and no one had the guts to turn the AC back on without my approval. Seeing her go through this torture at the age where she was supposed to be sitting at home, playing with toys was painful. What was her fault in any of this? Why did an innocent soul have to be put through so much misery? I used to attend every one of Maheen's therapy sessions because I didn't want to miss out on any part of her life even for a day. However, I never had the guts to see Maheen cry. Faiza always went inside the therapy room with Maheen, while I used to sit in the fourth-floor lobby with my tasbih (prayer counter) in my hand, praying to God to end this test that was placed on Maheen and her parents by God. Indeed, he is the one who places challenges on us and only he can provide relief.

After forty-five minutes, Faiza used to come out, carrying Maheen in her lap. Faiza used to cry too, but only behind shut doors. She was willing to go through anything for the sake of her daughter. Maheen's cheeks used to be red with anger and her eyes soaked in tears when she used to come out of therapy. I would hold her in my lap and kiss her forehead and a while later she would tap her hand on my shiny bald head and smile at me.

A few days later, Maheen fell in my room and tore her head open. The bed in my room had a wooden headboard, frame, and footboard. The corners of the footboard were raised and there was a metal flower on each of the corners. The tips of the flower petals were pointed and made a triangular shape. Maheen was sitting on one side of the bed playing with Mano, and Mano was sitting on the other side of the bed. Faiza's parents were over for dinner, and all of us adults were sitting outside in the lobby. I tried taking Maheen with me, but she refused to leave Mano. So I went, and the girls stayed back in the room playing. A brief second later, I heard Maheen screaming. Faiza rushed inside the room and all of us followed. Maheen was in Mano's arms crying, and Mano stood by the door crying too.

"What happened?" I panicked.

"Maheen fell back, and her head banged into the pointy petals at the edge of the footboard. "I am sorry, I didn't do anything, we were playing and Maheen suddenly lost her balance," Mano explained to me as she started crying.

"It's okay baita, it's not your fault. It happens, don't cry," I tried explaining to Mano. Faiza held Maheen in her lap for a while to try to get her to stop crying, but as soon as Faiza brushed her fingers across the back of Maheen's head, she saw the blood dripping down Maheen's head and onto her fingers.

Faiza began screaming, “She’s bleeding.”

I rang the bell to the servant quarter and called Sattar, and we all rushed our way to the emergency ward of National Hospital.

When we got to the emergency ward, all the beds were taken and the nurse on duty made Maheen sit on the chair in front of the “Emergency” sign. Maheen wouldn’t stop crying, and Faiza held her dupatta over Maheen’s head to try to stop the blood, but the bleeding had increased so much that it was dripping right down to the white tile floor of the hospital. Aamir, Salman, Mano, Shahrukh, Ahsan, Shafqat, and Nishat all stood there by Maheen’s side. All of them were crying. My blood was boiling out of anger.

“Why isn’t there a single doctor on duty or a nurse attending to her?” I screamed, but no nurse or doctor even turned around to notice. Ahsan went inside to find the head doctor on duty, but he refused to come to see Maheen. Not a single doctor or nurse was of any help. I was furious. I stopped the nurse passing by and asked her, “What is this? She’s bleeding, and none of you are available to help,” I said as I pointed towards Maheen.

“I am sorry sir, but she’s too young. The doctor on duty says he can’t do her stitches. You will have to wait till 5 in the morning for the other doctor to come in,” the nurse said to me and left.

“What in the world is that about? A patient needs medical assistance now, and you are telling me to leave this little girl here bleeding for the next seven hours because your doctor can’t do her stitches? Where is he? What kind of doctor is he? Tell me,” I said with my voice raised.

“Excuse me, sir, I will go call him for you,” the nurse said and never came back.

Shahrukh put his hands on my shoulder “I will take care of this,” he said to me.

“But what the hell is wrong with people in this country?

Doctors are supposed to save people's lives at all costs and what is this 'I can't do her stitches because she's a minor'? It's his duty to help her right this moment," I said. My heart rate was at an all-time high. The arrogant doctor came walking towards me in his white coat as he pushed his hair back with his fingers.

Shahrukh began arguing with the doctor. "How can you not do such a simple thing as putting in stitches? She's already lost so much blood," he yelled. The doctor wasn't ashamed of his behavior even a tiny bit.

"I will try my best," he explained and took Maheen back in the room. All of us waited outside for another fifteen minutes, and the doctor came back.

"What happened?" Faiza asked, wiping the tears off her face.

"Maheen won't let me touch her. I need one of you to help me keep her calm so I can do the stitches," the doctor said, looking at all of us.

"I will go," Shahrukh said, and he followed the doctor into the other room. Maheen was very close to Shahrukh, and she always stayed happy around him. Due to Farooq being in Thailand for his Oracle training, the only other person who could keep Maheen calm in such a situation was Shahrukh.

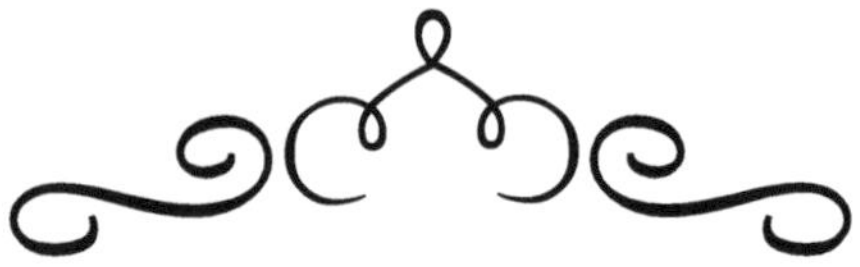

CHAPTER THREE

Maheen was three and a half now, and Farooq had finished his SAP and Oracle training course and was trying to find a job abroad with little to no luck. While their decision to move to Canada or the USA was still pending, Faiza and Farooq didn't want Maheen's education to suffer.

We decided to put Maheen's name on the waiting list for admissions into Defence Preschool, which was and still is the most Oxford-like school in all of Pakistan. It was one of the first schools in Pakistan to have preschool through twelfth grade under one roof and the first school that was recognized internationally by major universities because it offered International Baccalaureate programs. However, Defence Preschool was also one of the most expensive preschools in the country.

The average population in Pakistan that live in slums can't afford to send their children to school. Even if their children do go to school, they attend government schools. The atmosphere at such schools is horrible. Because of the nature of my job, I visited plenty of government schools in cities like Quetta and Sargodha where there were no facilities for children unless their parents could afford to pay a fee. Students didn't get desks or chairs; they had to sit outside and study. Classes often continued or ceased to exist depending on the mercy of the weather. The poor went to government schools and the rich went to schools like Glory College in Murree, whose principal was an old friend of my mine, and through him, I knew very well that merely good grades were not enough to get admitted into the school; family economic status mattered tons. There is no equal education for everyone. We were lucky enough to send our kids to the top of the top schools in the country, but things weren't always this way. When I was growing up in Faisalabad, I went to a government school. Throughout all my school years I used to sit on the pavement and learn; there were no desks or chairs. When I got to college and realized that I wasn't good at anything at all, I decided to join Pakistani Military Academy. After that came police life, but I only earned enough to make ends meet. I never took bribes like some of my own friends in the police did. All the wealth I had now wasn't mine to begin with; everything was Nishat's because she had inherited tons after her parents' death.

If one is born into a poor family, that status symbol won't leave them no matter how hard they work to change their fate. If a girl is born in a village in this country, she will probably never get the chance to even go to school because if she has brothers, her parents will do everything to pay their fees before even thinking about educating the girl. She will most likely be told to take care of the house. Sadly, these gender notions haven't changed no matter how much we say we are progressing in this country. Progression means the whole country as a nation is advancing together, but here in Pakistan only the rich are progressing, and out of the entire population of Pakistan, the percentage of people who fall under the category of "rich" are very few.

Private learning institutions in Lahore are great; they will give the child the opportunity he or she needs to succeed. However more than an opportunity to be successful, these schools are seen as a status symbol of wealth. Even Defence Preschool, part of Excellence Alliance, was a status-based school; it had less focus on giving all children the equal opportunity to learn and more focus on who's going to add value to the school through money. Anyway, if Maheen was going to live here, Defence Preschool was the best choice for her future. The only reason our family wanted Maheen to go there was that the school was recognized by universities abroad and had all the facilities of an American School.

Surprisingly, it didn't take long before Maheen's interview date had arrived. On the day of the preschool interview, Faiza had dressed Maheen up in a beautiful pink dress with frills and a matching flower headband. Faiza and Farooq had all the documents ready, Maheen's birth certificate, their educational certifications, tuition fee, enrollment fee, and the school required two passport size photos. The process of getting your kid into Defence Preschool was as hard as getting a US Visa for the first time, or harder. This school was the Ivy school for three-year-olds. The tuition cost just for preschool was about thirty thousand rupees, not including the enrollment free. I didn't care. If it was beneficial for Maheen, the money didn't matter.

The red brick building of the school stretched out for about two acres of land since preschool through twelfth grade were all in the same building. Faiza, Farooq, and I took Maheen inside, and we walked towards the main admissions office on the first floor. When we got to the lobby on the first floor, Faiza went inside the office in front of us to let them know that we were here for the interview. Farooq, Maheen, and I took a seat on the waiting chairs outside. Faiza came back walking towards us, "What did they say?" Farooq asked.

"The office lady said that the principal is busy currently; they will call us in when they are ready," Faiza said, and she took a seat next to Farooq and took Maheen from his lap.

After waiting patiently for about an hour in the lobby of the office, one of the personal assistants came out of the principal's office. "Come inside," he said. The three of us got up and went inside the main office from where the assistant led us to the principal's office. That's when I first met the principal and founder of the school, Ms. Khadija Abassi. She had bobbed hair and a very fake smile on her face as she sat behind her oval desk. Khadija was also, a relative of Nadeem's wife, but we hadn't come through that reference to get Maheen admitted; it was just a coincidence that Maliha and Khadija had family connections.

Something about Khadija's attitude annoyed me from the first second she spoke. "The examiner will interview your daughter, and if she doesn't meet our standards, I will not be able to help you." Khadija's tone had suddenly changed.

"Isn't that how it works?" Farooq asked curiously.

"I just wanted to clarify that your family reference won't help her get in." Khadija said sarcastically.

"But I am not trying to get Maheen admitted through reference or recommendation anyway," Faiza said.

Khadija ignored her. Her attitude was on a different level as if this wasn't some preschool but an Ivy league admission process.

A teacher dressed up in a white shalwar kameez came and took Maheen inside into one of the offices for an interview. No one was allowed inside, so Farooq, Faiza and I stayed in Khadija's office as she bragged about how students from this school go on to study in the U.S. in Ivy league schools. She said, "If your daughter doesn't pass the exam, we can definitely think of something, if you would be willing to donate to the school. It will only help us improve our facilities. You are understanding what I am trying to say right?" Khadija said, looking at Faiza and Farooq.

"Excuse me, what are you trying to say? That my daughter isn't capable enough for your school, but you will do me a favor if we donate to the school? That's ridiculous," he said.

"Don't get offended. I was just offering a solution," Khadija bluntly said. She just wanted our money.

A few minutes later, Maheen came back into the room with the teacher, and the teacher walked her to Faiza. "Ma'am, she got a 20 out of 20 on the entrance exam," the teacher said. Faiza and Farooq smiled.

"Really? Show me the results," Khadija said, panicked, as if she really didn't want Maheen to be a student here. She looked at the reports carefully and told us to go outside and wait for their decision.

"Abu, I don't like the principal's behavior towards Maheen at all. She's so full of herself," Farooq said.

"I didn't like the atmosphere," Faiza said.

Farooq and Faiza had decided that whatever the outcome here was going to be, they weren't going to put Maheen in this school. The assistant came back out of Khadija's office and called us inside again. We went in the office again, and Khadija was sitting at her desk drinking chai.

"Alright, so your daughter did great on the exam, but I am afraid we can't take her in right now," Khadija arrogantly said.

"But why?" Farooq asked. "Can I get a clear answer? She passed your examination," Faiza said.

"She passed the exam, yes, but I will be straight up with you, your daughter can't walk further than a few steps without losing her balance. How will she even excel at school?" Khadija said. My blood was boiling after hearing that. Faiza tightened her grip around Maheen, and Farooq's face turned red.

"However, if you really want her to be admitted, I can

honor our family terms if you are okay with paying extra money," Khadija said.

"Oh, so this is what it was all about," I thought to myself. I was DIG police, yet this woman was asking for a bribe to get my granddaughter into this school. Only I knew how I kept my cool in this situation, otherwise I literally wanted to shoot Khadija in the head. I have said it from day one, money talks in this country; money for people becomes bigger than respect and that is the saddest part.

"My daughter doesn't need you; let's get out of here," Farooq said as he stood up. Faiza and I followed.

It was decided that we were going to put Maheen in any school but not Defence Preschool. But destiny had something completely different written for her. Two weeks later, Farooq heard back from one of his job interviews in Guam, and they sponsored Farooq's entire family to move to the US. Without a second thought, Farooq accepted the offer, and a month later Farooq, Faiza and Maheen left Pakistan for good.

Once Maheen left, the house had become completely quiet. I was working, Salman was going to college, Aamir was busy with school, Nadeem had gone to America for his residency, and Nishat spent hours at home alone, or sometimes she would have a group of friends come over for dinner. Our lives felt so empty without Maheen. There was no one who I could play with for hours. There was no one who would barge into my drawing room and insist on sitting next to me as I watched Cricket. I used to have a drink or two while watching matches, and Maheen always noticed. She was such an inquisitive girl. She always asked me what I was drinking, and I always told her, "It's medicine." Every day when I got him from the police station there was no one to welcome me home by screaming "Dada(grandpa)" as soon as I would walk through the main door.

Nothing was enough to make Nishat and I miss Maheen any less. I used to speak to Maheen on the phone every day, which made me feel her absence even more. My heart wasn't in my work anymore. I wanted to be wherever my granddaughter was. As head of police, there was no way I could get more than seven to ten days off from work at once. I still had five years of service left before my retirement, but I had made up my mind. I filed a request for early retirement to spend the maximum amount of time in Guam with Maheen. All my friends and even Nishat thought that I should finish my remaining time in service. My friends told me, "You are crazy. Why would you let go of your job when not everyone could attain your position? And your pension will decrease." I didn't care if my post in the police was a dream to others. I didn't care that my pension would decrease if I took early retirement. I just knew that I didn't want to miss out on my granddaughter growing up. I wanted to be a part of Maheen's life, and if that meant I had to quit my job, then that was going to be it. And that's exactly what I did.

My request for early retirement was accepted, but I had to serve my final month in service before I could be addressed as Major Retired DIG Mazhar Qayyum. In the days leading up to my retirement, Nishat and I got our US visas, and Ahaya, who after retiring from the army had ventured into the traveling business now owned his own travel agency called Galaxy Travels, booked our tickets. Farooq and Faiza knew that we were coming, but I had told them to keep It a secret from Maheen. I wanted to surprise her. In November, Nishat and I flew to Tamuning, Guam. There wasn't much to look at during the drive from the airport to Farooq and Faiza's apartment. It was a single plain road with ugly green trees on either side. Farooq and Faiza lived in Oaka Towers, the apartment building faced Tamuning Beach. In front of the building were three community pools with a beach-facing view. The area was stunning. As I got out the car there was one thing I could not help but notice: the never-ending amount of tiny lizards on the footpath. Every time I took a step, I was afraid of stepping on one. "This is just like Lahore" I said to Nishat laughingly. I quickly slammed the door shut and rushed inside the building. I was eager to see Maheen. Farooq's apartment was on the thirteenth floor.

When we got up, I rang the doorbell, and Faiza came to open the door. "Salam (hello)," she said.

"Salaam," I said, putting my hand on her head blessing her, and dropped my suitcase in the middle of the hallway and ran towards the living room to find Maheen. She was sitting on the couch watching the Disney movie about the Native American girl finding love in a white colonizer. The movie was projected on the front wall through the projector which was placed in the back of the living room.

"Daa-da," Maheen screamed, looking at me as her eyes got bigger with excitement. I kissed her forehead and sat beside her. She made me watch ten different episodes of Dora the Explorer and then her favorite Bollywood movie Asoka, which was a Bollywood version of the story of King Asoka of the Maurya Dynasty. I never understood what fascinated Maheen as a four-and-a-half-year-old to get addicted to a movie about empire conflicts.

Every single day, Maheen and I sat in the living room and watched tv in the mornings before Faiza dropped her to preschool, and when Maheen would come back we watched tv together again. Whenever Faiza and Nishat went to the mall or grocery shopping, Maheen always stayed at home with me. She and I always had the best time together. Almost every other day, we would go swimming in the pool in front of the apartment building. Maheen had Dora the Explorer swim floats that she loved to wear to the pool all the time. And after our swimming trips, Maheen and I used to go down to the beach and walk on the sand. Maheen loved playing with sand; she had her little toy shovel and would always ask me to make a castle for her. I always did all the sand digging, but then Maheen would say, "Dada, I am tired of working now, let's relax." I used to start laughing at this four-and-a-half-year-old's effort to say words that were bigger than her and her diva attitude. She was a diva, the Mazhar family's diva. When the two of us were finished building sandcastles, Maheen would dig my feet in the sand and ask me to make a sand blanket cover over her, and the two of us would sit on the beach for as long as wanted, soaking in the beautiful sun in Guam.

In the evening, when Maheen and I would get back from the beach we always had her favorite snack, lemonade with macaroni and cheese. Maheen could eat macaroni and cheese any time of the day, and not just any mac and cheese, but only the ones that were shaped like seashells. Faiza used to bring them from the local grocery store. Once I was at the grocery store with Farooq and we picked up a different brand of mac and cheese. When I got home with it and showed Maheen, she threw it on the floor. When I asked her why, she said, "It's not shell shaped," and made a sad face. From then on I knew mac and cheese could only exist in a shell shape.

One day we were all sitting in the lobby in the afternoon. Maheen had just come back from school, and we were watching Shahrukh Khan's movie *Dil Se.* Faiza was feeding Maheen mac and cheese when Maheen's favorite Bollywood song *Chaiya Chaiya,* came on. Maheen suddenly got up and went right in the middle of the lobby, and started dancing, staring at us for attention. She wanted everyone to pay attention, so when Nishat started talking to me, Maheen came and tapped Nishat's knee, signaling her to pay attention. I started smiling.

Suddenly, I noticed that she had begun twitching her eyes.

Then she began jerking her arms left and right. “Maheen, Maheen, what’s wrong? Look at me,” Faiza suddenly cried out loud, tightening her grip around Maheen’s waist, but Maheen’s entire body was shaking at this point.

“Look at me, Maheen, look at me,” my voice got louder and louder. Maheen’s eyes went entirely out of focus. Her left eye looked up in space while her right eye looked at me. Her body was completely shaking and her arms flapped everywhere.

“Maheen! What’s happening to her? Call the ambulance, “Faiza began screaming. “Call the ambulance now,” Faiza cried again. My fingers shook as I dialed 911 on my phone. I heard Faiza scream again as Maheen had completely fainted in her lap.

When the paramedics reached us, they rushed into the apartment and picked Maheen up, strapped her onto the stretcher, and pulled her into the ambulance that was standing outside.

“I can’t leave her alone; I am going with her,” Faiza said as she followed Maheen inside the ambulance. She held on to Maheen’s forearm, and the paramedic shut the ambulance door on my face. I ran inside, called Farooq, and told him what happened. I put my shoes on, took the car keys, and Nishat and I rushed towards the car. I had never driven a car in the US before, but at this point, I had no choice. I had to make it to the hospital. Google maps did not exist, so I chased the ambulance bumper to bumper, breaking all the traffic laws in a rush to reach the hospital.

My hands were shaking as I gripped the steering wheel with all my force. I didn’t even realize that Guam had left hand driving just like the rest of the US, and I was used to right hand driving in Pakistan. I didn’t know incoming traffic verses outgoing; all I knew was that I had to follow the ambulance bumper to bumper even if the world was going to end today. There was only one thing going on in my mind. “God, don’t let anything happen to her. Please don’t let anything happen to

Maheen," I prayed under my breath.

After much chase, I reached the parking lot by the emergency entrance of the hospital. I walked towards the double doors. Farooq was already standing there panicking behind the ambulance as they pulled Maheen's stretcher out and into the hospital's emergency room.

Farooq ran inside with Faiza as they took Maheen in. I followed. Maheen was still unconscious.

I stood by Nishat's side outside the emergency, fiddling with my fingers and silently praying for everything to be okay. "Why all of this so suddenly?" I asked myself. Did she eat something she wasn't supposed to? I began strolling from one corner of the waiting room as one of the nurses came outside.

"Are you the grandparents of Maheen?" She looked at Nishat and me.

"Yes we are," I said, stepping closer to Nishat.

"She's regained her consciousness. You may go back now and meet her." Nishat and I walked through the narrow door into the emergency.

Maheen was lying down on the bed. "Dada, I want pudding," she said, looking at me as she reached her hand out towards me.

I kissed her on the forehead then looked at Faiza who was still crying by the side of the bed. "What happened to her?" I asked, looking at Faiza.

"Seizure," Faiza answered. "The doctors here said that we should take Maheen to a neurologist just in case to prevent another seizure in the future," Faiza added.

"Where's Farooq?" I asked. "He's still talking to the doctor," she said, looking back at me.

Nishat, Faiza and I stood there waiting for Maheen's drip to end. Farooq came rushing towards Maheen's bed and hugged her from the side tightly as he wiped his tears off his cheeks. The nurse came towards us with a sheet of paper in her hands. "You can take her home now. Make sure you pay attention to her moods, and the more relaxed she is, the better," she said. We brought Maheen back home, and she was completely fine. I couldn't understand what had even happened today. I just hoped that this would not happen again.

After much more research, Faiza and Farooq found a neurologist they trusted: Dr. Carlos, who was associated with the Neurology Clinic, and his office was located close to our apartment. At the doctor's office, there were chairs lined up in rows, one after another, kids play area to the left and reception desk in the back of the room. I sat down with Maheen in the little play area inside the doctor's office while Faiza and Farooq signed her in. The area had a mini bookshelf on one side and puzzle games on the other side. Maheen picked up a Barbie storybook and brought it over to me. "Read to me," she said. I grabbed the book from her hands and was opening it when the white door next to the reception desk opened, and a nurse in a blue and pink floral shirt and khaki pants called out "Maheen Mazhar," the voiced echoed in the room. I dropped the book, picked Maheen up, and followed Faiza and Farooq in through the white door. The nurse took Maheen's weight and led us into the room on the left. Faiza sat with Maheen on the bed while all of us waited for the doctor to come in.

I stared at the cartoon images on the wall, and then the door opened, and in came a tall man with broad shoulders and a mole on his face. "Hi, I am Dr. Carlos." He shook Farooq's hand, then Faiza's hand and finally my hand. "So, what's been going on? I see Maheen's report, and it seems like she's been having seizures lately," Dr. Carlos said.

"Yes doctor, that's our biggest concern..." Faiza said as she repeated Maheen's history as well as mentioned the trauma at birth.

Dr. Carlos pulled out MRI scans from Maheen's file and

took a minute to look at everything before responding. "Was there any kind of forceful pulling on the head during birth?" Dr. Carlos asked Faiza.

"Yes" Faiza answered.

"Hmm. This is not strange at all keeping in mind that she suffered massive birth trauma. Her brain is trying to adapt itself to the trauma it had to go through during the birthing process. Whatever was used to pull her head out of the birthing canal was used with too much force. It sort of shook things up a little bit. Because of the trauma, her brain has an increased level of neurochemical signals reacting at the same time. In other words, her brain is firing too many signals at the same time, and these signals are getting in each other's way, and they break out in the form of a seizure," Dr. Carlos said.

All of us listened to him very carefully. "Is she going to have this forever?" I asked curiously.

"I mean, it should die down as she grows up, but in some cases, it does become a permanent problem. Depends on the individual," Dr. Carlos answered.

"So, doctor, what should our next steps be as of now?" Farooq asked.

"I am going to put Maheen on a medication called Trileptal. I will give her the liquid version of the tablet since she's young. This will help prevent further seizure attacks, and for the next few years, we will be monitoring her through regular EEG exams every six months until we are a hundred percent sure that she will never have seizures again," Dr. Carlos said with a smile.

All of us were very satisfied with Dr. Carlos; everything he said made sense, but under my breath, I kept praying to God to end the test that he had placed on Maheen and grant her absolute health. Dr. Carlos handed Farooq a check out paper to give to the front desk as we left, and the three of us headed back home. Praise to God, for the next little while everything was smooth again. Maheen never had an attack again till the time I was there, and my prayer was always that may she never have one again.

One month later I went back to Lahore with Nishat because Salman and Aamir were missing us. A few months later we found out that Farooq was offered a higher-level job at Arthur Anderson in New York City, and with Faiza expecting a second child, he had decided to take it. In 2001, Farooq and Faiza moved to Staten Island, New York.

PART II
MAHEEN'S STORY

CHAPTER FOUR

For me, this story began when I was five years old. I opened my eyes and found myself at NYU Langone Hospital's Pediatric Neurology ward, laying on the hospital bed getting ready for an MRI Scan. My dad sat in front of me sobbing, his eyes were red from all the crying. I saw my Grandpa resting his hand on dad's shoulder as he stood behind him with watery eyes. My grandma was crying in the corner, wiping her cheeks with her scarf, and my mom was sitting beside me as she held on tightly to my right arm. I could see the tears dripping down her cheeks as if she had been crying for hours. "What's wrong?" I asked her as I stared into her eyes. It was just an innocent question. I wanted to know why I was in the hospital and not in school.

"Why is everyone crying and looking at me? What happened to me? Tell me," I said.

Mom bent over the hospital bed and kissed my forehead. "Nothing baby. You are my fighter baby, " she said, looking right into my eyes. I started smiling instantly. Those words made me feel so powerful as if I could do anything in the world. Those words suddenly made me forget the pain of having so many wires attached to me. I didn't know why, but hospitals made me sick to my stomach. It was as if I had this hatred towards hospitals since the time I had awareness of what it meant to be alive.

The nurse standing to my right had wrapped a grey pulse checker around my right index finger. I gazed a little bit higher, and there were two needles stabbed into my elbow crease that led to the IV drip to the right of my bed. "Get this off of me!" I started screaming. "It hurts. Get this off of me," I said. My mom started waving her hand gently over my head, trying to calm me down, but all I wanted to do was free myself from being attached to all these wires.

Another nurse walked into the room. "We are ready to take her back for anesthesia," the nurse said as she lowered my bed completely flat and raised the side bars of the bed to move me to the other room.

I glanced at my family one last time before being driven out of the room. I was hoping that my family would somehow stop all this from happening. But everyone seemed so helpless against the circumstances. My parents had this weird despair in their eyes as they had told me that all this was for my own benefit. But honestly, I hated it. I wanted to get up and run away, but the needles attached to me held me caged to the ugly bed. The two nurses began rolling my bed out of the room into the hallway. My family followed me down the hallway to the anesthesia room. The nurse took me inside a small room that had a tiny bed pushed against the wall. Behind the bed were a bunch of red and blue wires that connected to a rectangular-shaped monitor. I saw the long clear plastic tube of the anesthesia mask hanging on the left side of the cart, and I wanted to run away, now. The anesthesia specialist in the room detached my drip from my hand and moved me over to the smaller bed near the anesthesia machine. I saw my parents standing outside the door until the nurse slammed the door shut. I couldn't calm myself down; I kept staring at the anesthesia specialist and then at the ugly looking anesthesia mask hung right next to me. The nurse in the room tried to distract me from paying attention to everything that was happening around.

"Do you like pink?" she asked me.

"Yes," I answered, still peaking at the anesthesia machine on the other side of me.

"Do you like balloons?" the nurse asked again.

"I do," I said, looking at her and right that moment the anesthesia specialist came behind me and wrapped a rubbery string mask around my nose and then adjusted the sides of the mask on my face, making sure the rubber sides were bordering my nose but not on it. I thought I was going to suffocate. Not because I couldn't breathe but because of the sedative smell of the mask that I was breathing in. I was being caged into something that was the most traumatizing thing in the world to me. The anesthesia specialist could have given me injections to put me to sleep, and I wouldn't mind, but the two minutes between having the anesthesia mask on my face and completely knocking out were complete torture to me. I kept turning my head left, and right but the mask didn't come off, nor did the feeling of being caged. Slowly I was fading out. I couldn't even keep my eyelids fully open. I saw the nurse in front of me carrying something white, but everything was getting blurry by the second. All I remember before falling completely unconscious was that I felt as if someone was moving my bed from one corner to the other. The nurses were most likely taking me to the exam room. I had given myself away to the force of anesthesia.

The next thing I remember is waking up and wanting chocolate pudding. My dad was sitting in the chair by my bed.

Dada and Dadi stood right beside him, and Mom came running to me as soon as she saw that my eyes were open. "I want chocolate pudding," I cried. Chocolate Jell-O was my favorite. I wouldn't let Mom go from my side, so Dad ran downstairs to the hospital cafeteria to get me pudding. There was no pain; it was the disgusting anesthetic smell that was killing me. I wanted to vomit. If anyone was ever to ask me how anesthesia smelled like to me, I would say it was poison. It felt like as if that smell was sucking all the life out of me, and the taste of it in my mouth made me gag. Dad came back with two packets of chocolate pudding. Mom raised the hospital bed a little higher and helped me sit up with my back against the pillow. Dad ripped open the packaging of the pudding and began feeding me a bite at a time. Now I couldn't think of anything else except for how divine the chocolate pudding tasted. As each bite melted away in my mouth, the aftertaste of anesthesia faded away.

With half a spoon of pudding still in my mouth, I saw the nurse walk back into the room. Passing grandpa, she came in right by my bed. "Hi Maheen, how are you feeling?" she asked me as I savored the chocolate pudding in my mouth for a second longer.

"Okay," I said. I was annoyed. Why couldn't the nurse just leave? She spoke to my dad about how the reports would go straight to the doctor and handed him a check out form. "I want to go to Target," I said as my mom took off my hospital gown and got me into my own clothes.

"Of course, I will buy you whatever you want," Dada said as he walked up to me and put his hand on my head, blessing me. Dad checked out at the lobby, and the valet driver brought our car directly outside the glass doors of the NYU Langone Hospital building between 2nd and 3rd Avenue. I didn't want to go to the Target in the city. I wanted to go to Target near our apartment because that was where I always used to go to get a gift for no reason. We sat in the car and Dad drove us out of the city. Our apartment was a forty-five-minute drive from Manhattan, which was nice because we could come to the city whenever we wanted but still live in a suburban area. Mom and Dad used to say that Manhattan was the best place for opportunities in life but not for raising a family. There was no space in the city to play outdoors, and people looked at kids as if we were the most annoying creatures on earth. That's why we lived in Staten Island but Dad still worked in the city.

We reached Target, and Dada got out of the car, then I got of the car. He held my hand and took me inside the store. Mom followed us. I walked into the store and took Dada straight into the toy section where I knew they had toy high heel shoes. The heels were so pretty, and I was insanely crazy about them. There was Cinderella and her blue heels, Sleeping Beauty and her pink heels and finally my favorite Belle from Beauty and the Beast and her yellow heels. I began pointing my finger at a box that had all three high heel shoes. "I want this," I said, looking at Dada.

"Nope, I won't let you buy these," Dada said, looking at me as he shook his head from left to right.

"But why?" I cried.

Dada then looked at Mom who was standing behind us. "She will fall in these," I heard him telling my mom.

"No, I won't fall. I promise I won't fall. Can I please get this?" I insisted. I begged Dada, but he was stubborn about not letting me buy the high heel shoes. If he was stubborn about what he thought was right, then so was I. I started crying. Mom tried to console me, but I kept on looking at Dada with sad eyes thinking he would melt, but he didn't.

"I can't watch her cry, but I can't let her do something that will end up harming her," Dada said, and then he left and went back to the car as he told Mom to get me whatever I wanted.

I made mom buy me the high heel shoes anyway. We came back to the car, and I had hiccups from all the crying. "What happened?" my dad asked.

"She wanted to buy high heels, but Farooq, she will lose her balance. I can't allow that," my grandpa told my dad. Now grandpa was mad because I bought the shoes. But I wanted the shoes, and I wanted Dada to talk to me. The rest of the car ride home Dada didn't say a word to me, and I kept crying till eventually, I fell asleep. This was the first and only time I ever fought with Dada in my life.

Later that night when we came home, Dada came and sat right next to me on the couch in the living room as I watched TV. "I hate seeing you cry, Maheen, and I am sorry for not giving in to your wish, but I had to," he said.

"I am sorry for crying, Dada, but I love those shoes," I said to him.

"You can wear them when you get older, just not now, okay?" he said kissing my forehead.

"But I want to wear them now," I said. He didn't say anything to me, but I still knew he wasn't happy with my decision. I wore the heels around the house anyway. Even if I fell, I got back up and wore the heels again. I didn't care if I was going to fall a million times in those heels; that didn't stop me from wearing them.

A week later was my first day of kindergarten. Mom dressed me up in a white floral dress and she tied my hair in two pigtails like she always did. Both Mom and Dad drove me to school. My school was called "PS45." It was a red brick building that had blue doors. There was an ice cream truck that used to always be parked across the street from the school. The ice cream truck was the first thing I noticed, and once my parents and I got out the car I made them get me ice cream first thing. Mom got me my favorite chocolate ice cream sandwich from the ice cream truck, then she held my hand and walked me towards the school. I was fine till now. It wasn't really hitting me quite yet that I would have to spend seven hours away from my mom in a building that literally had no windows.

The entrance of the school was crowded with parents whose children would refuse to let them go. When Mom, Dad, and I got inside, I couldn't help but notice how old and dark the building was. All the walls inside the school were dark blue, and the classrooms on the first floor had no windows. There was a cafeteria on the right. Outside it there were benches, and directly opposite the benches was a blue staircase that led to more classrooms on the second floor. I did not want my mom to leave me like all the other moms were leaving their kids, so I tightly grabbed on to the side of her shirt. Little did I know, my parents were not just leaving me at school but leaving me with a surprise I never expected. As we stood there in the school lobby, a woman dressed in a white-collar shirt and a black blazer with curly hair walked towards me. She had a bright smile on her face and came straight towards me to shake hands with me. "Hi Maheen, I am Dianna, but you can call me Ms. D. How are you?"

I shook her hand, behaving like a good girl, but then I stared at my dad then at my mom from the corner of my eye thinking, "Who is this woman and how does she know my name?"

"The principal has sent me as Maheen's para," she said as she shook hands with my parents.

"Para what?" I thought to myself. It turned out that my dad had requested the school's principal to give me an aid who would hold my hand everywhere I go because my parents were scared that I would fall on my own. Everyone falls, it's okay. You fall and get back up again and get going. It didn't mean that I needed this woman to look after me.

Ms. D held her hand out towards mine, and I refused to hold her hand. I began crying. I didn't need a hand hold, in fact I didn't need anyone. If I had met Ms. D on my own, I probably would have liked her, but the fact that my parents forced her on me against my will annoyed me more than anything in this world. Throwing a tantrum on my parents wasn't quite successful in getting me out of the situation. They were parents, of course. They weren't my enemy, but I just didn't like the fact that they had done this to me. I knew how to take care of myself. I didn't need a hand hold. I didn't need anyone.

When we got to the classroom, Ms. D. sat me down on the table that had my name tag on it. The classroom didn't have typical desks; instead, we had long round wooden conference tables with about seven kids to a table, and the teacher had assigned spots for each student marked with their name tag. My main class teacher's name was Ms. Brown. Right next to me sat a girl named Nora who I started talking to right away, and we became friends instantly. On the other side of me sat a blonde girl named Kayla who got in trouble with Ms. Brown for using the s word in class. That first day in school we learned about how the apple represents a symbol for education, and we were asked to bring in an apple to school as our first homework assignment. The assignment was to bring a real apple to school so we could make apple pie.

The following day Kayla got in trouble again, because she brought a fake apple ornament to school instead of an actual apple. In my head, I laughed so hard at Kayla for not understanding such simple directions. If the teacher says bring in an apple to school, it means bring in an apple to school. Not a fake one. But then when Ms. Brown told Kayla that she couldn't participate in making the apple pie because she had failed to follow directions, Kayla's mischievous smile turned into a frown, and I started feeling bad for her. After the class had finished making apple pie and it was time to eat it, I cut my piece of pie in half and gave it to Kayla so she wouldn't feel completely left out while the entire class ate together. Ms. Brown was so busy putting up posters around the classroom walls as we ate that she didn't even notice.

On the other hand, Ms. D began to annoy me to my core. She used to follow me everywhere, and I wanted her to just leave me alone. During recess when the class used to go outside, Ms. D followed me like a shadow. On the steps, on the playground, on the swings, on the slides, the blacktop, everywhere, even when I was with my friends, Ms. D would be there. The lunch line was the only place Ms. D would leave me alone. I looked forward to lunch all the time because of that and also because the cafeteria in school used to serve the best grilled chicken sauteed in barbecue flavoring and white rice on the side. Schools usually never had the best food, but the grilled chicken at my school was unmatched.

One day Mom picked me up from school, and after getting ice cream she drove me all the way to NYU Langone Hospital. After reaching the hospital, Mom gave the car to the valet driver outside the hospital building and she took me to the eighth floor into the EEG exam department, in the waiting area on the eighth floor of the hospital. The seats in the waiting area were lined up in rows of five, and behind the seats was a giant glass window through which I could see the helicopter pad landing area of the hospital, and in the distance I could see the MetLife Building and the tip of the Empire State Building. While Mom and I waited for the nurse to call my name, I sat in the chair near the window and kept staring at the tip of the Empire State building as the clouds covered it on both sides, trying to hide its beauty, but the most iconic symbol of the city knew how to shine anyway. Despite being covered by grey clouds, the Empire State was still the pride of the New York Skyline, standing tall, unbothered by whether it snowed or rained or whether it was a cloudy or a sunny day.

Telling the world that no matter what kind of day comes by, it will always remain tall. That moment I felt like me and the building had so much in common. No matter what you put me through, I was still going to stand tall and strong. The Empire State building was how solid I aspired to be. I didn't want to be in the hospital; I wanted to run away, but in that moment as I looked at the Empire State, I realized if this building can stand through anything and still shine, so can I.

While staring at the Empire State, I turned my gaze down at the roof of the floor below us and noticed a large box with a circle, and inside the circle was a big letter H. "Mom what's this for?" I asked looking over at her as she was filling out forms.

"This is for emergencies, honey. When people get hurt and they need to be brought to the hospital right away, they bring them in helicopters because it's much faster and people can get treated right away," Mom explained to me. Staring out the window at the white cross, I couldn't stop thinking about what Mom had said. How scary it must be to rescue people from emergency situations. How people arrive in hospitals in every condition in every physical state. People die in hospitals while at the same time babies are also born in hospitals. A happy moment for someone somewhere may be the most dreadful moment for someone else. Hospitals just always made me feel very uncomfortable. I was lost deep in my own thoughts, and I didn't even realize that the nurse was calling my name.

"Maheen, let's go," my mom called. She held on to my hand and we started following the nurse out of the waiting area and into a hallway full of rooms. The rooms were numbered one to ten. The nurse took us inside Examination room #6. The door opened into a small room, which was the size of a storage room. There was a giant computer monitor that was set up on a table to the right of the entrance. Directly in front was a giant window covered with blinds; it was only a few feet away from where I was standing by the entrance. On my right was the EEG testing room. The door had a huge square glass window right in the center of it through which I could see the patient bed in the other room.

The nurse smiled at me as she took my mom and me into the testing room. The nurse went behind the door and picked up a large white trash bag which was overflowing with unopened toys. She walked back and stood right in front of me, pulled the bag open, and held it in front of me. Some toys were big while other ones were small, but I had already set my eyes on the Barbie doll figure whose sparkly silver top caught my eye in the chaotic pile of toys. "Once you are done today you can pick anything you want from this basket," the nurse said to me, putting the bag on the floor near the side of the bed. I was suddenly excited about this now. It didn't seem to be nearly half as scary as my other doctor visits. I knew I wanted to earn that Barbie toy in the end; that's what my mind was set on.

The nurse gently pulled my hair out from under my neck and scattered it all behind my head, away from my face and neck. Then she took a clear thick fuzzy gel and began applying it to the padded electrodes attached to the end of each wire. "Are you ready?" the nurse asked, gazing down at my face. I closed my eyes and nodded my head. She began attaching the electrodes in to my hair starting from the area between my forehead and my hairline. The cold jelly-like sensation on my head felt calming as the nurse gently placed the rest of the electrodes on my head, spread them out evenly across my whole head until no portion of my hair was visible anymore. I looked in the small rectangular mirror in front me and began counting the wires, but there were so many of them attached to my head, I lost count after ten.

"Alright, you need to make sure you stay as still as possible, alright? I am going to be at the computer outside. If you need anything wave at me. I will see you," the nurse said to me as she began heading out of the room.

"How long do I have to stay like this?" I asked the nurse quickly.

"About an hour. Try going to sleep; it may help you stay still," she said to me as she closed the door and left.

Still as possible? For an hour? On this hospital bed? "But I can't sit still for ten minutes," I thought to myself as I looked over at Mom. She smiled at me and put her hand over mine. The lights in the room dimmed and the exam begun.

"Beep." The first sound went off, and I closed my eyes because I was afraid of moving. There was a blue light to my right that kept flashing with every beep, and I could feel the intensity of that flash pierce through my eyelids. Every few minutes the machine beeped, and I felt like someone was tickling me under my hair as the wires vibrated. It was like a head massage, but more painful than calming. Every few minutes the nurse would peak in from the window and check on me by showing me a thumbs up or down, and I always gave her a thumbs up even though I wanted all of this to be over. I kept trying to distract myself by thinking about the Barbie doll, but every time I heard the long and sharp "beeeeep" sound screeching through my ears, I was reminded of how hard I was trying to keep still.

The hour passed and the nurse came back into the room to take the wires off my head. As the nurse gently took each wire off of my head, the gel of the pads stuck to my hair like glue, and it felt like someone was ripping my hair out of my scalp. "I am sorry, I am so sorry," the nurse kept saying to me as she pulled on my long locks. I could see pieces of my hair coming out as the nurse pulled each wire and my hair all covered up with the goo. My hair strands swelled up, framing my face as if something had just exploded in my hair. When I saw the nurse bring back the bag full of toys, I didn't care about my hair anymore. I took out the Barbie doll I liked. The nurse took a while longer to talk to my mom and then took us outside to show my mom something on the computer monitor. I don't know exactly what she showed my mom because I didn't see it. Then we were free to leave the hospital.

November rolled around, and Mom was in her last month of pregnancy with my baby brother due at the end of the month. Mom and Dad had everything planned out. His name was going to be Saad because my Dada really liked that name. My parents had already told the doctor that they wanted a C-section instead of going for a normal delivery because Mom was scared of giving birth again. A few days before Mom's due date, Grandpa Ahsan passed away from a heart attack. Dad, Dada, Dadi, all of us at home knew, but Mom had no clue about it. Everyone back in Lahore had kept the news hidden from Mom because she was at the end days of her pregnancy. Everyone wanted to save her from the trauma she was going to get after hearing the news. Every single day Mom spoke to her family in Lahore on the phone, and every single person from Aunt Mano to Grandma Shafqat kept lying to her thinking it was for the best. Whenever Mom asked, "Where's Dad? Why isn't he talking to me?" Aunt Mano and Uncle Shahrukh lied, "He's in Italy for a business trip. That's why he's not talking to you."

Mom believed it for the first few days, but she always told my Dad, "It's not possible for Abu to not talk to me for so long," and Dad always tried his best to change the topic. I knew he had died, but I couldn't break it to Mom. I was never able to spend a ton of time with Grandpa Ahsan, but I had some clear and sharp memories with him. He used to carry me on his shoulders all day long and sing "dama damn mast kalandar," which was Grandpa Ahsan's favorite South Asian folk song. Once all our family and Mom's family were together for dinner at Grandpa Ahsan's house and Grandma Shafqat had brought out her favorite set of dishes and plates made of Italian glass that Grandpa Ahsan had brought from Italy. The plates were firmly placed on their placemats around the dining table, and all of us sat down for dinner. Playing with it, the plate slipped out of my hands and broke into pieces on the floor. Grandma Shafqat screamed because her favorite plate broke, but I was laughing because I was amused by the sound of the plate cracking. Without even thinking once that Grandma Shafqat would get mad, Grandpa Ahsan gave me all the plates around the table, and as I broke each one, he laughed with me. In the end he said, "Nothing in the world is more valuable to me than Maheen's smile." Though all the other memories of that time of my life were blurry to me, this one was engraved in my head. Thinking about this, I used to sit leaning on Mom's nine-months-pregnant tummy without saying a word because Dad had told me not to.

Mom would ask me "Are you ok?" and I would just nod my head and say, "I just want to be around you that's all." It was hard because all I wanted to do was hug her tightly. Day by day mom became more skeptical, but before she got the chance to ask anyone any further questions she went into labor.

We took her to Queens Hospital, and on November 29, 2001, my brother was born. I remember Dad dressed up in the surgical blue gown and mask that the nurse had handed to him. Dad went inside the operation theatre for Mom's delivery while Dada, Dadi and I patiently waited outside. A short while later, Dad came outside with his mask still placed over his mouth, carrying my baby brother in his hands. Dad couldn't bring the baby all the way outside, so we just got to see the glimpse of my brother wrapped in a blanket from the window outside. Once Mom was moved to a room, all of us rushed to see her and my newly born brother. My brother was the cutest little baby ever, with fair skin, hazel brown eyes like my dad's and his tiny little hands and feet. Babies are such a miracle of God; it amazed me how tiny they are with the cutest features. Saad was lying on Mom's chest held by Dad because Mom was still under the influence of anesthesia. Dad stayed in the hospital with Mom for the next three days. I stayed at home with Grandma and Grandpa. During the day after school, Grandpa and I went to the hospital to see Mom.

After three days when Mom and Saad came home, Mom found out about Grandpa Ahsan's death. Aunt Mano, Grandma Shafqat and everyone back in Lahore called Mom one by one to congratulate her on Saad's birth. Yet out of all those voices there was only one voice Mom actually wanted to hear: her father's. Yet that was impossible. "It's been six days since Saad was born. How come Abu hasn't called to congratulate me?" Mom said on the phone to Shahrukh Mamu, who had no idea how to break the news to Mom, so he disconnected the phone. That was the moment Dad told her the truth. Mom cried her eyes out that day, and for the next several weeks she had become traumatized. She did everything like usual, taking care of me, taking care of Saad, taking care of Grandpa and Grandma. But she wasn't her usual self. Mom had completely stopped talking to her friends; she stopped going out of the house. She stopped speaking to her brothers for months out of the anger that they never told her the truth about Grandpa's death. Every time I ever asked Mom anything, she only give one-word answers. For a while, Mom had become completely numb.

On one hand there was the loss of a family member, the gap of which was impossible to fill. But on the other hand, there was the addition of a new family member, my brother Saad, which needed attention. The first day Saad came home I was so excited. I watched my grandma change his clothes, shower him, and change his diapers. There was a new toy in the house to play with. On his first day home, Dadi was trying to change Saad's diaper, and I insisted that I wanted to do it. I stood in front of Saad's bassinet, and the second I opened his diaper, Saad peed on my face. I quickly ran to the bathroom to clean myself up and I told Dadi to change his diaper instead. I liked holding him when he was asleep, which was almost all the time.

It took mom three months till she was finally able to come out of her state of shock and focus on normalizing life a little bit. I mean, once you lose someone you can't ever fully fill that void or forget about it, but as time goes on you are better able to put yourself back together, and that is what Mom was doing. Mom decided to change my brother's name from Saad to Ehsan. She wanted my brother to have the same name as her father, but she decided to change the spelling from "Ahsan" to "Ehsan." But Saad was already registered as my brother's name, so Mom and Dad had to go through the legal process of changing my brother's name on the birth certificate as well as his passport.

In February, Dada and Dadi flew back to Lahore. They always came for a while and went back, and I didn't really like it when Dada went back. We were all standing at the airport. As Dada and Dadi got their boarding passes and checked in their luggage, I had my eyes set on him. When we walked closer to the security line, I already knew that Dada was about to leave me. I kept looking at him; I didn't want him to leave. Mom and Dad knew I was going to cry, so they lied to me. Standing in front of the security line, my grandpa told Mom, "Take her to the bathroom so I can leave without her crying." Mom picked me up, and I asked her, "Where is dada going?"

Mom said, "He's not going anywhere. We are going to the bathroom." I stared at Dada the entire time when Mom and I walked to the women's room in the corner. By the time I came back from the bathroom, Dada was gone. Then my parents took me to Chuck E Cheese to make me feel better.

CHAPTER FIVE

In the summer of 2003, Kindergarten was finally over. On my kindergarten graduation I was the happiest, not because school was over but because graduation was the last day I had to tolerate Ms. D. After that day she disappeared from my life completely. She was probably making someone else's life miserable now, but at least she was gone from mine. I never held a personal grudge against Ms. D, but because my parents placed her in my life forcefully, I was never able to develop a liking towards her. I was glad I didn't have to deal with her anymore.

During that summer, Mom and Dad decided that it was time for us to move. Dad liked Virginia. He used to say it's subtle, calm, and the public schools in Northern Virginia were much better than those In Staten Island. Dad had visited Virginia quite a lot to see his college best friend Farid, who lived in a town named Centreville. During that summer, Dad went to Virginia again with the intention to finalize an apartment in the area of Centreville. Centreville had just the family feel Mom and Dad wanted. It was a suburban area but only a twenty- to thirty-minute drive away from Washington DC where Dad's new project was going to be. Dad had accepted a job offer from Deloitte Consulting. Life was going to change, school was going to change, and I would have to make new friends, but I was okay with that if Mom and Dad would just let me be. I was sad to be leaving my friends, but extremely happy that I didn't have to ever go back to the school where Ms. D was stuck to me like she was my mom.

Towards the end of the summer, Dad sold his grey Hyundai and rented out a huge U-Haul truck in which he took all the home furniture to Virginia. In the second trip he brought all of us in our golden Dodge Stratus. I can never forget that car. Not because I was emotionally attached to it or anything but because that car had a giant thick silver metal bumper protector that used to stick out inches away from the body of the car. I never had to bother reading the number plate of that car because I could recognize that unique silver bumper from miles away. I was excited for this move. The drive from Staten Island to Virginia was about four hours. My parents sat in the front, and my brother and I sat in the back in our car seats. Ehsan had a car seat; I had a booster seat. My brother's was on the left, and mine on the right. The car was packed with luggage, and extra home décor was placed right next to my feet.

At that time, four hours in the car felt very long. My mom had a mini DVD player hooked on to the back of her seat, so I watched *Dora the Explorer* the entire car ride. New York was urban, full of people. Though I didn't really care much about New York as a six-year-old, Virginia seemed quite the opposite. Since the time we had gotten off of the highway, there were only green trees and green grass plots around me as I looked out the window of the car and eventually, as we drove, communities of apartments and townhouses passed by. Traffic on the roads was nothing compared to New York. Everyone drove in their lane and under the speed limit, unlike New York where everyone just wants to squeeze their car into your lane. Honking in New York was the usual; it was as common and normal as brushing your teeth. Virginia was the complete opposite: this was the quiet, suburban city of rules. Here if anyone honked at you, people stopped their cars as if someone had just cursed at them. Mom and Dad loved how quiet and disciplined Virginia was compared to New York. I, however, didn't really care much.

When we finally reached our apartment, I saw a black and white octagon-shaped sign that said "Post Corner Trinity Apartments." From the sign, we took a right and there were two gates located side by side in the front entrance of the apartment community. The first gate was only for residents that lived in the community and only opened with a remote-control button that was attached to each resident's apartment key. Inside the community, the apartments were grouped into little huts. The longest hut was the community center, located to the right hand side as soon as one entered the community. There was a community pool behind the community center. "Look, Maheen, we can come here for a swim on the weekends," Dad said as we drove past it to get to our apartment. There was green grass everywhere along with trees and beautiful flowers planted along the sidewalks, and in the distance you could see the mountains meeting the sky as if the sky was the canvas and someone had drawn a beautiful painting on it.

In September of 2003, I started first grade at Bull Run Elementary. The school was about a fifteen-minute drive from where I lived. The building was brick, painted in beige and brown. All the doors on every side of the school building were green and numbered one through ten. Mom and I went inside the main office and walked towards the table that said "First Grade" on it. The lady behind the table asked me my name and handed me a sheet of paper. "You are in Mrs. Skeel's class. It's on the same floor, two hallways down past the staircase," the woman said, smiling at my mom. Mom thanked the lady, and she and I exited the office from the door that opened right in front of the stairs. As Mom and I were trying to find my classroom, I took a good look around the school, trying to get to know it better. The brick walls of the hallway had pictures of each graduating class from 1996 to 2000. Straight down the hallway was the school cafeteria, and opposite the cafeteria was the gym. On the other side were two hallways that led to the classrooms.

Mrs. Skeel had a roster list posted outside her door. Mom and I found my name on the roster and went inside to find the teacher. Mrs. Skeel was a very caring middle-aged woman with black hair and a broad physique. Mom met Mrs. Skeel, and then Mom helped me set up my desk. We set up my markers and colored pencils neatly in a box and the folders and papers we placed on top of the desk. Once I was all settled in to my new class, Mom kissed me on the forehead, and left. Later on that day, I found out that Mom didn't leave the school right away, but she stayed around in the office just to see if I was adjusting well to the new environment or not. But I was fine and loved my new class.

That year in school I received my first Blue and Silver Honor Award for Academic Excellence for all four quarters. The school year was basically divided into four terms, and at the end of each term your homeroom teacher chose who to give honors to. Blue and Silver Honors were principal awards that were given to students who were chosen for academic excellence, good character and behavior, and finally social service. Mrs. Skeel had told my entire class that we were going to the awards, but I had no idea I was receiving the award until I saw my parents at school on the day of the ceremony, standing right outside the cafeteria doors alongside other parents who stood by the cafeteria entrance greeting students as they walked through the cafeteria doors. I didn't know what category I was getting an award in, but I knew I was getting one. Parents sat down towards the back of the cafeteria, and the students sat in front with their class.

Our principal, Dr. Poole, began the ceremony with the kindergarten awards. The first grade awards were announced next. "The next award for academic excellence goes to Maheen Mazhar," Dr. Poole announced my name on the podium. This was my moment. I got up from my seat, walked down the main aisle and up on the stage to get my award and shook hands with the principal.

Everything was perfect, till one day Mom gave me a note for school saying that I would be leaving school early. When I came out of the building around one o'clock, I saw Dad getting out of the passenger seat of the car and walking towards me.

"How come he's back so early from work?" I thought to myself. Maybe all of us were going to eat lunch somewhere, was my wishful thinking. He met me midway on the footpath from the school to the car, kissed my forehead and took my backpack. I sat in the backseat of the car with my brother, who was softly asleep on his car seat. I immediately asked "Are we going out for lunch today?" I smiled, looking over at both of my parents.

"Yes, but first we have to go to the hospital," my mom said to me as she drove the car out of the school parking lot. The smile on my face vanished in a second. "How was school, Maheen?" my dad asked me. I didn't want to answer anything. I didn't want to go the hospital. I wanted to protest, sit there and not move. As we drove away from the school, I had never liked doctors in my life. They had never given me anything but suffering and pain. The only thing I wished in that moment was that somehow, I could just escape from the car and go back to school. I knew no one was my enemy, and my parents only wanted my well-being. But what about the price I always had to pay by going to hospitals? Nobody could understand how I felt because I was the one who had to go through the repercussions of all the doctor appointments my parents ever took me to.

The twenty-minute car ride felt like it had only lasted a few seconds when our car stopped at the parking garage of Peter's Children's Hospital. I wished time could just pause and the appointment wouldn't happen. Mom parked the car in the blue parking garage next to the Emergency section of the hospital, and my parents and I got out of the car and took the elevator up to the fourth floor where the pediatric surgery department was located. Mom with my brother in her arms, Dad, and I got off the elevator and took a left down the giant hallway that passed through all the operation rooms. To my left and right all I saw were nurses rolling patients from one corner of the hallway to the other. All the patients were bed bound and had oxygen masks on their faces, a look of despair on their faces. Others were asleep and had IV drips rolling along the side of their beds. I took a deep breath and held it in a bit longer. I was scared I was going to throw up any second. Though I was only six, I knew right then I could never be a doctor in my life. I hated hospitals with every drop of blood in my veins. I could stand anything in life but not being in a hospital, even if it was for a minor checkup.

My dad tightly held my hand and took me into the pediatric surgery ward. We signed in at the front desk, and the nurse in the blue uniform took me and my parents into the room in the back right away. Everything seemed so much like as if it was already preplanned. I was in the hospital for eye surgery because I had a lazy eye. The nurse sat me down in a small room by the pre surgery ward.

"Let's get her changed right away so we can take her in for

anesthesia," the nurse immediately said after taking my vitals and testing my pulse. Tears began dripping down my cheeks automatically as I looked over at my mom and then my dad.

None of this was my wish. Was asking for a childhood without one hospital visit after another too much to ask for? "Can we not do this?" I begged my parents as the nurse was busy on the computer next to me.

"It will be over before you know it, Maheen" my mom said to me. My entire body was shaking, and I felt the blood in my veins heat up underneath my skin.

"Maheen, when you wake up you won't even know that you had surgery," the nurse said to me as she opened the cupboard right next to the sink near the bed and handed me an all blue cotton surgery gown. "Here, change into this, and the anesthesia specialist will be here to get you shortly," the nurse said, placing the ugly bland robe in my hands. I stared at its blandness as I squished the fabric tighter between my fingers and thought about how I could possibly escape from all of this. Mom gave my baby brother to Dad and took me to the other side of the white curtain in the middle of room and changed me into the gown.

After a few minutes, a nurse in a green gown and a green surgical cap came in the room to take me along. "Ready to go back?" she smiled at me. This wasn't anything to smile about, I thought to myself. My dad held my hand tightly, and my mom leaned over to kiss my forehead.

"How long is it going to take? How strong is the anesthesia going to be?" my voice quivered as I

looked at the nurse. She picked up my file, placed it under her left forearm, and reached forward towards my hand with her right hand.

"It won't be too strong. The procedure is only a few minutes long; we just cannot perform it until you are asleep," she told me as she walked me out of the room. Both of my parents had their eyes set on me and I kept on looking back at them in the hope that one of them was going to save me from this misery that I was just about to go through. My mom followed us as the nurse led me to the other room.

"Please, I don't want to go through anesthesia again, please," I thought to myself as I kept looking at Mom. The nurse took me inside the mini room where the anesthesia pipes were placed alongside the patient bed, and the nurse attached wires around me in preparation for anesthesia. Just like last time when the nurse placed the ugly green squishy oval shaped anesthesia mask around my face, covering my entire face from the bridge of my nose, it felt like my soul was suffocating. I felt small and powerless in front of the strong smell of anesthesia that was taking over all my veins at this point. It was attacking my entire body. The lights on the ceiling directly above me were becoming blurrier by the second. I could hear my breath slowing down, dying out one second after another, yet I couldn't do anything but surrender myself to the effect of anesthesia. The nurse kept speaking, but slowly her words turned into noise. Within seconds, everything blurred away, and I was gone.

This time around I woke up within an hour of the procedure with no wires or anything; I was just extremely nauseous from the anesthesia. Mom and Dad sat to the right of me. It seemed like Mom and Dad had just cried since they both had puffy eyes. The nurse came through the door and came directly to me. She slowly and gently checked my eyes, and I was fine. However, I had anesthesia sickness, which was killing me deep down inside. The nurse checked my vitals and wrote something on her chart. "She can go now, no precaution needed with the eye or anything," she said looking directly at my parents. I could bear any kind of pain but I couldn't stand the aftertaste and smell of anesthesia. I felt sick to my stomach as if there was something in my body that my body kept rejecting but didn't know how to get rid of. Slowly and gently, Mom helped me come off the bed, and I changed back into my own clothes. I was ready to leave.

"You okay beta?" Dad asked me.

"Hmm," I said. I didn't want to talk to my parents. Why did they have to put me through this? They knew how much I hated hospitals, yet still. I wasn't talking to them because I was pissed off at them for doing this to me. During the walk from the hospital to the parking garage, I could only think about how passionately I hated hospitals and forever will for the rest of my life.

"What do you want to eat?" my mom asked me as we sat in the car. I was physically and mentally exhausted.

"I want naan. I need naan, or I will throw up," my voice barely made it of my throat.

From the hospital, Dad drove us to my favorite Afghan restaurant called Rose. We used to go there quite often on the weekends to eat kabobs and rice. When we got to the restaurant and the waiter sat us down, I put my head on the table and didn't want to talk to anyone. Mom and Dad kept trying to cheer me up by talking about shopping and shoes, but I didn't want to listen. I felt like gagging from the anesthesia aftertaste that was still in my mouth. The server walked over to our table with a basket of warm naan bread and placed it in front of me. Without looking left or right, I dug in to the naan, tearing a piece of it and dipping it in my favorite white sauce. With every bite I took, I felt myself coming back to life from the torture I had just gone through before getting here. My hatred towards doctors and hospitals had started becoming an innate response. Whenever I heard the words "doctor" or "hospital," my blood would start to boil. Even though the surgery was minor and not much aftercare was needed, the whole experience of going to a hospital was a trauma itself to me.

When I was in second grade, near Halloween, there was a Best Costume Competition at my school that used to happen every year. Last year, my classmate Laura had won first prize for the competition. Laura's dress was so perfect that she looked like a real Snow White. The dress was not one of those randomly put together costume dresses that one just creates at home because they didn't have time to go Halloween shopping. The dress was made up of yellow and blue organza with red and blue satin puffed sleeves and a glitter detail sat on the front. On the back of the dress was an attached red cape for extra decoration. The getup looked even more real because Laura had short but thick jet black hair just like Snow White's. I didn't like Laura because both of us were extremely competitive in class, but I genuinely admired her Snow White look. In first grade I didn't really care much about the competition, but now I wanted to win. I wanted my hair, my dress, and my look to be perfect.

I decided to dress up as Tinkerbell this year, and I was determined to win first prize no matter what. However, fate had something else in mind. On the day of the competition, I was standing on the tile floor in my bathroom, and Mom was doing my hair and makeup. She was trying to put my hair in a round high bun just like Tinkerbell's. Mom and I had searched a few stores to find a wig that would resemble Tinkerbell's hair exactly, but we couldn't find any. So Mom bought golden hair paint that she was going to spray in my hair for the night. I was happy with that because the golden paint would give the effect of fairy dust which worked perfectly with the Tinkerbell getup. I was standing in front of the sink, and Mom stood behind me.

"Can you give me the pins?" she said to me, pointing towards the edge of the sink where all the bobby pins were. I had stopped responding to her. I don't know what was happening, but her voice sounded like a screeching beep in my ears. My eyes began rolling, and my mom kept calling my name, but I was unresponsive. My body began to shake, and I fell backwards towards Mom. Mom screamed and began calling my dad out of panic. She took me in her arms and rushed me to the sofa in the living room. She kept crying and screaming my name loudly, hoping I would respond. I would open my eyes, but they barely stayed open. I was not the one in control of my own self anymore. I heard Dad's voice and Mom's cries, and I knew that they were both around me, but other than that I had no clue what had just happened. The last thing I remember is passing out on my mom's lap.

When I regained consciousness, I wasn't in my mom's lap but tucked in bed with Mom sitting right next to me. I thought I had gotten up right away, but it had been two hours since I passed out. "What happened?" I asked Mom as I looked at her. I couldn't remember how I had fallen unconscious, and I was having a bad headache. This was my second seizure, and Mom kept insisting that we go to the doctor's, but I didn't want to. I looked down at my dress. "My competition," I screamed.

"Maheen, it's eight at night. We missed the competition because you were not feeling well," Mom tried to console me, but I bursted out into tears. I couldn't believe I had missed the one event I was looking forward to for a year. My parents assured me that next year I could go again, but I couldn't stop crying.

Following the incident, my parents took me to another neurologist who ended up saying the same thing. "Give her some time; she will grow out of it." My parents patiently waited. I, however, was still mad at them for making me miss my school competition.

The following year October came again, and Halloween was right around the corner. So was the Best Costume Competition. This year nothing could have stopped me from winning first place. I took Mom to the Disney store at the mall, and we bought a Princess Belle dress because I loved Belle from Beauty and the Beast. I bought Belle's yellow dress and matching sparkly golden shoes. I had my hair curled professionally at the salon just like the way Belle's hair was curled from the bottom, and Mom did my make up at home.

Mom and Dad were just in their casual clothes but Ehsan dressed up as superman, which was his current obsession after watching Superman in the cinema with me just a week ago. As soon as we returned home after watching Superman, Ehsan was so inspired that he stood up on the wooden dining table chair and jumped off thinking that he would fly just like superman. That didn't really work out too well, and he fell right to the ground. When he came out all dressed up in a blue and red Superman costume with his red cape hanging out, I teased him about jumping off the table again. He walked up to me and started touching the curls in my hair. "Mao, you look pretty," he said cutely. I hugged him. It was my school's Best Costume competition, but the cutest thing was Ehsan being excited as if it was his own event, not mine.

The Halloween competition took place in the school's cafeteria hall. All the students were lined up in rows on the steps of the stage in the front of the room, and all the parents were sitting on the lunch tables in front. Our principal, Dr. Pool, had to choose three winners amongst all the students that were standing up on stage. I was looking down and then up at my family sitting at the first row of tables. Suddenly I heard my name being called from the podium. I was on cloud nine. I held on to the corner of my dress and walked right to the podium to get my prize. Dr. Pool shook my hand, and he put a badge on my dress that said "First Place Winner."

More than the basket, I was obsessed with the "first place winner" badge on my chest. It made feel so proud and happy. Even though the Halloween competition was not the end of the world, I just felt so satisfied knowing that I had done exactly what I said I was going to accomplish.

I proved myself right.

The summer between second grade and third grade went by in a blink of an eye with Dada, Dadi, and Aamir Chachu visiting us. Before I even knew, September rolled around, and I started third grade. My teacher Ms. Dent was never someone who made it to my good people list. She wasn't mean, but if you got on her bad side then you got on her bad side, and I never really felt any warmth or empathy towards her. Around midway through the school year, we had a math test in class on multiplying fractions. Ms. Dent's instructions were that half of the class was going to take the math exam before lunch and the other half of the class was going to take the exam after lunch. I was part of the group of students who took the exam first. I finished my exam around noon and went straight off to lunch. During lunch break, I sat with my friend Rachel at our usual lunch table. We were casually eating our lunch when suddenly Rachel reached into her backpack and took out her math practice worksheet. Rachel was part of the group of who were going to take the math class right after lunch, so she wanted to use the time to get more practice. "Can you help me solve this?" Rachel asked as she handed me the fraction worksheet.

"Sure," I said, taking the worksheet from her hand. I spent fifteen minutes trying to explain to Rachel that when you multiply fractions you have to multiply the numerators together to get a new numerator and then multiply the denominators together to get the new denominator. Rachel stared at me with a blank expression as if everything I had just said had gone past her head. I explained it again, but when Rachel still did not understand, I took her sheet from her again and started solving the problem step by step only so Rachel could understand how to do it.

Meanwhile, a girl name Kamini, who sat across from us on the other table, was trying to eavesdrop on my conversation with Rachel. Apparently Kamini was listening to Rachel and I this entire time, and after lunch she complained to Ms. Dent that I was giving away answers to the test during lunch. I was trying to help Rachel understand the concept of multiplying fractions, but never during our lunch conversation did we ever even speak of what was on the actual test itself. Maybe I shouldn't have done Rachel's homework, but I wasn't giving away test answers. Kamini and I had a history of always butting heads in class because we never liked each other, and I knew that this was her way of getting me in trouble.

When I got back to my class after lunch ended, Ms. Dent immediately called me and Rachel outside the classroom. I left my jacket on the seat and walked outside the classroom door where Ms. Dent was standing. "Were you two talking about the test during lunch?" Ms. Dent asked, looking at me and then at Rachel.

"I was trying to help Rachel understand concepts, but I didn't talk about the test," I blurted out.

Ms. Dent didn't really like my answer. "But you were still helping her," Ms. Dent said.

"I was helping her, but I didn't talk about the test," I restated.

Ms. Dent wasn't convinced. "Cheating will not be accepted," she said, putting her hands on her hips. "Both of you have to write a note to your mothers explaining what you did and have it signed by tomorrow. You may go back inside now," Ms. Dent said with a sigh. I honestly wasn't sorry because I knew that I didn't cheat. I went inside the class, wrote the note anyway because I had to, folded it in half and stuck it in my backpack.

I took the note home, but I wanted to find a way to get Mom's signature on it without her finding out that I had gotten in trouble. In previous school years if I ever got a bad grade, my teacher used to make us have parents sign the bad grade assignment. Two times in life that I did get a bad grade, I signed my report card on behalf of my mom. The first time it worked, but the second time I signed for my mom, I got caught by the teacher. Since that day I never copied my mom's signature again. So, signing this note as Mom wasn't an option anymore. I got home and saw that Mom was in her room on the phone with her friend. This was the perfect time to make her sign the note, I thought. I had a fantastic idea. I took out a piece of notebook paper from my backpack and gently placed it on top of the letter I had written. I made sure that the corners of both papers matched tip to tip so no one could tell that there were two separate papers not one. I grabbed a permanent marker from the kitchen countertop hoping that when my mom signed the note it would bleed through to the other side.

I walked into Mom's room with the marker and paper in my hands. Mom was still on the phone. "Can you sign this?" I said handing her the blank sheet of notebook paper. I didn't let go of the paper completely because she would know. My mom paused her conversation on the phone and said, "Why do you want me to sign this?"

"I just want to see how your signature looks," I said, smiling at her.

Mom immediately knew that I was hiding something underneath that smile of mine. Mom shut the phone down and took the paper from my hand and read the letter. She started laughing at me. "Maheen do you think I am stupid that I won't look at what you make me sign? I know you too well," she said to me as she signed the actual note and not the notebook paper. Mom didn't get mad at me for what had happened at school, but she did get mad about me not telling her straight up.

One day after lunch, my class was lined up by the cafeteria doors getting ready to go to recess. Rachel, the friend who I got into trouble helping, and I always used to hang out together, so this time I wanted to join Brittany's group and play with her. Brittany and I were friends, but her friend group didn't like Rachel. Brittany was standing in front of me in line, and her friend Valerie was standing in front of her. I went up to Brittany and asked, "Hey can I play with you guys during recess?" Before Brittany even got a chance to speak, Valerie came towards me and said, "No, you can't." Valerie was double my size; she was already five foot five and much thicker than I was.

"Why can't I?" I asked, and Valarie pushed me back with her hand and turned around to continue talking to her other friends. I didn't fall, but I went further back for a second and quickly caught myself. I was furious. Brittany just stood there in shock not saying a word. How dare she touch me? I thought to myself. I didn't look left or right I straight went up to Valerie and punched her in the stomach. The lunch lady on duty was looking at us all this time. She quickly interfered, and Valerie and I were both sent to the principal's office.

We went into the principal's office, and Dr. Pool made us sit at the round conference table in the room to discuss what had happened. Valerie and I sat three seats apart from each other, and Dr. Pool sat in front of us.

"Why did you punch her ?" he said, looking directly at me.

"Because she pushed me," I said, staring at Valerie then looking at Dr. Pool. He then looked at Valerie who was about to cry sitting crunched in her seat.

"Why did you push her?" Dr. Pool asked.

"Because, because I don't like her friend Rachel, and she annoys me, so I pushed her."

Dr. Pool sighed then looked at Valerie. "You need to apologize," he said. Valerie didn't say a word. "Now," Dr. Pool added. Upon the principal's order, Valerie apologized to me, and I was sent back to class. However, Valerie spent the rest of the day in the principal's office. That was her punishment. After this incident Valerie never even came close to me ever again.

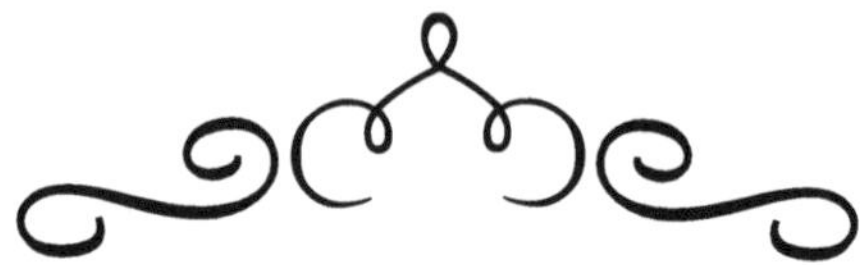

CHAPTER SIX

Sometimes in life we go through times that we wish we could erase from our memory forever because that's how painful they are. Even after those times have passed as soon as you think about them, all the trauma comes back. I no longer had to visit doctors anymore. My last EEG exam had come out completely fine. Life was good, but I hated talking about my past or thinking about all those hospital trips. I just didn't want to hear anything about doctors or hospitals anymore. My mind had formed ugly memories around those two words. Thinking about them was pure mental trauma. That's how I began to feel every time I thought about the first eight or so years of my life. Yes, I had an unconditionally loving and exceptionally supporting family who was there with me every step of the way. Yet still, my stubborn mind had begun to hate my past. It didn't want anything to do with it anymore.

Nothing much really happened in fourth grade. When I went into fifth grade, Ehsan was five years old, and he finally started Kindergarten at Bull Run. Ms. Lotz, who had been my fourth grade teacher had now become Ehsan's kindergarten teacher. I used to see her every day when I used to go visit Ehsan at the end of the day. When I asked Ms. Lotz why she had switched from teaching fourth graders to teaching kindergartens she said, "Little kids are innocent and so much more naïve. I prefer them over older kids." I laughed at her answer, but I guess it was true.

Every day at the end of school day I used to go to the kindergarten pod and pick Ehsan up, and we would head out for dismissal together. Sometimes Ehsan and I took the bus, but the majority of the time Mom used to pick both of us up from Kiss and Ride. Pick up and Drop off happened from the cafeteria. Ehsan and I had a Kiss and Ride number. We used to go and sit with all the other kiss and ride kids in the cafeteria and a faculty member always stood outside the cafeteria doors announcing numbers as cars approached. When our number was called Ehsan and I would come outside but until then I used to sit with him on the cafeteria table admiring school patrols who used to help with Kiss and Ride. As a school patrol, one had the responsibility of maintaining order within the school and making sure everything around the school ran smoothly. School patrols wore green belts that had a silver badge on them. Being a patrol meant having authority, and it seemed cool, so I wanted to be one too. However, to be a school patrol you had to be recommended by your teacher and take an exam. It was a long process that was handled by our gym teachers who also ran the student government program at school.

The same year, Mom started volunteering at my school during lunch. Mom used to come to school every day during lunch time and monitor kids. One day, during the lunch period, she met Aunty Nuzhat, another Pakistani mom who was volunteering in the cafeteria. Aunty Nuzhat had a daughter named Areeba, who was in the same grade as me but in a different class.

Apparently Aunty Nuzhat had been volunteering at lunch way longer than Mom, but surprisingly I had never noticed her till the day Mom introduced me to her. I was sitting with my friends at my usual table in the middle of the cafeteria and Mom came up to me. Alongside Mom was Aunty Nuzhat. She seemed quite older than my mom with short brown hair that had already turned grey from the sides, and she had a red sweater on. "This is Aunty Nuzhat. Nuzhat, this is my daughter Maheen," Mom said as she introduced me.

I smiled and said "Salam."

Nuzhat aunty smiled at me, and I turned back around towards my friends. "Wait, I want you to meet Nuzhat's daughter too. She's the same age as you," my mom said as she smiled at me.

"Do I really have to?" I thought to myself. I wasn't really in the mood to get up and leave my friends, but it was going to look bad, so I got up anyway, and Mom took me with her to one of the tables on the other side of the cafeteria where Nuzhat aunty's daughter was sitting with her friends. Mom introduced me to a girl with thick long hair up to her hips.

"Maheen, this is Areeba. Areeba this is Maheen," my mom said while Nuzhat aunty explained to Areeba how she ran into my mom. The two moms were more excited on making Areeba and I meet than Areeba and I were on seeing each other. I guess Mom was happy that she had finally found at least one Pakistani girl in my school the same age as me. I awkwardly said hello to Areeba and she awkwardly said hello to me, but it was such a weird meeting because our moms were literally forcing us to be friends, and who even likes forced friendships? When your parents ask you to become friends with someone, you automatically don't want to because you already have your friend group. Areeba and I just awkwardly stood there as our moms chatted away, and we never interacted with each other again the entire year because I never saw her again.

Close to the end of the school year, I was sitting in class, trying to finish my math homework when Ms. Johnson called me to her desk. I got up and went to the corner of the room where Ms. Johnson sat. She handed me an envelope, and I went back to my seat to open it. I tore the envelope open and found a letter inviting me to take the school patrol test. Ms. Johnson had recommended my name, and I was invited to the gym the next day to take the patrol test.

The next day I reported to the gym around ten in the morning for the patrol test. It was a good reason to skip part of class. Half of the gym was full of students who were there for the test.

"Only ten of you will be selected to become school patrols for the upcoming year," Ms. S said as she stood in front of us while all us students were sitting on the wooden floor of the gymnasium. Mr. Parker passed the test and a pencil to each student, and for the next forty minutes the gym had become completely silent. I quietly took the test and handed it in to Ms. M. Whenever any sort of timed tests used to happen at school, I never used to take the entire amount of time given. I didn't even double check my answers. The questions were all short answer like "What would you do if someone got into a fight in front of you?" And so on. I wanted to be school patrol, but I had to answer questions for bus safety procedures as well.

A few days later I got a letter in my classroom mailbox saying that I had made the cut. Ms. S and Mr. Peter had invited me to the induction ceremony for patrols which took place in the gym again. There were ten of us being awarded belts that day. Ms. S and Mr. Peter went over the Safety Patrol pledge and the ten of us stood there with our hands on our hearts reciting the pledge to keep the school safe. After the pledge, Mr. Parker walked up to each student, shook their hands and then put the yellow safety patrol belt on each student. I was so ecstatic about receiving that belt finally. I had seen students wear it around school all the time, and now it was my turn to wear it. The belt went around my waist, and a single yellow strap of it went across my shoulder. On the shoulder strap there was a silver badge that said "AAA" on it. After the induction ceremony ended, there were still a few hours left of school. However, I didn't take my belt off. I wore the belt the whole entire day in class until I had to report to patrol duty during dismissal. My first spot of duty was in front of the main office by the marble staircase. Since all the students going home on the bus used to exit through the main door by the office, that area was the most crowded during the morning and the afternoon. After finishing my duty, I picked up Ehsan and went to the cafeteria for Mom to come pick us up. Mom didn't know that I had become a safety patrol, but when she saw me wearing the belt she couldn't stop smiling. Once I got into the car, I took the belt off, folded it neatly layer by layer and put it in the back pocket of my backpack so that it wouldn't get dirty. It was mine now till the time I would graduate from elementary school.

The summer after fifth grade ended, Mom put Ehsan and I in Tae Kwon Do classes. There was a Tae Kwon Do center located near the Centreville Multiplex Movie Plaza about a five minute drive from where I lived. Twice a week my mom used to drive my brother and me to Tae Kwon Do lessons. I had to wear an ugly white uniform that felt like paper wrapped around my body. It was cheap quality. On top of the uniform, we had to wear our belts. Ehsan and I had started off with a white belt, but going up to the black belt was going to be torturous. Neither Ehsan nor I had started Tae Kwan Do with the intention to become a black belt. Mom and Dad thought that self-defense was an important skill to have, and Mom didn't want Ehsan and me to get bored during the summer, so Tae Kwon Do it was. Our lessons were semiprivate, so my brother and I used to be instructed together by Mr. Shim, the most disciplined Korean man I have ever seen. He always needed everything to be perfect. Our kicks, our postures, warmups, screams, everything. Whenever we were given a sequence with a punch or a kick we always screamed "Haeee ya" every time we made a move. If our "haeee ya" wasn't loud or enthusiastic enough, Mr. Shim would make us perform the whole sequence again. Our warm-ups were on the mat and with the punching bags, but then eventually we had to fight with other students.

School was going to start again in September but in August, I had my sixth-grade open house. I got to the school and picked up my schedule from the main office. Our schedules were set last minute by the main office receptionist, Ms. Doss. Ms. Doss knew me well by now. We had seen each other a million times. Ms. Doss loved me so much she had a picture of me and her from my Halloween competition placed on the side of her desk for the past two years. Every staff member in the front office knew me by face. I looked at my schedule to try to figure out my class. Since the population of the school was greater than the space of the building, sixth grade was outside in the trailers while all the other grades were inside. All these years I was waiting to be a sixth grader just so I could have class outside, but this year sixth grade had been moved upstairs on the second level while Music and Art classes had been shifted outside in the trailers. I glanced over at my schedule to find my homeroom teacher's name. I was placed in Mrs. Colontonio's class. I walked outside the office and went up the steps to the second floor. The second level was built in a shape of a rectangle, and the stairs were the middle of the rectangle. To the right of me was the fourth grade hallway. To the left of me was the fifth grade hallway, and all the way in the back was the sixth grade pod. It was called a "pod" because there were classrooms by the wall and seating spaces in the middle for events or just to sit and chill or have student teacher conferences. Mrs. Colontonio's classroom was the last classroom in the rightest corner of the second floor. There were only four sixth grade classes and teachers: Mr. Kelly, Mr. Decroo, Mrs. Parameter, and Mrs. Colontonio.

I went inside the classroom and walked straight over to the teacher's desk to meet Mrs. Colontonio. She was a middle-aged woman with long thick black hair tied loosely in a ponytail, and her thick golden glasses were resting midway on her nose.

"Hi, I am Maheen," I said as I shook Mrs. Colontonio's hand.

"Hi, welcome. You can walk around and choose where you would like to sit," Mrs. Colontonio said in her coarse voice that literally sounded like a man's.

The desks in the classroom were grouped in fours, and there were six tables altogether. Each desk had a sixth grade Welcome Packet placed on it. I walked around the room trying to figure out where I wanted to sit as I looked around to find familiar faces. I didn't see anyone in the classroom that I had known. I was standing by the table in the corner of the classroom, and I suddenly felt a hand on my shoulder. I turned around and saw Areeba. It took me a second to recognize her, but I remembered her from the time Mom made me meet her last year. "You are in this class too?" I asked as I smiled at her.

"Yup, do you want to sit together?" she said looking at me.

"Sure, where do you want to sit?" I asked Areeba. The two of us walked over to the table near the door.

"Here" she said. I put my stuff down on one of the desks, and Areeba put her bag down on the desk next to mine. In front of us sat two boys, Jared and Edger. Jared was a blonde hair blue eyed white boy and Edger was Hispanic. I didn't know them, nor did Areeba. Once we got settled at our desks, Areeba and I talked about how awkward our introduction was last year and began laughing about our moms trying to make us become friends. Little did I know that the girl I had resisted talking to last year due to mutual pestering by the mothers was going to become my best friend.

The school morning bell used to go off at 9:05. At 9:10 the morning news used to start on the tv in each classroom. I used to get to school at exactly 9:05, and I would sit at my desk waiting for Areeba to get to school. Areeba was always late, always, but as soon as she would get to the classroom, my chatterbox mouth used to go off. I didn't know how, but it was so easy to get along with Areeba. I didn't have to try to be friends with her; I just became friends with her. The actual class used to start at 9:30 AM, so from nine to nine thirty I was the one who talked, and Areeba was the one who listened. On the surface, Areeba was the quiet girl, but once I got to know her she was just like me. It just took her a while to open up with people. I was never the shy or quiet kind of kid at school, but I wouldn't open up to just anyone either. Areeba and I got along right away because we had so much in common, shared the same culture, and we both spoke Urdu. That was the best part because Areeba and I could always gossip in our language, and nobody knew what we were saying. Once, this Korean girl in my class, asked me how do you say "beautiful" in Urdu, and I told her it's "kutti," which means "bitch," and she believed me. She went around telling everybody that she was a kutti. Areeba and I laughed the entire day when we heard Sarah say "kutti." "Khoobsurat" is the word in Urdu for beautiful.

All the sixth grade teachers had set up their curriculums to prepare us for a smooth transition from elementary to middle school. Starting in seventh grade we would no longer have one homeroom teacher, rather for each subject we were going to have a different teacher and would have to switch classes. Our class was divided into four academic groups: A, B,

C and D. Luckily, Areeba and I were both in group B, which meant that we had all our classes together. Mrs. Colontonio taught science, Mr. Decroo taught math, Mr. Kelly taught history and Ms. Lilly taught language arts. Everyone had the same teacher for each subject however your group letter determined who had what class at what time of the day. My group had history first thing in the morning, then math, lunch, language arts and finally at the end of the day science with Mrs. Colontonio. I liked having her last because after science block ended Areeba and I didn't have to go back to class; we would already be in our homeroom class.

Every morning Mr. Kelly used to bore me with his history lectures. Areeba and I used to sit in the front row closer to the board, but that meant that we couldn't talk a lot during class because Mr. Kelly would notice. We had agenda books where we used to write down our homework assignments each day. Sitting in Mr. Kelly's lectures, I used to take my agenda out, open it up to an empty page and pass notes to Areeba. That notebook was how we talked during lectures. Thank God no one ever checked my agenda because Areeba and I used to talk so much rubbish about our teachers and classes, and we wouldn't even spare the kids that were in our class. Mr. Kelly had a crooked nose, so I always used to make fun of his nose. Mrs. Colontonio had a favorite blazer, which was the color of Pepto-Bismol, and she used to wear it so many times in the same week that Areeba and I had named Mrs. Colontonio "Pepto Bismol." After history, I had math with Mr. Decroo. His classroom was directly opposite Mr. Kelly's. At the beginning of each math class, Mr. Decroo used to walk around the room to stamp each student's homework. My math workbook used to be full of gossip notes rather than actual work. So, each time Mr. Decroo used to come by to check my work, I used to cover up the notes on the page with another sheet of paper just so Mr. Decroo wouldn't know that Areeba and I were passing notes in class. Surprisingly, I always got away with it.

Halfway through the year I had started developing a crush on Jared, the guy who sat in front of me in class. I thought he was the cutest boy with his sparkly blue eyes and sand-like blonde hair. I found him cute but never said anything about it, especially not to him. Only Areeba knew how I felt about him. Jared and I talked like normal classmates did; we did group projects together, helped each other with homework, but I never actually had the guts to tell him how I felt about him. Part of me wanted to tell him, but part of me didn't because at the time I didn't want anything out of it. It was just an innocent crush; I don't know how I would have felt if it progressed into anything more.

One day, after class had been dismissed, I was walking out the classroom with Areeba when I saw Jared walking down the hallway. He was probably going to his patrol duty because he had his green belt on. "Areeba, can you please tell him that I like him?" I said.

"No Maheen, I am not just randomly going to go up to him and tell him that you like him," she replied.

"I knew it is going to be awkward to just randomly stop a guy in the hallway and tell him that your best friend likes him, but I don't want to be the one approaching him," I said.

Finally, I convinced Areeba to tell Jared how I felt about him. I waited for Jared to cross the fifth grade hallway, and then I passed by him and started walking fast in front of him. From behind me Areeba called out his name, "Jared." Jared stopped as Areeba caught up to him. I really didn't want to be there or else it would have been obvious that I had told Areeba to do this. So, I went down the staircase to go get Ehsan from his class.

Areeba often went home with me after school to chill at my house, so after her conversation with Jared, she met me in the school cafeteria. "What happened? What did he say?" I asked Areeba smilingly.

"I stopped him and told him that 'Maheen likes you.' He smiled and said ok," she said, her breath was still heavy from running down the stairs and rushing to the cafeteria.

"Wait, he smiled?" I asked excitedly.

"Just a little," Areeba said.

"Thank you for doing this for me," I said. Areeba stared at me.

"If you make me do this again, I will kill you," she said, and we both laughed. My number was called, and Areeba, Ehsan, and I went outside to get in our car. I didn't really know what I wanted, but I was just happy that Jared knew that I liked him. The word spread like fire around school, and soon our entire class knew that I liked Jared, but Jared never encouraged me or anything; he just wanted to be friends. I was fine with that. The twelve-year-old me was just happy knowing that I didn't keep anything in my heart, and my crush was well aware of the fact that I liked him.

After finishing a half page of homework, I got really bored. I reached into my school bag, took at a piece of paper and started writing a note to Jared. On that piece of paper, I wrote, "Jared is hot, Jared is mine." I kept the piece of paper next to me as I finished my homework, but a while later I crumbled it up to throw away in the trash can. The trash bin in my room was transparent, and it had nothing in it. I realized that if I threw the note in my trash bin, Mom would notice it as soon as she would walk through my door. I squeezed the piece of paper tightly in my hand and went downstairs to throw it away in the large trash bin that was in the kitchen. Of course, Mom wasn't going to go through that trash in the kitchen, plus the bin was bigger so it would blend in, and no one would know, I thought to myself. I walked past our living room and made my way over to the sink where the trash bin was. I glanced over at the dining table, and Mom was on the phone with someone. I was sure that she wasn't going to notice. I opened the top of the bin by pressing on the lever by my foot, and I extended my hand out to throw the paper in, and I felt a hand suddenly grab my hand. I looked up and it was Mom.

"What is that? What's in your hand?" Mom said, her eyes bulged at me. My face had turned red, and she knew in a second that I was hiding something.

"Nothing," I muttered. I have never been a good liar. My face always said it all even if my tongue said something else. Mom snatched the crumbled paper out of my hand, opened it up and read everything.

Next thing I know, the Pakistani half of my upbringing came crashing, or should I say smacking on my face. My mother, the ever-gentle, ever-caring "mum," slapped me. Then the question followed "Who is Jared?" For a little context, slapping is part of the Pakistani parents' handbook on raising kids. Slap first, ask what they did wrong later. It wasn't abusive the way Americans would think of it. It's just what Pakistani parents do when their child does something wrong.

I only had a crush on Jared. I hadn't done anything that I had to be ashamed of. It was simply just a crush. Mom was in shock. She took me in her room and sat down on the bed as I stood in front of her. "How long has this been going on? Who's Jared?" my mom asked.

"Nothing is going on. I just like him and nothing more than that is going on," I answered.

She was so panicked and said, "Do you even know how big of a sin is to get pregnant before marriage? Are you crazy? Why are you getting into all of this at such a young age?"

Mom had started giving me an entire lecture. I was shocked. I was only twelve, and my mind hadn't even thought that far ahead. Mom had just turned an innocent crush of mine into something so serious. A thought like the one my mom was thinking about didn't even cross my mind. I wasn't even dating him, nor was I planning on it. But Mom's reaction shook me so hard. I knew Mom didn't mean what she had said; she had only said it to scare me from dating at such a young age.

Later on that night I was lying in bed with my lights turned off, thinking about what I had done wrong, if anything. Then my door opened, and Mom came into my room. She sat on the edge of my bed, kissed my forehead, and hugged me tightly. "Sorry I overreacted in the evening. I just wasn't thinking straight. I know you are a good girl," Mom said. I hugged her back. After that day, my Jared crush ended for good. Whenever I saw him, Mom's reaction would come in front of my eyes, and all the attraction faded away. Every time in my childhood I have ever tried to hide something from Mom it never worked out. Though Mom did overreact on my Jared crush, something amazing came out of all of this. Mom and I started sharing everything with each other. She became my best friend. I never hid anything from Mom again.

At the end of the school year, the music department in our school was doing a fundraiser for our annual chorus show in June. The entire sixth grade was invited to spend an evening at Chuck E Cheese to eat, which was a game arcade plus casual dining place. All the proceedings earned through food and games that night were going to go to our school. All the coin games were too childish for us, so I challenged Areeba to best of three on Dance Dance Revolution. I had won the first two rounds, and we were about to start the third round when the school principal and vice principal came and stood right behind us. I looked at them, smiled, and went back towards selecting the next song for our final dance off. Before I reached my hand out to press the "go" button, I heard the principal's voice from behind. "Can I try?" she said as I looked back at her. I was quite surprised. I had always thought she was the strict and uptight principal. She never smiled, and I had always seen her give detention to kids at school. I wasn't expecting this from her at all. "I want to play against you" the principal added as she pointed directly at me. Areeba got off her side of the stage, and the principal stepped forward on to the stage, all dressed up in her black suit and trousers as if she was still at school.

Everyone suddenly crowded around us as they saw that Ms. Kenney was about to dance. I chose the hardest level for the dance off. The music started and off we went. Ms. Kenney wasn't used to playing DDR, whenever the arrows on the ground lit up, she never followed through on time. I won again even though this time I wasn't trying to win. That day onwards if the principal ever saw me walking around in school she would always stop me, say hi, and tell her colleagues about how I was the girl who beat her in a dancing competition. Sixth grade was the most amazing out of all my years at elementary school.

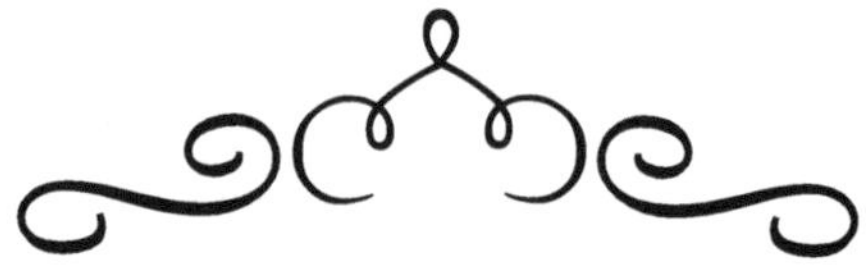

CHAPTER SEVEN

The summer after sixth grade ended, Mom and Dad bought a house in Fairfax, and we all moved. I was getting older, Ehsan was getting older, and we needed a bigger place for our family than a two-bedroom apartment. The new single-family house was only a ten minute drive from our old apartment, but the zip code was different and so were the school districts. I had to leave all my friends and classmates who I had known for years behind because they were all going to Stone Middle School while I was about to start seventh grade at Sydney Lanier Middle School. Everyone I knew in elementary school sort of vanished, except for Areeba. With her, it didn't matter whether we went to the same school or not, or if we met every week or not, we were friends for life. Everyone told me that the transition from elementary school to middle school was going to be a big one. Little did I know that my entire life was about to transform.

That something within me was about to change forever.

The first change started when Dad began dropping me off to school on his way to work every morning. I could have taken the bus, but this was the perfect way for Dad and me to get some father-daughter time together. The two of us always left home an hour before school started and made a stop at Starbucks or McDonald's to grab breakfast and coffee and chat about life.

The more time I spent with Dad, the more I started sharing with him in life. We were never the traditional father-daughter duo one would expect in the Pakistani culture. The conservative type where you aren't supposed to be friends with your parents. Of course, I respected him, but my father was my friend. Dad liked it that way too. He used to say that growing up in America things are different. You have to become your child's friend and become involved in their lives so they don't hide anything from you. Both of my parents were becoming more involved in mine and Ehsan's lives. They gave Ehsan and me our values but also made us comfortable enough to be able to share everything with them.

After coffee, Dad always dropped me straight to school. Lanier was about a twenty-minute drive from my house. The morning traffic to get to school used to be horrendous since there were three schools on the same road. Middle school started at 8:05 am sharp, which meant that I had to wake up around 6:30 am. Never in my life was I ever a morning person. I used to snooze my alarm a million times before actually waking up for school. Upon entering the school, the double glass doors on the left were the entrance to the main office; in front of the office was a wall. The actual school building started beyond the double doors in front of the library. The doors didn't open until 7:50 am sharp, so anyone who got to school before 7:50 always sat against the wall opposite the main office and waited with their Starbucks coffee cup in their hands until the doors opened. Everyone had coffee in their hands in the morning. I did too. It was the only way to get myself awake in the morning. Every other girl wore leggings, UGG boots, and a North Face jacket. The guys wore anything; they could care less. At 7:50 am the first morning bell rang, and the double doors in front of the library opened. Beyond the double doors and before the entrance to the library there was a long hallway that extended out like a T in two directions from the library. Both sides of the hallway led to student lockers and classrooms. My locker was down the left hallway from the library.

My counselor was Mr. Kamins, a man in his mid-fifties with a thick long white mustache that covered half of his face. Mr. Kamins was the one who guided me through the whole process of signing up for all honor courses in seventh grade. When I was signing up for all honor classes, Mr. Kamins had warned me that my course load would be way too heavy and that I should take it easy on myself. Mom and Dad told me the same thing, that it's the first year of middle school and I should take it slow so I could also enjoy, but I didn't listen to anyone. I was determined now. I didn't know what my long-term goal was in life, but in that moment all I knew was that I wanted to excel. Excel in whatever I had taken upon myself. Passion for anything is addictive. Once you set out to achieve something, passion doesn't let you stop until you achieve whatever it is you want. I didn't care if all honors was going to be a challenging curriculum; I was ready to take it on. This was the first time in my life I felt like my focus was becoming clear.

Beyond Mr. Kamins' office was a hallway that led to all the seventh grade English classes. The entire first level of the school formed a large square, cut in half by a main hallway that connected the two sides of the school. The library was the middle of this square. Down the left side hallway from the library were all the elective classes and upper-level math classes. All the lockers were blue (the color of the school) and were placed side by side in a straight line down every hallway. Towards the back of the first floor was the gym. Across from the gym was the entrance to the girls' locker room, a little bit further down the hallway was the entrance to the boys' locker room. The entire left side of the back of the school was the cafeteria. The only way one could access the second floor of the school was through one of the side hallways because the second floor had two sections that were not connected to one another. On level two of the building, one side was all seventh grade classes while the other side was all eighth grade classes. Thus, eighth graders and seventh graders barely ever interacted with one another, except for during lunch time or if they shared elective courses together such as Art or Computer Science.

From the get-go, middle school was already a different world compared to elementary school. Every time the bell rung after each class period everyone would rush to the hallway in the middle of the school and crowd around the lockers to talk and gossip. The hallways became so crowded that walking to class was impossible without unintentionally eavesdropping on a bunch of teenagers gossiping. I started observing everything, and the conversations were always like "so and so said this" and "so and so did that."

Or you would have a group of kids judging other people's outfit. "Did you see her dress? OMG, she doesn't know how to wear clothes. Aeropostale is so elementary; I only wear Abercrombie and Fitch."

I used to cringe hearing such conversations, and it always made me think I could never become a part of such culture. In fact, I always felt like the outsider. I mean, I could be wearing Gucci or Walmart if I wanted to. That was my choice, and it wouldn't change the person I was. So why was everyone so obsessed with brands and looks? Middle school felt like a coming-of-age/teen movie, and I felt like the audience watching it.

Soon enough, instead of becoming a part of this middle school culture, I found myself changing directions. The once carefree girl who was more focused on having a good time in school rather than her grades became more focused on herself. The social atmosphere at Lanier didn't appeal to me anymore. At Lanier, most kids had known each other from their elementary schools, and the social groups were pre-existing, and I felt like I couldn't bond with anyone beyond superficial hi's and hellos. Instead of trying to force myself to become a part of a specific social group, I began spending more time by myself, trying to figure out who I was and what I wanted in life. I missed my friends from Bull Run because those were kids who I had shared some of the most fun times of my life with. But without leaving my friends and my comfort zone, I wouldn't have started realizing the things I had begun to realize now, so leaving friends behind wasn't such a bad thing after all.

In this transition from elementary school to middle school I came to realize many things. I got to know what I believed in and what I didn't. I got to know what I agreed with and what I disagreed with. I began noticing things that I never had thought about before, like teenagers forming social groups and only talking to people in their own groups. Back at Bull Run, everyone hung out with everyone. There were no set groups. If you were in one group one day, you could be with another group the next day. At Lanier, everyone took social groups way more seriously than I had ever seen before. There were so many tiny cliques, and if you belonged to one clique you were only seen with them for the rest of the year and no one else. This whole new social group aspect at school made me realize that maybe our understanding of ourselves comes from external factors like our friends and the social groups we are a part of. But this is a notion that society has set in place for us; we don't necessarily think about this ourselves because from a very young age we are taught to always be a part of something, whether that be a friend group or society in general. Therefore, we become so busy defining ourselves through others, that the individual in us never gets discovered or doesn't get discovered till a lot later in life. I had suddenly started enjoying being by myself at this stage of life; I didn't want to be defined by my social group or my friends. Going to class and getting my work done on time was more satisfying to me than trying to fit into a group of teenagers constantly gossiping about others and fueling dramas as if they were not teenagers but Pakistani aunties at a desi party discussing others and their business.

In order to discover yourself you need to look within, which is something that you can't always do if you are always trying to find a group of people to fit in with. I guess we are never taught to look within, only taught to fit in. We are fed the notion that we are defined by the people around us and our circumstances, but the truth is nothing but you define who you are. Maybe all of this thinking was inside me all along, but I was just realizing it now because for the first time in life I had started looking within myself rather than focusing on the world outside. I realized that you get in sync with the voice inside you only when you stop paying attention to the world outside you. My vision in life was changing extremely fast, and I wasn't sure whether this was a blessing from God or all the trauma from my childhood led me to mature early. Maybe that's what experiencing pain and trauma at an early age does to you. It makes you start looking at the world with a lot more depth. Whatever the reason was, I was happy and unconcerned about fitting in. I spent my day walking around the school observing everything but fitting in nowhere, and my time in class lost in books.

Most of my classes were in the seventh grade hallway

straight down from the counseling office. During the fifth month of school, a new girl joined us in our science class. There was an open spot on my table, and Mr. Barker told her to sit there. I was going over my lab report when a girl with long frizzy blonde hair and sparkly purple UGGs came and sat right next to me.

"Hi, my name is Victoria, Tia for short," she said looking at me.

"Hey, I am Maheen," I answered. "Where did you move from?" I asked her.

"I just got into this class really late" Tia said. "Hey can you help me catch up on the lab?" she added.

"Yeah, sure I can" I replied. The entire time I kept on trying to explain pH levels to Tia, she kept talking about Pokémon, and everything she said went right over my head. It turned out that Tia was not just in my science class but also in my history and P.E class; thus, we began seeing each other every day, and I sort of just became a part of her friend group for the sake of passing time.

Tia had the craziest people in her group: there was Ella who was obsessed with Pokémon, and all she ever talked about were Pokémon cards. I didn't understand a word that girl ever said, but I always nodded my head as if I understood everything. Then there was a girl named Sarah who was a theater kid, and she made everything sound more dramatic than it actually was. Every time she spoke she had to mention High School Musical because that was her favorite musical, and the theater department at Lanier was going to perform it as their annual show. Sarah was chosen to portray the character of Gabriella, the main lead in the play, and she bragged about it every day. Theater plays were the least of my interests, so again I nodded my head to everything but never felt like I belonged anywhere here. And last but not the least there was Kylie who was super quiet and to the point but also the most normal of the group. Kylie was way too quiet, like to the point where whenever she would speak, it was hard to understand because she never said more than a word or two. People thought I was quiet, but I was only quiet by choice because I was observing everything around me; Kylie was the queen of silence.

So as time passed, these girls became my so called "social group." I never really intended on being part of one single group but it was middle school after all. My thinking didn't match with the people I was hanging out with, and I had started realizing that. I never needed a hundred people around me; I just wanted to be around people who were genuine and not fake or gossipy. There was more to life than gossiping and belittling others. Although Tia and I were two different worlds, at least I knew she wasn't fake.

Rumors spread like fire, and it made me think that what's the point of having fifty people around you when they don't even know you that well or if they are just there for the gossip or because they want news out of your life that they can then discuss with ten other people and soon without having said a word, you become the talk of the whole entire school? No thank you, that's not what I was at school for. I would rather only have a few people around me who I trust. I was becoming very clear on what I wanted from life by looking at everyone else my age who were mostly more invested in fake friendships that were only based on popularity.

Every day at school the social environment was the same. Crowd around and gossip in the hallways before the morning bell rang. Gossip in the hallways in between classes and gossip in the hallways once the dismissal bell rung at the end of the day. Soon came a point where stopping in between the hallways to talk to people or holding up crowds just to meet friends became pointless to me because I had seen so much of it every day. Each time the bell rang, I never used to crowd around the school to talk to people, instead I used to go to my locker grab my stuff and walk towards my next class. Middle school was the first time I saw people becoming fake. Certain people would be so nice to your face but then talk shit about you behind your back. Friendships didn't seem sincere, rather full of drama. Little did I know that my own so-called little group of friends who I had chosen to stay away from middle school drama would become infected by major drama too. Halfway through seventh grade, Tia and Sarah got in a fight over a boy named Carl. Carl and Tia were working on a group project together, but Sarah liked Carl, and so Sarah spread rumors around the school that Tia snatched Carl away from her, even though Tia and Carl never had anything going on. Despite not being directly involved in this drama, I unfortunately had to hear all about it since I was part of the same social group.

I just didn't understand the point of the whole drama between Tia, Carl, and Sarah. I mean God has given us the ability to speak, then why not just use our communication skills and sort everything out by speaking to each other directly rather than complicating life by spreading words about one another that aren't even true? When we are kids, we are blatantly honest. Whatever is in our hearts comes right out the tongue without a single thought. As we grow older, we naturally draw a shield in front of us to protect ourselves for any reason. Or we want to fit in so badly with a group that we change ourselves. Have you ever heard a child's conversation and the amount of honesty it has? That's because the child is genuinely inquisitive about what they are saying, and they are unconcerned with what the world will think of them.

As we grow older, we begin to have this need to fit in socially, and so we accept whatever norms society and those around us tell us to accept. Growing up is great, and understanding the world is great too, but why at the loss of our honesty? If you do not agree with something, say it. If you love someone, say it. Don't keep it in because you are afraid that someone else will think you are insane for saying exactly what you feel. If you do not like someone in your friend group, fine, but at least don't be fake to their face and talk behind their back. As we grow older, the image we portray of ourselves on the outside doesn't always reflect what's going on in our heads inside, and the situations I saw around me at school were proof of this. I wasn't mad at anyone, but I decided to distance myself from the group because I just couldn't put up with everybody in my group trying to be fake nice to each other, even though, on the inside Sarah wanted to murder Tia and vice versa. I stepped back to focus on myself, but I still always hung out with Tia during the day because I had classes with her, and I was happy having one sincere friend that I could rely on.

After coming back from school, I used to spend hours during the day studying in my room.

Mom and Dad would sneak into my room and always say the same thing: "Maheen, you are going to kill yourself with so much studying. Why don't you go out with your friends?"

And my answer to this was always the same: "I am happy doing what I am doing because this is what gives me inner satisfaction". Mom and Dad would still encourage me to go out more, but I realized that the magic wasn't in hanging out with people. The magic was in my mind.

As more and more of my time passed at school, I began developing opinions of my own which were different of those around me. In my Introduction to Foreign Languages class there were two Pakistani girls, Zoha and Kanwal who sat right beside me in class. Since the two of them were Pakistani as well, I thought maybe we would get along. One day after class, all three of us sat together at lunch, and Zoha started talking about her date. "Do you know he took me into the corner behind the school and tried taking my shirt off?" Zoha said so excitedly.

"Ooo, isn't that what you wanted? Score! Tell me more?" Kanwal asked as her pupils enlarged and her smiled widened. Everyone else sitting around us on the table was so engaged in the conversation, and here I was trying to laugh it off, but within I didn't find it funny or cool to say the least. Having a crush was a normal thing. Liking someone at this age was a completely normal thing. I did it too, but I thought it was disgusting of Zoha to be doing all that at such a young age. I found such conversations so stupid, and once again I felt so out of place. It wasn't the kind of company I wanted around me. There were bigger and better things to talk about than boys. I knew this was the age where all the "crush talks" were normal. But I had already passed that stage last year with the whole Jared episode. And in front of this entire conversation my crush on Jared seemed like the most innocent thing in the world. Such conversations couldn't hold my intention anymore. I wish more people talked about their goals, ambitions, and passions in life rather than a boy who tried to take a girl's shirt off.

Watching young teenagers, even my own classmates like Zoha and Kanwal, dwell on relationships was so weird to me. "Why involve yourself with someone at this age?" I started thinking to myself. This was the time one needs to work on finding your own self, and all these kids were busy finding someone else. That's another thing I never understood: how can you attach another life with your own when you haven't even found yourself yet. Nobody is mature enough at the age of thirteen; it's the hormones that speak at that age. Plus, the majority of relationships that started in middle school ended within weeks too. After a month of fighting with Sarah over Carl, Tia told me that she was done with him. I looked at her with my eyes wide open, thinking, "You ruined your friendship with Sarah over a guy, and you are not even into him anymore?" It all sort of just went over my head.

Why would you put yourself in something temporary

when you know it's temporary and in a few weeks you will be over them? So, Tia was just infatuated with Carl; it was nothing more than that, but her and Sarah had become so distant that even I couldn't get them to talk again. I began feeling like I didn't really fit in, and I was happy with not fitting in. My perception of the world was just very different from my friends now. When people interact with you, they know you at the very basic level of your conscious mind. They only know you through your actions or through the things you say. But what about the things you don't say? My mind was becoming the strongest part of me.

I became the quiet girl in class, and my class fellows probably assumed that I was shy, but that wasn't true. I wasn't shy; I just didn't need to be defined by my surrounding environment or another person. Age isn't always proof of maturity; maturity can come from our experiences in life, and my experiences in life along with observing those around me were turning me into the person I was becoming now. I loved being around people but only the people that I connected with. I didn't see the point in hanging out with people just for the sake of hanging out.

At the end of seventh grade a letter came to my house saying that I had been inducted into the National Honor Society for maintaining a 4.0 GPA the entire school year. Attached along the letter was my award certificate, which was signed by President Barack Obama. Though I knew that everyone who had a four point GPA must have gotten that letter, this was such an ecstatic moment for my parents. My parents couldn't help their excitement regarding the presidential letter, and I couldn't control my excitement about having done what I said I was going to do. I used to get obsessed with things I wanted to achieve. Not in a bad way, but in a positive way. In a sense, my mind would only focus on my goal and wouldn't stop thinking about it until I attained whatever it was that I had set my mind on. Too much of anything in life isn't good for you. However, obsession to a certain extent is important in life. It is what keeps you going; it keeps the hunger alive in you. The hunger to succeed, without which nothing can be achieved. School was never my passion. I was good at school only because I had set that goal for myself, and I had to achieve it no matter what. You must do what you have to do in order to do what you want to do. I had all my focus on school because I knew this was important for my future, so I could get to the part of my life where I could do what I wanted to do, which was still far.

Between seventh grade and eighth grade, I felt myself changing even more than before. I didn't care about what others around me were doing or how they were spending their time, or what the coolest teenager trend was or who was dating who. I kept myself at a huge distance from those things, they weren't my interest anymore. I think every time I thought about the painful memories of my past, it made me want something bigger, something a bit more meaningful from life. I wanted a life where my occupation would be my first love, where my work would excite me, and I would be filled with passion every single day. A life where what I did mattered, had substance. And to get to that point in life, I knew I had to focus on my academics, not on how thriving my image was in school. I wanted to be known for my mind, not for my face or my body, and I got that.

Everyone in my classes knew me as the girl who always got above a ninety percent on all her papers and exams. One of my guy friends, Christian, always joked around that I was the girl everyone wanted in their group for projects because if I was in the group then everyone would get an A. I smiled at that, but I also loved it. I loved being known amongst the guys for my mind and not for any other reason. When you get respected for your mind instead of any other superficial reason, it's a beautiful thing because at the end of the day your thinking makes you who you are, not your looks or body or outer beauty. Any girl can dress up and put make up on and look pretty and get attention. Teenage guys only talk about how hot or pretty a girl is, but to be known for your mind is something else. It's a soul fulfilling kind of feeling. Maybe I was a little old school, or this was just how my mind was processing the world around me now. Life had a very different meaning to me now then it did a year ago. As far as friends were concerned, I always hung out with Areeba outside of school, but keeping up with people just for the sake of keeping up with them wasn't my interest anymore.

I knew I had a higher purpose in life, and I had to get there no matter what all by myself. My parents always told me, "Maheen, it's not a race; it's a marathon." They told me I shouldn't overload myself, that I shouldn't take all honors again, but rather I should create time for myself to and keep everything balanced in life. I should have time for school but also have a social life and enjoy the teenage phase of life in general. Enjoy social life with who? People who have nothing better to talk about than boys and or other people? I felt like I was done with all that now. I wanted friendships of purpose, not fakeness. I didn't want to live the typical way everyone else lived: study till you're twenty-two, get a job, do your master's, earn a stable income, get married by your mid-twenties and raise a family. That's not what I wanted from my life. I wanted the world, I wanted excitement, the hustle of finding a purpose, and I was going to get it myself.

Boys, crushes, social drama, none of that mattered

anymore. The only thing that mattered was creating a life full of purpose.

When it was time to register for eighth grade courses, I took all honors again: Physics honors, English honors, Algebra honors, Civics honors and AVID, which was a program that helped students prepare for college. Now that eighth grade was about to start, all my classes were located on the second floor in Bevan Hall. Even my AVID class was in the same hallway. The only two classes I had downstairs were Algebra One and Spanish One. From day one of eighth grade, I instantly fell in love with science. Even though I had Mr. Savage's science class as my first class in the mornings, I used to always be alert in class, ready to answer any and every question. Every time Mr. Savage assigned a chapter from the Physics textbook, I didn't just read it, I memorized it so the next day I could be the one who spoke in class the most. I had turned into a science wiz. I was inspired by the fact that when scientists make a new discovery they are remembered for generations to come. My new aspiration in eighth grade was to become a scientist so my name could come up in a textbook for the generations to come. That had become my goal. I always knew I wanted to be somebody; I wanted to be somebody famous, and at this point in my life I wanted to achieve my fame through science. My friend Tia thought I was crazy for talking about science all the time, but I liked it. It motivated me to keep going, to keep working hard because I wanted something that would take a lot more effort to get compared to a typical job.

During lunch time I began skipping out on hanging out with Tia and her friends. Instead I would go find a quiet corner in the school library and use that time to do my science lab homework. It wasn't like I didn't like Tia, Sarah, or Kylie anymore, I just wanted to use my time more wisely by doing something that mattered the most to me: getting good grades. Time is all we truly have, and once time is wasted it never comes back. It's our responsibility to make the most of the time and opportunity we have in front of us.

After lunch period ended, Lanier had a tradition called Pride Time, which was a forty-five minute block where kids who had only A and B grades could go play games and socialize in the cafeteria; we called that SOARing. Students who had C or lower grades had to go to their teachers and work on improving in that class. Even though I had all A grades, I never used to go SOARing, though I had ten soaring cards from all my teachers, and I had saved all of them in my pencil pouch. SOARing cards were given out to students for grades and/or exceptional behavior and were meant to be used during SOARing to buy snacks from the cafeteria. My SOARing cards always rotted in my pencil pouch like souvenirs because during Pride Time I used to always sit in Mrs. Claire's Civics classroom and get all my homework done in school. How could I possibly let go of forty-five free minutes during school that I could use to get my homework done and out of my way so mentally I would be at peace knowing that I had little to no homework to worry about when I came home? If I had something that had to be done, I had to get it finished right away.

After Pride Time ended, I had AVID with Ms. Louise. AVID was an AP course elective that helped prepared you for college in advance. Most students took it in high school, but I was taking it now because my seventh grade English teacher had recommended me for this advanced course last year. Every student who took AVID had the same teachers for English, Science and Social studies. This was done on purpose so that during AVID we as students were able to discuss schoolwork because the AVID classroom was set up in a way that you would bring concepts from other classes and discuss them with your AVID group. Ms. Louise, had the class divided into tutorial groups, and each group consisted of six students and a discussion facilitator. Each day of class the homework was always the same, to bring a discussion question from one of our other classes. The idea was to gain a deeper understanding of the subject by re-teaching the topic to other group members or listening to others as they presented a topic within the tutorial group. The days where I had to explain a question and guide my group through the entire question were my favorite days of the week. I loved acting like I was the teacher, and I loved it when my classmates asked me to help them understand a topic.

Even the boys in my AVID group looked up to me to help them with projects and homework, and I loved being the girl who always answered everyone's questions regarding academic work.

After AVID, I had English. Everyone in my AVID class had Ms. Dunn as their English teacher, and we all hated her. Ms. Dunn was an unmarried middle-aged woman who always seemed very unhappy with life. All the kids in my class made jokes that she was unhappy because she was not married. Ms. Dunn was slender and had bobbed cut hair. She liked nobody and was always in a bad mood whenever any student spoke to her. She always treated us as if teenagers were all wild and had no sense in them. Talking to Ms. Dunn about grades was the worst possible thing one could do because she would instantly start yelling at you. Tia always sat next to me in class, and she never did her homework. Ms. Dunn used to call Tia out every single day of class and tell her to stay after to discuss her lack of attention in class. But Tia was Tia. No matter how many times Ms. Dunn lectured Tia on her work habits, Tia never changed her behavior. Tia and I talked about this almost every day. I always asked her, "Why can't you just pay attention in class and get Ms. Dunn to shush?"

And Tia always had the same answer. "I am too young to

be serious; I will do it later," and I always laughed at that. I guess life had only changed me so quickly, but I was happy it did. Ms. Dunn wasn't mean to me; she was really nice to me. Every day when I used to walk into the classroom in the morning, Ms. Dunn used to smile at me and give me the keys to her projector cart because it was my responsibility to set up the smartboard for her. Ms. Dunn had made me her helping hand, and I had nothing against her personally.

Midway through eighth grade, admissions to Thomas Jefferson High School became the talk of the entire school. Thomas Jefferson High School for Science and Technology was ranked the tenth best high school in the nation and the number one high school for science and technology in the state of Virginia. Admissions into TJHS were no less competitive than applying to an Ivy League College. A student needed a solid 3.8 or higher GPA, two well written teacher recommendations, and needed to pass the entrance exam just to get to the next phase of the application process. If one got through phase one, then phase two included an interview and another entrance exam that determined if the student finally got in or not.

Every year, TJHS received thousands of applications out of which only three hundred students were admitted after phase two of the admissions process.

I was ecstatic to apply to TJHS. This was my ultimate dream as a fourteen-year-old middle schooler. I had already spoken to my Algebra teacher Mrs. Laurdel and my science teacher Mr. Savage for my letters of recommendations. All I had to do was prepare myself for the TJHS entrance exam. I began to spend all my time after school preparing myself for the entrance exam. In fact, I had TJ Prep books that I ordered online and brought to school with me every day so I could read them in my free time or during lunch block. Mom and Dad were super happy and supportive that I was applying to TJHS. They put me in a TJ admissions prep course, which was offered by a learning center called Huntington Center located across the street from my house. Three days a week, I met with my tutor Sally, who helped me prepare my personal essay for admissions into TJHS.

A month before the TJ test, I went to go see Thomas Jefferson High School with Mom, Dad and Ehsan. The school was in Alexandria, which was a twenty-minute drive from where I lived and was bigger than any high school in the area. The building was triple the size of Lanier. When we entered, to the left was the library, to the right was the main auditorium, and in the middle was the information table. Mom and I walked up to the information table and grabbed a map of the school, as well the brochure for the program of the day. It was an open house where we could visit various classes and experience how life would be as a TJHS student.

Dad, Mom, Ehsan and I started walking around, and Mom noticed that the school had their own astronomy research lab, which was bigger than the size of the cafeteria at my school. Mom loved astronomy. If she hadn't had me so early in life, she would have become an astronaut. But she sacrificed her dreams so that I could become capable enough of fulfilling my own dreams. There could never be a more selfless love.

Past the astronomy lab was the Marine Biology Lab and then the Chemistry Lab and the Physics Lab. All the science labs were extremely high tech, packed with all the technological equipment needed for experimental learning. The hallways of the school were massive, and at the end of each locker row there were signs that read, "No carrying backpacks during the day." I kept wondering why because the school was so massive that anyone could easily get lost just trying to find their next class. What inspired me most about TJHS was that all the kids in that school were focused, they had goals in life, they knew exactly what they wanted from life and were working towards it to attain it. Maybe this was the place where I could finally be with people who shared the mindset I had about life, and that thought made me want to get admitted into TJ even more.

At the end of eighth grade came the TJ test, which was administered on a Saturday morning at Lanier just like an actual SAT exam would be. The first part of the test was an essay and the second part was multiple choice. The results were going to come in the mail within a month. But every day after school I used to check the mailbox outside to make sure I hadn't missed any letters. Finally, in May I found out that I had passed the entrance exam and was now a part of the six hundred students who had made it to the second round of admissions. It was so exciting. The interview process went by very smoothly, but at the end of the month when I took the second exam and the results came in, I had missed the ideal score by two points. Only two points: if I had gotten one more question right, I would have made the cut. Of course, it felt bad for a while. This was everything I wanted, everything I had worked for. I never wasted my time on social drama, parties, or other things like other middle schoolers did, so why weren't things working out for me? I began thinking what was the point of me working so hard when it wasn't even paying off? Whenever I complained to Mom and Dad, they always told me that I need to stop being too harsh on myself and relax because I had already given it my all and getting into TJHS didn't automatically guarantee a successful life. I understood that, but I wasn't going to get over it so easily, especially when I had prepped so hard for the test and had thought about not getting into TJ day and night.

Yet when you work so hard for something, and it doesn't work out, for some reason it's hard to think objectively about it. Negativity kicks in the mind, and you start to think that you failed. I cried for days over not getting into TJ. I didn't want to go to an average high school with average high schoolers; I wanted to go to a school which was focused and career oriented, which was TJ. If I had gotten into TJ, my life would find a purpose. I would be focusing on my goals and not be caught up with teenage drama. Mom kept telling me the same thing every day: that the high school I go to didn't matter, the college I go to is what really matters. I knew she was right, but college was so far away in the distance. I wanted everything to work out now. It took me a few weeks to finally not cry about getting into TJ, but I wasn't over it deep inside. I was even more determined now to succeed in high school.

Life gains meaning when you find your purpose, something that drives you every day and makes you look forward to tomorrow. Your family and loved ones are all important in life, and they drive you to be better every day. Without family, it's impossible to fly. But in addition to people, everyone needs a purpose in life to make tomorrow more meaningful. Maybe that's also why I didn't care who I hung out with at school anymore, because more than following people I wanted to follow and figure out my purpose in life. Everything that happened in my childhood was way behind me now. But maybe pain and trauma at a young age does have a purpose because now I had the wisdom to see what had meaning in life and what didn't. I didn't want to be around superficial friendships, I only wanted relationships in my life that actually had meaning. The world can see you from the outside. However, nobody but you knows the thoughts that go on inside your head. I no longer knew what it was like to not have a dream to chase or a goal to achieve.

Focus changes you, and it doesn't let you get distracted in

life. In elementary school, I was more concerned with having fun more than anything else, but this transition in life was important. Realizing my goals in life was important. My vision in life had become extremely clear. I was meant to chase my dreams, and everything else didn't matter. My parents mattered, but what friends or other people were doing was irrelevant to me now. When your vision in life is clear, what others are doing around you or what the world expects you to do—none of it matters anymore. All that really matters in the end is how true you are to yourself. My passion burned like gasoline. Without it, life wouldn't have the same meaning to me.

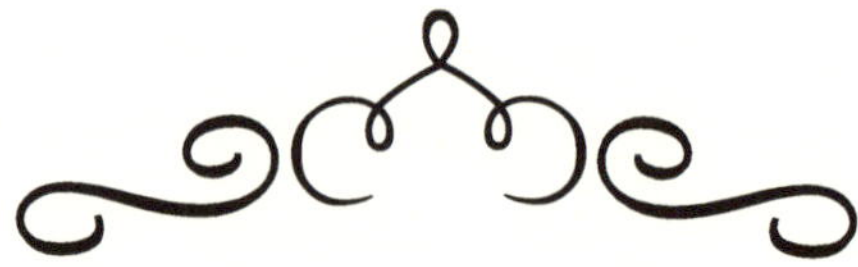

CHAPTER EIGHT

In September, I opened up another chapter of my life as I started ninth grade at Fairfax High School. The school was located straight down the main highway from my house. The winding road in front of the playing field led straight into the school parking lot. The first right turn was parking while the second right turn led into a curb that was designated for student pick up and drop off. The rest of the area was all student and faculty parking, which was marked by numbers. Seniors got top priority to choose their parking spot, then juniors, and if you were lucky enough to get your name chosen through a list during sophomore year, you got anything that was left over, and that only if there were any empty parking spots left. The long lanes in front of the main entrance of the school were all reserved for school buses. The school building itself was brick and glass, and the empty patio-like area in front of the main door had blue benches where students used to wait and hang out during the start and at the end of the school day.

Upon entering the school building there was a large hallway packed with benches where students used to sit in the morning waiting for the morning bell. Right from the first day of school as soon as I walked in the morning, I saw five different couples making out with each other on the benches in front of the main office. I kept my head away and just continued with my walk and sat at a bench near the office since here I was again, the observer, who noticed everything around her and was just trying to make sense of it all. I knew kids my age saw nothing wrong in kissing or casually getting intimate with someone. But I always wondered how could you kiss or make out with someone without having a proper emotional connection? I knew I couldn't, let alone kissing. I couldn't even imagine getting close to a man because I always thought that was something you do with the love of your life, not just any guy. How was it so easy for other people? I was American by the way I dressed, by the way I spoke, but I was old school when it came to love. Love was no joke or walk in the park to me. I was always told that love isn't shallow, it's not about sexual pleasure, kisses, hugs, or any of the superficial things that the world labels as love. Love to me was something very pure; it's supposed to come from the soul and be able to touch your heart. I could never in my life imagine kissing just anyone, without it meaning something bigger to me. Therefore, when I saw kids kissing each other in the hallways around the school it made me feel like I was not fully immersed in the American culture of casually dating, nor was I totally immersed in the Pakistani culture—I was stuck somewhere in the middle. I probably craved respect or a mental connection with someone more than I ever wanted the kind of "love" I saw happening around me in the hallways at school.

I hung out in the lobby till about 8:05 am, right before first period, still noticing people around me. Behind the bench where I sat was a wooden door that opened to a staircase that led up to the library on the second floor. Underneath the staircase was another bench attached to the wall, which was another popular area where you could spot couples making out. I often felt like I was born in the wrong generation. Maybe I was too old school, or my Pakistani upbringing didn't allow me to process how casually American teenagers treated something as serious as love. Could high schoolers even be in love? Was this all just a pastime for people? Because I for sure knew that it wasn't a joke or a game for a girl like me.

I got up and started heading to Ms. Eastman's English class. The school was big, and I had only visited once during orientation, so I kept the school map in my hand trying to find room B142. As I turned left from the main office, there was the counseling office, then the nurse's office, and finally, after the nurse's office was the career center down the hallway, left from the library stairs where all the classes started. The hallway ran straight down all the way to the end of the school, but along the hallway there were side hallways that we referred to as wings. First was the A wing, which was all foreign language classes. I had Spanish two in the A wing with Professor Cambel. A little further down from the A wing was the C wing, where all the English classes were located. Between each classroom wing were all the lockers that no one ever used because none of us had the time to go to our lockers in between classes. Everyone used to carry their backpacks with them all the time during the day.

Fairfax High School was constructed in the shape of a giant rectangle which was cut in between multiple times by various hallways. The C and D wing hallway was literally the middle of the school and the only hallway where all the other hallways intersected. When the bell rang, the intersection of hallway C and D had foot traffic coming from all sides of the school.

Students used to stand with their backpacks bumping into the person behind them because it would take five minutes just to pass through the amount of people that were all trying to cross the same hallway from four different sides. The other side of the school was built the same way with a long hallway running down to the back door of the school and mini hallways in the middle that had classes. Coming from Lanier which only had two hallways, it was confusing to keep track of where exactly each class was located.

After pushing through everyone crowded in front of the C wing entrance, doing nothing but talking to one another, I finally made my way to B142, where a woman around her thirties with brown hair and brown glasses stood outside the door greeting everyone as they walked in to the class. I said hi and shook Ms. Eastman's hand and walked inside the classroom and took the first seat in the first row near the blackboard. The classroom was only half-full at the time. I saw familiar faces from my old school, but no one who I connected with. I took out my folder from my backpack and began looking for the summer assignment which was due in class today. Over the summer, every student taking English Honors was assigned to read *To Kill a Mockingbird*, and it was to be discussed in class today. I never in my life enjoyed reading books; I never had the attention span to enjoy, but I wanted in A in the class, so of course I read the book to do my assignment. While I was busy getting ready for class, Tia walked into the room and sat on the chair right next to me and tapped my shoulder. "Hey," she said.

I suddenly looked over my shoulder and smiled. "Hey, so nice to see that we have a class together," I replied. I was suddenly so happy knowing that Tia was in my class again, and we could get through all English assignments together. On the second or fourth day of English class I began to notice that there was a cute boy named Feroze who sat in my row but all the way towards the other side of the room. He was tall, 5'9", much taller than me. He had thick hair that always used to be set back with gel and an extremely attractive deep voice. Feroze was smart. He always had something to say in every single class discussion, which was how I started noticing him. Plus, he was Muslim so even if I wanted to date him, I knew Mom wouldn't have a problem. But it wasn't my parents that stopped me from dating anyone in high school, it was my own thinking that stopped me. I didn't want to be emotionally attached to anyone yet because if I got emotionally attached, that would be it for me, but what if it doesn't mean the same for the other person? That used to scare me because what if I wanted something real but the other person just wanted something casual? So I stayed away from getting into a relationship.

Feroze and I used to talk as classmates during group projects, but it was never more than that. Plus, I had seen way too many "teenage love" scenarios happening around the hallways of school that I feared forming another one, so I never told Feroze I liked him.

I never understood the culture of hook ups, break ups, having casual sex, etc. It wasn't even about being from a Pakistani family. It was about the mindset I had. I didn't get the point of having any physical relations with a person without a deeper connection being there, and soul deep connections were not made in high school. I had to be attracted to someone mentally in order to be attracted to them physically. But everyone around me only seemed obsessed with physical aspects of a relationship. I could never relate to that. In the culture I grew up in, dating was a normal thing, but to me it was never as casual as kids my age had made it seem like. I was old school; I wanted to love one man for the rest of forever, instead of dating a bunch of them.

After Ms. Eastman's English class, we had Pride Time, which was the same concept from Lanier where we used to report to a teacher and use the time as study hall. For the first three months of school, no one was allowed to leave their Pride Time classes anyway, so the time was literally used as study hall. I used to just hang out with Tia and her friends and use the time to get my homework done. After Pride Time, I had AVID 9 with Mrs. Shafer in the D wing. AVID was fun in eighth grade, but in ninth grade it felt like a place where all the popular kids just talked about all the high school drama and social clique problems more than a class that prepared you for college. I was sitting in class one day, checking my binder for my notes when I overheard two girls in my class, Dina and Shra, talking about someone's boyfriend cheating scandal.

"Did you know Dylan cheated on Sarah?" Shra said to Dina.

"OMG, no way, how? What happened?"

Dina's jaw dropped as she was clicking away on her phone. "I am asking Emily for the whole story, but apparently Dylan called Sarah at five in the morning to break up with her, and she cried for hours," Shra said in the most dramatic voice ever.

I just sat there overhearing Dina and Shra go back and forth to unfold the whole break up story, and I kept thinking to myself, "This takes too much energy." There it was again, so much unnecessary drama, and I thanked myself that I was away from it. Social drama, so and so said this, and so and so did this took up so much energy, and if I was going to waste my energy, I wanted to waste it on something that was meaningful to me.

After each class period ended, everyone rushed out the door to gather with their friends quite like the way it was in middle school. However, at FHS each class had their own little corner where we gathered up to meet each other. There was a giant open square in front of the cafeteria, and it was divided into four sections. On the extreme left of the hallway was the freshmen corner where all the popular ninth graders hung out. Opposite the freshmen corner, near the trophy case was the sophomore corner. Near the cafeteria was the junior corner and after the trophy case was the senior pit where all the popular seniors hung out. The senior corner was called the "senior pit" because that area of the hallway was two steps below main level, kind of forming a corner on its own. As soon as the bell rang after every class, all the popular kids would come and stand in the freshman corner to come talk to one another. The popular kids were basketball players, cheer leaders, and people who knew each other from middle school. But the entire concept of high school popularity was one that I couldn't really understand. What even made someone popular and why? Being on a sports team or being known as a player amongst girls? Having the whole school know you but what for exactly? Nothing. It was just beyond me. From middle school to now, I had spent so much time on my own that social drama or social constructs within the school were of no interest to me. We all came to school to learn so why did it matter who was popular and who wasn't. How come students who played basketball and boys who spoke to girls were considered "popular," but someone who had good grades in class wasn't called popular but just a nerd? And what did "being popular" even mean when at the end of the day at 2:05 pm, once all of us left the Fairfax High School building, we were all the same.

Every time the bell rung, I used to walk around the halls with Tia, but whenever I looked at all the popular kids hanging out together talking about something dramatic, I always wondered what did anyone ever get out of being popular? What was even the point of being popular or not? Did it automatically make people smarter, or did it raise your GPA? Then what was even the point? Weren't we all the same at the end of the day, just regular high school kids? trying to figure out life. Popularity in high school was just a social label that I didn't even understand, but I knew that it didn't help you in your future, it distracted you. All the popular kids always focused so much on people, parties, fake friendships, and maintaining an image that people forgot that school is for learning and that there is life beyond their social status at school. You have a purpose behind coming to school, and that's learning, not being liked by two hundred people. Once the mindset of pleasing others or being liked by people becomes your only goal, you are no longer living to satisfy yourself, and that is sad. I always thought that people who take high school popularity way too seriously get stuck in that mindset high school phase forever, and they don't realize that in real life 10 years later, it won't matter whether they were popular in high school or the nerdy kid. What matters is what you do in the real world, but the popular kids never worried about that.

For so-called popular kids, high school seemed like it was their entire life. A place where they think they peaked the most in life. For others, high school is a time to figure out who you are. To figure out your goals, ambitions and plans. To experience a certain level of freedom, but through that freedom also figure out who you are and not only where you fit in the school but also in the world. I was part of the second group of people, still trying to work on myself rather than pleasing other people. Most high schoolers didn't want to look beyond the 3501 Rebel Run School building that consumed seven hours of our lives every day. Maybe teenagers forget that real life starts after the last period bell rings. Real life started outside our school doors, not in school hallways where anyone could act like the most popular person in the world. Whatever you are in school doesn't really matter. Who you are beyond school is the real you. How hard you work today determines what you hold in your hands tomorrow. However, in high school most people were more concerned with living a life that only looked good on the outside without thinking much about how that life felt on the inside. Instead of wasting my time trying to be a part of such a crowd, I used to pass by them and head straight to class. I just didn't care about being a part of a drama at all;

I was in school to learn. If I genuinely connected with someone, cool. If I didn't, then I didn't care.

During lunch I always sat with Tia and her friends; just like everyone else was still a part of their old social group, so was I. The school cafeteria stretched out all the way to the back of the school, and there were rows of tables placed side by side, and in the middle was a little stage where the leadership team used to do events during lunch. The leadership class was the student government at FHS that planned out school spirit weeks and any event going on in the school. Tia and I always sat on the tables to the left side of the stage. I was sitting at lunch with a few friends including Tia and one of her friends, Elena, when Elena's boyfriend came and sat next to her at our table. I was planning my birthday trip to New York with my friends in the summer, and it wasn't even final yet. We were just discussing the possible trip to New York after the end of the school year, and suddenly I heard Elena's boyfriend talking to Elena in the rudest manner ever.

"You can't go without me because I won't let you," he said as he looked over at Elena.

Tia and I looked at each other because both of us were suddenly shook by the boyfriend's words.

Elena nodded her head and smiled.

I was beyond shook at this point. I couldn't understand how on earth Elena's boyfriend could think he could control Elena's life already when he had only been dating her for a few months. It wasn't even like he was her husband. Imagine how controlling he would have been if he married Elena. That entire concept was beyond me. I could never imagine a guy telling me what to do and what not to. Even my parents have never tried to control my life. Yes, they have taught me the difference between right and wrong, but they never tried to control me, so if a guy ever tried to do that, I would never tolerate it. If a man could not handle my independence in life and respect my decisions, then I didn't think I needed him in my life.

Maybe it was the age that we were in, but high schoolers around me seemed infatuated with the idea of having a significant other in life that most people got into the wrong kind of relationship just because of social pressures or the idea that "because everyone seems to be dating, so should I." I never understood why being single was seen as such a bad thing. This was our age to find ourselves, to find our likes and dislikes, to focus on ourselves in life, and so many people were focused on finding a significant other. Therefore, relationships go wrong because people try to define their own value through someone else when in actuality your value and worth can only come from you. You must give yourself time to live for you so that you can be satisfied inside before attaching another life to your own life. It's more important to live for yourself before you live for someone else, and because of the way I was raised, this notion was just a part of me. Despite coming from a society that told girls to be a certain way, my parents never raised me like a typical Pakistani girl. I was raised with the belief that not only am I enough for myself, but that there is nothing in the world that I could not do myself. I didn't need anyone. I needed to fully love myself before I could fall for anyone else, and loving myself meant focusing on my life and my dreams, not boys and social popularity. After everything I had been through and seen in life, my self worth and independence could only come from me, not from another human being. What I had learned by seeing other people in relationships around me was that their partner's existence started defining their existence, or at least that's what I saw happening to Elena.

After lunch I had math in the H wing with Mrs. Laufer. Mrs. Laufer was a kind woman, probably in her late thirties or early forties, and she was pregnant, so halfway through the year we were going to get a substitute teacher anyway. Every time Mrs. Laufer would lecture us on solving geometric proofs, she spoke so fast in class that everyone used to get super confused and never understood the lecture. There were two girls who sat right next to me in class, and I had become great friends with them: Samantha and Sydnee. Samantha, Sydnee, and I always exchanged notes after lectures so we could help each other get the homework done.

One day in math class, Mrs. Laufer was going over the homework when I heard the guy in front of me talking to the guy next to him about how he took a girl on a date, but she refused to do anything with him, so he was bitching about her during our class lecture. At the end of the day, sex was all that mattered to high school boys, and I found that to be the most disgusting thing in the world. I understood that at this age being sexually attracted to someone was normal. But that didn't mean that sex was the only thing that seemed to matter. Once again, my Pakistani upbringing clashed with my "Americanness."

Two months later, along came Homecoming. The first week of October was always Homecoming week, and the first Saturday in October was always the Homecoming dance.

Freshmen year of high school, homecoming seemed like the most important event in your high school life. Literally every single freshman was obsessed with finding the perfect date, the perfect dress, perfect dinner venue, and of course the perfect homecoming proposal. Since it was such a new concept as a high school freshmen, I was intrigued by all the homecoming traditions. Preparations around the school had started weeks before the homecoming game. Homecoming posters were hung on thc walls in every single hallway of the school. A week before homecoming, the boys created posters to ask out girls for the homecoming dance. There was one proposal that year which became extremely famous amongst the entire school. A sophomore named Rohan was asking out a girl named Maria for homecoming by taking the help of Maria's best friend Hannah who was also Rohan's ex-girlfriend. During Rohan's freshmen year, Maria had helped

Rohan ask out Hannah, and now that him and Hannah had ended their relationship, Hannah was helping Rohan ask out Maria. The craziest part of this entire situation was that despite dating the same guy at two different times, Hannah and Maria were still best friends, and that's why this homecoming proposal became such a huge deal at school. I enjoyed observing everything, but I was so happy to be far away from all the drama at school.

During homecoming season in the fall, one would see a pair together, and by prom season in the spring, the girl would be someone else and the boy with someone else, and it was cool; it was normal. But to me, it was crazy. I used to wonder, "How in the world can people be this casual about relationships or switching partners so easily? How can you have feelings for someone and just wake up one day and not have them anymore?" Then that means you never had feelings for them. You were infatuated, with them. I could never imagine that. In my head, I wanted to be with one man for the rest of my life. But everyone around me changed partners as if it was as easy as changing clothes. Another common scenario in high school was going out with each other without being involved with one another. Why? I never understood the point of it. Why do it because everyone else is doing it? If you don't have feelings for someone, just don't go out with them, simple. Not having a boyfriend in high school or not wanting a boyfriend doesn't make you boring; maybe that's what others thought. I didn't understand why in high school the hype was so much around relationships and gossip and around who was dating who. Why was dating such a huge part of the American teenage culture?

One day during homecoming week, I was sitting in math class with Samantha and Sydnee talking about the homework while Mrs. Laufer was busy going over our lecture slides on the smartboard. Halfway through class, Mrs. Laufer paused and walked to her desk to pick up the manilla envelope which was laying on top of her laptop. Mrs. Laufer ripped open the manilla envelope and took out the white half paper slips and handed them out to the class. The white paper slips were voting ballets that had nominations for "Homecoming King" and nominations for "Homecoming Queen." Fairfax had a tradition where teachers recommended six senior girls and six senior boys to run for "Homecoming Queen" and "Homecoming King." Teachers always chose the kids who, according to them, were well rounded academically, socially, and were the most involved in extra circulars. Soon the intercom went on, and our principal Dr. Goldfarb started speaking. "We will now be playing the video for Homecoming nominations. Teachers, please tune in to channel six to get to contestants more in depth," he said. The video started playing, portraying each student, a little bit about their childhood and high school achievements. I had no idea who to vote for because I didn't know any of the seniors. I didn't pay any attention to the video. In fact, Samantha and I kept talking to each other about how we were even supposed to choose a candidate when we didn't even know anyone. The voting was anonymous, so I just circled random names, one for king and one for queen and put my sheet in the large brown envelope that was placed in the middle of the table. After all of us were done voting, Andy, the guy who sat in front of me straight up asked me, "Do you want to go to homecoming with me?" looking right at me. I paused for a second because I hadn't expected that at all.

Honestly, I didn't. Not just Andy, but I didn't want to be anyone's date for homecoming because going out with someone was not a casual thing for me. Sure, Andy was really nice, but I didn't have any feelings for him. What if at the end of the day he also wanted from me what I saw all the other boys wanting from every girl at school? "No, I am sorry, I can't. I am not planning to go to the dance at all," I blurted out.

Although I was going to the dance, I didn't want to hurt Andy's feeling either by saying, "I do not want to go with you."

I didn't care if it was just homecoming and not an actual date, but I could not be like every other American high schooler. I just wasn't. In fact, I could never date a guy without having super strong feelings or some kind of emotional connection for him. I was happy in my own life, and I was going to go to homecoming but with my best friends. After my answer, Andy had become quiet for the remainder of the class, and I felt bad, but I would be going against my own values if I had said yes. When the bell rung and I was packing my stuff to leave, I apologized to him once again and quietly went to my next class.

The following day was the Homecoming dance. The day of the dance I spent majority of my day at the mall to get my hair and makeup done. I never really dressed up for school otherwise. Not because I didn't like dressing up, just because I didn't care enough to do so. Either I could get up at five in the morning to do my make up to go school every day like all the other girls or I could use that time to sleep in. I preferred sleeping in. Many girls in high school dressed up every single day, and that was amazing, but a lot of people start depending on make up at this age to be more confident about themselves. I didn't believe in the idea that any superficial thing or product can give you confidence. To me real confidence was being content with whom you are inside, which meant that even if you had to walk out of the house in your pajamas, you would still embrace the world like you owned it. I enjoyed doing my makeup and dressing up for occasions, but not because I needed more confidence or wanted to impress someone. Make up will never give you the confidence that believing in yourself will. It was sad to me that there were girls in high school who thought that their self-value comes from looking a certain way or putting on makeup. That wasn't true. You want to be filled with beauty inside which reflects on the outside. I knew how I looked or whether I was pretty or not, but I wasn't just my face. I have always wanted to be known for my mind; my face could come later.

Around six pm, I was ready to go to the dance in my silver sequin dress, hair tied in a bun with curls hanging out on the sides and heels on. Tia's usual group and I got together before the dance for dinner and homecoming pictures at Tia's house. Homecoming pictures were such a big deal in high school; they seemed even more significant than the dance itself because everyone just wanted to get good photos that could be posted all over Facebook the next day. The pictures were taken either outside someone's house or at a country club before dinner. My group and I took pictures outside Tia's house and on the stairs near Tia's room. After staying at Tia's house for a while, at eight o clock Mom dropped all of us outside the Fairfax High School gym for the homecoming dance. "Go enjoy yourself. There is no rush to come home, but just call me whenever you are done," Mom said to me as she dropped me off at the entrance of the gym, which was made fancy with a red carpet and balloons. All of us got off, and I waved at Mom as she drove away.

At the entrance there were white and blue balloons hanging on both sides of a grey banner that read "HOMECOMING 2011" in blue print. Like all the other kids, we took pictures near the entrance and then went inside the gym. The middle of the gym was turned into a dance floor, and on the sides there were tables set up for people to sit and eat. At this point the dance floor was completely empty and there were only two groups sitting on the tables on the side. Liz and I started posing for pictures to kill time until the dance floor got more hyped. After a photo shoot session, the five of us went outside to get food from the food stalls. We waited a while before getting on the dance floor till I heard them playing Soulja Boy, and I took my heels off so I could dance properly. Tia, Liz, Sabrina, Elena, and I stood in the middle of the dance floor just enjoying ourselves and moving to the beat of the song. A few minutes later, I felt someone sneak up behind me. At first, I ignored it, thinking someone had accidently brushed passed me. But he was consistently just there, trying to dance on me. I pushed him away and he would come back. Finally, I went into a different corner of the dance floor because the guy was drunk, and he couldn't understand that I wasn't interested in dancing with him at all when he was trying to get on top of me. It felt awkward, but later while dancing Tia and I laughed about it.

About halfway through the night the DJ played "Cha Cha Slide," and everyone got into a line to dance as this was kindergarten again. "This is homecoming?" I thought to myself. Why was it so hyped up? Yes, it was fun to dress up and go out with friends, but we were literally just dancing in a school gym, so it wasn't something crazy like I had hyped it up to be. I thought it was going to be some huge experience that no one ever forgets in their high school life, but homecoming was so overhyped. My friends and I only stayed for an hour and a half, and then I called Mom to pick us up. I was done. The whole excitement of homecoming had been fulfilled.

When I was about to leave the dance, Salaar, a friend from Ms. Eastman's English class walked over to Tia and I. "Hey guys, I am hosting a huge afterparty at my house after this. Do you guys want to come?" Tia said no right away, but I wasn't sure if I wanted to. I mean I knew Salaar, but I also knew that he had probably invited all the popular snobby kids from school—everyone that I really didn't care about.

"Thanks, a ton, Salaar but I think I am gonna go home. I will see you at school on Monday." I smiled at him, gave him a friendly side hug, and walked out of the school with Tia. I wasn't too sure about house parties in high school. I sort of had an idea that's where things get crazy and inappropriate because during the dance, you are on school grounds surrounded by school faculty. What happens off school grounds no one is guarding. Therefore, homecoming after parties were where everyone went to do things they weren't supposed to do. Like if someone wanted to hook up or have sex , or even get drunk, they wouldn't do so at the dance but after the dance no one's watching.

After the weekend when I got to school on Monday, Salaar's party had become the talk of the town. Literally half our grade had gone to his party and the other half had already heard stories about how crazy it was. Everyone at school kept talking about how Salaar's mom was Muslim, and she herself had served alcohol to kids in her basement, and there were couples making out, and Salaar's parents knew all this was happening but were okay with this. As much as I respected Salaar as a friend, I just didn't understand the point of such parties and being wasted with alcohol or making out with someone that too was at someone else's house. Why did high school parties have to be so weird?

Everyone in my English class kept telling me, "Maheen, you weren't there Saturday night. You really missed out on the party." But I didn't feel that way for some reason. After hearing about all the things that people were doing at the party, I was proud of myself for not going. It didn't feel as if I had missed out on anything. I was very satisfied with myself and my decision, and I didn't care what anyone else at school thought of me not being at the party because on the inside I was satisfied with my own decision.

I was a mix of both worlds. There were parts of the American teenage culture that I never fully agreed with like making out, casual dating, etc. But at the same time, I wasn't the typical Pakistani girl who got along with other American-raised Pakistani girls. In fact, whenever I went to a Pakistani party with my mom and had to sit around other Pakistani girls my age, the things they talked about annoyed the heck out of me. One would think that meeting people that come from the same culture as you would hold similar values as you, but that wasn't necessarily true. Once during the month of Ramadan (Fasting) my mom took me with her to a friend's house for an iftar party and a Milad (Religious gathering). This was a gathering of about a hundred people in someone's house in Ashburn, Virginia. At the Milad, all the adults were sitting together while I was sitting with three other girls my age on the other side. All of us were gathered around an elder lady, wearing a scarf on her head and maybe in her sixties. The lady had a microphone in her hand, and she was explaining to everyone the power of prayer during the month of Ramadan. While on one side of the room this woman was speaking about religion, purity and good intentions, the girls I was sitting with, Mishal and Shanza were lost in a completely different world.

I was eating the leftover rice in my plate when Mishal started talking. "Do you know he tried to take my shirt off?" Mishal giggled.

"Who tried to take your shirt off?" Shanza asked anxiously.

"I don't remember his name, but he was cute. He took me into a corner behind my school building and tried kissing me," Mishal said as her cheeks turned red as she blushed. The two other girls sitting right next to me were listening so intensely to Mishal and her boy story.

I, on the other hand was just thinking in my head, "Why is she telling me all this when I just met her"? It was just awkward because on one side of the room everyone was talking about prayer and religion and then here was Mishal , talking about the details of her casual hook up. I wasn't the most religious person on earth, but I did have enough respect towards religion to know that Mishal's hook up discussion was not needed in this type of gathering. There is a certain level of respect that one should give to religion and elders. It's super disrespectful when someone in front of you is talking about God and you start discussing your intimate encounter with someone who wasn't even a potential significant other. Mishal and Shanza kept talking back and forth, but I didn't say a word and kept eating my food.

For the next hour, Mishal went through an entire list of boys that she'd dated, one after another. Arooj and Nadia were all ears while I didn't really give a damn. How come people my age always spoke about boys, never about their own passions, dreams, ambitions, and goals in life? All four of these things are so important to live a fulfilling life, and for me they came before boys.

I was zoned out from the conversation, thinking about my own view of life until Mishal suddenly added, "I think every girl or boy should try different relationships just to see what they like in the end."

That sentence burned me. What kind of value system was I being surrounded with? Did all teenagers think that relationships were like clothes that you keep trying on one after another until you find the dress you like the most? How can you possibly let someone in emotionally and then let go of them and repeat the process again and again? I could never do that. Maybe teenagers didn't care about the emotional attachment in a relationship. Maybe, for people my age relationships were nothing but a game. Maybe that was the reason why I didn't want one. You do not need to be in a relationship and then another just to try it out. Whenever it is time to be in one it will happen, but relationships are not meant for trial or experimentation—that just means you are playing around to have fun. Why was everyone at this age so obsessed with physical attraction and intimacy everywhere I went, whether it was school or worse, a religious gathering? Anyone can be physically attracted to anyone. A mental attraction and connection with another human being is what's rare to find in this world. A connection where you are in love with someone's mind and soul more than their physical body. Such love is rare to find, but it's what I believed in. I wished that more girls talked about their dreams and passions more than talking about boys.

When the night ended and I finally came home from the so-called religious gathering, I clearly told Mom about everything that happened. I also told her that I never wanted to go to such a gathering again. I went upstairs to my room, took off my heels, threw them on the side, changed my clothes, and started doing my homework. Though it was only Friday night, I always did my homework on Fridays so I could mentally be relaxed for the rest of the weekend, instead of procrastinating till Sunday night to do my schoolwork.

CHAPTER NINE

In December, Ehsan and I had two weeks off from school for Christmas break. Dad was sick and tired of the freezing weather on the East Coast, so Mom and Dad planned a trip to California for a family vacation. Our first stop was Las Vegas, and then from Vegas we were going to drive to Los Angeles because I really wanted to see Hollywood. It was my dream to be famous one day, and what better place to think big and dream big than Hollywood itself? Since middle school I had this desire to do something in life, to be someone and give life a purpose. Back then the dream was to become a scientist so that one day my name could appear in a textbook. When I got rejected by TJ, the dream of becoming a scientist slowly faded away, but I still wanted to do something big in life. When I got to high school, the passion inside me began to burn even more because I never enjoyed the things other high schoolers enjoyed. The image of the fast life from when I was a kid in New York City, staring at the Empire State building from the lobby of the hospital was still stuck in my brain. I wanted to be as famous and grand as that Empire State building.

Dad's paternal cousin Uncle Asad lived in Vegas with his wife and two kids, so we visited them first. As soon as our flight landed at McCarran Airport in Vegas, we rented a car and started driving to Uncle Asad's house. As we drove past the Red Rock Canyon mountain range, Dad told Ehsan and I to look out our windows to spot the views, but the sky was pitch black. We couldn't see anything. I wasn't really interested in mountains anyway. I was thinking about how inspiring traveling was. You go to a new place, have new experiences, and suddenly a part of you changes. Your soul has a new experience. Your energy shifts; everything around you remains the same, but something within you is completely different. I wasn't made to settle; I was meant to be free, to learn to use my wings and fly, to never stay too long in one place when it came to dreaming in life.

Finally, we reached Uncle Asad's house at one in the morning. Dad stopped the car by the gate and the security guard asked him the house number we were visiting. I looked over to my right, and Ehsan had already fallen asleep. We drove past the gate, and Dad pulled into the third driveway on the left where Uncle Asad and his wife were standing outside their door waiting for us. I got out of the car, woke Ehsan up, met Uncle Asad and his wife Reena, and quickly went inside the house. Mom and Dad came in later with the luggage. The first night at Uncle Asad's house after eating dinner, all of us literally crashed on our beds out of exhaustion. All four of us were in the guest room upstairs. Aunty Reena had given Ehsan and I each a mattress of our own while Mom and Dad slept on the queen size bed in the middle of the room. It was only a matter of two nights. Sleeping on the floor was no big deal. In fact, I enjoyed it.

The following day, Mom, Dad, Ehsan, and I went to the famous Strip, which was the heart of the city. The Strip was the most attractive road in Vegas lined up with casinos, hotels, clubs, and everything bling about Vegas. The neon lights on the street were never ending, and each hotel had a unique theme with a unique architecture.

Mom and Dad were never into gambling, however, the casinos on the Strip were a sight not to miss. The four of us walked down the strip to hotel Venetian. The most awkward part of walking down the Strip with my parents was that at every block there were posters of naked women glued to the back of trucks. As we kept walking along the block, there was a man standing outside of a strip club called "Gentlemen's club." He was handing out strip club cards that had pictures of naked women on them. As we walked past the man, he handed my brother a card, and before Ehsan could even reach his hand to grab it, Mom snatched the card from the man's hand.

"How dare you," she yelled as we walked past him, and he flicked his middle finger at Mom, and Mom flicked her middle finger back, and then we kept on walking as Mom told Dad what happened. Ehsan was only in fifth grade, and this was so awkward. He didn't even understand what had just happened, but later we all laughed at Mom's protective reflexes.

Venetian was a block away, and we just kept on walking straight without getting distracted by anything around us. Once we entered Venetian, the inside of the hotel felt like as if it was actually in Venice. The ceiling was painted shades of blue to mimic the sky. The walls had bright colored houses painted on the walls resembling small houses that you would see on the sides of a canal in Venice. There was a large canal built within the hotel that started from the corner of the lobby and then stretched all the way to the backside of the hotel, which was constructed to resemble the exact architecture of the city of Venice. The part of the canal that was near the lobby was covered by the hotel ceiling, but the back of the canal was openly flowing underneath the real sky. Mom, Dad, Ehsan, and I sat in a gondola and the gondoliers gave us an entire tour of the canal under the blue cloudy open sky. After the gondola ride, the four of us walked around the ground floor of Venetian to check out the shops. On the lower level of the hotel was a mall; we spent the rest of our evening shopping.

Mom and Dad wanted to go to the Paris Hotel to go on top of the miniature Eiffel Tower to see the fireworks and water show that happened at the dancing waterfront by the hotel. Ehsan and I gave each other the look. We didn't want to go on top of the Eiffel Tower; I wanted to stay in Venetian. By the time we walked to the Paris Hotel, the water show was about to start in ten minutes, and the line to go on top of the tower covered the entire block. Mom, Dad, Ehsan, and I decided to go stand by the fountain where the rest of the crowd was standing to watch the light show.

The next day, after having lunch with Uncle Asad, the four of us left Uncle Asad's house for Los Angeles. The drive was four hours long, but I didn't mind. I was thrilled by the idea of going to Los Angeles, the city of dreams for many. Places that made one dream big inspired me. Big cities have their own kind of energy, the kind that makes you want to believe that anything is possible. Living is about finding your soul, your purpose and following it through. Life to me was about finding purpose. Ehsan fell asleep halfway through the car ride while I spoke with Mom and Dad and listened to music. In LA, we were going to stay with Uncle Ahmed, dad's best friend from his school days. Uncle Ahmed lived twenty minutes away from Beverly hills with his wife Pinky and two kids Yasmin and Raza, but Ehsan and I had never met Uncle Ahmed's kids before. We reached Uncle Ahmed's house around eight at night. Dad parked the car outside their townhouse, and Uncle Ahmed came outside.

"Hi beta, how are you?" Uncle Ahmed smiled at me as I walked past him and towards the main door. His wife Pinky was standing by the door to welcome us all in.

"Salam," Aunty Pinky said as she hugged me, then Mom as

we entered in. I then hugged Yasmin, Aunty Pinky's daughter who was three years younger than me but super sweet to talk to. Ehsan and Yasmin's brother Raza began talking right away, and Raza took Ehsan in his room to show him his pet snake. Yasmin and I were standing in the corner of the lobby talking, but a few minutes later we also went into Raza's room. Right behind his door, Raza had a cage sitting on top of his writing table in which he had a green and yellow snake.

"Come here, take a look," Raza said, looking at me.

"What type of snake is this?" Ehsan asked as he stared at the snake.

"It's a baby python," Raza answered.

I stared at Ehsan, and he stared at me. The python was small, but I still thought that snakes were ugly and not to be kept in the house. Towards the far end of the room was another desk which had another cage full of reptiles. Raza walked over to the other side of the room and started showing Ehsan the turtle and gecko he had. In a way I was impressed with how passionate Raza was towards his pets, but I could never imagine owning a pet snake.

Yasmine and I got out of Raza's room, and Aunty Pinky was setting dinner on the dining table while everyone else was sitting and chatting in the living room. Yasmin took me into her room and started showing me her guitar. We talked about college and goals for the future. Yasmin wanted to go to UCLA, and that was one of my top choices too. While the two of us were talking about music programs at UCLA, Aunty Pinky called us outside for dinner. Uncle Ahmed worked at FedEx headquarters in LA, and during dinner he shared his experience of meeting Katy Perry.

After dinner was over, Uncle Ahmed took Mom, Dad, Ehsan, and me on a drive to see Beverly Hills at night. First, we drove by the ocean, then we drove across Beverly Hills looking at mansions that belonged to celebrities, producers, directors, writers and much more. The next day, Uncle Ahmed took our family to the Hollywood Walk of Fame where celebrities have stars on the ground named after them. As I walked around the area with Ehsan, I kept my gaze down looking at all the stars on the ground with names of extremely famous people. I felt so inspired. This was like a dream; I dream that I wanted for the longest time in my life. I had grown up being taught that one must have goals in life. You must dream, and for as long as I had been old enough to understand myself, I knew I was made to chase dreams in life. During my middle school years I used to watch a show on television called *Wizards of Waverly Place* in which Selena Gomez was playing Alex Russo, a girl who is from a family of Wizards but in the front of the world she's just an ordinary girl whose family owns a hot dog shop in Waverly Place, New York City. Inspired by that show, I always had this craze that I wanted to be on television. I wanted to be famous as an artist. Walking around Hollywood fueled the passion that already existed inside me.

In the world that we live in, a majority of things can be learned. It's one hundred percent true that with practice any skill can be acquired, but there are certain talents or "gifts" in life that are given to you by God. There are certain things in life that just are, and they do not need a reason for being. It's your calling, and you must find it. Everyone has a voice, a calling, a gift, and as individuals it's our job to figure out what that one gift or calling is. Most of the time, it's something that you are extremely passionate about. Something that you could do for hours while completely losing track of time. I never wanted to do a 9 to 5 job to be honest; I wanted to do something that excited my soul.

After the Walk of Fame, Mom, Dad, Ehsan, and I walked into the Dolby Theatre located in the Hollywood and Highland Center shopping mall, just a block away from us. We were only allowed to walk up to the area where the box office ticket booths were, and on the other side was a wall full of pictures of Oscars. The doors to the theatre were blocked off, but still I couldn't believe that I was standing in the exact place where the Oscars took place every year.

Everything about this place was so inspiring to me. It reminded me that I too had big dreams in life that I had to chase. It made me want the hustling kind of life, where I wanted to achieve everything that others thought was "out of reach." This was engraved in me since childhood; I always wanted to attain or do things others thought were not possible.

After the Dolby theatre, Uncle Ahmed took us to the area of Hollywood Hills. Uncle Ahmed's car was in front of us, and Dad followed behind as we drove through the hills of Hollywood. Ehsan and I were glued to the edge of the seats, peeking out the window to the ever famous Hollywood sign on our left which we had spotted from quite a distance. As the car got closer and closer to the top of the hill, I couldn't believe my eyes. Looking at the Hollywood sign, I got lost in my dreams. As we were getting closer to the sign at the top of Mount Lee, a bunch of houses kept passing by on the right and left.

"Look Maheen and Ehsan, these are houses of famous writers and filmmakers," Dad said as he drove to the top of the mountain so that we could get a good view of the Hollywood sign. I got even more excited. I was hoping I would see at least one celebrity during my trip to Los Angeles, but sadly I saw none.

Once we reached the level of the Hollywood sign, Dad stopped the car behind Uncle Ahmed's car, and we all got out to take pictures. The Hollywood sign was still at quite a distance from where we had gotten off, but it was directly at eye level. Mama and I began posing like crazy like we always did. After taking pictures, all of us got into the car again, and

Dad drove us to Beverly Hills. As soon as we entered the area of Beverly hills, Ehsan spotted a black and yellow two door Maserati that was parked outside the Hugo Boss store.

"I want that car," Ehsan said loudly, pointing to the Maserati.

"Work so hard that you can buy it, beta," Dad said, driving past the Maserati. That was the goal in life, to work so hard to get whatever you want, not just to get what you want but to live a life that feels good inside as well, and the way you feel good inside is by following your heart.

As we drove around Beverly Hills to get back home, I observed everything: the expensive, luxurious cars, houses, actually mansions, and all the designer shops, but more than all these materialistic things, the vibe of the place was attracting me. The entire car ride I kept thinking about how all the creative people lived in this area, like writers, directors, and all that they have contributed to Hollywood. It's never all just about glamour because dreams take every bit of sweat to come true. LA inspired my soul. It's the little things about a place or a thing that inspire you big. I wanted to look around the city and observe everything. I was even more motivated and passionate now about becoming something. There was one thing I knew I never wanted to do, and that was an office cubicle job where you are working nine to five every day and get a paycheck every two weeks. There's nothing wrong in doing such a job, but that's not what inspired me. I wanted the hustling life. Companies look at you through resumes, just how colleges look at you through your high school GPA and decide whether you are capable enough of getting the job or the acceptance letter from the college. It annoyed me that we lived in a society where everything goes by the numbers. Colleges judge students based on the grade point average they see on a student's transcript. Employers look at your resume for experience: how many jobs you have done in the past? How many years of experience do you have? And so on. At the end of the day, it all comes down to numbers. But what a school transcript or resume cannot indicate is the amount of passion a person has inside. Any two people who have the same exact credentials on paper can be completely different when it comes to the passion they hold. But sadly, there is no way that a piece of paper can measure the passion you hold within, and that's why I never understood this whole competition that we have in society to do well. Everyone has their own path in life, and not everyone in life is meant to do the same thing or choose the same path; then why does everything get judged through a standardized way? I didn't want to be defined by a number or any piece of paper. I wanted to be defined by my passion.

Passion is an extremely personal trait. All of us have it, but not in the same amounts or for the same things. Passion doesn't look at numbers or competition or society's expectations. Passion is connected to the soul; it's what you truly want from within. Passion doesn't look at experience, qualifications, or grades. Passion is the fire in your soul that comes from you. Yes, external factors can play a role in igniting it, but no one can teach you to be passionate about something. You either are passionate or you are not. I whole heartedly believed that no matter how impossible something may be, if you are passionate about it, you will find a way to make it happen.

One should never tell the world your big plans that may be unconventional; people question you. People say things like "this can't be" or "that can't be." But you can't always follow conventions. I could never follow conventions; I wasn't even born the conventional way. How can you expect me to follow conventions when I have been defying them by birth? You cannot always listen to people because you need to listen to your heart. Your heart knows no conventions, it can only feel. When you go after what your heart is in, you will automatically be successful. Not everyone in life wants a nine to five job.

Not everyone in life wants to be a doctor, lawyer, or a banker. Sometimes you dream of changing the world all by yourself because you know you can. My parents have always been super supportive of my dreams, but it always shook me that generally in the world when a person is struggling and dreams of the unattainable, people tell him or her to live by the conventions because a life lived in conventions is stable. However, when the same person follows their own vision in life and becomes successful, people who doubted the person become admirers. Take Steve Jobs for example: when Steve Jobs created the first Macintosh, nobody believed in him. Everyone thought that creating personal computers was pointless and creating a product that would stand in front of IBM seemed like a dumb idea, but look at Apple now. It changed the world forever. Most limitations in life don't exist in reality; they only exist in the mind, and the reason we can't achieve something is because we keep telling our minds, "This is impossible." But once you let go of limiting your mind, you open it up to the possibility of everything.

I don't remember becoming this way for a reason. I have always felt too deeply since the time I have been old enough to understand myself. There was just something inside me that valued dreams and ambitions and passion more than it valued fitting in with everyone else. I didn't understand the pleasure people got by just being like the crowd and following its footsteps by doing things that have already been done. We only live once, and why do we want to spend that life meeting standards that already exist? Why not create your own standards? Society gives us standards of success by which we measure our own success and failures. We are conditioned to judge ourselves through rules that someone else sets for us. How silly is that? But in reality, there is no one meaning-fits-all definition of success. Everyone has their own definition of success. For some people, success means financial stability, a high paying job. For others, success might mean a big house or holding a certain position within a company, like being in the C suite. How come in life, everyone always measures success with materialistic things or status? How come nobody ever asks, "Are you happy with what you are doing? Is your heart satisfied with what you are doing?" To me, self-satisfaction means success. But we live in a system where everyone is so trained to look at numbers or materialistic things that we totally forget that being happy and satisfied with your work is also a real thing too. I never understood why everyone in the world in general was so obsessed with fitting in with rules that they didn't even create for themselves; someone else did. I have never understood the human need to want to fit in and do what others are doing.

Why fit into a norm when you can stand out and be different? Success never comes by running after money, jobs, or fame. Success comes when you are completely in love with what you are doing. Whatever you do with passion will always be successful. Why? Because when you do something with passion, your heart and soul are in it.

After the LA trip and during the second half of the school year, I decided I wanted to start a charity club which was going to be organized and run by me. It was my way of trying to make a difference in society around me already. There was no such organization in school that focused on social change, and therefore, I wanted to be the one to start it. The goal was to create a club that would take initiatives to help the needy and homeless in the community. I called the club "Humans of FHS" and made pamphlets about the club so I could spread the word around school and get people interested. There were numerous student clubs in the school already that did fundraisers for the homeless, but my goal wasn't to just hold fundraisers or donation drives and then have everything sent over to an organization. I wanted to create a club where students could make a difference in someone else's life by actively engaging with the community themselves. I didn't want a club where everyone brings in food to donate and we tie food boxes and just give them away. I wanted a club where everyone would feel like they contributed something to someone else's life, not just by donating items but by getting involved personally with each activity. The leadership team was the one who approved the start of new student clubs at FHS. I needed at least a hundred signatures of students who would be interested in being part of such an organization. I also needed a teacher who would be willing to sponsor the club. Finding people was going to be easy, finding a sponsor who would be willing to commit time after school for a club was the hard part because most teachers didn't want any sort of extra responsibilities after school hours. Without further delay, I created brochures to pass around at school to teachers and students to spread the word. Every morning I used to walk around the school, asking people to sign the club sheet for me if they were interested. Within a week I had all the signatures I needed, but I needed a sponsor.

I started off by asking all my teachers, but most of them were already sponsoring other clubs. I didn't care how much time it would take to find a sponsor; I just knew I had to find one. I began coming to school ten minutes earlier than my usual time and went door to door, teacher to teacher, to explain my goal to them and why creating the Humans at FHS club was so important. Every single teacher I met rejected my idea. They either clearly told me no, or they would say, "I will get back to you," but never get back. None of that ever pushed me down though. I kept going from class to class, hallway to hallway asking every classroom teacher I could find. There is always a way for anything and everything that you really want. Rejection was disappointing, but it never scared me. Usually, rejections end up discouraging people, after hearing too many "no's," one starts to think that their ideas are not worth it. But that's stupid. If you believe in something, you have to go after it no matter what. Nothing stopped me. I kept going classroom to classroom every morning.

Till one day, I was walking around the school with fliers in my hand, and I knocked on door "D104." I walked in and saw Mrs. O'Neill sitting at her desk getting ready for her second period class. I walked up to her desk. "Hi, my name is Maheen Mazhar. I am a freshmen, and I am looking for a sponsor to help me start my charity club. Would you be interested?" I asked, handing Mrs. O' Neill the flyer and began explaining to her why this club was so important and that it would encourage students to become passionate about helping their community rather than just seeing community service as a duty.

Mrs. O'Neill read the flyer then said, "Thank you for this. Let me think about this, and I will get back to you soon," she said, smiling at me.

"Thank you so much, my email is on the brochure if you need it." I smiled and left to get to biology before the morning bell was going to ring.

The next day I started pitching my idea to other teachers once again. I thought I was never going to hear back from Mrs. O'Neill, but three days later I got an email from her saying that she was ready to sponsor my club. This is what I had wanted all along. I knew this was a very small example, but when you want something bad enough and you never give up on it, it always ends up working out. Even the universe falls in love with a stubborn heart who knows not to give up until they achieve what they have set out to achieve.

Mrs. O'Neill was sponsoring the club; I was the president of the club and Sydnee was vice president. The rest of the club committee was going to be formed after we would reach a certain number of participants. Sydnee, Mrs. O' Neill, and I filled out all the paperwork process to get the club running. In late January, we held our first meeting to discuss what the club is and where we were expecting to take it within the next year. Sydnee and I were surprised to see the turnout of fifty-five people at the first club meeting. This was an indication that we were going to grow even more by the end of the year. In the first meeting, I mentioned one of our first projects, the sandwich drive. Everyone was going to bring in something to donate, either cans of tuna or bread, and all the students would get together in the home-ec room to make tuna sandwiches for the homeless, and once all the sandwiches were made, we ourselves would take them to the homeless shelter to feed the hungry. This was one of our biggest successes as a club organization. Sending donations to help someone is a great deed, but helping someone by physically participating to help another human being—the joy of that is unparalleled.

A few months later, Dad's younger brother Salman and his wife Arooj came to visit us from Canada. A few years ago, Salman Chachu had moved to Canada with his family and every time Dada and Dadi visited us from Pakistan, Chachu brought his family too, and we all always reunited at my house. One day during their trip, Arooj Chachi, Dadi, Chachu, and I were at the mall. Mom was going to join us later as she had a doctor's appointment. Instead of coming to the mall, Mom went back home to rest. In the evening, when Sally Chachu, Chachi, Dadi, and I got home, Mom was sitting on the long chase near the window in the lobby. I ran and sat right next to her.

"What's going on?" I asked. I looked around and no one answered.

Dada and Papa started smiling at me. "You are having another sibling," Dada finally broke the silence and start smiling. I looked at Mom with a huge smile on my face. There was already that pregnancy glow on her face. Then I looked at

Ehsan and smiled. Another sibling was on the way, and Ehsan was overjoyed.

"Finally, you won't be the baby of the family anymore," I teased him.

"Whatever, Maheen, I really want a sister," Ehsan added after being his usual annoying self to me. Then everyone started chatting about whether it was going to be a boy or a girl. Brother or sister, I didn't really care. I was going to turn fifteen in the summer, and the baby was going to be due in November, so either way my new sibling and I were going to be fifteen years apart, so boy or girl, the baby was literally going to be like a child to me rather than a sibling. Everyone was extremely excited for a baby to come in the family since all of us had grown up so fast. Ehsan was in fifth grade, I was in ninth, and all my other cousins were closer to Ehsan's age.

During the times that Dada was living with us, every evening before dinner he would sit outside on the chairs in the balcony with his drinks and desi music playing on his phone. Drinking was a habit of his since his army days, but I never saw him being overly drunk ever. He enjoyed his drinks. I used to sit outside with him, he would have his drink, I would drink orange juice, and we would chat for hours. That day when he heard the news of another grandchild on its way, Dada prepared his two drinks and sat outside on the balcony again. I joined him and we talked, listening to music and staring at the community pool in front of the balcony.

"You know Maheen, when you were little, you used to come sit in the drawing room with me when I used to be drinking with my friends and watching cricket, and you always used to ask me, 'What are you drinking?' And I always tricked you by saying it's medicine." Both of us started laughing.

"Well now you can't trick me no more," I said laughingly.

"Of course I can't. You are one wise girl now Mashallah," he said, smiling at me and then picked up the peanuts from the tray in front of him. After a while, Dada always went into his storytelling mood. When I was younger these stories used to come out of children books. Now that I was older, these stories were ones that he had lived through while in the army. There were real war stories from the war of 1971 between India and Pakistan. Hours would pass by as Dada told me about all the things that he'd lived through, and I always listened with extreme admiration. His life wasn't easy; a soldier's life never is. Every time I heard one of his stories, I would always think that none of us could actually live the life Dada has lived as a solider in the army, fighting real wars and never knowing whether he would even come home alive or not. Summer nights with Dada were always story nights.

In August, just a few weeks before the start of tenth grade, Mom and Dad made a plan for our entire family to go to New York City. That was the one city my entire family was in love with, and it never got boring no matter how many times we went. Dad was already in New York for work that week, so all of us could easily spend some time together in the city. Dad had booked us all an apartment in New Jersey, from which the Freedom Tower across the Hudson River was clearly visible from the glass window in the lobby. Mom, Dad, and I were standing in the small balcony of the apartment admiring the entire view of the city of New York. I was so inspired by the city: the lights, the rush of passion through my veins. The New York skyline was one view in the world that looked more beautiful to me in person than it ever did on a postcard. Even though I had lived here as a kid, the city was so much more beautiful to me now than it ever was before. No matter how many times one sees the New York Skyline, it always leaves you inspired towards life.

Ehsan and I spent the whole night watching movies. Ten

minutes before, in front of Mom and Dad we were literally fighting in the lobby over the tv remote. Ehsan wasn't giving me the remote, and after arguing with him ten times over what movie to choose, I bribed him with ten dollars just so I could get the remote. But now that Mom and Dad were both in their room, the two of us were completely normal, and he was watching the movie of my choice. This was always the case. We fought and argued in front of others, but when it was the two of us by ourselves, we always got along. Even Mom and Dad used to laugh and always ask, "Why do you two always fight when we are around and become completely normal when we aren't?"

Ehsan and I also shared a certain look. If ever something funny, silly, or weird would happen, Ehsan and I would look at each other and be able to tell what we were laughing about or making fun of, and those sitting around us would never know why we are laughing. Siblings are a blessing; they are the first friend you make in life. One you can fight with all you want because you know they have no escape. They will still have to live with you no matter what. Fighting is just another way of telling your sibling you love them because you would never fight with someone who you don't care about.

The following day, we took Dada and Dadi to go see the city and the Statue of Liberty. We spent the first half of the day in Times Square walking around midtown. As we walked near the American Eagle Store on 45th Street, there was a yoga class happening right in the middle of Times Square sponsored by Aerie. Bright green mats were scattered around the area in front of the red Times Square stairs. There were about seventy women doing yoga at Times Square. After walking around a bit all of us went to go sit on the very top of the famous red staircase. Dada and Dadi loved the energy of New York; so did I. Dada literally used to say, "The energy in this city can make anyone feel alive." We were supposed to leave the city around five o' clock to head over to Liberty State Park for the Statue of Liberty cruise, but Dada and Dadi got so busy shopping that we left the city around seven and rushed to Liberty Park to see if we could catch another cruise. Unfortunately, there were no more cruises leaving the dock for the day. But we were in time to witness the sunset while looking at the Statue of Liberty. The colors of the sky began to change above Lady Liberty. There were shades of yellow, orange and red getting deeper and deeper before it all turned into dark night blue. The colors of red and orange behind the green lady liberty looked gorgeous. I took lots of pictures for them that day.

When we got back from New York, two weeks later Nani came over to stay with us. Mom was five months pregnant now, so having Nani over was extremely helpful. Nani stayed in my room while Dada and Dadi stayed in the bedroom in the basement. Nani and Dadi both took care of all the household duties while Mom could relax a bit. In the beginning of Mom's sixth month, we were going to find out if Ehsan and I were going to get a brother or a sister. I thought the baby was going to be a brother while Ehsan thought it was going to be a sister. Ehsan already had even decided to name the baby girl, Emaan.

I always asked him, "But what if it's a boy? What would you name the baby then?" and he always said, "No, it's going to be a girl because I want a baby sister."

The day of Mom's next ultrasound, Ehsan, Dad, and I went with her to Reston Hospital where her gynecologist sat. For the first time in my life, I was going to a hospital with a smile on my face, unlike my childhood when I was traumatized for life. Hospitals still scared the hell out of me. As soon as I went inside one it always made me feel sick to my stomach. But today was different. Today I wasn't going to the hospital to relive any trauma of my life. I was going there to celebrate the news of a new sibling on its way. This was the day of the big reveal. On our way to the hospital, Ehsan and I kept guessing the gender of the baby. The same conversation started again: boy or girl. Mom and I thought it was going to be a boy. Ehsan and Dad argued that it was going to be a girl. There was no other girl in the family after me and Nadeem thaya's daughter Zara, so Dad wanted another girl. Once we reached the hospital building, Dad parked the car in the Patient Parking Garage, and all of us went inside. When we got to the gynecologist's office, the nurse signed Mom in and took her right into the ultrasound room towards the back of the clinic. Dad sat with Ehsan and I in the lobby talking. Dad and Ehsan were the only two guys at the gynecologist clinic at the moment. On the benches around me I was surrounded only by pregnant women who had come to the clinic by themselves.

About twenty minutes later, the nurse came back to the lobby. "Are you Faiza's family?" the nurse said looking right at Dad, Ehsan, and I. "She's calling you all inside," the nurse added towards the end.

The three of us followed the nurse into the ultrasound room. When I entered into the room, the ultrasound screen was right in front of me. Mom was lying on the bed with a white curtain hanging on the side of the bed to cover her tummy. On the other side, the ultrasound technician was moving the ultrasound machine on Mom's stomach. "You are having a baby sister," Mom smiled. The nurse tried moving around the ultrasound machine to show us the baby and her hands and feet, but I couldn't tell one body part from the other on the black and grey screen. Dad, Ehsan, and I couldn't stop smiling.

The ultrasound technician kept moving the transducer probe around and guiding us through where the head of the baby was, the arms, the legs, etc. I still couldn't tell where the baby was. There were just black and white patches on the monitor that kept moving around in circles. But after the appointment when we went home, Mom showed me the printed images of the ultrasound. The actual pictures were so much better than the exam. The head, the arms, and legs of the baby were super clear.

CHAPTER TEN

During sophomore year, one day, I was sitting in Mr. Rubenstein's English class getting ready for the lecture, when Olivia, one of the popular white girls at our school, walked in with a bunch of happy birthday balloons in her hand. I knew Olivia since middle school, but now she was a completely different person since she was on the lacrosse team, and she only hung out with the so called "popular kids." Since it was her birthday, I got up and went towards the back of the room where Olivia was putting her stuff on the table. "Happy Birthday," I said, hugging Olivia.

"Thanks a ton, Maheen," Olivia said smilingly. Olivia's best friend Brianna was standing right across from Olivia and staring at me. I went back to my table and took out my binder from my bag as class was about to start. I was setting my papers on my desk, and I suddenly felt a hand on my shoulder. I turned around and it was Brianna.

She started whispering in my ear. "You know what I got Olivia for her birthday?" Brianna said.

"What?" I asked.

"Penis-shaped lollipops," Brianna giggled.

I wanted to puke in my mouth. "How can people possibly be so disgusting?" I thought to myself. Brianna kept smiling, but I didn't find this funny, amusing or something to be proud of. Such things disgusted me. Why in the world did I need to know that even? Why did high schoolers have to be so immature? We weren't babies, but tenth graders. We could at least have more maturity than discussing penis-shaped lollipops in English class. Why did everything in high school have to be so sexual?

Mr. Rubenstein came in the room and start writing on the smartboard. Brianna was about to rush to her seat, but then she came back towards me. "The party's this Friday, and there is going to be alcohol," she quickly whispered into my ear and left.

"Okayyyy!" I thought to myself as I was still a little confused to as to why Brianna was giving me all this information when I wasn't even a super close friend of Olivia's.

"Ok class, today we are going to do questions one through thirty in your AP questions packet," Mr. Rubenstein said. I searched for my packet but at the same time I kept on wondering why Brianna had told me so much about Olivia's party when I wasn't even going, nor did I need to know.

The following day I received a text from Christian, the guy who was in my AVID class in eighth grade. "Hey, are you going to Olivia's party?... Heard it's going to be lit," the text read.

"No, I am not going. I don't know Olivia like that anymore," I replied. The conversation ended there.

The weekend passed. Monday morning, I was back in Mr. Rubenstein's class. I sat at my desk and began opening my backpack to take out the homework that was due. Two minutes later, I saw Brianna walk through the door. She had a serious expression on her face, and she stared right at me. I smiled at her, but she didn't even react. Brianna came right up to my table. "Did you tell Chris about Olivia's party?" Brianna asked rudely. I put my pencil down.

"Hey, I didn't tell Chris about Olivia's party. He texted me asking if I was going to the party or not, and I told him I am not," I replied simply. But in my head, I was wondering why Brianna was asking me all of this.

"Well Chris told me that you spoke to him about Olivia's boyfriend and gossiped about alcohol at the party," she said, looking at me.

"What in the world are you talking about, Brianna? I don't even know who Olivia's boyfriend is, and why would I discuss what happened at the party when I wasn't even there, and Chris texted me a day before the party, not after, so how would I have known what happened and what didn't?" I said to her.

"What the heck," I thought to myself. Why was I getting involved in all of this when I hadn't even done anything? I wasn't even a part of Olivia's life. All I did was wish her happy birthday as any classmate would wish another. Brianna took her phone out and showed me the screen shots of the messages Chris had sent to her, saying Maheen had said all of these things. I was shocked. The messages were three paragraphs long and did discuss Olivia's party, but there was no way that the conversation that Brianna was showing me had actually taken place in reality. I took out my phone, opened up my messages, and showed Brianna the two-line conversation I actually had with Chris.

The same moment, Olivia came over to me, "Why did you talk about me like that?" she started. I then showed Olivia the message, but honestly, I had no gain in dramatizing the whole situation, nor was it my fault, so there was no point of saying sorry.

Our conversation was interrupted the moment Mr.

Rubenstein told Brianna and Olivia to go back to their seats as our lecture started. I, however, was furious at this point. I knew I hadn't done anything, so I wasn't going to apologize or calm the situation down.

Later during lunch time, I found out that Chris had talked shit about Olivia's party and her boyfriend in a conversation with a girl named Taylor but later Chris removed Taylor's name in his contact list and put my name on her number because he wanted me to look bad in front of Olivia. I didn't even understand what was the point of doing something like this, but to Chris this was the joke of the day. To me, this was so dumb because if you have the time to create and enjoy social drama, that literally means you have nothing better to do with life. I was mad at Chris but more than that felt sorry for him because what anyone thought of me made no difference to me since I already knew who I was or wasn't, but the fact that Chris had so much time to plan this whole drama out made me feel sad for him. My mind couldn't agree that someone would waste so much of their energy on such things when you can literally invest that energy to do something productive with your life. But no, apparently high school drama was more important to people rather than doing something useful with their lives. I hated being around such people and wasting time and energy on useless drama. This was one of the biggest reasons why I never wanted to hang out with people in the so-called popular group. My goals and mindset towards life had evolved drastically. I wanted real people around me, not fake ones that created drama as a means of passing time or gaining popularity. What surprised me the most was how immature a guy could be that he actually changed the contact name of the person he was talking to and sent a screenshot just to create drama between two classmates. I never understood what Chris was trying to gain from this. Chris wasn't like this back in middle school, but high school popularity changed him for the worst. Chris was the perfect example of the immature behavior that guys had in high school, and I found that so irritating. He gave me another reason to believe that high school boys were not to be trusted even as friends because people can switch on you any minute. It's true, you must experience things to learn from them. By going through this episode of high school drama, I became even more firm about my choice of never hanging out in the popular group or chasing certain people at school. I was much happier being by myself, focusing on my life, and having just a few people around me rather than being stuck in a crowd that had no purpose or meaning at the end of the day.

In October, when Homecoming came about, I went to the game with my friends, but I decided not to go the dance. I knew it was going to be the same as last year anyway, and I had already been there and experienced all of it, so I didn't see the point of going again. On the Saturday of the dance while everybody was getting ready and taking pictures and posting them online with the captions "Homecoming 2012," I was in my pajamas chilling on the couch watching Netflix. Nobody had told me not to go; I just didn't want to go. To be honest, I was over the whole homecoming hype. I liked experiencing things, but once I did them, I was over it. Mom and Dad never stopped me from going; I just didn't see the point anymore in dressing up like a doll just to dance in a school gym covered with balloons to make it look fancy.

When you are never stopped from doing anything and are free to make your own decisions in life, your urge to do things kind of dies out, in a good way, meaning you don't become rebellious or do something crazy, and this is the result of a very successful parenting. More than being my parents, Mom and Dad have always been my friends. They were the two people in my life who I could talk to about anything and everything. No part of my life was ever hidden from Mom and Dad. Some people, especially in our Pakistani culture have the mindset that parents should never be friends with their children because that produces a lack of respect for the parents from the child's side of the relationship. I disagreed with that, especially because I wasn't raised like that.

I was living under the belief that all Pakistani parents were as trusting and freedom giving as mine were until one day my classmate Kiran told me the story of her getting caught with her boyfriend by her mom. Kiran's mom was the opposite of mine: conservative and old school. Kiran wasn't allowed to wear short sleeves, leave the house late or even go out somewhere without her mom's approval. Kiran was dating a Pakistani boy named Bilal, but her mom had no idea. So, one day after school, Kiran and Bilal went to Kiran's house, and she sneaked Bilal inside her house while her mom was at work, and when her mom got back from work Kiran pretended like as if no one had ever come home with her. Kiran told me this story so proudly, but I never understood her. Maybe she never saw that what she was doing was wrong, but to me everything about sneaking a boy into your house without anyone knowing was wrong. I could never be like that, not only because I couldn't break my parents' trust, but also because my inner moral system would never allow me to do something like that. All of us have an inner voice that tells us right from wrong. Some of it is influenced by our upbringing but not all of it; part of it comes from yourself, from who you are inside. Some people listen to their inner voice more than the outside world, and that was me. I wasn't in a relationship because being in one didn't feel right to me at this point in my life. But even if I was to be in a relationship, I always knew that I would never hide it from my parents. The only time you hide something is when somewhere inside, you know you are doing something wrong. If you are not doing anything wrong, there is no point of hiding. If something is hidden or in secret, and especially if it's a relationship, then you are not giving it the respect it deserves.

November came around rather quickly. Mom's C section was scheduled for the nineteenth. The entire family was getting ready for the arrival of my baby sister. Dad took a week off from work near Mom's delivery date. Dada had taken responsibility of running all the errands outside the house. On November 19th Mom's surgery was at Inova hospital in Fairfax at eleven o clock. Mom and Dad had left for the hospital at 10 in the morning while Dada, Dadi, Ehsan, and I got there at 11 am. Dada parked the in the open parking right across the street from the hospital's main entrance and the four of us walked inside. The labor and maternity ward was located on the eighth floor, so we took the elevator near the check in counter and went up. Here I was in a hospital, not for myself but still thinking about how much I hated this place. Always had and always will. When the elevator doors opened on the eighth floor, there was a nursing station where two nurses were sitting in their blue gowns. I walked over to one of the nurses. "Excuse me, my mom's here for her surgery—Faiza Mazhar. Do you know if they took her back yet?" I said.

"Your mom is still in the pre-surgery towards the back. It's room 604. You can go see her," the nurse said. I started walking down the hallway behind the nurse's desk, and Ehsan, Dada, and Dadi followed. Upon entering the pre-op room, I saw Mom was laying in the hospital bed already for her operation wearing a white and blue surgery gown with her head covered in a surgical scrub cap. Ehsan and I ran to Mama's bed and hugged her tight and kissed her on the forehead. Then Dad pulled out his phone and started showing Dada and Dadi the pictures he had taken with Mom right after she got into the surgical gown. Then, Dad came towards Ehsan and me and started showing us the picture of him and Mom where Mom was sitting on the chair smiling, and Dad was standing behind her, kneeling on his knee to match levels with her.

"Look, your baby sister is going to pop out soon, inshallah," Dad said, pointing at Mom's belly in the picture. Ehsan and I started laughing. That's what I loved about Dad: he had no filter, and he could make anyone laugh anywhere. As we were talking, the nurse came in to take Mom into the operation room. Dad went with Mom, and the rest of us went back outside to sit down in the lobby past the elevators and in front of the nursing desk.

I sat on the chair next to Ehsan while both of us were on our phones. Dada walked towards the coffee machine in the corner to grab a cup of coffee. All of us sat there in the lobby for about an hour and a half, staring at the tv and talking to one another and spending time browsing social media on our phones. Surprisingly, we were the only family in the waiting room.

"Maheen , did you know that when you were about to be born, the entire waiting area was full of our relatives, and the nurses were so surprised to see so many people gathered for a child's birth," Dada said to me.

I smiled. "If that happened here, the hospital staff would freak out," I said laughingly to Dada.

Finally, an hour later, I saw Dad walking towards the lobby from the back of the maternity ward. A nurse was following behind him, rolling a bassinet. Dada, Dadi, Ehsan, and I had stood up from our chairs in excitement. I couldn't see the face of the baby yet as the nurse was rolling the bassinet towards us; all I saw was a tiny body wrapped in a blanket and the back of her head. The nurse walked towards us and stopped the bassinet right in front of where Dada, Dadi, Ehsan, and I were standing. That's when I saw my baby sister for the first time. She was deep asleep in the bassinet with her head turned towards the left. Everything about her was so cute: her little tiny eyelids that were completely shut, her tiny nose, and lips. Her little tiny fingers that were all curled up in a fist. She slept as if there was nothing else to care about in the world right now. I just wanted to cuddle her in my arms, but none of us were allowed to hold her just yet. She had to be taken to the nursery for her regular tests first. Overall, she was a very healthy baby weighing seven pounds.

Dada hugged Dad, then Dadi hugged Dad, and then Dad hugged Ehsan and me as we all congratulated each other.

"How's Mom?" Ehsan asked.

"She's good. They are just waiting for her to wake up from anesthesia to shift her to a room," Dad answered as he began showing Ehsan and me pictures of when Mom held Emaan for the first time in the operation theatre. The baby was all covered in blood when the nurse laid her on Mom's chest for the first time. Babies were so cute to me and truly a miracle of God. Babies are one of God's biggest wonders because you start off with a single cell, and nine months later you have a fully formed human being. And God has given this ability to bring life on earth to a woman, and yet in certain parts of the world like Pakistan there still existed the mentality that women are less than men or that their only job is to bear children. If a woman has been chosen by God to be capable of bringing life on earth, just imagine how powerful she must be. The nurse took Emaan to the newborn nursery room where they had to finish up taking her vitals. The rest of us sat back down in the lobby and waited for Mom to be shifted to a room.

"Excuse me, your mom was moved into room 621. You all can go see her," the nurse said loudly from a distance. All of us got up and walked to the room. As we got into the room, I put the flower bouquet on the table next to Mom. I kissed her forehead then walked over to my sister's basinet. She was deep asleep in her bassinet, which was placed right next to Mom's bed.

"Maheen, water," my mom called out in her sleepy voice. Mom was still under the influence of anesthesia. I picked up the glass from the side of the table and helped Mom drink out of it.

Seconds later Emaan woke up crying, and Mom wanted to feed her, so Dadi and I stayed in the room while all the guys left. The first day in the hospital, one by one all of Mom and Dad's friends kept coming to visit the baby. After dinner, Dada decided to do Emaan's Gurthi ceremony. Dad went to CVS to get a bottle pf honey as the rest of us chatted in the hospital room. Dad got back and handed the honey bottle straight to Dada. Dada got up from the sofa chair in the corner of the room and went to the bathroom to wash his hands. Mom was holding Emaan as she would wake up for a few minutes and then go back to sleep again. Dada opened the jar of honey, poured a drop of honey on his finger, and walked towards the bed in the middle of the room. Emaan's eyes were closed, but her lips were slightly open with one loosely resting on top of another. Dada quickly ran his finger past Emaan's mouth, and as she licked on his finger, the space between her eyebrows suddenly tightened, and she started crying as if she just had something really disgusting.

None of us had even realized that it was already eleven at night and family visiting hours had ended. Mom put Emaan to sleep, and Dada, Dadi, Ehsan, and I went home for the night. On our way back home from the hospital, we stopped at the Burger King drive through because the hospital cafeteria food was horrible, and Ehsan was still hungry. Since Thanksgiving break was only a week away, Ehsan and I had taken the entire week off from school so we could go to the hospital every day and spend time with Mom and the new member of our family.

I saw Ehsan suddenly maturing after becoming an elder sibling. He chose Emaan's name; the way he held Emaan in his arms and put her to sleep—Ehsan was doing everything. Ehsan was only four and a half years younger than me, but to me he always felt like a baby, and he was the baby of the house till now, but not anymore.

The next five days were spent making trips to the hospital and then back home at night. On the sixth day, Emaan and Mom were finally discharged. Dad and I had decorated the living room and Mom and Dad's bedroom with blue "welcome baby" banners and pink balloons.

Emaan's cot was all set in next to Mom and Dad's bed. When Mom came home with Emaan, it literally felt like all of us had gotten a new toy to play with and make us laugh. Each one of us was obsessed with holding Emaan in our arms. Most people would find it awkward to have a sister while you are in high school, but to be honest, I never felt that way. Whoever is meant to come in this world comes in this world. Emaan and I were fifteen and a half years apart, and it was so refreshing to have a baby in the house after such a long time. She felt like my kid to me rather than my sister because whenever I was too stressed about school or needed a break from my homework, I used to go cuddle and play with my sister, and it felt so good that all my stress would go away. Another plus point of having a newborn sister was that now Mom and Dad had another responsibility to take care of, which required a lot more attention, and so Ehsan and I used to tease Mom and Dad that now they wouldn't have time to keep a strong check on the two of us. We never needed a strong check because there were no such restrictions in our house. I just used the excuse as a joke with my parents.

After midterms ended in January, one day after Ms. McDowell's history class, I went to go meet my guidance counselor Ms. Emery to select classes for junior year. I walked into the counseling center, walked past the transcript office, and the third door on the left was Ms. Emery's office. I sat on the chairs outside her office and waited for her to call me inside. Ms. Emery was a really nice person, fairly young and an easy person to talk to. I loved meeting with her because she always welcomed me so warmly and spoke to me openly as if we were friends. I always came to Ms. Emery for academic guidance, but we would end up discussing life as well. I never had an issue with Ms. Emery; I had an issue with the standards of education. Ms. Emery walked out of her room and greeted me. "Hey Maheen, come in," she said standing in front of her office door. I went inside and sat on the black chair in front of her. Ms. Emery sat in front of her desktop and started opening my academic chart. "So, how's the year been so far for you?" she said as she reached towards the shelf behind her desk and grabbed a long green sheet of paper.

"Here you go. Why don't you read through this as I set up?" she said as she handed me the piece of paper. This was the "High School Diploma Requirement Sheet," and every year the school printed it in a different color. The front side of the green sheet had requirements listed for an Advanced Diploma and the Standard Diploma. The back side of the page was the entire list of courses for junior year. I was doing the Advanced Diploma because I was told that people who do the Standard Diploma don't get into a four-year college.

Ms. Emery turned her chair towards me. "Let's go over your Advance Diploma requirements: four years of English, four years of Science, four years of History, and three years of Math, two years of P.E"—which I was done with—"and three years of a Foreign Language." She concluded that I was done with two years of English, Math, and History. I needed two more years of English, Math, and History. For Science I only needed one year. I looked at the options I had for Science classes as a junior; the options were many. I could take Geosystems, AP Biology, AP Chemistry, Physics, AP Physics, Geology, and so much more.

I read the list and replied, "Geosystems." The class looked

interesting, and it would also end up satisfying the requirement for another Science course.

"Don't take Geosystems. That doesn't look impressive on college applications," Ms. Emery replied, fiddling with her pen.

"Why?" I asked.

"That class is too easy," Ms. Emery answered. Chemistry and Physics were never my cup of tea.

"What about Geology?" I asked.

"Umm, Geology doesn't count as a Science in the Advanced Diploma; it counts as an elective. Only in the Standard Diploma it counts as a Science."

I was so confused by now. There were choices, but I wasn't given the choice to choose my own class. It was being chosen for me by what the system deemed as right. I knew I had to fill my requirements, and meeting college requirements was important, and that's the only reason why I cared about doing well in school. I knew I had to do this to get to the point in life where I could do what I wanted to do.

But more often than not, the whole system made me feel like a robot. I felt that the system never gave us the opportunity to learn what we really wanted to learn and explore because we were so occupied fulfilling requirements—requirements that were made by someone else but were applied to my life and all other high school students' lives. I understood that requirements were important, but only to a certain extent. I thought school was about preparing us for real life, but high school was just about checking the boxes on the list so we could make it to college. Of course, making it to college was important, but why was everything a preplanned to do list? Why couldn't learning be made fun by letting kids create a curriculum that helps them achieve their specific goals? Not everyone has the same goal in life; then why have a one-size-fits-all sort of system to rate everyone by? I never said these things to my counselor, but I always felt them. No one had ever taught me to think this way. This was just the way I was. I thought too deeply about everything in life. In real life, there are no boundaries between subjects; you have to know how to apply your knowledge of one field to another. But in school, everything was so concrete; everything had to be done a certain way. Classes were all about grades and passing exams or memorizing. Anyone can memorize and pass a class, but that's not how the real world works. I wish my teachers in high school focused more on learning than they did on memorization. But at the end of the day, teachers get paid so little that all they care about is getting a decent passing rate for the final at the end of the year.

I understood that having a standardized curriculum is important so that everyone gets a complete and fair education. But not everything fits into a system; some people have passions, goals, and dreams that require focus, attention, and dedication. Some of us realized our dreams early on in life, and we didn't like wasting our time on things we would probably never need in life again after high school. The time I spent on learning about things I would never use in my life again... I wished I could have that time to use for music or something else that I was passionate about. Passion doesn't require a teacher; it's not a pass or fail thing either. Passion is an unstoppable fire that comes from within and urges you to do something great in life that no one has seen or done before. People who have a passion and a vision of their own always find a way to make their vision a reality. Such people never fit in to standards that other people set for them, and that's how I was. I knew school was important and I had to take the classes that complied with the school's standard, but I also knew that those who didn't fit into standards that society set for them knew very well that they had to find their own unique path to success, not standards.

"Thank you so much," I said to Ms. Emery as I stood up from my chair and got ready to go to my next class.

"You are welcome. Let me know if you need anything else," Ms. Emery smiled at me as I walked out the door.

While I was walking to my last class of the day, I kept thinking about how the school system technically killed creativity. The high school education system puts kids in a situation where they are nothing more than a number. First, you are defined by your grades. Even the classes you take are technically not decided by you because you must meet the standards set by the school system, or else you don't graduate. Then you are defined by the score you get on the SAT. Even when you do well on all of the above, when it's finally time to apply to colleges, you are merely just a number. You are just one out of the thousands of students who apply to college every year. This entire system of numbers is so deeply embedded in our society that there is no escaping it.

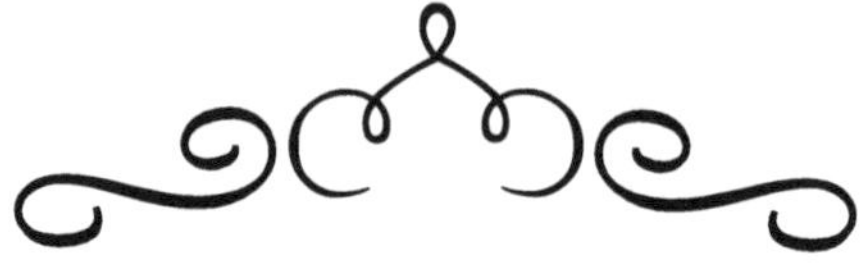

CHAPTER ELEVEN

During junior year, I had Fashion Academy first thing in the morning every single day. The class was located towards the back of the school near Mr. Hanrahan's classroom from freshmen year. Upon taking a left from the cafeteria there was a hallway, and my academy class was straight down near door 7. This hallway was home to all the ESOL classes and all the foreign kids. The entire hallway used to smell as if someone had dropped an entire gallon of men's Axe deodorant on the floor and I dreaded the smell. Every morning, while passing all the ESOL classes I witnessed the same thing. A bunch of couples sitting against the lockers, passionately making out as if this wasn't school but their house. You know what's better than making out with someone? Finding someone who you can have a mental connection with. Someone who just understands you at a deeper level. I craved that more than I ever wanted to get physically close to anyone. Yes, intimacy is important, but to me, it had no value without emotionally being connected to someone at a deeper level. And the more couples I saw casually making out with one another in the hallways at school, the more I realized exactly what I didn't want in my life. In high school every relationship was less about emotional attachment And all about physical attachment, or at least that's what I had noticed, not once but countless times throughout my three years at Fairfax High, and nothing was more disgusting to me than being physical with someone without an actual commit-ment.

One day during lunch time, my group of friends and I all sat around one of the black round tables in the lunchroom talking. Tia and I were doing our homework while Nick, Zaid, and all the other guys at my table were chatting about sex and money, the two things that my generation was obsessed with.

"What do you think is a good number?" Zaid asked Hannah.

"As in?" Hannah asked curiously.

"As in the number of people you have slept with," Zaid answered.

"I think eight," one of the other guys at my table answered. "Probably slept with ten already."

"I think seventeen," Ruby answered as she put another coat of lipstick on her already chapped lips. I stared at Ruby for a good minute before the question finally made its way to me. I didn't know how to answer that question, and I was hoping that no one would ask me it either. Are we animals or human beings? This wasn't the culture I belonged to.

It was my turn to answer. "Zero," I proudly answered with a smile, and everyone looked at me as if I were from another planet. Why was it so cool to sleep with as many people as possible but so not cool to be pure? Isn't it cool to be saving yourself for the love of your life. Wouldn't a man desire a woman who's never been touched before? Then why was it seen as not cool? Isn't that something to be respected? Then why did the culture around me applaud adultery and consider "purity" as having no experience. I absolutely did not give a damn, nor was I going to change my thinking for anyone's approval.

"Let's play never have I ever," Zaid said as he took out a large plastic bag which was filled brownies. Zaid opened the bag and offered some to everyone. Everyone took a brownie. "I am going to start," Zaid said smilingly. Whoever had done what the speaker was going to say had to take a bite of his or her brownie. "Never have I ever kissed two people in the same day," said Zaid. Everyone but me took a bite of their brownie.

"Never have I ever had sex with someone more than five years older than me," was the next answer. Everyone but Hannah and me took a bite of their brownie.

"Never have I ever found a friend's mom or dad sexually attractive," Hannah said. Everyone but me took a bite of their brownies. It was my turn to go.

"Never have I ever smoked weed," I said. Everyone but me took a bite of their brownies.

"Never have I ever made out with more than three people in a day," Ruby said. Hannah, Ahmed, Zaid, and Nick had a bite of their brownies. I just sat there staring at everyone else, thinking to myself that I really didn't belong here; I knew I didn't. Was there really nothing else to talk about in life than sex and how many sexual partners one's had? And how come having multiple sexual experiences and partners was such a celebrated thing in the American culture? I felt so out of place. I knew that I wasn't meant for such an environment. I felt so disgusted sitting there hearing people talk about nothing but the physicality of a relationship. I stayed quiet; this conversation wasn't worth me jumping in. Why did everything have to start with sex and end on sex too. Why couldn't it be cool to want to be with one man and one man only for the rest of your life? I didn't care about sex or the physicality of a relationship;

I wanted the kind of love that fueled your fire. The kind of love that wasn't interested in your body but in your soul. Something that added value to my life, not just fit me in to a "body count."

After the game ended, Nick, who was sitting right across from me began talking about these two youtubers who had apparently made a video about "Saving sex for after marriage." Nick went off. "Yo, these two Youtubers make videos about how you should save yourself till marriage, and it's effing absurd because what are you supposed to be do with the other person till then? Just talk while dating?" he said. Everyone started laughing in agreement with Nick while I just sat there with a straight face because I didn't find any of this to be funny.

A while later Nick's friend Josh goes, "Well, if you are not going to have sex with your date, what are you supposed to do? Just stare at them for effing nine years? I'd rather die," he said.

Everyone at our table had seem to enjoy the joke but me. I was the only one who sat there thinking no wonder I hadn't dated anyone yet because boys my age were super immature. I felt so out of place, but in a good way. High school boys always went for girls who were so-called "fun" or easygoing. Girls who didn't think much before jumping into a relationship because in your teens nobody is trying to get serious; everyone just wants to have a good time. Maybe a fling. If the definition of a fun and easygoing girl was someone who was easy to get and didn't care about the value of a real relationship, then I was more than happy to be boring and not easily approachable. I didn't know how to put my heart in someone else's hands and trust them enough not to break it. That was scary to me. I didn't want to be someone's temporary pleasure, I wanted to be someone's everything.

While everyone else at my table was laughing at the girls in the video because their boyfriends were okay with waiting to have sex after marriage, I was thinking I would have endless respect for a boy who could be with a girl without pressuring her or wanting sex from her. But that is a kind of respect you can never expect to get from a high school boy. A guy who can be with you through everything and still respect your decision of not getting physical with him isn't a guy to be made fun of or laughed at, that's a guy you respect. That's the kind of guy you do anything to keep. That's the kind of guy that is rare to find in a generation where everyone is so obsessed with physical attraction and people fall in lust before ever falling in love. Looking at people around me in high school, I wondered if anyone ever even knew what the real meaning of love even was. Real love makes you grow; it adds value to your life. Real love is felt in the heart. It's about wanting to be with someone even when it's inconvenient. Real love is not having sex. Sex and love are not the same. Sex is easy: you can have it with anyone. But love, love is rare. It doesn't happen with everyone. I guess nobody around me truly knew the difference between the two.

The bell rung, lunch was over, and everyone started heading to class. "I will meet you in class," I told Tia as I quickly rushed to the girl's bathroom. Right across from academy class was the girl's bathroom which always had long lines inside in the mornings. The lines were not to use the stalls but to look at yourself in the mirror. There were no mirrors on top of the sinks; the only mirror in the girl's bathroom was a long wall mirror placed on the side wall where the line of sinks ended. All the girls stood crowding around one mirror to fix their hair, their makeup, adjust their boobs. Literally there would be ten girls staring in one mirror at once trying to fix themselves. Some stood in the middle, others sat on the floor, and the rest of the girls stood on the sides of the mirror and would pop their head in from the side to look at themselves. The girls in the front often kneeled on the floor so the other girls could see too. Some girls used to take out their makeup pouches and start fixing their eyeliner and mascara. Others painted their whole face with make up in that one tiny mirror. I couldn't be bothered at seven in the morning about how my brows or haired looked. Who cared how you looked in school? It's not like I had to impress anyone anyway. This was a school, not a modeling agency. For some girls, their priority was to look good so people would notice them. I never gave two cents about looking good in school, especially for someone else.

After using the bathroom, I headed straight to Ms. Chang's academy class. Ms. Chang was a fashion design graduate from Parson's School of Fashion in New York City. She lived most of her life in NYC, but after having her first child, she moved to Fairfax to teach fashion. Most of the time I was the first one to enter the class in the morning because I never wasted time in the bathroom or the hallways. The rectangular-shaped classroom was humongous since it was the last classroom in the corner of the building. The room was divided into two areas: the first half of the room was the lecture area with the smartboard in the front of the room and a large rectangle-shaped table placed in the center with stools in each corner. To the left of the giant lecture table was Ms. Chang's desk. The large lecture table was no ordinary table, but it had grid rulers drawn all over its wooden surface and was meant for pattern making and fabric cutting. However, whenever we had lectures, this was the table where all the students sat to look at the smartboard. The second half of the classroom had square-shaped tables and adjustable chairs for every student. We all had assigned seats, and I used to sit on the back table with three other girls: Zilvia, Jasmin, and Natty. Jasmin seemed like a sweet girl; I had known her twin brother Jim for a while since he was in my algebra two class in tenth grade.

Zilvia was sweet. She was new, and we got along well. The third girl Natty and I could never get along because we both had the same exact headstrong personality. Zilvia was Natty's pet in the sense that Zilvia would do anything that Natty said, and I wasn't like that. I couldn't be friends with someone who always thought that she was above everyone else.

Natty thought she was some fashionista or something. She dressed up in heels and always did her hair and makeup every single day. That's not what I had an issue with. I had an issue with the fact that she considered herself the coolest and bragged all the time and didn't really think of others as anything. She never spoke to people that were not of her "league" because she was trying to fit in with the popular kids. At this point, popularity, and social standing between high school cliques wasn't my priority.

My only goal my junior year was to get good grades, get my SAT scores in shape and start thinking about the colleges I wanted to apply to senior year. I was always interested in the arts, such as fashion and music. I wanted to go to the Fashion Institute of Technology in New York City. New York University, UCLA, and Columbia University were other options I had in mind as well. I knew for a fact that I wanted to go to a college that was out of state. Virginia was an amazing and calm place to grow up in, one that was perfect for family life. I, however, wanted passion in my life. I wanted to explore the world on my own. I wanted to live a life full of purpose, one where I keep chasing a dream till I achieve it and then move on to the next. A lot of teenagers want to go to college far away from home just so they can get away from their parents. I never had the kind of parents you would want to get away from, but I had dreams that were way too creative for a place like Virginia. There was no better place in the world to pursue a creative career then in New York itself. In a city like New York, one could be anything. The New York life became my ultimate dream, I had to go back to that city no matter what. I wanted that energy, that New York hustle in my life that I had seen just a sneak peak of as a kid.

Everyone around me had told me that junior year was supposed to be the hardest year of high school. Junior year counted a lot because it's the last full academic year that colleges see on your transcripts while applying for admission, and in general, there is more pressure on you then previous years of high school. Regardless, I was taking three AP classes: AP US History, AP Language Arts, and AP Biology. I used to get over four hours of homework every single day. During the school day, instead of wasting time fitting in with people and gossiping during lunch, I started going to the library on the second floor to finish my homework during school hours. I had stopped hanging out with Tia and her friends because I had realized that my mindset and goals were very different from what they wanted. My goal wasn't to make my high school life the social popularity phenom that everyone else had going on. I wanted to make my dreams come true. Everybody in this world dreams, but that doesn't mean dreams come true. You must work hard and be different from the crowd to make your dreams come true, and that's what I was doing. Everything in the world starts off with believing. You must believe in your own vision before anyone else ever can.

During lunch I used to go upstairs to the library and sit on the computer doing homework and searching for colleges. NYU and UCLA had great business and music programs, plus their locations offered an environment in which any artist would love to thrive. Los Angeles and New York are two cities where the entertainment industry is so big and there is a myriad of opportunities to get into music or entertainment. If I was going to apply to a fashion school, I was going to apply to Fashion Institute of Technology in New York City. I always wanted to do something creative, but I had also never set boundaries for myself. I wanted to do it all: fashion, business, and music. I was still undecided because I didn't know how to just choose one and stick to it.

Right after lunch, I had AP US history with Mr. Heamker in room D111 in the history wing in the middle of the school. Mr. Heamker was probably in his early forties. He kept his entire head shaved all the time and wore thin black glasses. Mr. Heamker was sweet in nature. He would always stand outside his door and greet us in. I liked Mr. Heamker and the way he taught. He always explained things rather than just expecting you to know them, and he always let us do test corrections after school. Even if you got an eighty-nine on the unit test and you came after school to correct your mistakes, Mr. Heamker would add points back to your test grade. So, if you got a B + on a test, he would bump up that grade to a A-. I never got a bad grade in Mr. Heamker's class, but I always stayed after school to do my test corrections, even if they were only two questions long because I wanted those extra credit points.

After every six to eight weeks, Mr. Heamker used to change our seating charts and the layout of the desks in the room. Now the room was divided into rows of two all the way to the back where the teacher's desk was. I was sitting next to this girl named Danielle who I had never interacted with before. Danielle had blonde hair and blue eyes but was very tomboyish. I used to always see her dressed up in Bermuda shorts with a t shirt and belt or sweats. She liked being called Dani instead of Danielle, so I started calling her Dani too. In class, whenever Mr. Heamker gave out group work, Dani and I always did it together. Soon enough we also started working together on homework and long-term projects, and that's how Dani and I became pretty good friends.

Towards winter break our school always had a winter formal dance. One day in December I came into Mr. Heamker's class, took my seat, and began taking my history binder out. A few seconds before the bell was about to ring, Dani walked through the door and came and sat right next to me in her chair. While Mr. Heamker was getting ready to take attendance, Dani started talking to her friend Elise who sat right behind us. They were talking about some guy that Dani had met when she went rowing for the crew team. My tenth-grade chemistry teacher Mr. Martin was the coach of the Fairfax Varsity Crew team, and Dani had been a part of the team for a while now. Dani turned over to me and said "Hey, this is my boyfriend. I am going to the formal dance with him." I was busy reading my notes from last class, but I quickly glanced over to see the photo, and was I shook. Dani was dating Jared, the guy I liked and went to school with in sixth grade. What was surprising to me was how small the world is. I could have never guessed that Dani was dating Jared because he went to Westfield High School where Areeba went, and Dani was in FHS with me. It's so funny how we do silly things when we are younger and don't realize that they were indeed silly till we are at a different maturity level in life.

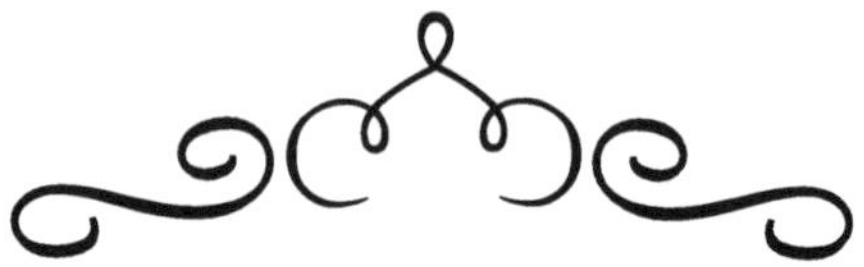

CHAPTER TWELVE

During the spring of junior year, I decided to manage the Fairfax Varsity Lacrosse team. The coach for the lacrosse team was Mrs. Shafer who had been my ninth-grade AVID teacher, and I had been in touch with her since then. On top of that, Sydnee and Samantha had Mrs. Shafer as their AP Psychology teacher, so whenever they used to stay after school, I used to stay after school with them. Sydnee and Samantha used to work on psychology while I used to finish my homework and help Mrs. Shafer with anything that she needed help with. One day after school, I was sitting in Mrs. Shafer's room when I saw a poster on the wall that said, "Varsity Lacrosse Interest Meeting."

"Do you coach Varsity lacrosse?" I asked, looking at Mrs. Shafer.

She ran her fingers through her blonde curls and answered, "Yes, I do. I need a manager for the team. Would you like to be one?" she asked, looking right at me.

"I would love to," I answered. Mrs. Shafer and I had always

gotten along super well, and I was really excited to be helping her.

From about early March I started staying after school with the lacrosse team almost every other day. I was Mrs. Shafer's right hand, making sure all the team members were doing what they were supposed to and that practices were running smoothly. Olivia and Brianna were part of the Varsity Lacrosse Team, and I had not spoken to them since a year after the whole Chris drama. But since we were all working together, we acted completely normal around each other, at least for practice. I was managing the team, and they were part of the team, so we couldn't really avoid one another. Every Tuesday and Thursday I stayed after school for lacrosse practice, and on Mondays I stayed after for my club meetings. School got out at 2:05 pm, but sports practices during the spring didn't start until 3:30 pm. During the hour and a half I had after school, I used to go to Ms. Varanawage's class to do math homework or test corrections. Whenever we had a test or a quiz in Precalculus and Trig, Ms. V always allowed us to do test or quiz corrections. If we did the necessary corrections, Ms. V increased our grade by a letter. Her full name was Ms. Varanavage, but all the students called her Ms. V. She was thin and she always wore turtleneck sweaters and baggy pants. I had her class fifth period on blue days, and I hated math so much that during fifth period I always stared at the clock in the room every five minutes, waiting for the clock to hit 12:05 so I could go to lunch and get out of math. The class was fine until the second half of the year rolled around and we began learning trigonometry. Where in the world was I going to need to use sin, cosine, and tangent of a thirty-five degree angle?

The very first trig assignment Ms. V had given the class was to memorize the unit circle. From day one of trig, I hated it. Ms. V had made us draw our own unit circle and label it again and again till we had the entire circle memorized. The example of the unit circle is very small, but in general schools test how fast we can memorize something and write it out on exam day.

Nobody cares about real world experiences or learning in a way that might help us in the future. Schools only test our memorization skills, not the way we see or think about a certain subject. When on earth was remembering a unit circle going to help me out, unless I wanted to become a mathematician or even an architect? Grades in high school were merely based on how much information you could memorize out of a textbook. But in life, there is no textbook you can follow and win, and memorization doesn't get you everywhere. In real life everything isn't black or white. Everything is connected; there are no boundaries between subjects, and you must know how to apply your knowledge of a single subject to another. In high school I just felt like a part of a larger system, as if life wasn't meant to be lived but to be planned out, and boxes had to be checked off as if life was a list of graduation requirements. Why? Why is there always a need in society to follow what everyone else is doing? People who hold passion create their own paths; they cannot be slowed down because of requirements.

School is important; it expands your horizons. Education changes your perspective on life altogether. However, the school system that I was growing up in was more focused on requirements and numbers than actual learning. It focused more on standards and passing exams than it did on learning or whether the student was enjoying what they were learning. My tenth grade chemistry teacher once told me how important it was for him that my entire chemistry class got above an eighty percent on the final exam. My teacher didn't want us to do well because he cared about our learning; he wanted us to do well because at the end of each school year, the FHS administration used to evaluate every teacher's performance to determine who would get promoted and who wouldn't. Promotion decisions for a teacher were simply based on the grades his or her students earned on the final. My chemistry teacher actually told my class that his end of the year evaluation mattered a lot to him, and we must do well for his evaluation. At the end of last year, when one third of my chemistry class got a seventy on the final, my chemistry teacher gave the class a ten point curve so everyone's grade would hit eighty percent. Everything was so much about numbers that most students including me cared more for our percentage in a certain class rather than learning something.

By the time I finished up my test corrections in Ms. V's classroom, it was time to go to the field house for lacrosse practice. The warmups took place in the gym itself, but the actual lacrosse practice used to take place outside on the field. After running for thirteen minutes exactly, our varsity team players all gathered around the field outside, and I took attendance first thing.

Literally every girl on the varsity lacrosse team was so annoying; all of them used to be discussing parties and what so and so did, and it felt like I was at a gossip meeting more than a sports meeting. About one third of our girl's lacrosse team were friends who belonged to the same social group. Since I used to be present at practice every single day, I saw how the team was divided. The so called "popular girls" used to hang out on one side of the field during breaks in their own little space while the other half of the team used to all get excluded.

Why did high schoolers think that hanging out in a certain group would validate them? Why do people always have a need to belong to a group? I could never do that. I could never seek my validation from anyone else but me. I have never understood why people have a need to fit in with other people and follow the norms in society. Who creates norms? People do, so it's fascinating to me how people are obsessed with following rules that other people have set for them. Being in a social group should not define you; your mind defines you. You can't live your life trying to fit in with people's standards or expectations. You only get one chance at life, and you should live it according to your own rules and standards. You don't need a billion people around you; you only need a few who are sincere. Most kids in high school aren't loyal friends; they are just there to have a good time. But I never understood the point of having a billion fake people around you when you can easily have a few trustworthy friends. A small friend circle is a happy friend circle; it's less chaotic and not full of drama, and at least the people that you hang out with are actually people you want to be around. You won't turn your back on them and bitch about them. I could never lie, nor could I ever pretend to be nice to someone to their face and then talk about that person later. I had very selected friends, but I liked that because I knew I could not pretend. I knew that high school wasn't all life had to offer; life was going to start once high school would come to an end.

In May of junior year my Fashion Academy class was having their annual fashion show in which only the seniors in Fashion Academy were going to be showcasing their very own collection. We were looking for models for the fashion show, and we had hung up posters around the entire school that said, "Looking for Models, five eight and above and can wear heels." The posters were up on every wall around the school for about two weeks, and I had so many of my classmates from Ms. V's and Mr. Heamker's class come ask me about modeling.

One day towards the end of April, I went into Academy Class and was setting up the designer's collections on the mannequins in the back of the room when I heard Ms. Chang say, "Alright everyone, leave what you are doing. We are going for auditions in the theatre academy room."

I left my half-dressed mannequin just the way it was and went to my desk to get my backpack. Our entire class was going to the theatre room on the other side of the hallway because the theatre room had a stage where Ms. Chang could make the models walk. The shortest way to get to the other side of the hallway wasn't walking across the school but cutting through the exit door. My class exited the school through the exit door right next to our classroom, walked past the trailers outside on our right side, and Mr. Douglas, the theatre teacher, opened the backstage door of the stage room for us.

As we entered, there was a mini hallway right before the stage entrance which was already packed with girls who had come to audition. Ms. Chang handed me and Natalie a bunch of slips and told us to pass them out to all the models. There were about thirty models waiting, and more were on stage already waiting to be auditioned. Each chit had a number on it, and Ms. Chang told Natalie and me to make sure only four models went into the stage area at once. I started handing out the numbers while Ms. Chang and all the senior students went on stage and took their seats. I looked around the room, and amongst all girls with short dresses and super high heels I saw a girl who had a black dress on and a creamed colored hijab wrapped around her head. She looked Arab, but I never asked where she was from. I was really impressed though, because it's true that beauty doesn't come from showing off your skin; it comes from whom you are and the way you carry yourself, and it inspired me that this girl was ready to go out there and walk in front of everyone while wearing her hijab and owning her identity and her values. Real beauty is honestly not about your skin or your outer appearance. Real beauty is about being happy, content, and comfortable with who you are inside and being able to show it off.

A few minutes later I heard Ms. Chang calling my name. "Maheen." I went backstage. "Can you come backstage and help dress models for the walk?" she said.

"Sure," I said, and I went behind the curtains where Yasmin was helping models dress up. A few minutes later, it was the hijabi girl's turn to walk the ramp, and I helped her quickly get into her outfit.

Ms. Chang announced "Dunia" on the microphone, and the girl looked at me then at the mirror on the wall, quickly pulled her head scarf off and threw it on the floor of the dressing area and walked out on the ramp. I was shocked for a second. The headscarf was laying in my feet, and Dunia was walking the ramp, twirling her hair, and there weren't only girls in the room; there were men sitting down at the judges' table too. I don't think anybody else really cared that Dunia's head scarf had come off, but I was in shock.

Dunia came back into the room after her ramp walk, changed her clothes, grabbed her scarf from the floor, tossed it in her black tote bag, and left. I was still a little shocked because I did know that when you wear a hijab, you cover yourself for God. You cover yourself from men that are not part of your close family, and you do it not for the sake of convenience but for God.

"What kind of a hijab comes on and off?" I thought to myself. The hijab isn't something you just say you will do one day and take of the next day; that's insulting the whole concept of what it represents. Once you take on the decision of wearing the hijab, you have the responsibility of holding up its respect through your actions in life, and Dunia had just now violated that by taking her hijab off per her convenience. I was no one to judge anyone, but rather than wearing a hijab for the world, I'd rather not wear it all. Sometimes, girls who come from very conservative backgrounds do such things. They are forced by their parents to wear hijabs when they do not want to, and when you are forced to do something, your heart isn't there anyway.

When the Fashion Show auditions ended and we are all in the girls' changing room backstage, I saw Dunia putting her hijab back on in front of the long mirror by the bathroom stalls. I was still very intrigued by why Dunia had taken her hijab off for the show and put it back on after she was done modelling, so I went up to her and asked anyway.

"Hey, if you don't mind me asking, do you wear your head scarf all the time?" I asked.

"Nope, not all the time. I don't even like it to be honest. I do it for my parents, but when I come to school, I mostly take it off," Dunia said to me casually as she adjusted the pins on the left side of her head scarf. "It's so annoying, dude. Like my brother, he's a guy, so he gets to do whatever he wants. He literally comes home at three in the morning, and that's okay, but when I leave the house, I have a hundred rules to follow," Dunia sighed and then walked over to the table in the middle. "Anyway, ok bye. Got to run to my next class now," she said as she picked up her bag and smiled at me as she left.

"See ya," I said as I gathered my belongings and got ready to leave too. On my way to my next class I couldn't help but think about what Dunia had told me about her parents forcing the hijab on her. Coming from a culture where every other parent is conservative like Dunia's, it forced me to think that I was indeed extremely lucky to have parents who never imposed anything on me. I was raised Muslim and I loved my religion. I looked towards God for guidance because everything that existed in my life was because of him, but I never saw religion as something that restricted my life or something that I had to rebel against. My parents gave my brother and me the same exact values and never even differentiated between the fact that I was a girl and he was a boy, even though that's also something that happened in South Asian families a lot. I felt like the luckiest desi (South Asian) girl in the world because even though Mom and Dad were born and raised in Pakistan, they never believed in the constraints that existed within the Pakistani society itself, and I was finally realizing how this wasn't something that I should be taking for granted but something that I should be cherishing.

Two months later, it was that time of the year again where I had to go to Ms. Emery's office in order to select my classes for the next school year. I couldn't believe that I was already going to be a senior in the fall and that three years of high school had just gone by in a blink of an eye.

After Mr. Heamker's class I went straight to see Ms. Emery. I sat on the bench outside her office and saw a blue sheet of paper hanging on the billboard right in front of me. I got up and walked closer to the board to get a good look and recognized that blue sheet of paper very well from all the years before. It was the list of graduation requirements broken down into two halves: half of the sheet was for the "Advanced Diploma student requirements" and the other half of the sheet was "Standard Diploma requirements," and under each of these headings were categories labeled as "Math, English, Science, History, and Electives," and under each sub section were like two choices of classes. This sheet was my biggest pet peeve about high school because every teacher or counselor used to say, "You have options. You can explore any courses you want," but the truth was you could only take the courses you were given approval to take. I found that really annoying because other people were telling you what to do in order to get where you wanted to be. No one else knows how much passion you carry inside of you, and yet all of us are constantly told to follow standards. Why? If everyone follows the same standards, no one will ever be successful or different. Everyone will just be stuck in the race to check the boxes and fulfill requirements.

Ms. Emery finally came out. "Hi," she said, looking right at me.

"Hi," I said.

"Come inside," she said as she turned back towards the door, and I followed her in. I sat on the same chair in the corner as always while Ms. Emery sat at her desk, and the process repeated just like last year and every year before that.

Ms. Emery looked at her computer then looked at me again. "Do you know what you want to study when you go to college?" she said. For me it was always clear that I wanted to do something creative, something that excited my soul. Up till this point music was something that I would find myself in. However, studying music doesn't get you anywhere. All you could do with a music degree is go into music education, and that's something that would kill all my creativity together. Fashion and Business were the top two fields I was really interested in. More than sewing and creating designs, I was interested in the business side of fashion, the marketing and branding of a product. Business in general had its own appeal to me; you can literally apply business to anything in the world and one day be able to create something of your own.

"With a business degree, there is no limit to what one can do and can't do," I thought to myself. "Fashion and Business," I said, answering Ms. Emery's question.

"Great," Ms. Emery answered, and then she pulled out the sheet of requirements again. THE SAME EXACT BLUE SHEET THAT WAS HANGING OUTSIDE ON THE BOARD. I sighed.

I signed up for AP Literature, Physics, Statistics, AP Government, which was being offered online, and last but not least, Economics and Personal Finance. Econ and Personal Finance was something new. It was the only class that I hadn't seen on the blue sheet in the years before.

"Is this a new requirement?" I asked Ms. Emery.

"Yes, this was just added by the school board this year as a part of the Advanced Diploma because recent studies show that high school graduates that do not continue to higher education are not prepared enough by high schools to handle their finances properly."

"Wow," I said, but in my head, I was thinking for once there was a class that made sense and would be handy in daily life for anybody. "Because when in my life am I ever going to need a protractor to measure the angle of a triangle in my day-to-day life?" I thought to myself. Most of my classes were already decided; I just had two electives to fill in my schedule. I decided to take Business Management, as it aligned with my desire to go into business later in life. All my requirements for graduation had been successfully met, except the classes I was about to take senior year. I had the option of taking "late start" on blue days, and I signed up for it. So next year, instead of coming to school at seven in the morning, I would come in around 8:45 am before the start of third period. This meant getting a whole hour and a half more of sleep, which was going to be amazing.

As senior year was approaching, time to take the SAT exam was coming closer. The SAT is one exam, but in high school and the society we live in it seemed like the most important thing in the world. Doing well on the SAT would make your life and if you didn't do well on the SAT, well then no good college for you; you can successfully start working at McDonald's then. Or at least that's how much we were pressured to do well on the SAT that it felt like if not this, then McDonald's was going to be our future. The SAT, along with your total grade point average was crucial to what college you get into. The higher the SAT score the better college one has the chance of getting into. The SAT is a standardized test that measures how prepared you are for college said every high school teacher ever. But it's not. In my opinion, a single exam cannot determine your future. It's not the entire measure of your intelligence. You are so much more than your SAT score. An SAT score maybe able to measure a person's level of writing, reading, vocabulary, or math, but it can never measure the amount of passion you have towards life. Each college has a certain range or an average range of SAT scores that they accept or reject. The average SAT for an Ivy League college was above a 2000. A good SAT score for a school like New York University required students to be in the top eight percent of all SAT test takers. The higher the score the better. In state universities such as Virginia Commonwealth University and George Mason, an average SAT score was around a 1500.

Students could take the SAT however many times they wanted to, if they were willing to pay the fifty-dollar fee to register for the exam. Did I agree with the concept of a standardized test determining my life decisions for me? No, I didn't. However, they could take my money until I got the score I wanted. Wait, Mom and Dad's money to be precise. Standardized tests were a way for colleges to have something to compare students by, but that's the whole point. No individual is actually "standardized." There is no one clothing that comes in one-size-fits-all; then how can you measure everyone's intelligence through one single standardized test? Everyone has different strengths and weaknesses, and none of us are the same. If we were all the same, the world would be full of only doctors, or only lawyers, then who would do all the other jobs? If it was left to South Asian parents, the world would only consist of two professions: doctors and lawyers, with the odd IT professional running between with a failing marriage and a kidney. Why is every high school kid and their academic success measured by the SAT when none of us have been created the same way? Instead of fitting into standards, it's more important for every individual to find who they are, what they love, and embrace it. I didn't believe the notion that my SAT was going to determine my fate.

Nonetheless, I was stuck in a system where I had to take the test despite disagreeing with it. I was going to take the SAT twice: the first time to see how I did and the second time to see if my score improved or not. Since the SAT was a timed test, and it was engraved in every high schooler's mind that this test determines your future, the pressure of doing well was really high. Older people around me used to say that even though you are allowed to take the SAT as many times as you want, taking it more than a second time never improves your score.

I had about two months to go before the SAT exam, and I had bought every SAT prep book from every single academic publishing company out there that published an SAT prep book. I was all in, not because I was forced to by my parents or anything but because I had taken this on as a challenge and wanted to get the absolute best score on the SAT no matter what. I began spending countless hours in my room after school doing practice SAT exams after finishing up school work. I gave up on going out with friends just so I could use that time to get a little bit more studying in. I didn't even meet Areeba for a month, even though we literally only lived ten minutes away from one another. Some days when I was so into studying that I wouldn't leave my room, Mom and Dad would come inside and beg me to go out with friends or just take it easy and enjoy my life. But I was too focused on preparing myself for this test that according to society and high school teachers was going to be the so called "prime factor" in determining my fate after high school. I found it extremely funny how the SAT was such a huge factor when it came to college, yet in high school no teacher or class ever focused on it. You had to focus on it yourself. If you tried to take the SAT the way you would take a high school test, you would fail miserably. For the longest time I tried studying for the SAT by applying concepts I had learned in school, such as applying proofs to a geometry problem. It took me a while to realize that the SAT could not be cracked with concepts learned in school. When we memorize things in school, we use a different part of our brain to retain information. During the SAT we are asked to use logical reasoning, not memorization, which happens in a different part of the brain.

In school all anyone ever cares about are the grades you get. You are taught to pay more attention to the grades you get rather than paying attention to what you have learned. No one cared about truly doing well; everyone just wanted the 4.0. "Doing well" has a different definition for everyone. A 3.7 seven GPA might be well for somebody but not enough for another person. If you had a 4.0, you were considered smart as hell by your parents and society, but if you didn't have a 4.0, you were automatically stupid. You are judged by the world by your GPA. What society doesn't understand is that in school you can memorize book chapters and get exemplary grades, but in real life you cannot memorize a book and succeed. I have always disagreed with the whole phenomena that SAT and grades "define" you and your future. No, your hard work and dedication will decide your future.

And then finally came the first Saturday of July, the day of the SAT. The only Saturday of my life where I had to wake up as early as 5:00 am just so I could get to school for the test before seven in the morning. And, of course, by the time I got up, got dressed and came downstairs, Mom was already in the kitchen making a banana milkshake in the corner. I got to the dining table and a breakfast plate of eggs and French toast was already waiting for me. I sat down to eat, and Mom brought over the banana milkshake.

"You have a test today. Eat properly," she said as she sat down with me while I ate. Before any big test, Mom always made sure I was stuffed up because on normal school days I often skipped breakfast in a rush to get to school on time. I finished my breakfast, gave Mom a big hug, and left the house at 6:30 am to get to school on time. When I got to school, there was a long line right outside the main office where people were signing in. When I got to the front of the line, the lady checking everyone in checked my ID and told me to go to room C104 where the test was being proctored.

I got to room C104 and sat down at one of the empty desks. There were probably ten kids taking the SAT in the room I was in, but over two hundred kids were taking the test in the entire school. First the exam protector handed out the SAT test booklets and scantron sheets. Then she went over the instructions of the test. We were given twenty-five minutes to finish the essay and twenty-five minutes to solve thirty math problems, which was fine too. But twenty-five minutes to read long passages and answer questions about the readings seemed too little. Even if you want to do well and can do well, it becomes hard to focus because your mind starts focusing more on how much time you have left on each section rather than focusing on answering the questions right. The test started, and for the next three and a half hours, my butt was stuck to my chair, turning the pages and pacing myself through each section of the test. Every time I started a new section, I always stared at the clock to see what time it was and how much time I had for that section because I was scared of not finishing each section within the given time. On the test, you are not penalized for not answering a question, but you lose a quarter point every time you get a question wrong, this is why it's so important to keep track of time because you want to spend it on the questions that you are a hundred percent positive about. Three and a half hours later when I was finally done with the test, my hand felt like it was going to fall off with all the writing I did. I silently prayed under my breath, handed my test to the proctor at the door, and walked out to go home. I was hungry again from all the test anxiety, so I decided to get a sandwich from Subway on my way home. When I got home, the first question my parents asked me was "How was it?"

"Good," I said, or at least I hoped I had done good. Then I

went to my room to take a big fat nap because I could not think about the SAT anymore.

The weekend passed just fine, but then on Monday when I got to school, everyone around me was literally asking each other the same question: "How did you do on the SAT?"

I was in English class when I heard two Indian boys talking about the SAT. "Yo, I have a 4.0 grade point average already. I just hope I get a perfect score on the SAT because that would mean I could get into any college I applied to," the guy behind me said to the guy sitting right next to me.

"Good luck dude, but like even if you don't get a 2400, you will still get in. I know someone from my business class. He's a year older than me, and he got into Georgetown with just a 1900 SAT score, which is on the low side for their average acceptance rate," he said.

"Nah dude, I can't take chances with luck. I need to fit right into their acceptance rate," the guy behind me said.

And for the next several minutes these two guys kept on talking about SAT scores, GPA's and college acceptance. I had heard this debate over grades and test scores so much over the past six months of my life that I was so done. Yes, all of this was extremely important, and that's exactly why like every other high school kid, I too was putting in so much effort into it. Even I had good grades but in my opinion, having a 4.0 GPA didn't measure how smart you were; it measured how well you could memorize information. Yes, colleges look at your GPA and SAT scores for admissions, but you are so much more than just a number. However, our system in high school and every teacher ever had emphasized the GPA and SAT scores so much that it felt like you were merely a number to the world. If your numbers aren't amazing, colleges won't even bother reading what you have to say in your personal essays even though your essays are the one thing that describes who you are beyond numbers. The essay is literally the only part of your application where you aren't being judged by numbers. In my opinion numbers can never accurately depict a person's mind or depict a person's will power or entire skill set in life. A piece of paper with your grade point average, a standardized test, or merely a number cannot describe a person. Yes, it's a process that all of us had to get through to get into college, but your grades or SAT scores cannot define you or your entire worth in life. That is wrong. With so much pressure of doing well in the numbers game, all of us somewhere felt that how we performed on the SAT or at school would decide our destiny. Yes, it was important to do well, but that mindset that numbers decide who you are was what I had a problem with. You create your own destiny through hard work and dedication.

Life is not a race; you are not an SAT score or a grade point average. I wish I could tell this to parents, teachers, and other high schoolers like me who were all stuck in this race of numbers: that you are capable of anything and everything, and you can be anything in this world. Even if what you want to do doesn't already exist, it's still possible if you believe in it. Everything starts off with a belief. You must believe in your dreams and yourself no matter what the world says or thinks. If that belief inside you is strong enough, you will cross any mountain or hurdle in your way with ease. If you deeply, truly want to do something in life, you will find a way to make it happen. People who cannot follow their own dreams will often tell you not to follow yours. Such people would say, "Stop dreaming and live-in reality." But what even is reality? Reality is a perspective which is never the same for everyone. Reality is a perspective that you create for yourself, so whatever you choose to believe in will become your reality. It doesn't matter how impossible something may seem; if you believe in what you want with all your heart, someday that will become your reality. But if you keep sticking to the idea of impossible, you will never see the magic unfold in front of your eyes because your mind will be too focused on the limitations of why something can't happen rather than the endless possibilities of why it can. Impossible is nothing but a human-created limitation of the mind.

Summer of 2014 went by in a blink of an eye with staying home with family and writing my college personal statement since that was our official summer assignment for AP Literature. During the same time, Mom and Dad wanted me to start planning college visits and see various campuses before I would apply for admission. I didn't really care about the colleges in Virginia. I wanted to go away from home for college to experience life on my own. I wanted to get out of my comfort zone. I wanted to go to college in New York City; that was my dream. During the last week of August, before the start of senior year, Mom and Dad took me to New York to visit the Fashion Institute of Technology (FIT). If I was going to go study fashion, I wanted it to be at FIT. I had an information session and campus tour of FIT arranged for my entire family.

Dad drove our entire family to New Jersey on a Friday night, and the information session was on Saturday at noon. We were staying in Newark, New Jersey near the Newport Shopping Mall, in the same apartment building where we always stayed each time we came to New York. Every time I thought of New York City, there's only one word that always came to my mind, and that was passion. In my opinion, if there was an emotion embedded within the atmosphere of NYC, it was passion. The fire that comes from within to do something in life and to make it big. From far away it seemed like anyone could be anything in this city. The energy, lights, tall skyscrapers, people, fashion, business, media, everything was in New

York, and that made me feel like there's nothing you can't possibly achieve in this city if you are willing to give it your all. The city was a symbol to me of endless opportunity, dreams, and desires. It was interesting to me how I had lived in New York City as a kid, but I never saw it the way I was looking at it now. The five-year-old me didn't care about such things, but the eighteen-year-old noticed everything in life. I loved how people in New York never stopped; they were on the go twenty-four seven because they had dreams to turn into reality. Living here was a dream I wanted to achieve. It felt as if I was made for New York. I didn't see myself living in a place like Virginia forever. I wanted to do something creative with my life which wasn't possible living in Virginia because Virginia mostly had government-related jobs.

The following morning, Dad and I woke up super early and got ready by 10 am. The city was only a fifteen-minute ride on the PATH train, and the Newport PATH station was less than a two minute walk from the apartment building. When my family and I used to come to New York City as tourists, we always only went to the Times Square area around 42nd Street and 7th Avenue, and that's it. We had never explored any other part of the city, so I had no idea where anything else in the city was. Dad and I walked out of our apartment and crossed the street to cut through the Newport mall into the PATH Station. Newport Station at ten in the morning was crowded with people in suits and ties like bees around a sunflower because a lot of people worked in the city but lived in Newport. While Dad and I waited for the train, standing on the 33rd Street platform, I looked around and noticed the crowd around me. While most people were dressed in shorts or dresses as maybe tourists, there were so many people who were wearing proper suits and ties on a Saturday morning.

The PATH train was going to take us directly to 33rd Street station near 7th Avenue, and FIT was located on West 27th Street, literally a five-minute walk from the station. The East and West side of New York City was confusing because we weren't sure if the 33rd Street station was on the West side or East side. It turned out to be on the West side, where we had to go. First stop on the Subway was Christopher Street, then 9th Street, then 14th Street, 23rd Street and 33rd Street. I was excited to be visiting FIT, a school I had heard so much about in a fashion academy class and more so after knowing that Michael Kors and Calvin Klein were FIT grads. The image I had of FIT was that of an extremely fancy fashion school. The school even had their own fashion museum which was located right on campus.

The last stop of the PATH train was 33rd street. Dad and I got off the train and walked straight to get through the scanner machines. Thirty-third Street was Herald Square where the world's largest Macy's was located. Towards the right of the station exit was the entrance to the 34th Street Herald Square station where the N, Q, R, B, D, F trains ran with in Manhattan. Dad and I went straight out the exit stairs and came out in front of the Harold Café between 6th and 7th Avenue. From the corner of the café, we started walking straight to get to 7th Avenue, famously known as the Fashion Avenue of New York. In the hustle and bustle of people while crossing 33rd Street, it was hard to pay attention to directions because I was paying attention to the life that this city had. Once we got to 7th Avenue, we took a right and started walking along the side where the street numbers were decreasing. While walking, I noticed that everyone around me walked in the same exact manner. Gaze straight, no left, no right, and people walked fast as if they were missing their train, which could have been the case for some, but everyone on the block was walking the same way. I loved the hustle life. The streets of New York were the sound of hustle: hundreds of people crossing the street all at once. Their walk wasn't lazy or casual but fast and powerful as if they must be somewhere right away and they could not afford distractions. As Dad and I made our way down from 33rd Street to 27th, each block had tons of restaurants and cafés, and every one of those cafés had long lines all the way out to the sidewalk just of people who wanted to get in.

The blazing hot sun rays were piercing through my skin. Here or in Virginia the sunlight is the same, but since you are always on your feet in New York, it felt stronger. The cars passing by kept honking, and I started to wonder, "Can New York even be New York without all the street noise?" The sweet smell of honey-covered nuts went right through my nose as I walked right passed the "Nuts 4 Nuts" stand right at the corner of the street. All the food stands had a red and yellow striped umbrella on top of them. Some of them had blue and yellow umbrellas on top of them so anyone could spot a food truck from a distance. Dad and I had reached the intersection of 28th Street and 7th Avenue, and we still had about thirty minutes before we had to check in at FIT. Dad and I walked past Madison Square Garden and Penn Station. The directions to FIT were on Dad's phone, and Google Maps kept telling us to keep going straight. Dad looked at the time and decided to get coffee before reaching the university. As we walked down 7th Avenue, three different Starbucks were on the same street, but Dad wanted something different. Just a block before the FIT campus on 7th Avenue was a café called "Paris Baguette." Dad and I went there instead. The café was small and there was no space to sit on the first floor, so we went up to the third floor. Even the third floor was packed with people drinking coffee and eating breakfast in the morning. Since there were no tables available, Dad and I sat on the bar stool seats facing the large window on the side of the café. I ordered a white mocha for myself, and Dad got his regular coffee and a croissant. Dad and I sat there and casually discussed life and looked at the view of Fashion Avenue from the cafe. Cars rushed by. Countless numbers of people were walking on the sidewalks. In front of me were advertisements for various fashion brands hung on the billboard.

"How are you so grown up already, Mashallah?" Dad said, looking at me with his deep hazel eyes. I was lost deep in my own thoughts and sipping my tea, but I started smiling. Directly outside the café window was a "Parson's School of Design poster." I saw FIT as Parson's competitor, but I was never too crazy about Parson's. Then Dad started telling me "Do you know when I first came to America, New York was where I got my first job in a company called Arthur Anderson, which used to be one of the 'big five' accounting firms in the US but had closed in 2002?"

I smiled. "I know. See, you started off in New York, and here I am trying to start off my life in New York too," I said. Dad's office used to be in midtown too, on West 57th Street and 6th Avenue. Dad himself had walked all these streets with passion, and now he couldn't believe that it was my time to go and prove myself out there in the world.

It was almost 11 am. We finished our coffees and walked out of Paris Baguette and down towards West 27th Street. After crossing Potbelly Sandwich on our left, on the right came a small beige building that took up the block of 27th Street. In front of the building were black gates, and right next to the sign was the FIT logo in blue and white. The gated area looked too small to be a college campus, so I thought maybe one of the FIT buildings was located here and the rest of the campus was spread out throughout the city. Dad also thought that the gated area was too small to be the entire campus, so he asked the security guard standing outside the gate, "Where is the main FIT campus?" The security guard began pointing to the black gates behind him, reiterating the fact that this was it. "Thank you," Dad said to the security guard, and then Dad looked at me. "Is he serious?" Dad quietly whispered to me.

We walked through the gates, and there were literally five small grey cemented buildings placed one after another in a shape of a capital U. Those five buildings pretty much made up the entire FIT campus, and two out of the five buildings were residential halls. The first building to my right was the welcome center. Dad and I walked through the glass doors of the welcome center to check in for the information session. The welcome center was pretty decent. Outside of the building itself was all glass, and the auditorium was huge with about three hundred seats. At 11 am, counselors gave everyone a short information session on degree types, majors, and the FIT experience. At FIT, every student finished their associate's first as a degree in the first two years and then bachelor's for the last two years. One was also given an option of doing their associate's in one subject and then doing their bachelor's in another. I looked at Dad and tried reading his face because I knew that in his head he wasn't really impressed with the information session and the FIT glamour vibe, but Dad never said anything to me because in the end, he would agree to whatever I agreed to. After the admissions counselors were done speaking, current FIT kids were called up on stage in order to share their experiences with us. Almost all the student speakers were those who commuted every single to FIT from New Jersey. Students from various majors displayed their works on the projector for all the potential students to see.

After the presentation in the welcome center, Dad and I were free on our own to explore the campus, so we started walking around one building then on to the next. All the buildings were interconnected with each other through black solid double doors that resembled those of a hospital ward. FIT wasn't fancy at all; the hallways were plain with unfinished paint and cracks on the wall. The hallways looked unfinished like walking down a basement that hasn't been renovated in years. The double doors that connected every hallway to the other were all black and rusty and had to be pushed open. The classroom doors were grey, but they resembled hospital room doors more than they looked like classrooms. Every building had an auditorium and a common room then a bunch of study spaces near the building entrance.

The school was dominated by females. Everywhere I went within campus, the majority of the students were all girls, and the guys were really sweet. Everyone was dressed up as if they were going to fashion week right away or a fashion company was about to hire them right there and then. A part of me loved it, but then another part of me felt like the environment was too specifically concentrated on just one thing. I couldn't yet decide if this was truly it or not, but nonetheless being at the hub of everything fashion was exhilarating.

The campus tour only took thirty minutes because there wasn't much to see anyway, except for the FIT Fashion Museum. The Fashion Museum at FIT was located right at the front near the black gates. The exhibits in the museum were beautifully laid out. There were two floors, and each floor had collections displayed by various designers. The only reason I wanted to see the FIT Museum was because of Calvin Klein, who was also a FIT grad. In the FIT museum, Calvin Klein had his own display of formal coats and dresses, which took up the entire studio downstairs. He was the most inspiring to me because he was a FIT alum that had a brand that was globally very well known. Glamour, fame, fashion, success: these things look extremely appealing on the outside, but none of them are things that come easy. Behind every success story lies a story of struggles, of various failures and bad attempts; only then does success come. And just getting an education from a certain school does not make you successful.

Hard work and talent gets you places where you want to go.

After looking at the entire fashion museum, Dad and I decided to leave the campus. "Are you sure, you are done? Do you want to see anything else?" Dad asked me.

"No," I said as we came out on the street and started walking around. The plan was to meet Mom at the original "The Halal Guys" Gyro food cart by the Hilton on 6th Avenue and 53rd Street. Dad and I walked to the Herald Square station and took the D train going uptown. Dad and I were on 34th Street, so we took the Uptown D train to get off at Bryant Park. Mom, Ehsan and Emaan were waiting for us at the Halal Guys cart right in front of the Hilton Hotel.

Dad and I got off the train at Bryant Park and started walking down 6th Avenue towards 53rd Street. All the buildings in midtown seemed to be having a conversation with the sky. All of them were so tall that one had to stand still and raise their neck all the way up just to be able to see the tip of the building, and more often on cloudy days the tips of tall buildings used to be hidden within the clouds, but thank God today was a sunny day. As I was crossing the intersection between 52nd and 53rd Street, I saw Mom standing with Ehsan in the gyro line as they were almost ready to give their order. This was one cart in New York that had endlessly long lines no matter how bad or good the weather was. Even in the winters, people stood in hour-long lines just to get a gyro. The dish was very basic: chicken over rice, but the sauces that were used in the gyro were out of this world. My personal favorite was the white sauce.

Dad, Ehsan, Mom, and I got gyro and sat down on the benches in front of the Halal Guys Cart to eat, and Emaan was sleeping in her stroller.

"How was it?" Mom asked me. I didn't hate it, but I had mixed feelings. FIT was definitely not what I had imagined it to be.

"It was ok," I answered and took another bite of my food.

Then Ehsan asked me, "Do you think you would end up coming here?" I knew I wanted to come to New York for sure, but looking at how specific everything at FIT was it felt like maybe it wasn't exactly meant for a person like me who wanted to do so much in life.

"I will apply and will see," I answered.

"I like that answer. Keep your options open," he smiled. I didn't disagree with him. The following morning, my family and I left for home as school was about to start on Tuesday. Even on the car ride back I kept thinking about NYC. I was a person who followed her heart no matter what, and whatever felt right to my heart was right, and if something didn't feel right to my heart, then it wasn't for me. I don't know why, although the spark was there, I wasn't getting the click from my heart about FIT. The kind of feeling that makes you want to say, "This is it." If I couldn't feel it, I was not going to do it.

CHAPTER THIRTEEN

The first two months of senior year were all about filling out college applications. I had a long list of colleges that I was applying to which included Harvard, Georgetown, Columbia, NYU, Princeton, James Madison University, University of Virginia, UCLA, FIT, Stanford, and last but not the least, George Mason University. Mason was only five minutes away from my house, and it was the school that every South Asian kid in the greater Washington DC area went to. I used to go to Mason for music lessons after school, and I had seen the campus. Mason's campus used to be full of South Asian kids, and all the faces seemed so familiar because I had lived my entire life in this area. I wanted a change; I wanted something more from life. Mom and Dad insisted that I apply to Mason as a backup option in case all else failed. But that's not what I wanted. I wanted to explore the world, to go out and explore life on my own.

Once a week Dad and I used to go sit at the local bookstore café near my house and plan out my college applications and essays. Most of the schools I was applying to all took the Common Application, which is an application that you only must fill out once and you can send it to all the schools that accept it. The personal essay for all schools on the common app was the same. However, each school had additional essays that were specific to that school, and those essays took a while to plan. Colleges like UCLA, James Madison, FIT, Georgetown University, and George Mason did not except the common application, so Dad and I used to sit down and look at each college's application at a time and plan everything. Dad and I used to grab a table in the mini-Starbucks inside the bookstore, and we looked at each school's website and application and planned for me to write each school's essay differently. I loved sitting with Dad and filling in little details like extra-circular activities for each application. It was such a little thing, one that I could do on my own, but I loved Dad being there by my side supporting me through each step. He empowered me to follow my dreams. It made me think about how lucky I was to have a father who encourages me to live life my way. A father who was brought up in Pakistan with a Pakistani mindset but gave his daughter the utmost freedom to do whatever and everything she wanted without fitting in to the stereotype of a typical Pakistani Dad. There was nothing more empowering in the world than knowing that Mom and Dad were always there to push me, to become the air beneath my wings and help me fly higher. I didn't need anything else.

On grey days I had Business Management and Law first thing in the morning with Mrs. West in the D wing. Her first name was Melanie, and she had the squeakiest voice I had ever heard in my life. The business classroom was set up like a computer lab instead of an actual classroom. There were computer stations for each student and a chair in front of each computer station. The first half of the semester in class was all about business management; the second half of the year was going to be about business law and ethics. Every day in class, we had the same routine: walk into class, log in to our computers, then take a piece of paper out for the morning warm up. The warm up was always written on the board, and I always started doing it right away. The rest of the class used to be power point presentations accompanied by a lecture. Mrs. West always made all of us open our blackboard accounts on our computers, as she always posted lessons for each class online in blackboard under the assignments tab. Blackboard was an online system every public school in the county had, and it allowed for students to access all their class materials online. Whichever PowerPoint was up on the big screen in front of the room we would just have to open the same Power Point on our screens and follow along. From 7:05 to 8:35, Mrs. West lectured nonstop. I used to get so bored after a certain point that I used to pull out my phone and start checking Twitter and count down minutes for the class to end. The lecture wasn't even engaging; we had to copy the slides down word for word, but that used to become tedious after a while.

After Business Management I had Pride Time, and after Pride Time, I had AP lit with Dr. Hrabak. After October, my AP lit class was pretty much done with working on college essays. The class had moved on to reading *The Invisible Man* by Ralph Ellison. The story of *The Invisible Man* revolved around a man who overcomes alienation, invisibility, and defies a society that is unable to recognize a black man as a person, an individual who has all the rights that others had during a time when African Americans were considered inferior. The book explored topics such as race, identity, ideology, and stereotypes. This whole idea of identity was really interesting to me. If you think about it in a deeper way, God has created all humans equally; he never differentiated people. In fact, even religiously, God keeps all his creations in a space of equality.

But us humans, what did we do? We created categories such as "race," "color," "sexuality," and even "gender." Being female or male is one thing, but humans created the ideas of what it means to be man or woman, which we more commonly call culture. God created land, but humans divided it by countries. This is your side, that's my side, and because you are not on my side, you are different. A good example of this is India and Pakistan.

When Pakistan didn't exist and India was under British rule, Hindu, Muslims and Sikhs used to live together often under the same roof. Nobody cared about the other person's religion—everybody lived as one. But then the British made Hindus realize that Muslims are way different than them and should create their own country. Thus, when India gained independence from Britain, Pakistan was created. A border was established between Lahore and Amritsar, and the Hindus stayed in India, and the Muslims migrated to Pakistan. The differences that started off as religious differences soon became political because business got involved and so did economic factors.

Today, two million Hindus live in certain parts of Pakistan, and the largest minority living in India are Muslims. In fact, in India, wherever there is a temple on the same block you will also see a mosque. It's no longer even about religious differences anymore; it has become about "being" Pakistani and "being" Indian. For a single second, let's leave religion completely aside: what is the difference between being Pakistani and being Indian? Pakistanis speak Urdu while Indians speak Hindi, but in actuality both languages are basically the same unless you want to speak poetic Urdu or poetic Hindi. If one person can understand Hindi, they can understand Urdu. Indian people value culture more than anything, and so do Pakistani people. Indian food and Pakistani food are almost the same. Pakistanis eat samosa chat, and Indians eat somosa chat as well. Women and men in

India wear shalwar kameez and so do men and women in Pakistan. We may come from different religions or may have different traditions, but the majority of us talk the same, look similar, dress similar, and share family values. So why so much fuss about Indians and Pakistanis being different? Why do Pakistani people think that Indians are so different than us, and why do Indian people think that Pakistanis are different? Just because of a line that dictates "this is my land" and "this is your land"? Why can't we respect each other's differences and identity and just accept each other's similarities and differences. Indians should be proud being Indians and Pakistanis should be proud being Pakistani, and all we have to do is give each other respect. But it's not that simple. We forget that we have the same culture, language, traditions, land and even the way of living.

All the difference us humans fight over are differences that are given to us by our creator and not by our own choice. You don't choose whether you're born into a rich family or a poor family: God chooses that for you. Yet in society we have categories for everything: socioeconomic status, color, race, power, etc., everything is categorized. We as humans like pointing out who's rich and who's poor. Secondly, there is our religion, which the majority of the time is handed down to us by the family we are born in. A baby born in a Sikh family will likely be raised as a Sikh, and a baby born in a Muslim family will most likely be raised as a Muslim. Yet when it comes to religion, we blame people for being from a certain religion as if they chose to be from that religion. Yes, people can change their religion, but my point is at birth we don't get the choice to decide what religion we want to be a part of. Last but not the least: race. Race is another concept that this world discriminates people over, but race is also given by God at birth. We don't decide if we want to be black or white or South Asian. When race, religion, status, and identity are things that are mostly given to us by a higher power, why do we have so much ego of wanting to be superior to anyone else? Why do civilizations in this world have a need to prove that we are stronger and better than someone else? Why can't humans treat other humans equally when all humans are created by the higher power. I have just always been very inquisitive about such topics, and it was something that boggled my brain. We are all human; just respect each other and live.

Dr. Hrabak used to assign us two to three chapters of *The Invisible Man* per week, and when we would come to class there was always an AP style essay we had to write. Dr. Hrabak gave us a prompt every week that would be related to the chapter we had read for homework. In the essay we had to analyze whatever the prompt asked for and were also required to pull out quotes from the assigned chapters and use them as evidence in the essay. To be honest, I never used to read the assigned chapters in their entirety. I have always been a curious thinker but never an amazing reader. I have never enjoyed reading in my life, whether it be for pleasure reading or assigned reading; my mind just doesn't like it. I used to just go on Marknotes.com and read the three-page summaries for each chapter, and that worked for me every single time. Dr. Hrabak never found out that I never actually read the chapters because I always made enough notes to be able to answer questions during class discussion.

Our class had B lunch, so around midway through the class we would leave our work in the middle to go eat lunch. I didn't like eating lunch at school, so instead of going to the cafeteria to socialize with people who didn't even matter, I used to go to the library or the career center during lunch time to do my homework. Often the library computers used to be full of students working during lunch time so I used to go to the career center. The career center was located right next to the counseling office, and Ms. Kim, the career center specialist, used to always be sitting at her desk in the back corner of the room.

Towards the right wall were three computers which were always free since not many people used to come here, only the ones who wanted career advice from Ms. Kim would come in during lunch hours. I used to sit at the first computer towards the wall and spend my entire lunch time searching majors and student life at NYU. NYU was my golden dream. The school had every kind of opportunity an artist would ever want to be exposed to. There was the Steinhardt School of Music, Tisch School of the Arts, that had every single major related to any of the creative fields. Then there was the Gallatin School of Individualized Study that interested me the most. Gallatin was an interdisciplinary school within NYU that allowed students to create their own major. Since I was stuck in that traditional mindset of following standards I didn't really agree with, I loved the idea of going to a college where I could create my own degree and follow my passion the way I wanted to rather than being stuck in a system again where requirements mattered more than actual learning. I was in love with the idea of having the freedom to study what I really wanted to study rather than being stuck in a requirement system again.

I would go back to Dr. Hrabak's class and finish up whatever we were working on before lunch. Since the weather was still decent in October, Dr. Hrabak used to take our class outside in the front patio of the school for book discussion. All of us used to pick up our desk chairs and carry them outside to the front of the patio where buses usually lined up for dismissal. Dr. Hrabak's instruction was to always sit in a circle during a class discussion, so all of us used to put our chairs in a big circle before sitting down for discussions. Everybody had to speak at least once and contribute to the discussion, or else Hrabak would deliberately call our names and ask questions. A lot of times what I wanted to say about something, someone would say the same thing, so I always used to try my best to speak in the beginning so no one took my point from me. Class discussions used to be a lot of fun outside, but once the weather began to change, it became a lot harder to go outside, and indoor class discussion got super boring really quick.

Sixth period ended around 12:35 pm, and my eighth period was AP government online. Ms. Emery had told me that online classes can be usually taken at the library at the computer station, so I used to go to the library to attend my online class. There was a link on blackboard through which I used to access the "Apex online class learning system." All of my AP government course material, textbook, and assignments used to come up through Apex, and all I had to do was do the assignments in a timely manner. My online professor for AP Gov't used to hold a virtual class every Tuesday where I would have to login to APEX video live and listen to the instructor lecture. It was never a face-to-face class; whenever I logged into the virtual class all I would see on my screen was an electronic white board on which my professor wrote on while lecturing. The virtual lesson used to be like a conference call between me, the professor, and twenty other kids who were taking AP gov't online. The teacher would put up notes on the virtual class board and ask questions. It was important for every student to answer the questions because that's how each student earned their "class participation" grade.

At 2:00 pm I used to log out of my class, pack my bag and rush out of school. I used to get home around 2:20 pm or 2:30 pm and ate proper food. I had started working at the mall at the American Eagle Outfitters store to gain experience. So, two hours after school ended, I used to go to work. I worked at American Eagle Outfitters as a sales associate. The job had purely come to me by luck. From the past one year I had been applying for a job at AEO, but everyone at school who had worked there already used to tell me that it's hard to get hired. If they didn't call you for an interview within a few weeks, that meant your application was discarded. The last time I applied was the beginning of August, and I did get an interview call. When I went in for my interview, the general store manager at AEO, who was a lady with short blonde hair and tattoos around her body, automatically hired me without any questioning. She started giving me an orientation, and my interview day automatically became my first official day of work. My shifts were seven to eight hours long. I came home from work around dinner time and used to have no energy at all after an entire day of standing on my feet and folding clothes all day long. I used to eat and then go to my room to study, even though my brain used to tell me to just go to bed. Working in retail was not a fun job to have, but it was necessary. It made me realize that this wasn't what I wanted to do all my life, so might as well work hard now and get an education so that one day, I could actually live the life I wanted to live.

On blue days I didn't have to go to school till eight forty-five in the morning, which was amazing because I got two extra hours of sleep compared to the normal school day. The doors on all sides of the FHS building used to remain open for teachers to go in and out of the building during the day and for students who had to leave school early or come in late. But within the past year a lot of seniors and juniors who had their cars on campus would leave school during lunch and never come back, and the administration team found out about this. This year the doors used to get locked by seven fifteen in the morning and then only open at two o five for dismissal. If anyone wanted to go in and out of the school building during the day, they would have to use only the front entrance. When I used to get to school around eight fifty, before the beginning of third period, I used to go up to the front door, click the black button on the side of the door, and the intercom connected me to the lady sitting in the front office. On top of the first door was a camera through which I showed her my late pass, which Ms. Emery had given me, and the office lady opened the door for me. By the time I got in the building, the third period bell would ring, and I would head over to Mrs. McCullen's economics class.

In Mrs. McCullen's Econ class I sat in the second row next to Sydnee. Mrs. McCullen was probably in her late fifties or early sixties. She had extremely short grey hair with front bangs that leaned towards the right side of her forehead and was super thin. You could see her bones popping out through her skin whenever Mrs. McCullen wore shorts to school. But as a person Mrs. McCullen was the sweetest high school teacher I had ever met. To her we were not just students who had to fulfill a requirement for graduation; she cared about our learning and was always there to help. Mrs. McCullen used to hand out note sheets every class that went along with whatever power point she was presenting that day. The first half of econ was always lecture-based where the class just sat in their seats and took notes as Mrs. McCullen presented the PowerPoint presentation on the smartboard. The second half of class was always some sort of group activity based on the lecture that was given on the day. Usually, it was some sort of poster or presentation that we would have to make in a group then present it to the class during the last fifteen minutes of class. For most of the group activities I used to just partner up with Sydnee, Lucas, and Susan. Lucas and Susan sat right behind Sydnee and me, so it was just convenient to work with people who were already near you. Around 10:15 am near the end of class, Mrs. McCullen always gave out worksheets which were to be done for homework.

The bell for fifth period rang at 10:20 am. Cydnee had A lunch, so she went straight to the cafeteria after third period. However, I had Statistics with Mr. Whalley during fifth period. Mr. Whalley's classroom was located directly opposite Mrs. Laufer's classroom in the most crowded intersection of FHS. I came out of Econ, took a left, and walked straight down the hallway crossing all the world history class, and then would take the first right towards the math wing. Stats was the first classroom on the left side of the hallway after the multipurpose room where all the marketing classes were taught. I used to be one of the first students lined up outside Mr. Whalley's room before the fifth period bell rang. There was one another girl who used to line up outside the door with me. Her name was Madison. Everyone in the class used to call her Maddi. Mr. Whalley himself used to arrive to class super late because he didn't have a third period class. He used to be in the teacher's lounge grading papers till five minutes before class.

My entire Statistics class was full of all the snobby kids at my school who thought that they were the shit, and all of them were friends with each other. There was Dina, who I never in my life got along with because of the amount of arrogance she had in her. Then her best friend Aminah, who had failed three classes up till now but yet somehow, she still thought she was "cool" because she hung out with all the so called "popular" crowd. I didn't really understand what popularity meant when you are failing your classes and are on the verge of not graduating. Popularity in high school didn't mean anything, but to the popular kids it was everything. When you go out in the real world, high school popularity doesn't count for anything. How could you be ok with failing? How could you be ok with going to community college not because of any financial reason but because of grades?

Not everyone can afford college, and that's very understandable, but what I couldn't understand was how could you be ok with failing so many classes and act like it's no big deal because your social life is everything? I never understood why high schoolers thought that their social lives were everything even though they were not. There has to be some goal or motive in life that one should constantly work towards, and none of that existed in the popular kids at school. Aminah, Dina and their friend Luv always used to make fun of Mr. Whalley in front of his face every time Mr. Whalley stood in the front of the room trying to teach. Mr. Whalley was probably in his fifties, super tall, thin, and talkative. I loved it when he would start teaching us but then go on about his own rants and stories.

On Blue days as well, I had B lunch, so around eleven o' clock Mr. Whalley would let us go to eat lunch. After lunch time was over there was still an hour left of class, but we never had much to do. Most of class was note-taking, and then the last thirty minutes we were free to do homework. I used to get my homework done early and still have fifteen minutes left in class to be on my phone. School was still my top priority; I wasn't compromising my academics for anything, but I guess I was developing senioritis slowly because school seemed easy. Fifth period ended at 12:35 pm and for my last class of the day I had Physics, which was outside in the bleachers near the field house. The population of FHS students and teachers was increasing year by year, and there was no space for all the Science classes to fit inside the school building, so all the Physics classes were moved outside in the trailers behind the field house, which was literally the opposite end of the school from where I was.

Mr. Peterson was my Physics teacher, and his classroom was the first trailer behind the field house. Mr. Peterson always used to stand outside his classroom door greeting every student that walked into class. The trailer was white and in a rectangular shape, almost like the back of an RV truck but bigger in size. The trailer had seven oval shaped tables that sat four students each. I used to sit with Sydnee and another girl named Kayla who I didn't really know that well. The fourth girl that used to sit at my table was some Arab girl who couldn't really speak English that well, nor did I ever talk to her. Physics was all lecture, no group work. As soon as the bell rang at 12:45 pm, Mr. Peterson came into the room and walked around the class to check homework. After checking homework, Mr. Peterson always went over the homework to see if anyone had any questions, and then after going over the homework, Mr. Peterson started the rest of the lesson for the day. I didn't mind Physics. I liked it better than Chemistry, but I was never passionate about it. It wasn't education that I disliked; I hated the fact that majority of learning was basically based on memorizing things and presenting them, and I was more the creative type of student than the follow the book kind. More than reading a textbook, I wanted to create work of my own. Reading textbooks wasn't engaging enough for me. At 2:05 pm when the bell rung, I used to rush out the door and not think about physics ever again.

Then came mid-November. Two weeks before college applications were due, my advisor Ms. Emery recommended that I go see Mrs. Kim, the career center specialist just to talk about my future and college applications. I already knew what I was doing with my life and the colleges I was applying to, but I still went to meet Mrs. Kim, just in case she had insight about something that I didn't have. One day during lunch I went to go meet Mrs. Kim in the career center. Mrs. Kim sat behind her computer in the middle of the room. I pulled up one of the chairs from the student tables in front of the room and sat right beside Mrs. Kim. Mrs. Kim pulled her blonde hair back and reached for her glasses that were on the table. I handed Mrs. Kim the paper in my hand which had all my selected colleges listed on it. Mrs. Kim glanced at the paper really carefully then used my student ID number to pull up my transcript through the school system. "You have stellar grades," Mrs. Kim said as she looked at me smiled. I nodded my head.

Then Mrs. Kim glanced at the paper in her hand began reading my college list out loud. "Princeton, Harvard, NYU, Columbia, FIT, GMU, JMU, William and Mary, UCLA, Stanford, Georgetown, George Washington and Cornell." Mrs. Kim paused for a second and looked down before continuing. "Don't you think you are aiming too high, Maheen?" Mrs. Kim added. Aiming too high? No, I wasn't aiming to high, this is what I wanted from my life I thought to myself. "I think you should add schools in the list that you will get into for sure, like schools that don't have really high criteria for acceptance. Here, look at VCU. It's a really good option," she said. Mrs. Kim began showing me Virginia Commonwealth University's website. I had heard of the school through my classmates, but my mind was somewhere else by now. I didn't think I needed a backup school; my grades were already amazing. Mrs. Kim couldn't decide my fate for me, then why was she telling me to add more schools to my list? Mrs. Kim kept on telling me her suggestions, but in my head, I was already zoned out because I was going to do what I wanted to do anyway. VCU was just never an option to me. Why would I aim low when I knew I was capable of more?

The time for our career session was coming to an end. "Thank you for the suggestion. I will come back again," I said and walked over to class.

The rest of the day I kept thinking about VCU. My classmate Natty from Fashion Academy, her dream school was VCU because of its Art Program, and I used to think, "How can VCU be a dream school when it is a backup school?" The school one would go to when they have no other option. I don't know what made me do this, but just how I half-heartedly filled out the application for George Mason University, the same way I added VCU to my Common Application. I don't know why I did, but I did. It wasn't like I was going to go to any of those schools anyway. I had taken my time on writing all the essays for each college I was applying to and had sent everything in on time. George Mason and VCU were the last two applications that had to be sent. For the George Mason application, I wasn't excited at all, but I still sent it in because my parents had told me. The VCU application I filled out at three in the morning literally the day it was due. My personal statement was already done, but I had to write two essays that were specific to VCU. One of the essay prompts was to describe how you would overcome a challenging situation in life. That essay was extremely fun to write because I was all about facing challenges right in the eye. The second essay prompt was what threw me off. The prompt stated, "Write an essay about why you would do well at VCU and how will VCU prepare you for reaching your life goals?" How was I supposed to give in an honest answer for this specific question when deep down inside VCU wasn't the place of my dreams, and I knew I couldn't excel there? My heart wasn't in it, but I kept writing just to fill up the twelve hundred word count required for the application. Without even spell checking what I had written, at 4:00 am in the morning I submitted my application to VCU.

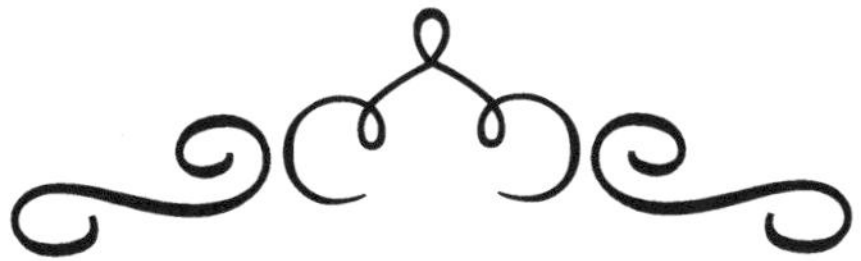

CHAPTER FOURTEEN

Halfway through senior year, all seniors at my school were suffering from senioritis because college applications were now all sent, and college decisions were not going to come out until April, so everyone thought they didn't have to put in effort anymore. I was getting a little lazy too. A lot of times I went to school late and missed half of second period. Every time a student was late to school, they had to go to their sub school office to get a late pass to get into class. Sub schools were divided by alphabetical order and last name. My sub-school was Sub school three and Mrs. Brian was my sub-school lady. I knew Mrs. Brian well because her son Melton was my friend since seventh grade. Every time I got late to school Mrs. Brian always excused my lateness. She never believed that I was the kind of student who would skip class on purpose. Not going to lie, I did skip second period a few times but never to do something I shouldn't have done. If I ever skipped second period, I used to go to the career center and catch up on homework. I was still getting in all my work in on time, but I was mentally so ready to be done with high school and start a fresh chapter of life.

Every night, I began to sit with the Quran opened in front of me and read it for thirty minutes and then prayed for whatever I wanted. I hadn't become religious suddenly, but if going towards God meant that he was going to help me achieve my goals in life, then I was all for it. We take so much time to please people, or we tend to depend too much on circumstances. We forget it is indeed God who created whatever circumstances or people are there in your life. We try to please the world all the time; aren't you going to take some time out to please God? And so here I was trying to please God so that maybe he would listen to me. The release date for college admission decisions was April 1st, and as the day got closer and closer, I became more and more impatient and anxious. I used to come home from school and wait for the mail every single day, just waiting for that one acceptance letter from NYU or FIT. The admissions decision for NYU was going to be released via email, so I began refreshing my email ten times day.

After weeks and weeks of praying and hoping came the first shock of my life. Around the first week of April, I kept checking the mailbox every day to see if any college letters had arrived or not, but each day I found nothing. Mom's birthday even passed, and I found nothing. Then one day I came home from school and made my way over to the dining table where Mom had put all the mail. I picked up the pile of envelopes and started going through them. "You are not going to find anything here," I heard Mom's voice from behind me. I turned around and saw her coming towards with an opened white envelope in her hands. "Here," she said handing it to me with a blank expression on her face. No smile, no nothing, which got me a little tense.

I took the envelope and pulled out the letter which said, "We are sorry to inform you, but we cannot offer you admission at our school at the time, but we wish you all the best for your future endeavor. Sincerely, Georgetown University's admissions committee." I read the letter and looked up at Mom.

"The letter had come in two days ago, but I didn't tell you because I wasn't sure, how you would react to it. I know you were looking forward to it all this time," Mom said to me. I hugged Mom. Of course, getting your first college letter as a rejection is not a good feeling at all, but hey, this was only one out of many colleges that I had applied to, so I wasn't completely shattered or anything. There was still a lot of hope, and my dream schools were still in the game so, everything was still ok. I looked at the Georgetown letter again and what I couldn't stop laughing at was how nicely and kindly colleges reject you. First, you are the one doing everything they asked you to do, and then when they reject you, they sugar coat their language like "We are really sorry that we can't offer you admission right now." They say it like as if students will believe them. Like hello, I know you are not sorry that you couldn't accept me because at the end of the day, I am just a number for you, nothing more.

Two days later, an acceptance letter from VCU came in the mail wrapped up in a white packet that was two inches thick.

Mom and Dad were ecstatic because this was my first acceptance letter from any college. However, I wasn't too excited about it. I didn't even understand how I got accepted because I didn't even apply with all my heart anyway. I wasn't being arrogant or anything, but I genuinely did not want to go to VCU. My expectations from NYU started to get even higher because the last thing I wanted was to go to college in Virginia, and going to VCU meant seeing all the kids from my high school again, being in the same exact environment all over again, which was exactly what I didn't want from life.

As the day of the NYU admissions decision release date got closer, my time spent praying increased. Yes, there were other colleges on my list as well, but I didn't have the kind of feelings attached to them compared to what I felt for NYU. If NYU happened, I would literally feel like all the sacrifices and efforts I have made in life thus far would pay off. NYU would be my ultimate reward. Next in the mail came the acceptance letter from George Mason University. Again Mom and Dad were extremely happy, but I was waiting for something else. My prayers Increased. Nothing was on my mind other than NYU now. I didn't care about senior beach week or a graduation party or anything, I just wanted what I wanted. Days passed and rejections started coming in. FIT had rejected me, Harvard had rejected me, Stanford, Princeton, Columbia, William and Mary, UCLA, George Washington, and Cornell all came back as rejections. To this Mom and Dad said, "Rejection is a part of life. Facing it is inevitable. It's okay, you did your best." I was fine. I guess I was. I mean, not all hope had ended yet. I still had NYU to count on. They say, "Don't put all your eggs in one basket," but now all my eggs were in one basket. All my hopes and prayers were stuck on one thing.

Then finally came the day when NYU was about to release their admission decisions via email. They had said that they were going to release their admissions decisions at 4 pm. I was so anxious and excited for it, I kept on checking my mail throughout the school day. My mind wasn't on my classes at all; my mind was on my phone. I came home around 2 pm that day and I still had two more hours to waste before the big news. I decided to call my friend Areeba and talk to her on the phone to keep myself distracted till 4 pm. Finally, the clock struck 4, and I made Areeba hang up on the phone and rushed upstairs to check my mail on the laptop. I opened my mail and saw the NYU "admission decision" email in my box. In a second, my heartbeat reached the sky, and I felt like my heart was going to drop right out of my chest.

I closed my eyes. "This is it," I said to myself and opened them again and finally got the courage to open the email. And there it was:

"Dear Maheen, after careful review of your application and academic credentials, we are sorry to inform you that we are unable to offer you admission to NYU, at this time. Sincerely, Dr. Cabbott."

The next second tears had started falling down my cheeks without me even realizing it. I was shattered. It felt like all my dreams were broken in one second. All the hard work I did felt like it had gone down the gutter. No one else was at home at the moment, and here I was crying in my room to myself nonstop. Nothing that had happened in my life up until is point was ever able to break me or shatter me, but for some reason this broke me inside.

I was so frustrated that I started questioning myself. All my high school years I did everything to make sure that I would get into the college of my dreams. I had sacrificed my entire social life, I never partied or did anything insanely crazy like every other kid. Then why me? What was even the point of me making all those sacrifices and being so uptight about my academics? I should have gone to the parties. I should have gone to beach week, damn it. I should have just enjoyed my life like every other teenager because clearly being focused and keeping distractions away never paid off. I always prioritized the important things in life, I had stellar grades, gave my all to my studies, yet things didn't work out for me. All the kids at my school who partied and never spent a minute focusing on their future, were they better off than I was? Because everything was working out for them just fine. Even my prayers to God didn't work, so what was even the point of that? Imagine spending every second of every minute working and dreaming about just one thing, and that one thing never ended up happening. I didn't even know how to feel anything anymore.

When Mom and Ehsan got home in the evening, I was sitting on the couch with all the lights shut off. "What happened?" Ehsan came up to me and asked. He knew something was off from my silence. "Maheen, what happened?" Ehsan asked as he sat down next to me. I hugged him tightly and broke down into complete tears. I was holding it in for so long, but at this point I just couldn't. Mom came running from the kitchen and the door just opened as Dad got home.

He came upstairs and saw me crying and panicked. "What's wrong?" my dad said, looking at me frightened, and then looking at my mom. "Will someone please tell me what happened?" my dad said.

"I don't know; she didn't tell me anything," Mom said.

Dad came up to me. "What happened. Did NYU say no to you?" Dad said, looking at me. I wiped out the tears from under my eyes and turned my gaze up to look at him.

"How did you know?" I asked, looking right at Dad.

"Maheen, I am your dad. I know you don't cry so easily in life, so the girl who could go through hell in life and not complain, when she cries, it's got to be over something that meant a lot to her," my dad said looking at me. I hugged him in tighter.

No one better than Mom and Dad knew how hard I had worked during high school. They had witnessed all the sleepless nights I had spent in my room studying for exams. Junior year was so much pressure that I even used to sometimes end up crying while doing my homework because I had so much work, yet I never complained. I did everything

I was supposed to do in the expectation that it would pay off in the end, but apparently life doesn't always happen according to us. But why doesn't it? Why is it always the good people who get tested the most in life?

"It's ok, Maheen. Certain things in life don't work out the way we want them to. Such is life," Dad said. But I constantly had this question of why? Why do things come harder to those who give their all to it?

"Why do things not work out for those who deserve it? Shouldn't it be the opposite? Shouldn't things be easier for those who give it their all?" I said to my parents.

That night I spoke to Dada on the phone in Pakistan and told him what had happened, and he said only one thing to me. "You can only try, Maheen, whether your efforts become successful or not is not in your hands. It's in God's hands. You tried and you should be happy that you gave it your best. If it didn't happen, maybe it was written for you yet. Maybe something better is written for you. Trust God."

"Hmm," I answered him back. I knew what he said was Important, but like why did I have to be the one to always wait for everything in life or show patience all the time? Why was I taking everything in life so seriously when nobody else my age even cared about these things? Why did I have to think so deeply about everything in life? Why couldn't I be more carefree and enjoy my life as a teenager? Maybe I was too serious in life, and maybe this wasn't the way to be.

I felt like nothing was working in my favor. I began hating this entire college process. A student spends his or her entire time working to beat the system, working to getting good grades, yet someone else gets to decide whether that student is good enough for something or not? How is that even fair? I understood that colleges get hundreds of thousands of applications every year and you can't admit everybody, but how is that fair to someone who has done everything that was required but still doesn't make it through? Colleges weigh people in numbers, and there are a billion kids out there who have the same SAT score or GPA number, but the thing is, not everybody has the same amount of fire in them. You cannot measure the passion within a person, and my passion burned like hell fire. I wasn't going to stop here.

It took me a few weeks to get over the NYU decision, but deep within I had turned extremely negative. Every time my dad dropped me to school in the morning, the entire car ride I used to complain to him about how much school sucked or it's too early in the morning. I started complaining about every single little detail about life. When you put all your energy into something and that something ends up not working, it drives you crazy. Instead of looking at why something is possible, my mind started to look at the limitations of everything. I even stopped praying for a while because I felt like my prayers weren't being answered.

I was so tired of looking at the NYU rejection letter in my inbox every day that one day I decided to print the letter out. I took the letter downstairs and started searching for tape in the kitchen area. "What are you doing Maheen?" My mom looked at me from the living room.

"I am trying to find tape. I need to tape this" I said.

"Tape what," my mom came up to me and took the rejection letter from my hand and started reading it. "Why did you print this out?" Mom asked, looking at me.

"Well, I am going to frame it," I said, looking at Mom.

"Wait, what? Why?" Mom asked.

"Because I am going to reapply as a transfer student and make this happen. Do you see this dean's name? Shawn Cabbott," I said to Mom, pointing at the dean's signature at the bottom of the letter. "Well, this guy is the one who sent the rejection letter, right? Well a year from today, he will be the same person who will send me an acceptance letter."

Mom started smiling. "I love that, Maheen. I love it," Mom said, smiling at me. I took the tape and went upstairs to my room and framed the letter right on top of my bed. I had nothing personal against the dean himself, but like since he was the one in charge of sending out admission decisions, it was my new goal that I had to get an acceptance letter from the same man who had sent me a rejection letter. And just like that, out of failure a new goal was born, another reason to work hard again day and night, and the framed letter on top of my bed was a constant reminder of what I had to work towards now.

By the end of May, I had to inform VCU that I was accepting their offer of admission, and at this point I was okay with this because now I had a new dream in mind. I was going to spend a year at VCU and transfer out to NYU. There isn't just one way to get somewhere. So what if it didn't happen the first time around? That didn't mean that I couldn't make it happen. I went ahead and finally committed myself to Virginia Commonwealth University. In the middle of May, after I had officially accepted VCU's offer of admission, Mom and Dad planned a trip to Richmond so that I could see the university's campus. Dad was more excited about seeing VCU than I was, and I know he was doing it to make me excited for VCU because even though it wasn't what I wanted in life, this was reality. The first few weeks after receiving so many rejections I felt miserable, but life has a rule: it moves on. I had mentally accepted the fact that I was going to VCU, but that didn't mean that I would stop dreaming or running after those dreams. I had only seen pictures of VCU online, and it looked as if it was in a very urban setting, busy roads and several buildings lined up one after another. It looked like a proper city of lights. The drive from my house to VCU was about two hours long. We left the house by 5 pm, and by the time we reached there, it was already nighttime because traffic on Highway 95 was insane. Dad drove the car directly towards the heart of Downtown Richmond, where all the corporate buildings were. It was like a mini city within a more suburban setting. At night you could only see the lights of the VCU hospital building. I couldn't tell what all the other buildings were in the dark because not all the streetlights were lit. Dad took a left into the public parking garage near our hotel and the five of us got out of the car. We walked out of the garage and onto the side street where there were tons of clubs and restaurants lined up in a single line. When I got on to the street, all I saw around me were college kids all dressed up and enjoying their Friday night. Girls were mostly in dresses and heels and the guys were in nice plaid shirts and jeans. Almost every restaurant around the street had waiting lines that covered most of the space on the footpath. We were staying at the Mary Hotel right in front of Buffalo Wild Wings.

We reached the hotel lobby. Mom and Dad checked in to the hotel while Ehsan and I decided to just take a stroll outside. There were huge buildings around me but no actual campus, which made me curious because I was trying to find the "VCU School of Business" where I had been accepted. I took out my phone to use my Google Maps to locate the School of Business, and my maps showed me "twenty-two minutes away."

"Shoot, Ehsan, I think we are on the wrong campus," I said as I showed Ehsan Google Maps on my phone. VCU had two main campuses, MCV (Medical College at VCU) and MP Campus (Monroe Park Campus). My family and I were on the MCV Campus, which was the campus for graduate students. Monroe Park Campus was the undergraduate campus.

"Does dad know?" Ehsan asked.

"I don't think so," I said. Ehsan and I came back to the hotel. Dad had already checked in to the hotel and the keys were in his hands.

"Dad, we are at the wrong campus," I said to him as I showed Mom and him my Google Maps.

"Damn, why didn't we think about that before?" Dad said, putting his index finger and thumb on his nose. It was already around ten at night, and our bags were checked in, so the five of us decided to spend the night here and then go see the Monroe Park Campus tomorrow.

The next morning Mom, Dad, Ehsan, Emaan, and I left the hotel around 11 am to go to the Monroe Park Campus. The Monroe Park campus was nothing like the MCV campus. The MP campus was located within a residential neighborhood of Richmond about twenty minutes away from downtown Richmond. The neighborhood within which VCU was built was referred to as the Fan District because when seen from an arial view, all the campus building created a fan shape. When we got to main campus, all the buildings were very spread out from one another. Dad was using his GPS to take us to the School of Business, which was isolated completely from the rest of the campus, and one had to cross the highway just to get to it.

Across the street from the Business School was an upperclassmen dorm attached to Chili's restaurant which was a part of campus but not really because the restaurant was open to anyone who wanted to come in.

Finally, we reached the School of Business. The elongated building, stretched out alongside the highway in the shape of a giant triangle, was home to the School of Business on the front side and the School of Engineering towards the backside. Dad drove the car around the entire building, but there was nowhere for visitors to park. Across the road was prepaid parking, which was part of the city of Richmond. Dad decided to park the car there.

The building had five floors in total. All the classrooms and offices started on the second floor and went up to the fifth floor. Mom, Dad, Emaan, Ehsan, and I took the stairs up to the second floor to look around the building. All the classroom doors were locked and there was not a single person around.

"Why is there nobody here?" Ehsan's voice echoed throughout the second floor.

I was wondering the same thing till I realized that the spring term had just ended and the summer term had not started yet. It was 4:25 pm, and the security guard on the first floor had told Dad that the business school will be closing at 4:30 pm. Dad, Ehsan, Mom, Emaan, and I began making our way out of the building. I wanted to see the rest of the Monroe Park Campus, but because of lack of time we had to head back home. Mom and Dad were satisfied. I don't know whether they liked Richmond or not. They were happy looking at the Business School.

A month before high school graduation, I received an email From VCU regarding "New Student Orientation." The new student orientation was going to be in the summer, and I was given the choice to choose my own orientation date out of a list of several dates throughout June and July. The orientation was going to be two days long; I would have to stay on campus for the night and come back the next day at night. Each new student would be assigned housing for a night in one of the VCU dorms, but the requirement was that we had to find a roommate ourselves. I was on the "VCU Class of 2019" Facebook group, where people who were accepted to VCU from all over the country would interact with each other. One day at school, I was sitting near the window in the library doing my physics homework when I received a Facebook Messenger alert on my phone. It was from the VCU Group. Some girl named Aleena had reached out to me saying, "Hi, what school do you go to?"

I replied to her saying, "Hey, I go to FHS," then asked her what school she went to.

Aleena replied, "James Madison High School," and she got admitted into VCU as a biology major on the Pre-Med track. We started casually chatting on Facebook throughout the day. Aleena didn't know too many people who were going to VCU, and the people who I knew that were going to VCU, I did not want to associate with them. The both of us were just trying to get to know more people at VCU before orientation. A week later, Aleena messaged me on Facebook once again asking me if we could possibly plan out our orientation dates together and be roomies. Aleena seemed like a nice girl, and she was fun to talk to. Of course I didn't know her that well, but being roommates with her was going to be better than being roomies with a random person. Aleena and I coordinated and selected Thursday June 23rd as our orientation date since it was exactly a week after my high school graduation and one week before Aleena's graduation.

A few days after graduation it was already time for me to go to VCU for New Student Orientation. The first day of orientation was for newly admitted students and their parents, so Dad and I drove to Richmond. We left early in the morning around 8:30 am because Orientation was going to start at 11:00 am. Richmond was only a two-hour drive from my house, and that made my parents happy because they could come see me often. I didn't know how I felt about that. I loved Mom and Dad more than anything, but I was dying to be on my own now. Once we were on the highway, we went straight on the road for about two hours, talking about life and watching Aamir Chachu's interview on my phone. Aamir Chachu was one guy in my family who I thought was exactly the way that I wanted to be. He didn't live life in a conformed way bounded by standards, rather he knew how to turn his vision into his reality, and he did. Chachu was a banker in Dubai, but he hated the nine to five robotic routine of the corporate world. His passion was PR and Event Management. Without a proper PR background, blindly following his passion, Chachu took the risk of following his heart and created his own PR firm which was solely run by him in its initial days. Today, Chachu was amongst the top three PR Gurus in all of Pakistan, and that was all because he wasn't afraid to follow his heart. It was my belief in life that if you follow your heart, you will always end up being successful because you are not actually chasing success, you are trying to find fulfillment in what you are doing, and when you enjoy what you do, success follows.

Everyone used to say that VCU is a city campus, which the MCV Campus was, but to be honest the Monroe Park campus was more like a college town surrounded by residential neighborhoods and a few shops. Not all the building but some of the VCU Administrative office buildings were also built in a way that they resembled the houses rather than university buildings. The VCU administrative offices looked like small, tiny colored houses attached to each other in a straight line going down the entire street. Dad and I had to report to the student commons, so dad parked the car in the parking garage past all the administrative offices.

The student commons building was a dark red brick building exactly in the center of the VCU Campus. It was home to all student activities and clubs. I got out of the car, took my suitcase out, and walked through the black sliding doors of the student commons, and Dad followed behind me. Upon entering the commons, to the left was Subway and Pizza Hut accompanied by tables and chairs. Chick Fil A was in the middle, located just a few steps up from Pizza Hut, and then there was the "Student Information Center" in the back right corner of the commons near the door that opened towards the other side of the campus. I walked up to the information desk and started speaking to the lady in the red "VCU" shirt.

"Where do students go for orientation?" I asked her.

"Just wait by Chick-Fil-A. We are just waiting on everyone to get here, and then we will start," the lady said to me politely.

Dad and I walked over and sat on the table right in front of Chick-Fil-A.

"When is Aleena coming?" Dad asked me. I was literally just in the middle of texting Aleena to ask her where she was. Just as I was about to answer him, I saw Aleena walking into the Commons with her mom.

"She's right there," I said to dad as a pointed towards Aleena and waved at her. I recognized them right away because I had gone through Aleena's pictures on Facebook when we connected through the "VCU Class of 2019" page. Aleena had long jet black hair, a tan complexion, and brown eyes. Her mom had the same exact features but with short hair. Aleena waved at me and came walking right towards us because she had recognized me from Facebook as well.

Dad and I got up and met Aleena and her mom. "Hi, I am Maheen's dad," Dad said to Aunty.

"Hi, I am Aleena's mom," Aunty said. The two started briefly talking while I began chatting with Aleena.

"Hey, how are you? It's so nice to finally meet you, although we have spoken to each other so much over text," I said laughingly.

"Yup, definitely doesn't feel like we are just meeting for the first time," she said, and it was true. Just within those few minutes me and Aleena had gone off on a tangent of our own, and I could already tell that orientation with her was about to be so much fun.

"So, what's your major beta?" Aleena's mom asked me.

"Business," I answered smilingly.

"What's Aleena's major?" my Dad asked.

"Aleena's doing Pre-Med. My elder son also did Pre-Med

from here. Now he's attending med school at the MCV Campus," Aleena's mom told Dad. "Ok, I am going to leave now. I will come tomorrow to get you," Aleena's mom told her. Aleena nodded her head.

"Are you not attending the parent orientation?" I asked Aleena's mom.

"No, I already did for my elder son and it will be the same thing again, but I hope you and Aleena have a good time," she said as she said goodbye to the three of us standing there and left.

A guy in a red VCU shirt with a megaphone in his hand came towards the center of the student commons and began talking loudly through the megaphone. "Will all the parents, please come here for parent orientation." I hugged Dad, and he kissed me on the forehead before we parted ways. I took my suitcase and went down the black stairs in front of me to the basement level, and Dad went to join the parents' orientation group which was gathering up in the center of the student commons. The first thing new students had to do upon getting to the basement was to drop off all our luggage in the conference room. Checking in to the dorms wasn't going to happen until eight at night, and the entire day ahead was full of activities. Aleena and I both had suitcases that were pretty big to carry around the whole day, so we got in the line to check in the bags. The student worker at the table took my purple suitcase from me and give me a pink ticket with a number on it so I could easily get my bag later in the day.

The first item on the to do list for the day was "All student orientation," which took place in the group lecture hall on the second floor of the student commons. After that, we were going to be divided for our department specific orientation. Aleena and I went to the second floor to grab seats in the lecture hall. During this presentation, the VCU administrative staff as well as admission counselors went over rules, regulations and procedures of the school and discussed graduation requirements. VCU's president, Dr. Rao welcomed us as the class of 2019, and afterwards the VCU Police Chief and Public Safety in Charge came up and spoke to all the new students about being safe around Richmond. VCU was very much a college town but not isolated from the rest of the world. Burglaries and gunshots were extremely common around the campus area. The homeless community was very much a part of our own VCU community. The chief of police explained to all the students there is no need to get scared of the homeless, rather we as students should look out for them because we cannot ignore them; they were spread out all throughout the fan district. What I appreciated the most was that there was no sugar coating on the facts. The chief of police explained how safety is important because a lot of things happen, and he put it out there openly that it is your responsibility as a student to stay safe around campus. At least the police officer wasn't showing off how safe the school is, rather he was telling the bitter truth: you are responsible for your own safety.

After the safety presentation had ended, all of us students were divided into groups of seven based on our majors, and each group had an orientation leader. My orientation leader was Sasha. She was a junior at the VCU School of Business. The group I was in had three other girls and three boys. The next two hours were all about games and getting to know the campus better. Sasha took my group out the back door of the student commons where there were stairs, and a plaza area for students to sit outside was located under the stairs. The chairs and tables had been removed because the school was making minor improvements to the back side of the student commons. On top of the stairs of the plaza was a statue of Rodney the Ram's face and ears. Rodney the Ram was VCU's mascot, and one of the most important school traditions at VCU was that every new student must go and touch Rodney's ear with their right hand and make a wish for the next four years. The joke was that if someone missed out on touching Rodney's ear their first day on campus it meant that they would not graduate on time. All of us stood in a line and one by one everyone touched Rodney's ear. The whole incoming freshmen class was participating in this tradition. I didn't know that Dad was there too, standing at the bottom of the stairs with all the other parents ready to high five all the kids as they touched the Ram's ears and walked down the steps. I touched the Ram ears, but I didn't make a wish. My heart knew it didn't want to be here. I just simply came down and high fived Dad then went to stand alongside the rest of my group.

Post following Ram traditions, we walked straight down the street from the student commons toward James Cabell Library. The library was under renovation now as VCU was redesigning the entire Cabell building. The library building was made from solid cement and had no windows at all but solid cement panels running vertically down the building at each corner. More than two thirds of the building, including the main library entrance, was all covered in scaffolding. Towards the side of the library facing the dining hall were two temporary doors to allow traffic in and out of the building as the main entrance of the library was all under construction. The ground on which the library was built was all red brick covered with patches of tan cement cutting through the red bricks horizontally. "The red brick is iconic to VCU and deliberately planned by the VCU development team, so wherever you see red brick that symbolizes campus property, everything else is part of the city of Richmond," Sasha said as we kept walking.

From that point on, I started paying attention to the sidewalks to follow along what was part of campus and what wasn't. All the sidewalks from the student commons to the VCU Barnes and Nobles all the way on West Broad Street were all red brick. However, the apartments directly opposite VCU

Barnes and Nobles called "Rams Apartments" had solid grey sidewalks with a bunch of restaurants around it.

Sasha took us inside the library through the temporary wooden doors that opened in front of Shafer Dining Hall. The entrance opened right into Starbucks. Past Starbucks was the circulation desk. When my group walked up to the circulation desk, one of the librarians got up from behind the circulation desk and began giving my group a tour. The first floor was mostly for computer use, the second floor of the library was collaborative study, the third floor was quiet study, which meant that students on the third floor could only whisper. The fourth floor was silent study. As soon as the elevator opened up on the fourth floor, just a few feet in front of the elevator were the doors to the silent study spaces. Sasha took us inside. Half of the floor was blocked because of construction, but inside the quiet room there was pin drop silence. Students were still working, but there wasn't even the sound of keyboards clicking. The guy sitting on the table in front of where I was standing suddenly dropped a pencil, and everyone in the room stopped for a second and turned around to look at him as if he had just disturbed the entire floor. The fourth floor was the scary kind of silent and not where I would ever work in the library. Once we got out of the library, one of the girls in my group and I started talking about how scary it would be to study on the fourth floor and be scared to even sneeze because that would turn heads.

After the library tour ended, it was time to meet parents at the Shafer Dining Hall for lunch. The Shafer Dining hall was located directly opposite James Cabell Library. In front of the entrance of the dining hall there were bold yellow, life size block letters that spelled "VCU." These giant size bold letters were the most iconic thing on campus and the one place everyone took pictures on campus. Behind the large "VCU" logo were black tables and chairs covered with black umbrellas so students can eat their food outdoors directly under the sun. The maroon Shafer Dining Hall building was shaped like a rectangle but cut directly in the middle by a semi-circle. I reached the main entrance of the building and directly behind the VCU letters I saw Dad standing with a VCU bag in his hand. I walked up to him, hugged him, and took a peek inside the bag. The bag was full of papers he had gotten through the information sessions. Dad's orientation was done, and he had to go back after eating; I had to go check in to my dorm for the night. But before parting ways, Dad and I went inside Shafer Hall to grab a bite.

As soon as we went up, the staircase ended directly ahead of us. There were two desks, one to the left and one to the right, where two ladies with "VCU dining" shirts on and hairnets on their heads were letting everyone into the dining hall. I didn't have a VCU ID yet or a meal plan, but my orientation leader had given me lunch, dinner, and breakfast vouchers till tomorrow. Dad had gotten his own lunch voucher from the parent's orientation. I handed the vouchers to the lady behind the computer, then Dad and I began walking around to find something to eat. The dining hall was huge with never ending food choices, or at least they looked never ending. First there was a fried chicken and pasta station. Next to the pasta station was the sandwich station. Right in the middle of the dining hall was the stir fry station and pizza bar. Towards the back of the dining hall was the cereal and juice station, and to the left of the cereals was the dessert bar. The tables were spread out throughout all the food stations and extended all the way towards the far back end of the building. Dad and I got pizza and sat on the bar stools right next to the pizza bar.

"So, you will be coming to eat here every day in the fall, huh? It's nice you will get a lot of options," he said to me.

I nodded my head.

Dad took another bite of his pizza then started looking around at all the kids eating lunch with their parents in the dining hall. I think Dad couldn't believe that I had reached that age already where I was going to be out of the house finally. He didn't say anything, but then two minutes later he put his pizza slice down on the plate and said, "Look, you are going to be college now, and Mashallah I know you are going to be a responsible kid, but just with freedom comes responsibility. I don't want you ending up in a situation that you shouldn't be in," he said.

"Yes," I said laughingly. I knew Dad was just being a parent and telling me all these things, but I knew that inside me, I never cared about doing what everyone else does. I was only going to do what felt right to me. Of course, I wanted to experience college life, but that didn't mean that I couldn't be responsible about it.

After having lunch, it was time for Dad to leave for home. I had to go get my bag from the basement of the student commons and meet Aleena at the dorm we were staying at. I hugged Dad and handed him all my orientation paperwork that I didn't need anymore. He kissed me on the forehead and left, and I waited for my group and my orientation leader outside of Shafer Dining Hall.

When Sasha and the rest of my orientation group came over, all of us walked back to the student commons to get our bags. All orientation students were staying in the same dorm building on West Franklin Street, which was a fifteen-minute walk from the student commons. We walked back towards Shafer Dining hall, and after Shafer we took a right. I was so lost around the VCU campus. I had no clue whatsoever of all the street names we passed in order to get to West Franklin Street. We kept walking straight down after taking a right from Shafer Dining Hall. After a few blocks came a park where the grass was dusty green, trees were a few and to the right and left were a bunch of benches. The walking trail within the park was unpaved and all the mud kept rubbing against my sneakers. To the left and right the benches were filled with people smoking weed. They stared at us students walking down the park as if we were a different species altogether. Homeless men and women in ripped clothes, bare feet and satchel bags were lying down on the grass and the benches, wherever they could find any empty space. This was Monroe Park; the park was very much in the center of the VCU's campus and that's also where this part of campus got its name "VCU Monroe Park Campus." This was the same park the VCU police officer had referred to when he was talking about the growing homeless population around VCU during the auditorium presentation.

The park ended right at West Franklin Street where there were two red brick buildings attached to each other like two large towers. The first building was Brandt Hall. It was shaped like a tower that had windows facing the front of the building, and the roof of the building was curved with "VCU" written in black right on top of the entrance. There was an entire line of students standing in front of the side entrance waiting to check in. After searching the crowd, I found Aleena toward the back of the line and stood with her so we could get a room assignment together. "How was your day?" I asked her as we waited in line to check in.

"It was good. I think I need a nap now," she said. "How was yours?" she said as we moved forward in line. I was up since the morning, and by now I was exhausted.

"Not too bad," I answered.

It was our turn to check in, the lady sitting behind the white desk checked my ID, then she checked Aleena's ID and handed us two blankets and the keys to room "15E." Without paying much attention to the rest of the building, I walked with Aleena through the back door and straight up the elevators to the fifteenth floor. Upon getting off the elevator on the fifteenth floor, on the wall across from the elevator was a billboard all about "VCU events and student policies." There was a sign that said "Sober it up," which was all about alcohol policy in the dorms. Of course, if you are a freshman and you get caught with alcohol on campus, then it's no fun anymore. The other poster on the billboard talked about sexual consent. "What does sexual consent look like?" and "No means No." We took a left from the elevators, and suite "15E" was the last door down the hall. There were four suites in total on each floor, one in each corner. The floor was a mixed gender floor. The suites on the left of the elevator were all guy suites and the suites to the right of the elevator were all girl suites. Each suite had four rooms with a common space in the middle. Each room had two beds and two writing tables. The beds were placed against the wall, and the writing tables and chairs were pushed into the wall behind the beds. Each room had its own sink, but the bathroom was shared by two rooms.

There were two wooden cabinets on each side of the sink to hang up clothes, but none of us really needed to use it since we were only here for a night. I dumped my suitcase on the floor and made my bed with the sheets the receptionist had given us at the entrance. Then I came outside into the common area to see who else was in our suite. When I came outside from my room, there were two girls sitting on the blue sofa in the middle of the lobby area. There was Nicole who was from Ohio and was going to be studying Pre-Med, and then there was Beth who was also on the Pre-Med track. Beth, Nicole and I sat there talking until someone knocked at our door. I got up and opened the door and Sasha peeked in to ask, "Any of you want to go to the gym tour?" she said. All of us nodded our heads because none of us knew the campus and of course, all of us wanted to go see it.

I quickly went into my room, got my sneakers on, and Aleena, Nicole and Beth went downstairs towards the main entrance where everyone was gathered outside for the gym tour.

As Sasha got everyone together, she started leading us towards the gym, which was quite a walk from our dorm. The streets around Brandt Hall were pitch dark, no streetlights whatsoever. It was only eight o' clock at night, but walking through the park at night seemed sketchy. There were no lights or even a single sound of life in the park. All the streets around campus looked the same at night anyway. After a twenty-five-minute walk, we finally reached Cary Street Gym. The VCU Cary Street Gym was no ordinary gym; the school had transformed an 1890's era building that resembled the structure of a European store into a gym in 1879. The building had a gabled roof and exposed steel framing inspired by markets in Italy because the building had served many purposes in the past. The red brick walls of Cary Street Gym used to be the house to an open market back in the 1800's, an auditorium for performances, and finally before turning into a gym, the building was used as a garage for postal trucks.

The auditorium structure of the building had never been changed, the only difference now was that instead of the stage there was a rock-climbing wall, and instead of seats were treadmills and a running track. Aleena got on to the treadmill in her flip flops, and I got on to the one next to her. Nicole and Beth also got on the two treadmills right next to Aleena and I. A few minutes later Beth spoke up. "Look at all those basketball players lifting weights," she said, looking down ahead.

"Why don't you go lift with them?" I jokingly asked her.

"Me? No way. I am going to look like a fool lifting twenty-five-pound weights in front of men who can lift 200," Beth explained.

I didn't say anything to her, but I thought to myself, "Why do people care so much about what other people are going to think or say of them?" People will always have something to say about you anyway, but that does not mean that you should make your decisions based on what others will think. To me that was the biggest stupidity of people my age. They thought so much about what others would think of them that they forgot to be themselves. You should live your life according to yourself only. If I went downstairs and I only lifted twenty pounds while everyone else was lifting two hundred, I wouldn't be embarrassed or ashamed of myself. Even if a good looking guy saw me messing up, that was nothing to be embarrassed of. To me, that wouldn't change my own image in my head.

When we got back from the gym, it was ten thirty at night, and I was so tired I fell on the couch. I had literally been up since seven in the morning and had constantly been on my feet all day. I wanted to crash on my bed, and that was it. From eleven to five in the morning there was a party downstairs in the lobby of Brandt Hall for all of us incoming students. Aleena went inside our room to get dressed while I knocked out on the couch. When she came back, she patted my shoulder. "Maheen, wake up," I heard her say. I suddenly got up and saw Aleena in a mini dress on and a full face of make up on as if she was going to a club. Everyone was so hyped up for this party. I looked around and even Nicole and Beth were all dressed up to have a fun night. "Aren't you coming to the party?" Aleena asked.

I was so exhausted that I had no energy to force myself to get up, dress up, and go to the party. "No, I think I will stay here. I am tired," I said. She asked me a billion times if I wanted to go to the party, but I was so damn exhausted that I really wanted to go to sleep. Even if I did go to the party, I wouldn't have enjoyed anyway. I never go to bed before 3:00 am, but that night as soon as Aleena left, I went in my room, laid on my bed thinking I would check Twitter and Instagram on my phone and within five minutes I passed out. I didn't even have the energy to get up and turn off the lights in the room. I was so deeply asleep I had no idea what time Aleena came back at night.

The following morning at 6:00 am sharp, the VCU housing lady started knocking at our door because breakfast was going to be served at Shafer Dining Hall exactly at 6:30 am. I woke up and got ready, then Aleena woke up and got ready.

"Why didn't you go to the party even though it was so lit?" Aleena asked me as I stood in front of the mirror doing my hair. "Everyone got crazy last night. Of course there was no alcohol, but there was weed," Aleena continued. "There was a guy at the party who kept on lap dancing on all the girls one by one," she said as she got up to go to the bathroom.

I don't know why, but I just couldn't be like everyone else. Lap dancing or getting extra clumsy around guys that I didn't even know was not my thing. I had no regrets of not going to the party. None.

And then Aleena said it from the bathroom again, "It was your first college party; you are insanely crazy that you didn't go."

"Lol," I answered. To be honest, sure it was my first college party, but I wasn't desperate to go to a party like all the other kids were. And honestly that stupid party in the lobby of a dorm wasn't worth sacrificing my sleep for anyway. This was just the beginning of college; there were going to be a million opportunities for me to party ahead. Of course, I wanted to experience college parties, but I never understood the fun in having a random stranger get mushy with you or like being desperate to party. I wasn't some desperate child who had just gotten freedom being away from home.

After eating breakfast at Shafer Dining Hall everyone got divided up into groups by their respective major. Each group was then going to their designated school to register for classes in the fall. I was in a group of fifty other kids who were also business students and from Shafer Dining hall. Sasha began guiding us to the School of Business. It was a long walk from Shafer Dining Hall to the business school. We crossed the road to get to the student commons, passed Harris Hall and the GRC dorms on the right, then kept walking down towards Main Street. Then came the highway, and across the highway was the VCU School of Business on West Main Street. The advisor meetings were being held on the second floor of the business building in room B202. All the incoming freshmen were lined up alongside the door, and there stood an assistant at the door who would tell each student when to go in. When it was my turn to go inside, the business school advisor told me to take a seat on one of the computers in the room. There were seventy computers in the room and all seventy kids being "academically" advised at the same time.

Right next to the mouse pad on the table was a sheet of paper with instructions on how to sign in to the VCU system and register for class. I followed the instructions and used the number on the back of my VCU ID that I had just received this morning to log in. "Hi my name is Ms. Lopez, and I am your advisor here at the business school. I will be helping you enroll in classes today. Everybody is going to enroll in "Business Management, UNIV111, Microsoft Word, Excel, University Advising, Precalculus, and one elective of your choosing," the lady standing in the middle of the room with a yellow shirt and curly hair screamed into the microphone in her hand. What kind of academic advising was this where there were no one on one discussions with students about their own specific interests? Where everyonc was taking the same classes even though not everyone has the same goals in life? In high school, we were always told that college has so much freedom: you can choose your own program of study, you can decide your classes on your own, but here it was again, those standards that everyone had to follow no matter what. You pay so much tuition money for college, yet you would think that the academic advisor is there to help you individually achieve your future goals. How come it's our life but someone else tells us how to live it or how to pursue our education. Everyone in this world is different. Not everyone wants to be a doctor, or a lawyer or become a top broker on Wall Street. As a society and a school environment, we talk so much about diversity, about being who you are and being true to that. We respect it when people come from different backgrounds and cultures, yet when it comes to education we become so systematic that we place everyone in the same box even though not everyone is meant for the same box. Not everyone is meant to walk the same path in life. None of us are built the same way, and that's where the beauty of being human lies. A person may be good at math, but another might suck at it, but that doesn't mean that they are dumb. Maybe they are good at something else, but they won't know that because they don't have the freedom to pursue an education that fits their personal needs. Everybody MUST follow standards because, damn, they are REQUIRED. When my entire schedule was already planned out for me, what was even the need to give me ONE elective of my choice? Damn, so much freedom.

Ms. Lopez kept calling out class titles with their course numbers, and I kept adding those courses to my schedule. Sitting in that room I felt like just another machine in a factory or an assembly line, required to do all the same damn things everyone else in the room was doing. I thought that maybe after high school I would finally have the freedom to choose my own classes as well as plan my own higher education, but no. Even in college the system doesn't leave you. Yes, you chose your major, but your degree requirements are chosen for you. The entire system wasn't wrong, it was just me who didn't want to fit in the system—any system for that matter. I believed in freedom.

After everyone was signed up for classes, it was finally time to go home. I met Aleena outside the student commons where her mom was going to come to pick us up. Mom was going to come directly to Aleena's house for tea. Aleena's mom came to pick us up from campus and took us to her house. When Mom reached Aleena's house, Aunty and Mom started having long chats while Aleena and I were showing my younger sister Aleena's pet rabbit. Later as we all sat in Aleena's living room chatting, the first thing Aleena said to Mom was "Aunty, she didn't even go to the party yesterday. She was sleeping," in a shocked voice.

Mom looked at me suddenly. " Maheen, why didn't you go to the party?" she said.

"I was so tired, Mom. I slept," I said laughingly.

"I am probably the first mom who's disappointed that her daughter didn't go to a college party," my mom said laughingly. Parents usually have a problem with their kids partying too much. In my case, it was the exact opposite. My parents always pushed me to party, but I was the one who wanted something else from life. I didn't want to be stuck my entire life in a system where you follow rules set by other people and then go out to parties to find your own life. I wanted to work so hard that my life itself could be a party. Plus, I was going to do everything, but just when I felt it was the right time and place for it. Now wasn't.

CHAPTER FIFTEEN

A month before going to college, I was lying in my bed, checking Instagram, and Mom and Dad walked into my room. "What's up?" I asked as I got up from my bed.

"Check your email," Dad said smilingly.

I logged into my Gmail right away, and the first email that popped up was Dad's. It read, "fwd.: British Airways Confirmation." I clicked on it, and it was a ticket to London. The smile on my face went from one ear to another.

"You are going to London; you need to chill out and stop taking life too seriously," Dad said as he hugged me. I hugged him tight and then hugged Mom. I knew I was supposed to be moving on with life, but more than me, Mom and Dad knew that a part of me was still upset about the whole college application process and rejection letters. There wasn't much I could really do about it, so the London trip was organized just so I could get my mind of off what had already happened and focus on what was to come ahead. Traveling alone was always something that excited me; I loved it. In my opinion, travel is how you find yourself and connect to your soul. Sure, going on trips with friends is fun, but growth only occurs when you learn to be with yourself and be happy with yourself. During the first week of August, I flew to London for a week. I stayed in Wembley, at Khawar dada's (dad's uncle) and Riffat dadi's house. The best part about Khawar Dada's house was that it was located two minutes away from the Wembley Park Tube Station. I would wake up early every day, get dressed and leave to tour the city all on my own and then come back home at night.

When I got back from London, two days later it was time for me to move out for college. Surprisingly, I wasn't that upset anymore about not getting into the colleges of my dreams. Maybe that was all I needed to realize that even after not getting what you want so badly, life still moves on. Traveling made me realize that the world is a lot bigger than just things going on in your life. Sometimes you get stuck on all the microscopic details in life that you do not see the bigger picture. Traveling allows you to gain that bigger picture and look at life with a completely different lens. That nothing really matters, and everything will be ok.

A few days after I got back, I found out that Mom and Dad had already gotten a studio apartment for me in the "Rams apartment complex," which was a commercial property located within the VCU college campus. VCU had no such policy that all freshmen had to live on campus. There were so many off campus apartments within the area that everyone had the option of choosing whatever was convenient for them.

The next day, I had breakfast with my entire family, and then around 11 in the morning Dad and I left for Richmond. On our way, Dad and I started talking about college and how everything was going to be so new.

"Are you excited?" Dad asked me.

"Yup," I answered.

It was a beginning of a new chapter of life. Before getting on the highway, Dad drove right past University Drive; I saw the huge green George Mason University sign to my right as we were turning left onto 1-95 south. I looked at the GMU sign and thanked God that I wasn't going there. As we started driving on the highway towards Richmond, Dad began telling me about his college experiences and how he was still studying for his final MBA exams when I was born. "I used to pull a lot of all-nighters because it was easier to study when the entire house would be sleeping, but then your Mom would come downstairs and push all her hair in front of her face to scare me in the dark," he explained to me. I laughed. Then dad started telling me about how crazy college boys were in Pakistan and how all of them were only interested in girls and not their studies. "Dating in Pakistan wasn't like dating here, Maheen. In Pakistan the guy could only flirt, the guy would give a smile and maybe the girl would smile back. During the time I went to school, people didn't really go on actual dates. The guy would find out what restaurant the girl is going to with her family, and then the guy would show up at the same restaurant with his family, both would stare at each other from a distance, and that was a date," Dad said.

"How innocent," I said. It was innocent to me. Growing up in the American dating culture, casual hook ups, sex, and physicality of a relationship is all I got to see and hear about. It was nice to hear something so innocent such as just getting happy by seeing the one you like from a distance. I always thought that my generation had lost the value of many things in life, and one of those things was love. Love doesn't have to always be adulterated, but that's all I got to hear in my school life. Sometimes I used to think that maybe if I was born in my parents' generation then people around me would give value to the same things I gave value to.

"However," Dad added, "when guys used to tell their friends, they always exaggerated what had happened and tell a false story.

"The same thing happens here," I said. "Guys only want something that they could discuss in front of their friends and look cool. They are so immature at this age," I added.

Just then my phone rang. "It's Dada," I said, picking the phone up. "Hello Dada," I said.

"Hello Mahu, have you reached your university, or are you about to?" he asked on the phone.

"On our way," I said.

"Good luck," Dada said.

"Thank you, Dada," I said.

By the time I got off the phone, we had already reached Broad Street. A bit further down Broad Street was the VCU School of Arts building for crafts and material studies. Directly across from the craft and material studies building on Broad Street were the Rams Apartments. On the top of the blue and grey were apartments, and on the ground floor there were many restaurants and shops. There was a pizza shop in the corner called "Xtreme Pizza," then there was a nail salon and a dry-cleaning store and a few shops after was my favorite place, "Tropical Smoothie Café." The parking for the apartments was on the back side of the building. To the right of the Rams Apartments was VCU'S own Barnes and Nobles, which was the main bookstore on campus. It was literally across the street from me, so I could go there any time to study and just get coffee.

Dad parked the car near the main entrance of the apartment building, and I went inside to go get a cart for all the heavy items I had. Inside the building, there was an elevator on the right that led to the apartments, and past the elevator was the main desk where I was supposed to pick up my keys from. I told the girl my last name and that I was checking in to the apartments. She gave me my keys and a large blue cart for my luggage. I rolled the cart outside to my car where Dad was already unloading my bags from the trunk. Dad held the cart from one side while I rolled it from the other side, and we brought it into the apartment building and went inside the grey elevator to go to the second floor where my apartment was. When the elevator door opened up on the second floor, in front of the elevator there was a little lounge with sofas and study tables with a vending machine and snooker table on the second floor.

My apartment number was 214, which was all the way at the end of the hallway, right next to the stairs. The lock on my door had a magnet that I had to match with the magnet on my key before I could use my key to get in the door. I opened the lock on the door, and Dad pushed the blue cart in. Inside the apartment, the first door on the left was the bathroom, and straight ahead was a narrow hallway that led to the rest of the apartment. At the end of the narrow hallway on the left was the kitchen with a stove. The fridge was all the way towards the end near the window that looked out towards the bus stop on Broad Street. The breakfast table sat directly in front of the window so one could enjoy the view outside while eating. Further down right from the breakfast table was the writing desk which was also wooden and had a wooden chair pushed in front of it. In the last corner of the room near the larger window was a twin size bed, and directly next to the bed was a wooden closet that had a double door hanging space for clothes, and towards the bottom it had three chest drawers for storage.

Dad unzipped the comforter bag and took out the sheets while I put the mattress pad on the bed first. I was still making my bed when Dad went and stood behind the chair of the breakfast table and began looking outside. "Maheen, come here and see this. Where are we?" he said as he looked at the window and laughed and then looked at me. I left the comforter half undone on the bed and went towards the window. Down below at the bus stop there was an obese woman whose jeans were pulled down to her lower thighs and her pink underwear barely covered her behind. She just stood there waiting for the bus around a crowd. This was a shocker for my dad because he wasn't used to seeing such things publicly, nor did Dad truly trust the area. Richmond had a very mixed crowd, some of whom were highly sophisticated and in some areas not at all. My area was a bit sketchy, or at least so far it did seem like it.

"You sure you want to live here for the next four years of your life?" my dad turned his head and looked at me.

"You are saying as if this was the college of my dreams," I laughed, then Dad started laughing too.

Next, Dad and I set up the kitchen. All the cabinets had to be dusted first because God knows how long the apartment had been left closed. Then Dad and I put cabinet liners in each cabinet before putting any crockery in it. After the kitchen was done, the bathroom was next. Dad attached my shower curtains to the rod on top of the tube, and I had to set up all my bathroom supplies neatly in their place.

Around ten o clock at night Dad and I were done setting up all the basics in the room. The room wasn't perfect, but it had all the basic things I needed to start living here. When we had left the house in the morning, Dad had told everyone that he was going to stay with me in Richmond for the night and everyone else was supposed to come meet us tomorrow because August 15th was Mom and Dad's anniversary. Since the apartment was already set, Dad and I decided to go back home, so at 12 o' clock midnight Dad and Mom could be together.

I picked up my keys and my laptop bag from the breakfast table and left everything in the apartment the way it was. Dad and I walked towards the car, and in the meantime Dad's phone started ringing. Dad picked up the phone on speaker. "Hello," he said.

"Hello," Mom answered.

"How's setting up the apartment going?" Mom asked.

Dad and I looked at each other for a second. "It's going well," Dad answered. We got in the car and started driving back home. When Dad and I got closer to home, Dad stopped the car at Wegman's, our local grocery store, to get a cake, balloons, and cards. Dada kept on calling on Dad's cellphone, so Dad ended up eventually telling Dada that we were coming back home. Mom still had no idea.

Dad and I reached home just four minutes past midnight. Dad parked his black Mercedes in the community parking four houses before our house so Mom wouldn't see our car from the windows in our living room. Dad held his laptop bag while I held my backpack, and both of us walked to our house and rang the doorbell. At first no one came to open the door, and it was visible from the window on top of the garage that all the lights were off. Dad thought Mom was going to come and that she would be surprised to see Dad and I back home. But that's not what exactly happened. Dada opened the door, and the first thing Mom said standing by the staircase was, "I knew you guys were coming back." It's been really hard for anyone in the family to keep anything a surprise or a secret from Mom because somehow, she always finds out everything.

I hugged mom tightly and wished her "Happy anniversary," and Mom, Dad, and I came upstairs to cut the cake with the rest of the family. Alongside Dada and Dadi, Nani was also living with us for a few months. She used to share my room with me.

Ehsan, Emaan, Dada, Dadi, Nani, Mama, Papa and I went to the kitchen area to cut the cake.

The major celebrations were going to happen tomorrow in Richmond since I had to be on campus for the start of welcome week.

The next morning everyone in the house was ready by 11 am to leave for Richmond. My entire family and I left the house for Richmond around 12 pm, and we reached my apartment around 2 pm. Dada and Dad unloaded the remaining suitcases from the car, and I led everyone into the building and up the elevator. The plan was that everyone would see the apartment first and then go out to a restaurant nearby to celebrate Mom and Dad's wedding anniversary. When we got into my apartment, Dada sat down in one chair at the breakfast table and Dadi sat in the other. Nani stood near the window gazing outside towards the crowd on Broad Street. "I love this place," she said to my mom. Nani always loved places with a crowd, where you can just get out of your apartment and walk out into a crowded space where there was life. She hated quiet places. In terms of being in a noisy place, this apartment was perfect because every time the AC was turned off, one could hear the noise of cars honking and people fighting on the streets. And Broad Street was packed with cars and people 24/7 because all the restaurants around that were open till four in the morning.

"Mao, is this your house?" Emaan kept asking me as she kept strolling around my apartment.

I nodded my head, and from that point on Emaan start calling my apartment "Mao's house."

Mom began opening the black suitcase that Dad had placed by the kitchen wall. Ehsan and I began helping her. Mom took out all my clothes and accessories one by one, and I just hung them in my new closet, which wasn't the most ideal closet because of its very small size, but nonetheless everything was so exciting. For the first time in my life, I was about to live away from my parents and be completely independent. I am not talking about independence in the sense of freedom because even while living with my parents, I always had my freedom to do anything and everything I wanted. Now I was going to become more independent in the sense that I would have nobody to rely on except for my own self, and that's exactly what I wanted.

After setting up my closet, Ehsan and I went downstairs to check out the rest of the building and the laundry system. The laundry room was located in the basement level. However, each floor had a laundry card machine located near the elevator where you could add money to your laundry card. I added twenty dollars on the laundry card from the machine on my floor and went to the basement to check out the laundry room. The entire basement was only for laundry. There were about twenty-five washing machines and twenty dryers. Each machine had a card slot where the payment had to be inserted before starting the machine. Honestly, I had never even put detergent in the machine. Let alone that I didn't even know where detergent goes in a laundry machine. But all of that was about to change now.

When Ehsan and I came back upstairs to my apartment, everyone was ready to leave for dinner. Dad and Mom had selected a Chinese restaurant just a little bit of a walk from my campus around Cary Street. I didn't know the area at all yet, so I kept looking out left and right on our way to the restaurant so I could familiarize myself with the area a bit. Even though the drive from my apartment to the restaurant was only a few minutes long, I kept noticing the streets around me and realized that Broad Street was literally the liveliest street around VCU. All the other streets around the VCU campus were super quiet and sketchy with people randomly sitting on street edges looking at you with their eyes popping out of their eye sockets. The smaller streets outside the campus were all residential neighborhoods with single family houses and not that many streetlights. In high school I knew so many people who were super excited about going to VCU because it was in a city environment, but when I came to VCU, I found it to be quite different. It wasn't a proper city to me but a suburban area trying to make itself a city. Yes, the VCU Campus itself was crowded and like a city campus because all the buildings were spread out throughout different areas, but once you got away from the campus area, you would end up in some random neighborhood of Richmond with no street lights whatsoever. It wasn't exactly what I had expected it to be but nonetheless it was better than all the other Virginia colleges like University of Virginia, Virginia Tech, and James Madison University, all of which were in completely isolated areas of Virginia like Blacksburg and Charlottesville. Charlottesville and Blacksburg were suburban towns covered with grass literally in the middle of nowhere. There was literally nothing in these towns other than college campuses which would get so sickening after a while. I wouldn't have been able to handle being literally in the middle of nowhere because I liked having life around me. And if VCU was comparatively quiet to me, I thanked God that I didn't get in to James Madison university because I would have hated Fredericksburg. That town had nothing other than a college campus created in the middle of a bunch of fields.

After having dinner at Good Taste Chinese Restaurant, Dad dropped Nani and me back to my Apartment, and now it was time to say bye. I was excited for the beginning of this new chapter of life, but of course there was a part of me that felt so heavy saying goodbye to everyone.

Since the apartment was all mine, I decided to keep Nani with me for the time being. Mom and Dad were trying not to think about this day all this past year, and now here it was actually happening. The only thing that stopped mom from crying a waterfall was the fact that I was keeping Nani. Mom could go home and sleep in peace knowing I wasn't completely alone in a new place where I didn't know a single soul. Well, I knew Aleena but she lived quite a distance away from me. In my building I didn't know anyone yet.

Nani slept on the bed that night, and I laid out a mattress for myself on the ground in front of the wooden closet. All night long I could hear cars honking and people yelling at each other across the street. All the noise was annoying because I couldn't fall asleep, but also nice because Nani wasn't going to be living with me for long. I kept twisting and turning in bed. I don't know if it was because of the bright lights coming in through the tiny spaces in the blinds on the window in front of me or I was just too excited about this new phase of life. High school was a different world altogether, the image you create for yourself once in high school is the image that lasts throughout high school. However, college is a place where you get to reinvent yourself, go out of your comfort zone and just start fresh. I spent the night thinking about all the things I wanted to do. A lot of people who went to high school with me came to VCU as well, but I didn't want to see those people ever again, not because I hated them or anything, but if I was going to stick around with the same old crowd from high school, how was I ever going to grow as a person? I wanted to get to know as many new people as possible. Fairfax High School was very small compared to VCU, and everyone in high school never tried stepping outside their own little niche social group. This was college; kids from all over the country were here.

I spent the next few days getting used to my new apartment, getting groceries and toiletries and walking around the area to get a better idea of it.

On the day before the start of college classes, I was in the kitchen making breakfast when suddenly my phone buzzed. I put my cereal bowl on the counter and picked up my phone to check who had messaged me. It was Aleena, the girl I had shared a room with during college orientation. She texted me, "Hey, I am near you, can I come by? I have a friend with me too that I want you to meet," Aleena wrote.

"Sure" I replied. I quickly finished my breakfast, and Nani woke up to have hers.

There was still some time left before Aleena and her friend were coming over, so I went to the Barnes and Nobles directly across the street to get Starbucks and print out a list of textbooks that I had to buy before the start of classes. Inside the Barnes and Nobles was a massive book section that took up about half of the store, then there was a Starbucks right in the middle with a mini cafeteria area with tables for people to sit and work on. On the other side of Starbucks were computers for student use. The second half of the store which covered two entire blocks on Broad Street was all dedicated to textbooks, school supplies, and VCU merchandise. I quickly grabbed two "tall white mochas" from Starbucks and was making my way back to the apartment when Aleena texted me again. Aleena couldn't find the entrance to my apartment, but she was right in front of Tropical Smoothie Café. I walked passed the main entrance of my apartment and down the hallway towards Tropical Smoothie Café. Aleena was standing right by the entrance of the café with a friend of hers.

"Hey," I said as I hugged Aleena from the side, making sure the coffee in my hand didn't spill, and then she introduced me to her friend.

"This is Sama, my best friend and roommate," she said.

"Hi, I am Maheen," I said as I hugged Sama.

"I have heard so much about you," Sama replied. Sama was about six foot one, light skinned, and her weaved hair went down to her hips. All three of us kept talking as I led Sama and Aleena back to my apartment.

"So what major are you?" I asked Sama.

"I am a fashion design major in the school of arts," she said as we got into the elevator to go up to my floor.

"That's cool, are you taking any fashion classes this semester?" I asked her as we got off the elevator.

"No, I can't take any fashion classes until I finish my Art studio classes," she said. VCU had this rule for all art related majors that everyone had to complete Art studio classes regardless of their major. These classes including drawing, painting, sculpting, etc. Thank God I wasn't a design major because as much as I would have loved to be in the School of Arts, I sucked at drawing, since always.

Aleena and Sama came into my apartment. "Wow you are so lucky you get your own kitchen and bathroom," Aleena said barely seconds after walking into my apartment.

"Hello," Nani's voice came from across the room.

"HI," Sama and Aleena replied.

"How's your dorm set up and which dorm are you in?" I asked Aleena as she and Sama took a seat on the breakfast table while Nani and I sat on the bed.

"I am in Brandt Hall, right next to Monroe Park, and I am in a suite with two other girls, so Sama and I have to share a bathroom with two other people," she said.

"K, so are you all moved in?" I asked Aleena.

"Yeah, my parents came this morning to help me move in and they are coming back soon with food, so I will need to head back in ten minutes. I just wanted to come see you and say hi," Aleena said.

"Hey, we are going out tonight around campus. Do you want to come with us?" Sama invited me with an enthusiastic voice.

"Are you guys going to a party?" I asked looking at Aleena and then looked at Sama.

"No, but we are going to try to find one. You should definitely come," Aleena said.

Aleena was literally the only person I knew at VCU so far, and Sama seemed pretty chill, so of course I was going to go with them. And this was going to be my first college party, so hell yes, I was going.

"Cool, I will join you guys," I said.

"Sounds awesome. I will text you when to meet up," Aleena said as she got ready to leave.

"See ya soon," Sama said as she hugged me and the two of them left. I was excited about the night. I opened my closet and began searching for what I was going to be wearing at night. I took out my long black T shirt dress that I had just gotten from Forever 21 and paired it up with some nice silver jewelry to make it look a little fancy.

I was so excited about finally going out, I started getting ready two hours before it was actually time for me to meet Sama and Aleena. Finally, around 8 pm, I left my apartment and started walking towards the student center, which was literally a straight walk from my apartment, but it took about fifteen minutes to get there. Aleena had told me via text that there was a dancing competition going on on the ground floor of the student center and I was to meet her there. I walked into the student center and went down the stairs to the ground floor. There was a DJ playing songs, and the empty space below Chick-Fil-A was turned into a dance floor and was crowded with students. There was barely any space to walk, let alone dance. Nonetheless I found Aleena and her friends. There was Sama and another girl from Aleena's dorm. The four of us danced for about half an hour before Sama and Aleena decided to leave.

"Hey, let's get out of here and go somewhere else," Aleena said, and she pulled me alongside her and Sama.

The three of us walked out the student center and crossed Monroe Park to get to Brandt Hall because Aleena had to pick something up from her room. I went inside Brandt Hall with

Aleena and waited by the front desk while Aleena quickly ran up to get her bag. Amongst the crowd of students running in and out of the dorm, I noticed Natalie, the girl I hated in my fashion academy class, then I saw her friend Jasmine, and within fifteen minutes I probably saw half of my entire high school in that one dorm building. Everyone that was walking out of the dorm at this time was all dressed up, most likely were trying to party before the start of classes.

Five minutes later I saw Aleena coming back towards me. “Hey, there are other people going with us too,” she told me. By the time all of us were about to step out of Brandt hall, there were fifty freshmen gathered up, trying to go out together. Aleena and Sama knew a few people, but I didn’t know anyone. I started walking with Aleena, and she introduced me to Allison and Katie who Aleena knew through her Pre-Med program. All of us walked down Monroe Park and then towards the side of the highway. I didn’t know the area at all, so I just went wherever Aleena and Sama were going. Monroe Park was pitch dark at 10 pm. There was not even a single streetlight along this park, and on the other side was the highway. Every time VCU would send out an emergency alert via text it was always about a shooting near Monroe Park. In the past twenty-four hours, I had already received two alerts on my phone regarding “shots fired near campus,” but I never told Mom and Dad because they would freak out super easily.

After an hour had passed by walking around different neighborhoods around VCU the entire group decided to walk past Monroe Park again and go towards the other side of the campus to see if there was a frat party that we could get into. I couldn’t believe we had just wasted an hour only on trying to find a party and were still walking. A part of me thought this was so stupid, but another part of me wanted to go to my first college party.

After about another hour and a half of casually walking

around the streets of Richmond, our group finally found three house parties, all happening in upperclassmen houses on the same block. The houses seemed like actual frat houses which were rented out by fraternities and sororities for the purpose of partying. Outside all the party houses there were a bunch of drunk upperclassmen, mostly guys standing by the doors trying to get people to come in. I wasn't getting a good feeling about this. I mean the idea of walking into a random person's house just to party seemed a bit desperate to me, but so far, I followed along. About half of us fifty freshmen were allowed to enter one of the upperclassmen parties and the other half of us were told no. I was sort of getting irritated by this extreme desperation of a bunch of freshmen to find a goddamn party. It felt like everyone here had run away from home solely for the purpose of partying. No frat house in that neighborhood allowed us in, so the remaining twenty or so of us kept walking, and by now it was past midnight for sure.

After walking a few more blocks, Sama saw another house with bright disco lights and music so loud that one could hear it three blocks down the street. When I finally walked up to that house, there were two guys standing outside the door with beer cups in their hands.

"We will only let the hot girls in. The less clothes the better," one of the guys at the door screamed.

The other guy standing at the door was literally checking girls out to see who to let in and who not to. Something felt weird as if my instinct was telling me something wasn't right. It just didn't feel right. I wanted to have fun, but something inside me kept telling me that this wasn't the way to have fun. This didn't feel right, like the time in high school when that boy asked me to go to homecoming with him but I couldn't because I wasn't the kind of girl who could engage in anything casual. For some reason I was getting those vibes again. How could I just walk into a random person's house with a bunch of crazy drunk boys when I didn't even know who those people were? If I knew them, it would have been a different story.

A voice in my head kept telling me, “Maheen, you just need to get out of here.” I don’t know what it was, but every time in my life I was ever about to get into something that I shouldn’t get into, I started feeling it in my gut. My instinct always told me what to do. My intuition said no, and I couldn’t go against that feeling. Whenever I have been in any situation where I have been unsure or uneasy about something, God has always guided me. Whenever my inner voice has told me that something isn’t right, it’s like a warning sign and I have never ignored it. It’s like God guiding me right from wrong, and that feeling is so powerful that I couldn’t ignore it. Also, I didn’t understand the point of having fun with a group of people who I didn’t even know. Yeah, sure, I knew Aleena and Sama, but I couldn’t just trust random people at a party, especially when everyone was going with the intention of getting drunk or hooking up. I didn’t even understand the fun of going inside a party like that. Sama and Aleena kept telling me to go inside with them, but I had to follow the voice inside me.

“Hey you guys carry on. I have an 8 am class tomorrow, so I better be heading back home now,” I said to Aleena and Sama as I saw the guy at the front door walking towards me. I didn’t have class the next morning, but I wanted to get out of the situation.

“Are you sure you are leaving us?” Aleena asked.

“I am sorry. I got to go.” I hugged Aleena and left. It was 1 am and I didn’t know the way back to my apartment and my phone was dead. I made my way back to Shafer dining hall. Luckily, I saw a girl in a hoodie standing by the large yellow “VCU” letters outside the doors of the dining hall. I approached the girl and asked her if I could call “Ram safe” from her phone because Ram safe would know where the Rams apartments are. Ram safe was VCU’s bus service that ran during the night for safety reasons because burglaries and gun shots were a common thing.

The bus picked me up, and my apartment was the last stop on the bus route. During the whole bus ride I felt so good for some reason. It felt like my heart knew that I had done something right by leaving the scene even though I didn't get to experience my first college party. Such parties were going to come and go, but for this feeling inside me, I could give up anything. It's said that your intuition is made up by your experiences in life; it's there to protect you. When something doesn't feel right, you should follow that feeling because what you feel inside about a situation is almost always right. Your intuition is the soul guiding you right from wrong, and it's completely up to you whether you want to follow the crowd or your own voice. I didn't care what Aleena thought of me that night; I just knew that I felt good making the decision I made, and I had no regrets about it.

When I finally reached my apartment, it was around two in the morning. Nani was still up on her iPad. I called Mom and told her everything about the night. She laughed about it but was happy that I had done what felt right to me. The next day, when I woke up, I picked up my phone and saw an alert message from VCU that said that "there has been a sexual assault incident in the 1400 block of West Franklin Street."

When I read the entire address of the house, I was shook. The address was of the same exact house that I had chosen not to go into last night. I was freaking out now. I wanted to know what had happened. I picked up my phone and called Aleena to confirm if it was the same house. It turned out that the house was the same and the girl that got assaulted by an upperclassman was someone that Aleena had known. Some guy at the party had mixed drugs in the girl's drink and then assaulted her. I felt terrible, disgusted. Something like this shouldn't happen to anyone. But at the same time a part of me felt so blessed that I had come home last night and missed the party. It could have been anyone in that place of that poor girl. My inner voice was my faithful guide. In a lot of places in life

I have listened to myself instead of to the world around me, and every single time I have listened to my own soul more than the noise of the world, it has always turned out to be the best decision I have made.

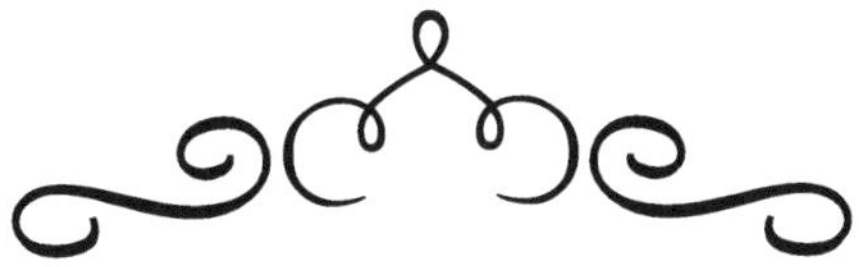

CHAPTER SIXTEEN

It was finally my first week of classes at VCU, and I was sitting at a roundtable in the lobby of the College of Science and Arts building waiting for one of my orientations to start. There were still 45 minutes before the lecture, so I began checking my emails on my phone.

Moments later, I saw a guy with black shirt and khaki trousers walking towards where I was sitting. I got busy on my phone again, but then he came right up to me. "Are you in the politics course this semester?" he said very randomly without even saying hi first and casually sat down in front of me. The way his eyes looked at me and the way he spoke to me gave me the hint that he was checking me out because I could feel his eyes scanning me down from head to toe.

"No, I am not actually. I am here for an orientation," I said.

"So am I," he said excitedly.

"Okay" I thought.

"So, what's your major?" he asked me.

"For now, it's business," I said. "What's yours?" I asked

him politely because I didn't want to be rude to him, but I still didn't want to encourage him.

"Political Science," he said.

"No wonder he had asked me if I was waiting for the political science lecture here," I thought to myself.

My emails got left in the middle, and for the next forty-five minutes as the guy spoke to me nonstop. When it was finally one o' clock, I had to interrupt him. "Hey, I am really sorry, but I have to go to class now. It was really nice meeting you," I said, trying to end the conversation nicely.

"Oh, no worries. Can I please just get your number?" he said to me right away.

I had been nice to him, but there was no way I was about to give him my number, so I thought why not just give him a fake one?

"My name is Ethan; what's your name?" he asked me as I gave him a fake number.

"Maheen," I said.

"Maheen, you have beautiful eyes," he said to me randomly.

"Thank you," I said as I got up, grabbed my backpack, and started heading down the stairs to the auditorium. Ethan followed me, asking me how many kids were going to be in the class. I told him I didn't know, which was true. I actually didn't know how many people were going to be at orientation.

"I will see you soon," Ethan said and just went left, as I went right into the auditorium for orientation. I sat in the third row. The next thing I knew, Ethan came and sat on the seat right next to me literally five minutes later. He started smiling at me. I smiled back, but I didn't say anything.

Soon, the presentation started and Charlene, the Student affairs in charge of CAS began talking about safety on campus. After 2-3 slides, Charlene stopped in the middle of her presentation and told everyone to save the 212 number on the screen in our phones as the VCU contact number for all emergencies. After the one minute pause in the auditorium, Charlene moved on to safety in the city, how at night one should always walk around with a buddy. Then Charlene went over living on campus, housing expectations, how to meet with advisors to register for classes for the next semester.

During the final moments of the presentation Ethan asked me, “Do you want to go walk around the campus with me?”

Honestly no, I didn’t. I didn’t want to give him any sort of hope because after seeing all the boys in high school, I didn’t know if I could trust boys my age.

“I am sorry but my grandma’s visiting me right now, and she’s waiting to have lunch with me after this. I can’t, sorry,” I said.

“It’s ok,” he said. The presentation continued, and there was pin drop silence between Ethan and me.

Later on, Charlene presented the wellness center slide and talked about how mental and physical health is crucial in college. One of the Wellness counselors at VCU stood in front of the podium and started talking about the “sexual conduct” course that every new student had to complete just for safety reasons. It’s a requirement in college to take the sex course so you are aware of the differences of giving consent or not. After explaining the course, the wellness counselor moved on to the resource center slide, which said that “the resources center is your one stop for everything you need. It even provides condoms.” After reading that line from the board the wellness counselor added, “We even have colored condoms, just if you are feeling extra.”

I was in shock at that statement. We lived in a world where casual sex was sort of just the norm, I thought to myself. That made me wonder how come colleges can give out free condoms to men but not free pads to women. I understand that stopping pregnancy at this age is of importance to some people, but it’s simple to do that. Don’t have sex, and you will avoid an unwanted pregnancy. Abstinence can be practiced, but periods, periods are unavoidable for females, so how come schools don't offer free pads and tampons to girls? In my opinion, you can easily avoid sex by just not having it, but you can't really stop your monthly cycle. Sex is a choice, but periods are unavoidable natural occurrences, so if schools can promote condoms so much by giving boys free samples, why not also take the initiative to provide free pads for the convenience of girls? A girl needs pads more than a guy needs a condom, so why this inequality in our schools? It was what it was, but how did this make any sense at all?

Orientation was over, but classes for the fall semester were going to start in two days. The last two days of welcome week were super busy because all VCU clubs and student organizations were having their interest meetings. The first day I spent going to various club meetings and organization meetings, all of which were held in the student center building. The Student Government Association meeting and the Pakistani Student Association meeting were both on the first floors, in the classrooms corner towards the back of the student center. I was a hundred percent sure I wanted to join SGA at VCU. The Student Government at VCU was broken down into committees: there was the Student Affairs and Transportation Committee that dealt with extracurricular activities for students and safety around campus. There was the Academic Affairs Committee that dealt with any student concerns related to academics. There were several other committees as well, but I only focused on these two because they were the ones that interested me the most. Finally, I signed up for the Student Affairs Committee because I thought I would get the chance to add many more changes to campus. I already even had a suggestion for SGA ready in my mind, to add more streetlights around campus so at night students don't feel unsafe walking back to their dorms or apartments from any of the campus buildings.

After the SGA meeting ended, the Pakistani Student Association meeting was in the classroom just across the hallway. I went inside the classroom, and the guy standing in front of the podium greeted me. "Salam sister," he said.

"Salam," I said, and I walked up the steps and took a seat in the second to last row. Shortly after I sat down the guy sitting right next to me started talking to me.

"What part of Pakistan are you from?" he said smiling at me with crooked teeth.

"Lahore," I answered, trying to be as nice as I could because I wasn't interested in making conversation.

Throughout the presentation the guy kept staring at me and later he goes, "Are you single?"

"What?" I blurted out loud in the middle of the PSA presentation, and everyone in the room stared at me for a second. I didn't say anything, and the presenter went on. Shortly after the presentation ended, the PSA team in the front of the room went over the activities for the year, which included dances and most interestingly "a brother and sister bonfire." Because we were all Muslims, in PSA everyone referred to each other as brother and sister because it was a way of giving each other respect. Minutes later when the presentation ended, two senior members of the PSA announced that they were getting engaged during the bonfire meet up this year. Everyone started rooting and clapping, and I sat there quietly thinking to myself that I didn't fit in here. My goal of joining PSA wasn't to end up coming out as a senior engaged or in a relationship. I wanted to join the PSA because I thought that we would do meaningful things like talk about poverty in Pakistan and how we can help or educate young girls or boys back home who do not have access to education in the villages of Pakistan. But here I was hearing stories about how couples met through PSA and were now getting engaged.

As soon as that meeting ended, I walked out because instantly I had realized that this wasn't worth my time.

Back in high school, Fairfax had a Pakistani Student Association as well, but I never joined it because students used to go into the organization single and three years later come out engaged or in a relationship with each other. More than focusing on promoting Pakistani culture and increasing diversity, people that were part of the PSA were more interested in "Halal dating," basically, dating someone who's Muslim and of the same cultural background as you. I saw myself somewhere in the middle. There were things I didn't admire in the American culture, and there were things that were just not for me in the Pakistani culture. I spoke Urdu, my parents used to take me to Pakistan every summer, so I knew my culture. But I was raised in America where we always had exposure to everything. I wasn't raised like a normal Pakistani girl who is taught in the back of her head that one day she would get married and her husband will be her top priority. No way.

The PSA group at VCU was full of students that had just come from Pakistan as international students. Kids who have grown up in Pakistan have a very different mindset compared to kids who are Pakistani but have grown up in America. There wasn't much exposure in Pakistan, and that's why when kids came abroad to study, they got distracted easily by their surroundings. A lot of schools in Pakistan were still all boy or all girl schools, and so when a guy or girl from Pakistan came to America to study, of course attraction to the opposite gender happens and one gets distracted, it's normal. Every time I saw a Pakistani guy trying to flirt, I would literally want to run away. It's not just the boys; the girls who have lived in Pakistan mostly and then come to study abroad have similar issues. The girls in Pakistan are usually, not always, but usually raised in very conservative environments and aren't allowed to do things on their own. When such girls come to study abroad, they know that no one is watching them, so they do things that someone grown up in America would never do. I wasn't trying to demean anyone; everyone has the right to live how they want and do what they want. I never blended in with people who came from Pakistan. I never blended in with anyone, and I was okay with that. In the meeting some people were discussing religion, but by the end they started flirting with one another. If you are going to flirt with each other then simply do not call each other "brother" or "sister" even out of respect because that's clearly disrespecting the actual relationship. If someone were to ever ask me to rename the Pakistani Student Association at schools and colleges I would have named it "the Rishta (marriage alliance) group" where people came for "Halal dating."

The next day I went to the student center in the evening again, this time to check out sororities and fraternities. VCU as a university had a huge focus on Sorority and Fraternity life. Almost every other student was part of a sorority or a fraternity. Out of curiosity of trying everything, I wanted to attend the information sessions for some of the fraternity and sororities just to experience what all the sorority hype was about in college. Sorority life has always been such an "American thing," or should I say a "white girl thing." Majority of sororities were almost always made up of all white girls that were mostly blonde. That notion broke for me when a came across a South Asian sorority at VCU called "Kappa chi Gama." It was the only sorority on campus that was made of a diverse group of girls, mostly Indian and Pakistani. This was very appealing to me because then again, I thought how cool it is to have a sorority that will be just like me, culturally and value wise, because a sorority full of white girls was not my cup of tea.

At 7 pm, Kappa chi Gamma were having their interest meeting in the auditorium of the first floor. The auditorium was located directly on the right past the entrance doors of the student center. I was there at 7:50 pm waiting for Sama and Aleena. Aleena had texted me earlier in the day that she was going to attend this meeting with me. We were both just really intrigued by the idea of a South Asian sorority.

The auditorium was huge, and we were just a few people. There were three girls sitting a few rows above me and four girls sitting on the right-side seating of the auditorium. There were five girls on the stage who were all Kappa chi Gamma girls. Aleena came rushing through the door and straight towards me. She was coming from the Indian Student Association meeting she had gone to with another friend of hers. Aleena came and sat right next to me, and the meeting started. The president of the sorority, Sara came up on stage started her presentation on the South Asian sorority. Sara herself was Pakistani. Her other friend who was doing the presentation with her was Indian; her name was Anita.

"Welcome to Kappa chi Gamma's Fall 2015 rush week," the two girls said together. After that, each existing sorority member introduced themselves. There were only six girls in total from different countries within South Asia.

"So, once you are a part of the sorority, you will be living with us at 8 ½ Canal Ctreet," Sara explained. She went on with the presentation, and a while later something tripped me. "There is a monthly fee to be in the sorority. Once you get accepted by us, you will need to pay three hundred dollars to us each month to stay in the sorority," she said.

That sounded a bit crazy to me. Why would you pay to be in social group? That's like paying to have friends.

Towards the end of the meeting Sara explained the induction process. "So one of us senior members of the sorority will become your Big, and we will choose who to train as our Little. Then there will be a few competitions, and then we will decide who to induct into the sorority," she said.

I looked at Aleena, and she looked at me for a second. I didn't really know how to feel about this. A part of me said no, but then another part of me wanted to try it out because at the end of the day, it was my first week of college and this was college life.

The next day after my English class ended, I walked to the Student Commons to grab brunch. I got my sandwich and sat down at one of the tables right in front of Subway.

Seconds later I saw Sara walking towards me with her Pizza Hut box in her hands, and she came right up to my table. "Hey, you are Maheen right? I saw you at the meeting yesterday," she said to me as she smiled and sat on the chair in front of me.

"Yup that's me," I said as I wiped the buffalo sauce off my face. Within fifteen minutes Sara took my entire interview: where I was from, where my family was from, and she told me that her family was from Lahore as well.

"Hey, why don't you give me your phone number? We are having an ice cream social at our apartment, and I would love for you to join," Sara said. She took my phone number and offered to pick me up from my apartment for the event, which was tomorrow night.

"I will let you know," I said as Sara had to leave to go to her next class. She smiled at me, threw away her pizza box in the trash can on the side and walked away. I wanted to go; I wasn't a hundred percent keen on joining the sorority, but I wanted to go just so I could meet other people. What Sara never told me was that the ice cream social was part of rushing, (the process in which a new girl entering a sorority spends a week with the sorority girls before becoming a part of the sorority.) Completely unaware of that, I was excited about meeting more people at VCU.

The entire rest of my day, Sara kept texting me nonstop asking me to give her my address. I couldn't answer her texts right away because I was in lectures all day long, but she kept on texting me every hour so, and every time it was the same exact text: "Hey what's your address? And don't worry, I will come pick you up myself," just copy pasted and sent at different times.

Finally at night I texted her back telling her my address. I texted Aleena as well asking her if Sara had done the same thing to her, and Aleena replied back to me saying, "Yeah, she's just like that. She even added me on Facebook, but I barely even know her." I guess Sara was desperate to have as many girls as possible to come to the sorority event.

The day of the ice cream social I only had one class during the day "International Relations" in the social sciences building right behind Cabell Library. The class was in a typical college lecture hall with about three hundred students. Most of my classes this semester were all set up in a lecture style except for my English class, which was only twenty students. On the first day of lecture for International Relations I learned an important lesson on the American education system. Near the end of his lecture, the professor announced, "There will be a quiz next week in class on recognizing all two hundred and forty-seven countries on a map and labeling them. You can use Google to study."

That was my first college assignment ever, and what shocked me the most was that in twelve years of grade school no teacher had ever taught us basic world geography. Yes, there were social science classes all throughout grade school, but all of them were always based on American history or the American Revolution. In World History class back in high school I did learn about other countries like Japan, England,

France, but the only reason we learned about these specific countries was because of the US's involvement in world affairs with these countries. No one ever taught us world geography in school.

After my classes ended, I went back to my apartment and took Nani to the South Asian grocery store right across the street because Nani wanted to buy mango pickle. I got home around 7 pm and got dressed because Sara was coming at 7:30 to pick me up. I told Nani I would be back in a few hours and she could eat without me. At exactly 7:30 pm, Sara was outside my apartment building waiting for me in her white Honda Accord. I walked up to her car and saw that there was already someone sitting on the passenger seat, so I got into the back of the car. In the passenger seat was Alexa, a white girl also a freshman. To the left of me was Sahar. Sahar was a sophomore who had just joined VCU and was also from Lahore. Right next to Sahar was Disha, a Punjabi girl with thick long braided hair. I introduced myself to everyone.

While Sara was driving all of us to 8 ½ Canal Street, Disha started talking to me. "What's your major?" she asked me.

"Business," I answered. She herself was a psychology major. After fifteen minutes of the car ride, I realized we had left campus far behind us and even the VCU Business School had been far left behind. I was more focused on the route now than on socializing.

Sara drove into a dark alley and parked the car outside an all-black door that said "8 ½ Canal" on it. Alexa, Disha, Sahar, and I got out the car and began following Sara into the building. This entire time Sara kept on repeating herself about how much fun it is to be living with her sorority sisters. Though the building gave an extremely sketchy affect from the outside, the lobby inside was very nicely furnished with white leather couches with black cushions. We crossed the sitting area and followed Sara into the elevator, since the Kappa chi Gamma apartment was on the fourth floor.

The four of us got out the elevator and started following Sara down the hallway. 410 was the exact apartment number. Sara knocked on the pitch-black door, and Ankita opened the door. Ankita was a junior who had been in the sorority since her freshmen year. Then there was Kinjal in the kitchen with Rimsha preparing snacks. All the girls that were senior members of the sorority lived in this one apartment together.

"Take a seat," Sara said, offering us to sit down. There was only one sofa in the living room, so Sara brought additional chairs from her room, and all of us sat down and casually started talking. I kept thinking to myself, do I really want to limit myself to just being friends with these five girls for the rest of my college experience? I didn't. I wanted to hang out with other people too. But I also just wanted to see what a sorority life was about. Whether I wanted to join or not was something I was going to decide later.

Meanwhile, Rimsha brought S'mores from the kitchen for everyone. They were fresh, hot with melted chocolate coming out of the crackers with every bite. The conversations happening in the room were something else, and instead of saying anything I was focused on eating my s'more. Disha started talking about her weed addiction, how she smoked all the time but her parents never knew. Then Kinjal started talking about her boyfriend and their sex life. Right after that Sara started talking about how her dad found out about her boyfriend and how she didn't care about what her dad thinks. Then Sara brought up the story of how her dad found out about her smoking ,and he's completely fine with it.

Every single conversation in that room was either related to drugs or to boys. I felt like I was in high school all over again. I was all about big ideas, being independent and changing the world and stuck in a room with people whose lives were miles away from words like passion, ambition, and a purpose in life. I honestly felt like I was stuck with people who had no goals or ambitions in life except for talking about drugs, boys, and parties. I didn't say anything unless I was asked something, but I kept smiling acting like I was enjoying. I did talk to Sahar that evening because she seemed normal to me compared to everyone else. We spoke about life and our future post-graduation rather than boys, sex, or drugs.

The night didn't end here. Later Kinjal went into the kitchen and made vodka shots for everyone. When Kinjal came back into the living room and offered me one, I directly said no, not because of any other reason but strictly because I have always believed that one does not need to drink to have fun. If I wanted to drink, I could have because no one was watching me. I mean, someone watching wasn't even the issue because in my house, I had seen my grandfather drinking, and it was never a big deal. But here, I didn't want to do it. I didn't think I needed alcohol to have fun. My definition of fun wasn't any of this. I'd rather go on an adventure with my close friends than sit here and drink with a bunch of girls I barely knew. If these girls were close to me, maybe I would have taken a shot, but I was meeting all these people for the first time. I didn't even get to eat dinner; it was 11:30 pm, and I was living on nachos and s'mores. I wasn't even close to my apartment that I could just go back, and Ram Safe didn't provide service to 8 ½ Canal Street. So, until the party was over I had no choice but to stay in the apartment with everyone else.

Finally, around 1 am, Ankita was going to drive everyone home.

"Are you sure you are not too drunk?" I asked Ankita laughingly because I wanted to make it back to my apartment alive.

"No, I can take up to eight shots," she answered me. I picked up my bag, met Sara and all the other girls and rushed out of the door.

On the car ride back, before reaching my apartment Ankita asked me, "Did you have fun today?"

"Yeah," I said in a very unenthusiastic voice.

Her car stopped right in front of my apartment, and I rushed out of the car, said goodbye, and went upstairs. I had never been happier to be back in my own space. Sororities were so effed up, I thought to myself. Whoever decides to join one is basically paying a monthly fee to have friends and to be a part of a certain social group. That was so dumb, and on top of paying fees, you don't even get to choose your friends. Once you sign up for a sorority, you are stuck with the same people for all your four years of college, and there is no going back. There was no way I wanted to be stuck with Sara, Kinjal, Ankita and Rimsha for all my undergrad years. Being in a sorority meant eating with your so called "sisters," living with them, going to the gym with them, studying with them, basically being socially limited only to them because sorority girls only hung out in their sorority. They never had any outside friends.

My goal was to make new friends in college, not to tie myself down to only a certain group of friends, so I decided to get even more involved in club activities at VCU. I began going to every single SGA Student Affairs Committee meeting which took place in the Student Commons Conference Room every Tuesday and Thursday evenings. There were ten other members in the student affairs committee, and after about the third or fourth meeting I had become the student liaison between VCU police and the student body. My job was to work with the VCU police to ensure student safety around campus and make sure any student concerns regarding safety issues are heard by the VCU Police Department.

Mom and Dad were very happy to hear that I was working with the VCU police, and I really enjoyed this job because I knew I was doing something worthwhile with my time, something that was making a difference in other people's lives and changing the VCU campus for better rather than sitting with a bunch of girls and wasting my time talking about meaningless things.

Life went on the same way until late September when Nani had to go to Texas to visit Tariq Mamu. Mom, Dad, and I decided that I would break my apartment lease and go into the typical dorm life. I applied for housing on campus through VCU. I didn't get to choose my dorm yet because the lady that worked in the Residential Life and Housing Department had told me that at this point housing offers would only be made to students based on availability of the rooms.

In less than a week I received a call from VCU Housing regarding rooms that were still available on campus. There were three different options available, a triple room in Johnson Hall that had three beds in one room and communal bathrooms. And the other two options were in Brandt Hall, where I had stayed with Aleena during orientation. I knew right away that I was going to choose Brandt Hall. When I received the email notification for room availability I told my parents right away. Mom and Dad both told me to accept the Brandt Hall offer and get the keys as soon as possible.

I emailed VCU housing right away and accepted my housing offer. Within a few hours I got an email saying I could get the keys to my dorm tomorrow, but I would have to pick them up from the Residential Life Office which was in the upperclassmen dorm near the VCU School of Business and Chili' s Restaurant. After attending my management class, the next day, I crossed Main Street to get to the Residential Life and Housing Office. I entered through the two glass doors and turned right towards the "Residential Housing Office" sign. There were two students sitting behind the security desk in front of me.

"I am looking for the housing office," I said looking at the guy in the red t shirt behind the desk.

"It's through that door," he said pointing at the tinted glass door ahead of me.

I went inside, told the lady my name and that I was here to pick up the keys to my dorm. The woman had an envelope with my name on it right in front of her. She reached for the envelope and handed it to me. The envelope had my room keys in it. "Thank you," I said as I thanked her and took the keys and began heading back towards campus.

On my way back while I was crossing Monroe Park, I thought, "Why not drop by my dorm and see the room and meet my roommate?" My biggest concern wasn't whether I had a roommate who partied or not; I was just hoping that my roommate would not turn out to be someone who constantly brought her boyfriend over in her dorm all the time. I have always been the kind of girl who values her privacy, and since always I have found it so disgusting when people start making out or get physical in public. It just puts you in a very weird space if you are sharing your space with someone and they start doing private stuff in front of you.

I crossed the park and made my way inside Brandt Hall. After the entrance was the security desk where all students had to check in before entering the dorm building. Students who lived in Brandt or Rhodes scanned their ID on the black scanner towards the side of the desk to check in. But because I wasn't fully registered as a student living in Brandt Hall, I went up to the guy in the red "VCU Housing" shirt who was sitting right behind the front desk. I showed him my VCU ID. "I am just moving into the building very soon, but right now I am just here to see my room," I said. The guy took my ID and made me sign in as a guest. I walked past the front desk and took a left after the clear marble-covered wall and went towards the elevators for Brandt Hall. If I had gone right from the same marble wall, I would have entered Rhodes Hall—that's how closely connected the two buildings were. Brandt was literally packed with freshmen constantly walking in and out of the building. Past the marble wall were three elevators in total, but there were so many students waiting to go up that

I had to wait for two groups of students to go up before I could get a turn to go up the elevator.

The elevator almost made a stop at every floor before finally reaching the fourteenth floor. I got out of the elevator and turned right. The fourteenth floor was built in a rectangular shape. There were four suites in total, one in each corner. The brown envelope in my hand that had my keys in it said "14E," but the suites had no numbers on them. I walked up to the first suite on my right. The wooden door to the suite had name tags on it of each person living there. The names of the roommates were written side by side. There was "Colleen and Hailey," "Dani and Tina," "Sophie and Dina," and my name was paired with a girl named Hannah. I took the key out of the envelope in my hand and opened the door to the suite. Upon entering the suite there was a mini lobby area with a black table placed in the left corner. There were two rooms near the black table and then two rooms on the opposite side of the suite and each room was marked with a letter. My room was E.

I went up to my door which was the last door down the mini hallway. I knocked first, just wondering if anyone was there or not, but nobody answered. I knocked again and just as I was about to reach for my other key, the door opened and there stood a girl with thick long brown hair in her pj's. She was fair skinned and had freckles on her cheeks, just around the sides of her nose.

"Hi, I am Maheen. You must be Hannah," I said smilingly as I reached my hand out towards her. The online VCU portal had already told me the name of my roommate. Hannah looked at me awkwardly at first because she wasn't really expecting a roommate and nor did she know that I was going to be her roommate.

"Hey, yeah, I am Hannah," the look in her eyes was asking so many questions like why the hell was I here.

"I am your new roommate," I said as I walked in through the door.

"When did this happen? I was expecting a girl named Lilly because that's what it said on my online housing portal. Did you apply for housing late?" Hannah said as she went back to her desk near the window to close her laptop.

"Yeah, actually just got this room assigned to me today," I said to her as I looked around the room. Starting from the entrance door, the brown wooden door on the right was the bathroom, it was shared with the room next to us. On the left, right after the entrance was a wooden closet, which was Hannah's. After her closet was the sink area with a mirror right on top of the sink. Directly after the sink was the wooden closet that was going to be mine.

"Nice. I got really surprised to see you because I was expecting someone, but nonetheless, yay! I finally have a roomie," Hannah said smilingly to me as she stood by her bed.

My bed was against the wall. The gap between the two beds was a little less than four feet. The beds were high and each bed had a wooden chest drawer placed directly beneath it for extra storage space since the closets were small.

"I am glad you think that way. What's your major?" I said to her as I stood near my desk and chair, which were right behind my bed. Hannah's desk was placed right behind her bed too, but she was lucky she had the side with the window view.

"I am on the Pre-Med track concentrating in biology, what about you?" Hannah said to me as she was fixing the pictures she had put up on the wall behind her bed.

"Nice, I am a business major," I replied.

"So, I can't stay for long because I have to go today, but I just wanted to know how our other suite mates are?" I asked Hannah.

"They are nice, so far. Dani and Tina are the ones who share the bathroom with us because they are right next to us, and then Colleen Hailey, Dina and Sophie are on the other side," she said.

I nodded my head. "Well, I really wanted to meet them, but they aren't here, so I will just wait till I move in to say hi," I said to Hannah.

"When are you moving in?" she asked me.

"On Sunday," I said.

Hannah and I exchanged phone numbers. I said bye to her and left because I had to go back to my apartment and help Nani pack her things since she was no longer going to be living with me. The following weekend, I moved into Brandt Hall.

I had early morning classes; therefore, I used to say bye to my suitemates early and go off into my room. I never used to sleep early, but I enjoyed laying on my bed and browsing my phone. Plus, I didn't know everyone's schedules, so I wanted to shower before anyone else did. Since the bathroom was shared and I didn't want anyone else using my shampoo or body wash, I had a basket I used to bring in and out of the bathroom and a spare towel that I kept in the bathroom for the purpose of cleaning the wet floor after showering. After my shower I got in bed and Hannah had come back by now, we talked for a bit, and then I went off to sleep. At four in the morning the fire alarm went off in Brandt Hall, and the noise woke me up. Everyone was running out the building. I didn't even grab my keys or my ID. I literally got my shoes on and ran out the door. Half asleep, I had to run down fourteen staircases to get out the building. I followed the crowd outside from the backdoor of the staircase on the ground floor and out to the patio in front of Brandt Hall. The resident assistant standing outside told us to cross the road and stand near the entrance of Monroe Park. Everyone standing outside kept complaining about how this was the tenth time the fire alarm had gone off in the building since the semester started. A lot of the students left to go to the dining hall across the street where there was an IHOP open twenty-four hours.

I stood there right next to Hannah, hating this drill because I had to be up in the next four hours for class anyway. I saw a girl standing in front of us who only had a towel wrapped around her and half of her hair was wet. Oh my god, that was my biggest fear, what if you are in the shower and the fire alarm goes off? I laughed about it with Hannah later.

Later Hannah told me that every week VCU was required to do a fire drill in the dorms as practice and the fire alarm would go off at very random times of the day.

After twenty minutes of standing outside, the RA finally announced through his megaphone that everyone could now line up to go inside. The RA's were only letting a few people enter the building at a time just so the elevators wouldn't get so crowded all at once. If I lived on the second floor or even the fifth floor I wouldn't mind taking the stairs back up, but there was no way any of us in my suite were willing to go up fourteen flights of stairs. Hannah and I simply just waited for our turn to enter the building. When I got inside the building, I heard the security man saying that this was no fire drill, but someone had purposely pulled the fire alarm as a freshmen prank. That pissed me off so much, I literally wanted to find that person and kill them for ruining my sleep. I didn't understand how eighteen-year-olds could possibly be so immature. Nobody found this to be funny. I got upstairs, got back in my bed, and went to sleep hoping the fire alarm would not go off again.

In the morning I got up at 8:30 am to get ready and leave at 9:00 for my 9:30 am class. My class was in Harris Hall, and the walk from Brandt Hall to Harris Hall took about a good twenty minutes, so I used to put my headphones in my ears and my music loud to walk around campus. From Brandt Hall I used to take a right and walk straight for about three blocks before turning left for Shafer Dining hall. I used to walk past Cabell Library then go across the street to cross the student commons and Harris Hall was directly behind the student commons, on the other side of the road. I always got to class five minutes before time and sat near the window in the second row.

There was a light skinned girl who always sat next to me in class named Bridgette. She seemed like the really quiet type of girl, but Bridgette and I had become good friends since the beginning of the semester. Bridgette was also studying biology on the Pre-Med track. I don't know how, but I always got along well with the pre-med kids. Literally all the friends that I had made this semester were all Pre-Med students with me being the only business major amongst them.

Out of all my classes this semester, English was my favorite because my professor Dr. Walker was the kind of teacher you only got once in a lifetime. Dr. Walker never forced guidelines on us; she always told us to enjoy writing and write about the things we were passionate about. Dr. Walker was the one who made me realize that writing is not a standardized thing, rather a work of art that's completely your own. True writers write from within, and I realized that only after sitting in Dr. Walker's class. In UNIV111, which was the name of our course, there were no exams throughout the semester, just class participation and three major essays that made up your grade for the semester. Each essay had to be seven to eight pages long, but the prompts were never restricted to the typical styles of writing in high schools. The very first essay that Dr. Walker had assigned in her class had to be about an obstacle in your life and how you overcame that obstacle. I had so much fun writing that essay because I could literally take the prompt in any direction. In my entire life, I never enjoyed writing until now, because all these years in grade school writing had to be done according to what your teacher required, the typical five paragraph writing. Dr. Walker told us to forget what we had learned in high school and follow what comes from within. Dr. Walker usually gave us two weeks to write an essay and during class she made us do all kinds of readings and research projects, but not the boring kinds of research projects. Three weeks into the semester we were watching a video about types of college campuses and overall performances of students in class. The video talked about how university professors don't really care about how well students do in class after getting a tenure because a tenure ensures that the professor's job is secured. The video also talked about party and sports culture of universities and how it affects student performance. Every lesson that Dr. Walker planned was about some intriguing topic, and I always had lots to say about it.

I always used to raise my hand in class to participate in discussions. Dr. Walker's class ended at around 11 am. I used to be starving by then. Bridgette and I would walk to the Commons together from class, and Bridgette would get in the line for Pizza Hut and buy food for the whole day. Bridgette was thin as a stick, but she ate as if she was feeding four people. All the left over food Bridgette took back to her dorm because she hated leaving her dorm unless she had classes. I never understood that. If I had to stay in my dorm all day long, I would go insane. I loved walking around campus while listening to music and just observing the world around me.

From the Commons I walked back towards my old apartment and got Tropical Smoothie Café almost every other day. My order was always the usual: chicken caesar salad and a regular mango magic smoothie. Hannah used to tease me on buying Tropical Smoothie every day because I never went to the dining hall to eat, even though I had a two hundred meal plan for the semester. I liked the grilled cheese or the chicken steak at the dining hall, but I couldn't get myself to go there every single day to eat.

After finishing my breakfast-actually-lunch from Tropical Smoothie, I used to go to Cabell Library to get my homework done. There was a spot in the library after Starbucks where there were all glass windows, and one could see the park behind the library. I used to take my laptop and go sit near the window to work so I could enjoy the sunshine at the same time. I used to come to the library every day whenever I had time in between classes because it was central, close to all my classes, and I couldn't get myself to work in my dorm since my bed was right next to my desk and thus I would get lazy. I liked Cabell library. I could work there and chill there. When I had to study, I used to just take the elevator up to the third floor and find a desk. The area directly in front of the elevator on the third floor was filled with single office style desks and black comfy rolling chairs. The third desk down from the elevator, facing the rest of the third floor was my favorite. Whenever I wanted to write I sat at that specific desk.

Writers have really weird habits; I know I did. If I ever had to write an essay, the third desk on the third floor is where I always went. The rest of the time I had in between my classes I used to work on finishing my two online courses. Microsoft Word and Microsoft Excel were two courses every business student had to take regardless of their concentration; these courses were offered online and were module based. Each week I had a module and textbook reading due for Word and another one for Excel. On the third floor of Cabell is where I did my online homework. Directly behind the elevators there were long, comfy leather accent chairs and an ottoman to put your feet on in front of every chair. I used to sit on the purple chair and put my feet up on the green ottoman every single time I worked on my online classes. The online modules for Word and Excel used to take an hour each because I wasn't the kind of student who could do a part of the assignment and leave the rest of it for another time. Once I started an assignment, I never got out of my chair until I had completely finished it. At first, I thought taking a class on Microsoft Word was really stupid because of course I knew how to use the program, but once I got started on the modules, I learned that one could do a lot more complicated things on Word than I thought. There was only one thing annoying about the online program where I was taking Excel and Word: the modules used to be very poorly organized. Every time instructions popped up on the screen, I would follow them and press every key accordingly, but the online learning program would never recognize my work as complete. Every freshman in the school of business was taking Word and Excel, and all the people in my management class were having the same issues with the program that I was having.

My biology lecture and math class were in the same building, South Harris Hall, which was an extension of Harris Hall. Harris Hall and South Harris Hall were connected via a walkway through the second floor, but students weren't allowed to use that walkway. We had to cross the street in order to get into the building, which was super annoying because if I ever wanted to rush from one lecture to the next, I had to walk out of the building and walk across to get to the next building. I didn't even understand the point of the bridge when it wasn't even useful to us. The only difference between Harris Hall and South Harris Hall was the size of the classrooms. South Harris Hall had all lecture halls with the capacity to seat two hundred students in one room. The lecture hall for bio was so big that it had three different entrances from where students would enter in. In bio, I used to sit towards the back of the room, and honestly the room always used to be so crowded I never used to pay attention to who was sitting around. I would just go to my biology lectures, take notes and come back. It was only last class when I noticed Abby and Olivia sitting right behind me in my biology class. The same Olivia and Abby I knew in Fairfax High School. Midway through class I turned my head towards the back of the room and saw Abby staring right at me. I stared back at her for a second. Olivia was busy on her phone, but later on, I knew Abby would tell her that she saw me. VCU was so big I thought I wouldn't be able to spot that many people from high school, but little did I know my classes and the building I lived in were full of people I knew in high school.

After Bio I had Math, which I hated the most. I hated sitting in a dark and creepy lecture hall that looked like an overstretched movie theatre and listen to the teacher lecture math to three hundred students at once. Bridgette was also in my math class, and we sat together since the first class, which made class a bit more bearable. Right next to Bridgette sat a girl named Katie who later became good friends with Bridgette and me. More so with Bridgette than with me. When the three of us hung out it, everything was fine, but Katie and I would never hang out by ourselves. It didn't work somehow. With certain people you can only hang out with them in a group because one on one you would never click with one another. The math lecture used to run from 6:20 to 8:50 pm every Tuesday and Thursday, and by 8 pm my brain used to be fried. I used to fall asleep on my seat, and Bridgette would tap my shoulder to wake me up. Both Katie and Bridgette knew that I was so clumsy in that class that I always dropped one thing every class, either my pencil, notebook or the graphing calculator—something always fell. The chairs in the lecture hall were padded like the ones in a movie theatre, but there were no real desks in front of the chairs to write on. There was only a mini table attached to the hand rest of each chair. The square shaped table was barely eight by seven inches, and every time I tried taking notes, I dropped one thing or another, and Katie and Bridgette always teased me about it which was funny.

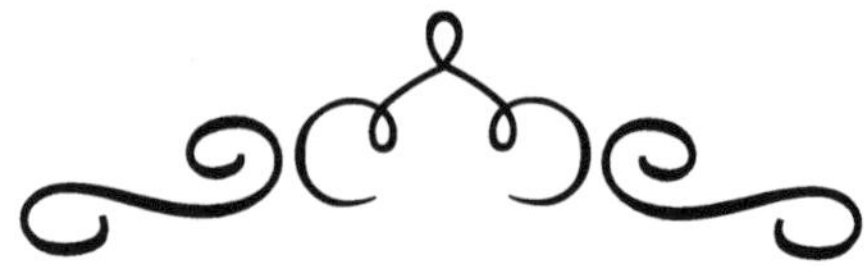

CHAPTER SEVENTEEN

I was getting ready to go the library when Hannah came up to me while I was making my bed.

"Hey, I just wanted to let you, my boyfriend Nate is coming over tonight to see me," Hannah said smiling at me.

"Sure, no worries," I said to her and picked up my backpack to go the library. I spent the entire day in the library and in the evening after going to the gym, I got back to my room around 8 pm. I unlocked my door, and Hannah's boyfriend was sitting on my desk while Hannah was doing her make up. When I walked in and he saw me, he awkwardly got off my desk and moved to Hannah's desk.

"Hey guys," I said politely.

"Hi," Hannah's boyfriend said awkwardly. His voice sounded like he was five.

"This is Nate. Nate, this is Maheen, my roomie" Hannah said officially introducing Nate and me.

I smiled and said, "How are you Nate?"

"I am fine. How are you?" he said as he fiddled with the

pens on Hannah's desk.

"I am good," I said as I reached under my desk to take out my biology textbook. I had two chapters of reading for Biology due on Monday, and I didn't want to think about homework over the weekend, so I sat on my desk to start reading.

"What are you doing?" Nate spoke to me again in his high-pitched voice.

"Just getting my homework out of the way," I said. He looked at me as if studying on a Friday night was an abnormal thing to do.

"So, what's your major?" I asked him.

"Oh me," he said pointing at himself, "I don't go to college. I don't know what I want to do," Nate said shrugging his shoulders.

"I am convincing him to do Pre-Med too," Hannah's voice echoed from near the sink. I nodded my head, but I couldn't understand how someone like Hannah who was just so dedicated and passionate about her life was with someone who had no idea of what he was doing in life.

I went back to reading my textbook and making notes while Hannah and Nate got into a fight.

"You need to wear this or else we won't be able to get in at the party," Hannah said to Nate as she handed him one of her loosely fitted sweaters. Apparently Hannah, Nate, and Colleen were going to a frat party on West Franklin Street.

"Why does Nate need to wear your clothes?" I asked Hannah out of curiosity.

She turned around and looked at me. "The Frat boys won't let us in to the party if they see a guy with us, so Colleen and I decided to make Nate wear my clothes, but you can still tell," she said to me.

Right after Hannah finished talking, Colleen walked into the room. "I have found a solution; I am going to do his make up like this," Colleen said pointing at a picture on her phone as she showed it to Hannah. Hannah and Colleen dragged Nate in front of the mirror above the sink and began doing his make up. I was just shocked at the amount dedication Colleen and Hannah had for this party, to me it almost looked more like desperation then dedication.

Soon, Nate had deep red lipstick on and layers of foundation covered his skin, and his hair was covered under a white cap. With make up he even looked like a girl. With his thin body structure, even Hannah's sweater was big on him.

As Hannah, Colleen and Nate were getting ready to walk out, Nate came up to my desk randomly. "You shouldn't be studying. That's so boring," he said and walked out the door.

"Bye Maheen," Hannah said while shutting the door closed.

I knew that what I was doing wasn't boring. I knew my priorities, and I was only focusing on them. I already knew that I didn't want to be stuck at VCU and Richmond for the next four years. If I did, my passion and creativity would die. I knew I wanted to transfer out of VCU next year, and for that I needed to do well in school. I wasn't studying on a Friday night because I enjoyed it. No one "enjoys" studying. I did it because it was a means to get the future I wanted. You can't expect to get a result from anything without putting in the effort, and dreams don't work unless you do. Ambition requires sacrifice. It requires endless hours of dedication and a certain extent of obsession towards whatever it is that you want to be successful at. I wanted to get to that success in life and then party. I wanted to go out and go crazy too, but at the right time and with the right people, not with people who were not on the same mental frequency as me.

I agreed that frat parties were a huge part of the college experience, but I hated how people thought that the only definition of "having fun" is going to a frat party. How could you enjoy going to an unknown person's party with unknown people around you? That to me was basically desperation to party. I preferred being around people who were my friends, even if that meant just chilling and having a good time with them over dinner. I just couldn't understand why people thought that going to a frat party and getting drunk to the point where you have no sense of what you were doing was seen as cool. I didn't see the fun in that. You don't need to drink it to have a good time. The high a person gets from substances is just an illusion that doesn't even last long. The real high in life comes from experiencing new things, going on adventures, following your passion, and doing something nobody thought you could do. I loved doing things that nobody thought I could do. I think that's what gave me the most amount of "high" in life.

When I finally finished my work and got myself into bed, I started browsing NYU on my phone. I knew I wanted to get into NYU, so I used to go on YouTube and watch videos of the NYU campus, imagining that someday I might be there. Then I watched admission videos on how to get into NYU. Nobody at VCU knew I had the intention to transfer because I never liked telling people about my future. When you tell people your goals even before you achieve them, often the thing you are excited about never ends up happening. I never liked being loud about my intentions; I believed in actions. When I would achieve the things I had always wanted to achieve, the world would find out on their own, and I wouldn't have to say a thing.

While I was on my phone, I got a text from Sara, the Kapp chi Gamma sorority girl. The text read, "Hey, we are going clubbing. Do you want to come?"

Even though I had made it obvious to her a long time ago that I didn't want to be a part of her sorority, she still texted me every single day. I swiped up and pretended like I didn't see her message.

Sara and her sorority girls went out every single night, sometimes it was for drinks, other times it was the club, but literally every night. Whenever I checked Snapchat, all Sara ever posted was her and her girls getting drunk. This wasn't an occasional kind of thing; every single day it was the same story just a different location. Some days Sara posted snaps of tequila shots and another day she would post snaps of being at a strip club. I used to laugh so hard going through Sara's, Ankita's and Sahar's snap stories because all of them always posted the same exact videos and images that the other person had already posted. Going out is fun, depending on where you are going, but not every single day. Even if you are going to a club, cool, but doesn't that get boring too? Anything you do excessively loses its charm. To me, if you go out less like once in a week there's an excitement to it; you look forward to it. Going out to a club every night and drinking every night wasn't cool. It's literally wasting yourself away.

A few minutes later, I got another text, this time from Aleena: "Hey, I am just chilling in my room. Do you want to come over and chill?" it read.

I was done with work, so of course I wanted to. This was the kind of fun I looked forward to, rather than going to a frat party. I was still in my pj's, but I didn't care. Aleena was in the same building anyway. Her dorm was on the eleventh floor. I picked up my keys and just showed up at Aleena's room. She was just chilling in her room with music on while Sama was standing in front of the mirror getting ready to go out.

"Where are you going?" I asked Sama as I stepped in.

"It's a week before Halloween, and there is a party in Mansion, so I am going there," Sama said as she finished applying eye pencil under her eye. Mansion was a night club right next to our campus. I had walked past it a billion times before but it always had the weirdest crowd hanging outside and waiting in line to get in. The area around Mansion always smelt like weed, and the guys who stood outside the club checking out everyone that walked in looked as if they hadn't showered in ages.

"Come sit with me," Aleena said as she was sitting on her bed with her laptop watching "Bigg Toss," an Indian reality tv show in which ten contestants must live in a house together for three months. The show was the Indian version of the Australian show *Bigg Brother.*

"I need to tell you something," Aleena said to me as I sat with her. "Later," she added. Aleena was upset at Sama because Aleena didn't want to go to Mansion, and Sama was forcing Aleena to go with her before I had walked into the room. The two of us spoke in Urdu since Sama was right in front of us. Aleena and I were talking for a while, and Sama chimed in. "You know I just had my first kiss today," she said, walking towards her desk to grab her make up bag.

"With whom?" I casually asked since I thought maybe Sama was dating someone that I didn't know about.

"I saw him for the first time today, at the bar across the street. I had to kiss him because everyone has had their first kiss, and I needed to experience it too." Sama said as she finished applying bronzer on her dark brown cheeks. I went silent for a second. I didn't say a word back to her because I knew that Sama's perspective and my perspective were a world apart from each other.

Sama left for the club and Aleena and I spent the next two hours venting, talking about everything: college, life, friends, fake friends, drama, everything. Then Aleena started playing Bollywood music on her laptop and the two of us just started dancing in the room, having our own little party while we had the dorm all to ourselves. We danced in her room until three in the morning when Aleena's phone rang. One of her friends was super drunk and had fallen on the street and needed her help. Aleena and I immediately left Brandt Hall to go find her friend while she stayed on the phone with him. We walked past the student commons and towards the 7 Eleven towards the end of campus. Right in front of the gas station before 7 Eleven, Aleena saw her friend Deonte laying on the floor. Aleena and I rushed towards him, Aleena pulled Deonte's right arm while I pulled his left arm, and we got him off the footpath. Deonte was so drunk he couldn't even walk on his own. Aleena held on to him from one side, and I held on to him from the other, and we started walking Deonte back towards Brandt Hall because he lived on the same floor as Aleena. Deonte wanted food too since he hadn't eaten dinner, so Aleena and I took him to the IHop in the campus restaurant building first. After stuffing an omlette and chicken tenders in his stomach, Deonte told Aleena and I that he had gone to a party with his friends, where his friends made him drink then left him alone.

"It's ok, we got you," Aleena assured him.

After Deonte was done eating, Aleena and I dropped Deonte to his room.

After safely leaving Deonte in his room, I said goodbye to Aleena and decided to go back to my room since it was five in the morning already. On my way to the elevator, I kept thinking about Deonte. What was the point of being so drunk that you would fall on the road and not know where you were? I didn't see the fun in that. Luckily, he was conscious enough to call Aleena, but I would hate to put myself in a situation like that, ever.

I got back to my dorm. Hannah and her boyfriend were still out. I got into my pajamas, brushed my teeth, and decided to call it a night and go to bed.

Usually on Saturdays and Sundays I used to wake up late and then hit the gym for about an hour to workout. Then during the day Hannah and I used to chill together, and in the evenings, I used to go out for dinner with friends or go to the library to do work. Every day when I left Brandt Hall in the morning I always had my headphones in and music on. I loved walking around campus, listening to music, and admiring my surroundings. I used to walk straight down Franklin street from Brandt Hall and go to the IHOP on the opposite side of the road for breakfast. I always got a grilled cheese sandwich from IHOP because their eggs used to be too watery. In the same building there were two other food vendors: "Cannes," which was a fried chicken place and Croutons, which was probably the healthiest salad bar on campus. After the first week of school, I never went to Shafer Dining Hall anymore because the food there was awful. Everyone who had meal plans either went to the IHOP building or the Student Commons to eat. Sometimes the lines at IHOP used to be so long that one had to wait outside just to get in. If I was getting late for class, I would just skip eating and go to class.

Wherever I went on campus, whether I was in the library or casually walking around campus or coming back from the Cary Street gym, I always used to have my headphones in my ears and my music blasting at full volume. I was a huge day dreamer, with headphones in my ears I never used to be in the current moment. I used to be daydreaming all the time of being in a more exciting place. While walking around the streets, I used to imagine being in New York City. It was my biggest dream to go there and prove myself in life. While walking around the VCU campus I used to visualize myself being in New York City. I wasn't dreaming because I lived in my own world. No, I was dreaming of something better and bigger because I knew that I was capable of achieving it. I wanted something more from life, which I wasn't going to get at VCU.

In my free time I was either in the library planning out what I wanted from life or having dinner with a friend or at the gym. Exploring Richmond for fun wasn't really on my list of things to achieve. I did enjoy hanging out with Hannah though because after living with each other we had become great friends. Near the VCU arts Pollak building was a restaurant called the Village café. They served the best milkshakes around town. Hannah and I used to meet up after class and talk for hours while drinking shakes. The milkshake used to come in steel glasses like the ones people in Pakistan drank lassi (typical Pakistani breakfast drink) in, and it had about thirty ounces of milkshake in it. The white chocolate marshmallow milkshake was heavenly. I used to chug it down my throat as if it was beer. Going out to eat was probably the only attraction around town.

VCU was a big school, however since there wasn't much to do around campus except for hanging out with friends, and that too at the same hangout spots, everyone pretty much knew each other. People used to hang out with each other and then come back and discuss about the same person that they were just sitting with moments ago. The fakeness was to a level that I couldn't take. It reminded me of the popular crowd in high school who used to sit together and smile at your face but then backbite you as soon as you left the crowd. I had grown from that. I didn't want it anymore. That's why I didn't like being around such people.

Even in college, it seemed like everyone just wanted to fit in and be a part of a group, and that feeling of belonging was something that everyone was looking for. Maybe I was too, but I knew I didn't belong here; I was just making the most out of it so I could get to the point where I could live the life I craved for.

So, in my suite, Kylie and Dina were the so called "popular girls" because they never missed a single frat party on campus and almost every freshman at VCU knew them. Hannah wasn't really their friend, but she used to hang out with them thinking she was. I myself had been in her position back in high school, so I knew that they didn't consider Hannah a friend. Then one day, Hannah and I were at the IHOP dining hall getting cookies.

Standing in line we saw Yasmine. Hannah went up to hug Yasmine right away, and I just stood there not even bothered to say hi. This was the same Yasmine, the one that I never got along with back in high school when we had Fashion Academy together.

After Hannah and I had gotten our cookies and were going back to sit at one of the tables and eat, I asked "How do you know Yasmine?"

"Yasmine is so nice. She's Sophia's friend, and I have met her a few times. I want to meet her more though," Hannah said eating her cookie. "You know her?" she asked curiously.

"I know her from one of my classes in high school," I said casually without telling Hannah my opinion of Yasmine.

"Oh nice," Hannah said. "Maybe we should all hang out sometime," Hannah added.

I nodded my head in silence. Hannah wasn't like Yasmine or Sophia; Hannah was a lot like me, determined and focused in life. I don't know why she wanted to be friends with Yasmine and Sophia so badly. Sophia used Hannah whenever she wanted as per her convenience, to get her food or do her homework, and Hannah used to do it. Sophia only called Hannah when she needed a favor, and Hannah would always give her that favor thinking she was a friend. And whenever Hannah tried texting Sophia to make plans, Sophia always made an excuse not to meet Hannah. I could see everything that was going on. I saw that Hannah wasn't considered a friend but a side kick, but Hannah couldn't see that. I tried telling her to not expect much from Sophia, but you can only help someone so much by giving them advice. Whether they want to follow that advice or not is up to them. After we finished eating our cookies, Hannah and I headed back to the dorm.

A few days later, after having dinner with Bridgette, I was back in my dorm, tucked in bed watching Netflix when around midnight Hannah rushed into the room with Dina who went straight into the bathroom. I could hear her trying to vomit. Hannah filled an empty bottle with water from the sink and rushed over to Dina. I got off my bed to see what was going on.

When I got to the bathroom Dina was sitting on her knees, facing the toilet with her head bowed down literally inches away from the toilet seat.

My voice rose. "What happened?" I said.

Hannah turned her gaze up towards me. "She's had too much alcohol, and she keeps vomiting," Hannah said.

Dina was gagging in the background trying her best to vomit again.

"Where were you guys?" I asked worriedly.

"We were at a house party, and I was drinking too, but none of us realized when Dina had too much." Hannah said.

Just then, Colleen, Hailey and all the other girls in my suite came running to my room to see if Dina was ok. Her vomit was still stuck, and she kept gagging inside the ring of the toilet. After constant failures, Hannah decided to help Dina by grabbing her toothbrush from the brush bowl on the sink and sticking the back end of it down Dina's throat to make her vomit. Dina screamed loudly, "What the Faaaahh," and before she could finish her sentence, that trick worked, and all the vomit came running out of Dina's mouth. Vomit was all over our floor and the toilet seat. I felt so disgusted just looking at it.

"Why drink so much?" I thought to myself? You do not need to drink to have fun, or even if you do want to drink, why drink that much? Why couldn't college students do things in moderation? Why was it always one extreme or the other?

"Are you feeling better now?" Colleen asked Dina as Hannah was helping Dina wash her face.

"Yo, I am. It was such a sick night," Dina said.

Now that I knew she was okay, I calmly went back to my bed as Dina kept going on about how amazing her night was. Why was it always weed or alcohol or clubs? Colorful disco lights, super loud music, going crazy on alcohol? Sure, these things are fun, and everyone experiences them, but what annoyed me the most was that people around me were stuck just in these things. No one ever talked about their ambitions and life plans as much as everyone engaged in party culture. Indeed, there is nothing wrong in party culture, but to me it could never be the only thing in life or my only goal. However, whenever I looked at the people around me, I always felt like everyone was just obsessed with partying, fake relationships and fake friendships. People gossiped more than they spoke about attaining their dreams. People spoke about drinks and frat boys more than they ever spoke about their passions or life goals. Maybe partying was a huge thing for college kids, but how come nobody realized that we had our entire lives to party and waste ourselves? This was time to do something, to achieve something. Drinking, partying, smoking, those are all fun, but they are not soul fulfilling. You can only get temporary happiness out of those things. And maybe that happiness will last you a few hours, maximum a day, and then what? That fourteen shots of vodka won't even keep you happy for fourteen days. A day later the effects of it will start to fade, and then what? You will be left wanting more. Well, when you do something with passion and purpose, the feeling of self fulfillment never fades. That's what I wanted. Above all, how could you call a night "fun" when you ended up throwing up in the toilet and passed out? And the next morning, could not even remember what happened? That was above my understanding.

A few days later, I was in Aleena's dorm with Aleena and Sama. The three of us were sitting at the table in her common room doing homework. I was writing my UNIV 111 paper and talking to Aleena who was sitting right across from me.

Suddenly Deonte came through the door. "Hey, they keep bothering me," Deonte said in a low voice.

"Who?" Aleena asked as she raised her eyebrows.

"Nick and all the guys in the other suite," Deonte said as he rushed back out. There were five guys who lived in the suite across from Aleena's room. I was still doing my homework, but Aleena's stepped outside for a second to see what was going on. Taj, an Indian boy with a turban was standing in the hallway laughing, and then he came right into Aleena's suite following her, then into her room to mess up her things. Taj and Aleena were friends and apparently, he was getting back at her for something she had done before. Taj went into Aleena's room, threw her pillows off her bed, and ran back to his dorm. Aleena got pissed off. "Come with me," Aleena said, looking at me, and she pulled Sama along too.

I followed Aleena to the boy's suite, but for a second, I stood outside. I didn't know anyone on her floor. What was the point of me going into someone's room just like that? I thought to myself for a second. Nonetheless I went inside with Aleena. All the guys were sitting in the common area of the room watching tv, the center table in the room was packed with bottles of vodka, cans of beer and chips and the classic red cups that are famously used at college parties. Aleena rushed into Taj's room to hit him on the head, and the two were fighting as I just awkwardly stood behind her.

"Hi," I said to the guys sitting at the table, and they said hi back, but I didn't know anyone there except for Nick who was in my International Relations class. "Don't these kids realize that if the RA walks into their room randomly for any reason all these people would get kicked out of the university?" I started thinking to myself.

Maturity says even if you want to do such things, you do it somewhere else where you are not going to get in trouble. But I guess you cannot expect a bunch of freshmen college boys to be anything near the word "mature."

Without saying anything further to anyone, I walked out the door with Aleena and back to her dorm. Later, Aleena told me how Sama and her always have this chasing and teasing game going on with the boys on the floor. Then out of nowhere Aleena brought up Nick's story, how once Nick had taken a girl out on a date for dinner, had paid for the dinner and the girl's Uber ride, but at the end of that night the girl told Nick that she didn't want to do anything further with him, and since then Nick calls her a bitch because he had spent a hundred dollars on Uber and food that night and didn't end up getting what he wanted from the girl. I wasn't really surprised after hearing that. I mean what else do you expect from a college boy? They don't date for love; they date you in order to get closer to you. Most of the times all college boys want is sex, and when they don't get it, it's over. This mentality of college boys was exactly what scared me about boys and relationships.

Every other day when I got back to my suite, Hannah had the same exact story to share with me. Our suitemate, Dani, (who shared the bathroom with us) had a boyfriend named Sam who used to be in Dani's dorm twenty-four hours a day. I didn't see him around as much as I heard his voice from our wall, that connected to Dani's room. Hannah and I used to get really annoyed when Sam used our bathroom, especially because he used it all the time. Dani, Hannah and I lived here and Sam didn't, nor was he paying for our bathroom supplies, so of course it was annoying. We were all girls, and we needed our privacy. It wasn't even like Sam used our bathroom occasionally, but it was every single day. Dani and Sam used to shower together, and Hannah and I would be able to hear them screaming and shouting while being in the shower.

Hannah and I used to make fun of Dani and Sam showering together because the shower in our bathroom was so small that barely one person could stand under it without running into the wall, let alone two people showering together.

This was just a trailer; there was worse. The wall in my room, behind Hannah's bed was connected to Dani's room on the other side, and whenever Dani had sex with her boyfriend, Hannah and I heard every bit of the pounding. The bed in Dani's room used to bang against the wall making extremely disturbing sounds. Imagine studying for your biology exam and suddenly you start hearing a bed banging against the wall and someone moaning. It was sickening. Often, I used to be out of the room, and when I would come back Hannah used to tell me "an episode of sex in the city was aired again today" as a joke. But sometimes Hannah and I both used to be in our room, and as soon as we would start hearing Dani and Sam banging the wall, Hannah and I would blast music in our room and start singing on top of our lungs just to give Dani the message to shut up or keep her business to herself, but that almost never stopped Dani from anything. When the music wouldn't help, Hannah and I used to hit the wall hard with a textbook to get the message across on the other side that you are actually being really loud. You can't really control what other people do in their life, but neither Hannah or I needed to know when Dani was or wasn't having sex. That never stopped Dani as well. Dani and I had nothing against each other personally, but she knew that her habits irritated Hannah and me a lot. However, if Dani and I saw each other outside of our suite she always had this fake smile on her face, and she used to become all sweet pretending as if nothing had ever happened.

It was a day close to the end of November. Classes were finishing up and finals were around the corner, so everyone was busy studying. Apparently, Dani had a huge fight with her mother after which Dani kept ignoring her mom's phone calls the entire day. I was at the library the entire day, and when I got back to my dorm, I found police in our suite. Because Dani chose not to pick up her mother's phone calls, Dani's mom had filed a report to the police to check whether her daughter was okay or not. When I got into the dorm, the police officer was standing in our common area asking Hailey questions about Dani and how Dani usually behaves around everyone in the dorm. Everyone else in my suite had rushed out the door with their giant black mysterious bags full of alcohol and weed because none of the girls wanted to get caught by the police for possessing illegal drugs and alcohol. We were all underage, but I knew for a fact that everyone in my suite except for me drank. I casually walked into my room, and I got a text on my phone from Hannah which said, "Hey I saw the police coming, so I left since I had alcohol stored in our room. Let me know when they leave, and I will come back ☺."

"Okie," I replied. I knew Hannah kept alcohol in our room. She hid it in the air vent on the ceiling.

I got changed and was going to lie down in bed and watch something when I heard a knock on the door. "VCU Police," the officer behind the door yelled out.

I left my bed sheet half undone and hustled to open the door.

"Hey, are you Dani's suitemate?" the police officer threw the question at me as soon as he saw me.

"Yes, I am," I answered patiently.

"Do you know her well?" he asked.

"I don't really interact with her too much," I answered.

"How about Dani's boyfriend. Do you know him?" the police officer asked me.

"He's always here, but I have never spoken to him," I said.

Maybe I did speak to Sam once when he said hi and I said hi back. He had a really squeaky voice, almost felt like a fourteen-year-old girl speaking, and Dani always bossed him around like crazy.

The officer kept making notes on the notepad in his hands. "Do you have a roommate?" the officer asked, peeking his head into the room.

"Yes, but she went home," I answered. The police officer abruptly left without saying anything, and I shut the door closed. Thank God Hannah had left the room with her alcohol bottles, or else if the officer had inspected the room and found Hannah's alcohol, I would have gotten stuck in that mess for no reason.

Since Dani, Hannah, and I shared one bathroom we each had to contribute getting toilet paper. We had a monthly system in place where one month I was responsible for toilet paper, another month Hannah was, and then Dani. It was Dani's turn to provide bathroom supplies.

One day I got back from working out. I rushed into the bathroom and there was no more toilet paper. It was not my responsibility to provide toilet paper this month so without even using the bathroom I decided to go to Dani's room to ask her to refill the toilet paper. Dani had barged into my room earlier in the semester at 2 am, but I wasn't going to go down to her level. I got out of my room and went to politely knock on Dani's door.

"Dani are you there?" I said as I knocked on her door.

"Hey, yeah. The door is unlocked. You can come in," I heard Dani's voice from the other side of the door. I turned the door handle and went inside, but what happened after that I had never expected in my life.

The room was pitch dark with only the bathroom light coming in from underneath the bathroom door. "Hey by the way, Sam is here" Dani said.

So far, I hadn't seen anything because I was searching for toilet paper. I looked up and there was Dani and Sam in the blanket with Dani on the bottom and Sam right on top of her. "Hi," she said to me. Dani was in the middle of having sex, and I stood there for a second in shock, with my gaze down on the floor, thinking why the hell did Dani tell me to come in firstly?

"Um, sorry um, I just needed toilet paper since we ran out of some," I said as fast as I could.

"Sure, it's underneath the sink," Dani called out as she giggled. I quickly grabbed the toilet paper from the cabinet under the sink and rushed into my room through the bathroom.

"What the hell was that about?" I thought to myself." Did I actually just walk into my suite mate's room while she was having sex with her boyfriend? EW."

More shocking than that was the fact that Dani was the one who told me to come in. Any doubts that I had were confirmed when I heard Dani moaning while I was using the bathroom. That was super disgusting and annoying, but when Hannah came back I told her and hysterically started laughing because I couldn't believe what had happened. Although I was laughing at what just happened, deep down inside I was like, this random sex and hook up culture I could never understand in my life. I never did and I never will.

CHAPTER EIGHTEEN

This semester of college was coming to an end in the first week of December. While most of my friends spent their nights at the Mansion Club partying, I was spending hours in Cabell Library working on final projects and studying for my final exams. VCU and the city of Richmond were my reality, but was I truly happy? I didn't know. A part of me was here living this life, but a part of me knew I didn't belong. The thought of spending the next three and a half years of my life in a college town amongst people who knew nothing more than partying and drinking was depressing. The thought bothered me that what if I didn't get into NYU, then I would be stuck here too, in the same environment, and maybe I would lose the spark of doing something in life. I couldn't lose that spark. It was what I was born for. That spark was what made me who I am.

The night before my biology final exam, I was sitting on the first floor of Cabell Library from 2 am to 6 am, making sure I had accurate notes from each reading chapter because the final exam was going to be cumulative. I wasn't killing myself; it was just how I worked best because if I had gone through the chapter readings ahead of time I wouldn't remember anything. I was sitting at one of the computer tables near the elevators when I heard a loud scream from behind the bookshelves. The noise seemed to be coming from all the way on the opposite side of the first floor of the library. There were a few other students sitting around me on their computers, and everyone paused to look around and see what had happened. I didn't see anyone near the bookshelves, but minutes later I saw a VCU police officer walking in through the main entrance of the library and two VCU police cars parked directly outside the glass window behind the computer stations.

The police had caught a student from behind the shelves and was dragging him out the front door in handcuffs. The guy who was handcuffed kept screaming, "He f*cked my girlfriend. He f*cked my girlfriend." Apparently, a student had caught his best friend and his girlfriend having sex in the library behind the bookshelves. Out of anger, the guy who was arrested by the police punched his best friend, and that's when the rest of us heard the screaming.

What shook me the most wasn't the fact that two students were having sex in the library and got caught. That by now was no shocking news to me. What shook me was that the student who was arrested kept blaming his best friend for having sex with his girlfriend but didn't say a word to the girl.

Honestly though, his girlfriend was having sex with the best friend. It wasn't forced, so it was consensual, which makes it the girl's fault too. If she was faithful to her guy in the first place, why would she ever have sex with her boyfriend's best friend? It was common sense. But it's true that common sense is not that common after all.

Young people make love using the excuse, "Oh, it

happened accidentally," when nothing happens accidentally. Things take conscious effort. Having sex with someone just doesn't happen out of thin air. But when two people want to do something with consent, it takes effort from both sides, so to me the girl was unfaithful to her boyfriend to begin with.

When I left the library, the guy who had been arrested was standing by the police car with a policeman on his side, and he was still screaming, "I won't spare you." But his girl and best friend had already left.

The day my finals ended, Mom came to pick me up. I was going home for winter break, and at this point all I could think about was being home and not stressed out about school. Mom picked me up from Brandt Hall. I didn't bring home much with me: just a suitcase, because I knew I was going to be back on campus in a month anyway for the spring term. While we were leaving Broad Street trying to get on the highway back to Fairfax, Mom drove by Mansion where the lines extended with all VCU students waiting just to get inside the club.

"College kids are so crazy," I said to Mom as I told her about most of my friends partying during their final exams.

"There's something greater waiting out there for you. Maheen, you are going to do everything just at the right time and place and with the right kind of people," Mom said to me.

"I really hope so," I thought to myself. I wanted to be around people that were on the same mental wavelength as me. I guess I just had to wait for my time. But it was hard to think that way. It was hard to wait when you have known for the longest time exactly what you want from life.

After spending New Year's at home, I was back in Richmond for my second semester at VCU. My routine was slightly different this semester because I had been accepted into the School of Arts for my double major in fashion and business. I had switched my major just in case if I had to spend the next three years of my life here as well, at least I wouldn't be dreading my degree.

My advisor at the VCU art school had told me that I had to fulfill my art history requirements. The Art History class was only offered on Tuesdays and Thursdays at 9:30 in the morning, but that was conflicting with my English class with Dr. Walker. VCU had a rule that whoever was your UNIV111 professor, he or she had to be your UNIV112 professor. Out of all my professors I liked Dr. Walker the most, and she loved me too. She didn't want me to leave her class. Technically, I had no choice but to leave her class and register with another professor. But then a few days later I received an email from Dr. Walker saying that she had fought with the Dean to keep me as a student and she had found a space in her 2 pm class even though the section was already full. I was extremely happy to be in Dr. Walker's class, however this meant that I wasn't going to see Bridgette in English class anymore. Thank God Bridgette and I still had math together.

9:30 in the morning I had my "Computers for Fashion" class in the Pollak building. The Pollak building was the actual VCU Arts building that housed all the departments within VCU ARTS. Out of all white cement buildings in front of Cabell Library, the Pollak building was the only red brick building with no windows on the first two floors. The building had two entrances, one from the side near Shafer Dining Hall and the other entrance was on the side towards the main road that opened up towards the Village café where Hannah and I used to go get milkshakes all the time. Each floor of Pollak had faculty offices and classrooms dedicated to a specific program. The first floor was home to the photography department, the second floor was home to the graphic design department, the third floor was home to the interior design department and finally the fourth floor was home to the Fashion design and merchandising department. I had two classes this semester on the fourth floor of Pollak, one of which was "Computers for Fashion." The second class I had on the fourth floor of Pollak was the "Introduction to the Business of Fashion," which was all about the economy of the fashion industry and how fashion plays a role in the economy of the world.

Every morning when I used to walk to my classes, I always had my headphones in and my music blasting loud. Every other college kid listens to music while going to class, but I wasn't just listening to music. I was lost somewhere in my own world, visualizing everything that I wanted in my life. I used to think about New York City, I was walking around Richmond, but I used to visualize myself walking around New York City. One of my fashion professors told me about how one of her students from the past was now working as a fashion photographer in New York and had gotten the opportunity to be one of the photographers for the Met Gala. Of course, my dream wasn't to become a fashion photographer, but I still thought that it was inspiring that someone from a small town like Richmond had gone up to New York and had made a name for herself. Being a recent graduate from a college in Richmond and being at the Met Gala was a big deal. I have always been an obsessive dreamer because I knew that dreams come true. Whatever you believe in will eventually come true. I wanted everything that was unimaginable. I wanted everything I was told I couldn't have, and I wasn't going to settle without attaining all of it. I have never known what it is like to live life without a passion, without dreams. Passion is what keeps you going on in life. I was never the kind of girl who waited for things to happen; I knew I had to make everything happen in my life.

Back in high school, I had tried being realistic. What did it do for me? Nothing. Every time I thought realistically, things never worked out my way. My mind always used to dwell on reasons why something didn't happen rather than making it happen. It almost felt like I was setting myself up to not succeed because I used to limit myself with all the thoughts of why something wouldn't happen. I wasn't even conscious of the fact that my mind had turned negative. In my head I used to think of the worst case possible and my fear of failing would come true. Why? Because instead of following my own voice, I was believing in what other people thought was possible or not possible. This world teaches you that there's only one way to do something, there's only one way to attain something in life, and everyone starts to follow that way. For instance, in high school grades are huge; SAT scores are huge. There is a lot of emphasis on the fact that you need extracurricular activities to get into a good college, and if you don't have those things checked off like a list of to do's, teachers tell you that you will never get into a good college when there isn't only one way to get somewhere or to do something. Why is society so obsessed with conventions? Why are we always told to color inside the lines when we can color the whole page?

I hadn't experienced all of life yet, but there was an important lesson I did learn from my exposure to life thus far. I learned that realism and conventionalism are limiting while delusion is infinite. Limitations breed negative energy because when you focus on limitations your mind will always think of all the ways something cannot happen. But delusion is infinite because delusion believes in reaching the goal. Delusion does not care for how the goal is achieved. Delusion opens all sorts of possibilities, all sorts of ways for something to happen. Delusion works because when you are crazy enough to think about something constantly, your frequency meets the frequency of the universe, and in return your mind attracts whatever it is that you are thinking about. All you must do is believe in your vision. If you are crazy enough to believe in something, you are crazy enough to make it a reality. It's simple. If you want to understand the universe, you need to understand frequency. You, me, everything in this world has a frequency, and the frequency you send out into the universe is the frequency you receive in return. This is how negative thoughts come true because the universe is responding to those negative frequencies. Ever feared something terribly and your biggest fear came true? It's because in your unconscious mind you gave your fears too much attention. You were so worried about fearing your fear that it came in front of you. Therefore, we should always think positive because you never know which thought of yours the universe might respond to. Not everyone will believe in everything you believe in. But that's okay because you don't need anyone else to believe in your vision for it to be real. Your vision is only yours, and all it needs is your attention and belief, no one else's.

I had work study during my second semester at VCU, and I decided to take up a job of an assistant in the economics department at the School of Business building. The Economics Department was located on the sixth floor of Snead Hall, and I had my own little office right outside the program coordinator's office. The program coordinator's name was Ann Nordin, a tall, skinny women with completely grey hair. I directly worked with Ann, and she managed the entire economics department in Snead Hall. I used to work every Tuesday and Friday. My job was to make Excel files for Ann and attend phone calls. I also directly worked with all the economic professors at VCU, so if any professor ever needed photocopies or files I was their go-to person. The Economics department office was in the corner towards the right of the elevators on the fourth floor of Snead Hall. The first desk through the wooden door was my desk, and to my right was

Ann's office. To the left of my desk was Carol's office.

Carol Scotese was an assistant economics professor at VCU. She was the only professor who had an office inside the economics' departmental office. The rest of the thirteen economic professors had their own separate offices across the sixth floor. What I disliked the most about my job was that professors would make me grade exam papers of their students. Some professors would just come up to me with a stack of papers and an answer key sheet for the exams, and I had to grade everything. I hated how the grades of other students were in my hand, and the professors would never even bother to double check the student's paper again.

The rest of the time at work I used to be making Excel sheets. On a slow day at work, I used to work on my transfer essays for colleges in New York. NYU was my top priority, but I was also considering Parson's and FIT just in case NYU didn't work out again. During my workday I was allowed an hour of break, so around 12:30 pm I used to go downstairs to the café located in the lobby of Snead Hall and get myself a sandwich. I would bring the sandwich back to my office and start working again.

I once took a writing workshop at VCU which was taught by a professor named Ms. Mason. The name of the class was "Creative Writing," but ironically, I had no creative freedom in that class whatsoever. Everything I wrote in my workshop class had to be MLA format, double spaced, "critical writing" that had to follow the prompt we were given word by word. In MLA formatted papers one is supposed to put the page number and their last name as the header on each page of writing. In my class every time a student forgot to put their name and page number on EVERY page, Ms. Mason always lowered the student's grade by an entire letter. This was so unfair because in a "creative" class your thoughts and creativity should matter so much more than following standards. In fact, art comes from within; it has no standards. No writer in the world writes to be like that other writer. No painter in the world just wants to be a shadow of another painter. People create art to express themselves, to break norms in society and to express things they cannot say otherwise. By making everything standardized, teachers block our creativity. Ms. Mason's requirements regarding writing reminded me of my high school English classes where all my teachers emphasized that students should know how to write a five paragraph paper with an introduction, three supporting paragraphs and a conclusion. No one ever cared about the content of our papers, which to me was a much more important part of an essay than form. This whole concept of standardizing everything made school more like a burden than something enjoyable. When we are so drowned by the responsibility of meeting a certain set of standards how are we supposed to enjoy learning? Everything became a requirement that we had to just get through rather than learning that can be enjoyable.

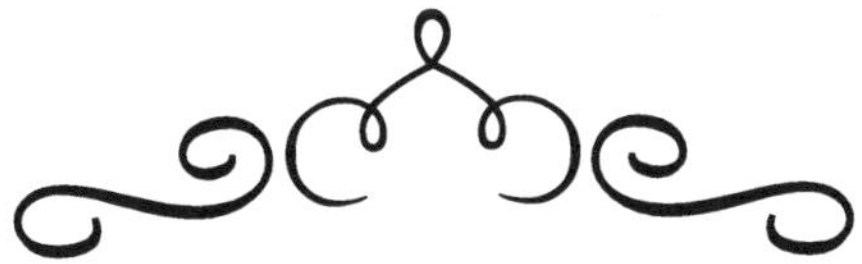

CHAPTER NINETEEN

During the last two months of the semester, the only thing I could think about was New York. Was my dream finally going to come true, or was I to spend all my undergraduate years at Richmond, alongside people who were not on the same mental frequency as I was? The majority of the people who are okay with living an ordinary life by following standards will always tell you what you are trying to do is impossible.

When I mentioned to Hannah that my plan was to transfer to NYU, the first thing she said to me was, "Isn't that school like super hard to get into? It's almost as competitive as Ivy League schools." She paused and then continued, "How are you going to get in? What's your back up plan?"

Of course, the backup plan was VCU and fashion. However, I wasn't the kind of person to rely on my back up plan. I had to make my plan A work. Sure, nothing happens overnight, but just because you fail once doesn't mean you let go of the dream altogether. Backups are needed only when you stop dreaming. Until your dream is alive, there is no such thing as a backup because something may not work now, but it will one day. Nothing in life lasts forever, and that is a good and bad thing at once. In general, most of the world is very realistic, we are expected to be practical all the time. Get a job, something that pays well, and then worry about dreams.

Hannah was only looking at the fact that it was really hard to get into NYU. While that is true, my mind was only focused on getting into NYU. If it was written in my fate to get in, then how hard admissions were or were not didn't matter. But if it was not written in my fate to go to NYU, no power of mine could make that happen. The least I could do was give all my energy into positive thoughts, rather than breeding negativity. The rest was in God's hand. But after God, it's in your hands to make your reality, not anyone else's. And even God can only help you if you know how to help yourself. You cannot sit on your couch day and night dreaming about ruling the world and not do anything to achieve that. Nothing changes by just hoping and doing nothing. But if you have a dream, then you must take the risk to chase it too. Dreaming is not craziness; dreaming is essential to being alive. Sure, dreams don't always work out, but you would never truly know that unless you try. I believed in daydreaming. Those who daydream never lose sight of their goal because they are constantly thinking about whatever it is that they want to achieve. Believe it or not, daydreaming keeps you focused if you are daydreaming while putting in effort into what you want. It's a mutual effort. For as long as I have known myself, I have always been this way. Whatever I want becomes my dominant thought till the time I achieve it. It has always helped me keep my focus in the right place.

Two nights before final exams, Hannah, her group of friends, and I were chilling on the patio outside Brandt Hall. We all sat around one of the black round tables near the sidewalk, talking and enjoying the warm spring weather. Hannah and I were doing our homework while Nick took out his bag of weed brownies. The brownies were bite size and in a zip lock so no one would be suspicious. Nick opened the bag and offered everyone. Everyone took a brownie but me. I just could never stand the smell of weed let alone put that in my body.

I dug my head back into my notes and kept listening and talking as the conversation moved forward. The discussion went from school and life and suddenly it elevated to the topic of relationships. Nick (the same guy who was complaining over the girl who left him after dinner without even having sex with him) began talking about this couple who had apparently made a video about "Saving sex for after marriage."

Nick started talking. "Yo these two girls make videos about how you should save yourself till marriage, and it's effing absurd because what are you supposed to do with the other person till then? Just talk while dating?" he said

Everyone started laughing in agreement with Nick while I just sat there thinking nobody here actually realizes the value of true love. I didn't say anything, but I kept listening to everyone talk.

A while later Nick's friend Josh goes, "Well, if you are not going to have sex with your date, what are you supposed to do? Just stare at them for fucking nine years? I'd rather die" he spoke. Everyone at our table had seem to enjoy the joke but me. I was the only one who sat there thinking no wonder I hadn't dated anyone yet because boys my age were super immature. I thought after high school guys would mature a little, but no. All of this was still the same that I had seen in high school. After looking at the boys around me, I wondered if I ever even did want to date anyone. I would never give my heart away to any boy who was anything like the boys I saw in college. That's like signing yourself up for a heart break or a one night stand, none of which I wanted in my life. Was a real connection too much to ask for in a culture that was obsessed with sexual pleasures? Why couldn't there be a boy who would value you for more than just your body? I wanted to be liked by a boy for my mind and soul, not just my body.

It was already the middle of April, and the semester was ending in two weeks. Yet there was no reply from NYU regarding my application. Slowly I was getting tired of anticipating a decision every day as if it was the only thing that I was looking forward to. People praised NYU for its prestige and fame around the world. To my friends at VCU and everyone who knew I was transferring, NYU was just a name. People saw it for its ranking, especially Pakistani people. Indian and Pakistani people think that the name of a college is everything. If you go to Harvard, automatically your life is made. Sure, going to Harvard opens endless opportunities for you, but simply going to Harvard won't make you successful. If you go to Harvard but spend your day sleeping and never take advantage of opportunities around you, you won't be successful. It's not a name or place that makes you successful, it's how much effort you put into something that makes you successful. To me, NYU wasn't just a prestigious name, a brand, or a number. I did not want to go there because it was one of the top schools in the nation. I wanted to go to NYU because I personally wanted to go there. NYU inspired me artistically. I felt like if I could be there, eventually I could make my dreams real. It was the NYU vibe that attracted me. NYU was a way for me to my dreams. I wanted it to be in New York City. I wanted to be in an environment that inspired me to think big and step away from the little things of daily life and change the world. I no longer wanted to be in an environment where people had no capacity to think beyond frat parties and relationships.

CHAPTER TWENTY

Everyone in this world seems to have their own opinions about what is possible and what isn't, about what is reality and what isn't. But the truth is that there is no universal definition of reality or possibility. Reality and possibility are perceptions that are unique to every single individual. My version of reality will never match your version of reality. My thoughts on what is possible and what isn't will never match yours. This is because reality is a perception that the mind creates depending on what it thinks. If you think that something is impossible, it will be impossible because what you think about something becomes the lens through which you see the world. When you think about how impossible something is, your mind is only focused on reasons why something is impossible, therefore even if possibilities exist your mind will never see them. On the other hand, if you think that whatever you want is possible, you will automatically begin to see ways in which things are possible. This is because your mind is focused on finding ways to make something happen rather than finding excuses why it can't happen. Your life reflects what you are holding in your mind. Whatever your mind believes is what it will see in life. Therefore, when people tell you to think "realistically," don't listen to them. Because you oversee creating your own reality through the thoughts that you hold in your mind. I wish I had realized this back when I was in high school and everything around me seemed negative. But then you don't realize anything until God wants you to realize something. Maybe by going to VCU and kind of going through numerous college rejections and feeling like a failure, everything was supposed to happen this way so that I could realize the things I now did. Maybe coming to VCU was crucial for me to become aware of things I had never thought about before. Because everything in life happens for a reason. The good in your life and the bad, the setbacks and the comebacks all have a reason. We might not know the reason behind something when it happens, but once you come out of it, you know it has to happen. Maybe I had to face hardships in my childhood so I could become the girl I was today. VCU had to happen because God wanted me to learn certain lessons along the way. Or maybe VCU was the lesson that you won't always get what you want in life. Sometimes you must put up with what's in front of you and make the most of it.

Walking on the streets of Richmond, New York was nothing but a dream. I wanted to go there but I didn't know that all the daydreaming I used to do about New York while walking around VCU was going to become my reality. I never knew before how strong your thoughts can be. That's when I realized that by being negative in high school, I wasn't doing a disservice to anyone but to myself, that negative thoughts can only give you negative outcomes, never a positive one. I guess I was so sick and tired of the whole system and the competitive race we are put in since high school to compete for colleges that I took all those failures to heart. I used to always think about the worst of everything without realizing that when I thought negatively about something I'm sending conscious energy to that thing. Energy doesn't care if it's positive or negative; energy only knows to attract energy that vibrates at the same frequency. Therefore, we as people need to be aware of the thoughts that we are thinking and sending out in to the universe because what we send out is what comes back to us. This isn't the only perception out there in the world but once you start believing in this, you will see the magic unfold in your life. If you don't believe in the power of your thoughts, you won't notice how making something your main thought can bring it in your life. This is the power of believing, believing in God and believing in whatever it is that you want in life. Even if you are the only one who believes in something. This is also a way of life; it surely has become my way of life. Life is not as complicated as we make it in our heads.

It's true that nothing in this world can bother us as much as our own uncontrolled thoughts. If you can control your thoughts, you can control your life, and that's probably the biggest lesson life itself has taught me.

In the beginning of May, my first year at VCU ended, and I went back home for the summer.

Just a few days after coming back from college, my parents sent me to London for a solo holiday. Mom and Dad knew how much I wanted to transfer out of VCU, and I was always thinking about that. When you have given everything to something, it's hard to let go of it.

I had always been an all or nothing kind of soul. But when I went to London, I decided to completely forget the expectations I had of getting a "yes" from NYU. I decided to let go. I didn't want to spend every day of my vacation constantly checking my email for a response from NYU. In fact, I even shut my phone off completely and kept it away. Instead, I was using a local Nokia phone that my cousin who I was staying with had given to me. I needed it. I wanted to be present in the moment, enjoying Oxford Street and Central London for the next few days rather than thinking about college. I could figure that out after getting back. So, the next five days of my life in London were spent shopping on Oxford Street, walking around Hyde Park, and touring the State Rooms of the Buckingham Palace.

Honestly, life was tension free and amazing for the time I was away.

Two days after I had come back from my solo trip to London I was sitting on the couch in the living room watching a show on Netflix with my brother. He was more into the show, and I was more invested in browsing my phone. Mom and Emaan were at the gym while my Dad was at work. I had not checked my email since the time I had come from college, so while chilling on the couch, I randomly decided that I was going to check my mail. I logged in to my email on my phone, and the system wasn't logging me in for some reason. Ehsan was still watching Netflix, and I went upstairs to open my email on my laptop. I logged into my email, and I couldn't believe what I was looking at.

The first email in my inbox was from NYU. It read, "Congratulations, Maheen. We are delighted to inform you that you have been accepted into New York University."

I froze completely, my pupils enlarged, staring at my computer screen, and my fingers didn't move from the mouse pad. For a second, I couldn't believe my eyes. I had no idea if this was all a dream or reality. I blinked my eyes and looked at the screen again, just to make sure that I hadn't read anything wrong. Out of pure happiness and excitement I began yelling Ehsan's name, and he came running upstairs to me.

"What happened?" he asked as he entered my room. I was so excited and filled with happiness, I jumped on Ehsan and hugged him super tight for the longest time. Ehsan looked at me like, "What the hell is she doing?" Brothers love you but they do not like hugs, but I was so happy I didn't let go of him for the longest time. "What happened?" he asked me, as he still didn't know why I was so affectionate suddenly.

"I got into NYU," I told him with a huge smile.

"You are kidding me, right?" he said calmly.

"No, I am not. Look," I said, bringing the laptop closer to Ehsan so he could read the email himself.

"Damn this actually happened," Ehsan screamed with excitement. I was blank in shock. I was so happy I didn't know how to respond. I started crying.

"Silly girl, why are you crying? Let's go tell Mom and Dad," Ehsan said.

Ehsan and I first told Dad over the phone about getting in to NYU, but Dad thought I was joking with him. NYU is almost every South Asian parent's dream for their child. The moment was so surreal for all of us that it was hard to believe right away. For my parents, I was the first child in the Mazhar family who was going to be attending a highly prestigious American university. For me, this was proof that dreams do in fact come true. NYU was all I had ever thought about while at VCU, and now my dream was standing in front of me, not as a dream but in the form of my very own reality. I still couldn't believe that I had finally done it. Next, I called Mom and she was like, "No, this can't be true."

"It is," I smilingly said to her on the phone. None of us could believe it. This had always been the dream, and it was hard to believe that what was only in my thoughts till yesterday had become my reality today.

When Mom and Dad came home at night and I showed them the actual email, that's when it really hit them that I had got in to NYU. Dad was more excited about me going to NYU then even I was. Not once did my parents think about the money or tell me that NYU is too expensive. My parents weren't filthy rich; they always gave me what I wanted but also taught Ehsan and I to value things in life. NYU's tuition was expensive as hell, but not once did my Dad say, "No you are not going there. Save money." He supported me more for NYU than he had ever even supported me for VCU.

From the next day Dad sat down with me to plan out my whole degree. Mom, Dad, and I went to the local coffee shop near my house, sat down and discussed school. Then dad started looking for apartments for me in New York. He was more excited about this new NYU chapter more than any one of us in the family.

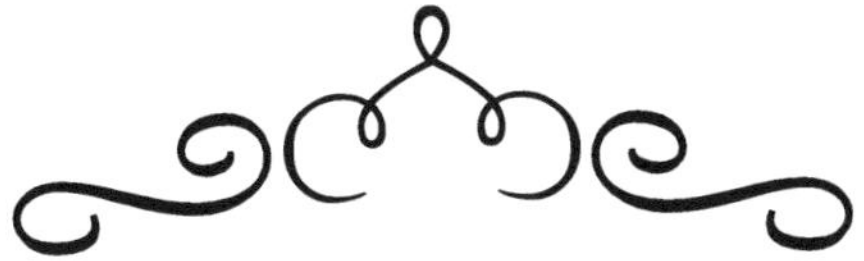

CHAPTER TWENTY-ONE

The summer that I got into NYU, Dad was working for a firm called FTI Consulting, and his project was moved to the company's New York office. While I was getting ready to go to school in the city of dreams, my dad had started travelling to New York on the weekdays to attend meetings. Both of our destinies led us back to New York. In the middle of August, my parents, grandparents, and I all went to New York City so I could see the NYU campus and register for classes.

On our way to New York City from Virginia, we stopped in Jersey City to meet one of my grandparents' old family friends who lived in New Brunswick. We reached my grandfather's friend's house around 7 pm, and though we had only stopped to say hi, the family insisted that we stay for dinner. When I went inside the house, there were so many older desi (South Asian) aunties and uncles sitting in the living room, and all their kids were in their late twenties and married. I didn't know anyone's name, so I just kept saying hi to everyone I saw out of respect. When dinner was served, all the adults sat at the main dining table, which was placed right next to the kitchen. All the kids sat around the square table which was placed in the living room. I was sitting at the dining table eating dinner; Mom was sitting on the chair next to me feeding Emaan. Suddenly an aunty in a white beaded Shalwar kameez and hair pulled back in a small ponytail came and sat down next to me. She was probably Dadi's age.

"Maheen, this is Aunty Zara. She was your dad's fifth grade teacher," Mom said, introducing her to me.

"Oh nice," I said, hugging Aunty Zara out of respect.

Aunty Zara sat herself on the chair next to me and started talking. "Your dad was the best student I ever had in my teaching career. He would memorize a speech on the spot and recite it in the class so perfectly," Aunty Zara said to me smilingly. She went on for the next fifteen minutes talking about all of Dad's accomplishments. Aunty Zara seemed so fond of my father it felt good to hear. I always knew Dad was really passionate about education. He always wanted to be the best at everything.

I was eating while talking to Aunty Zara, and suddenly she threw the question at me: "You are all grown up now Mashallah. What are you doing with your life, beta (child)?" She stared at me without even blinking for the longest time. Her eyes were literally scanning me like every desi aunty who scans a young girl for a rishta.

"I am studying fashion and business, and I just got into NYU," I replied to her question as I took another bite of the chicken that was on my plate. Aunty Zara suddenly went quiet for a few minutes. I didn't know what to make of it, so I started playing with Emaan.

Then suddenly, Aunty Zara spoke up again. "Beta, that's ok but at the end of the day you are a girl. You need to keep in mind that one day you will have a family and you will be married, so you need to take care of your house and your husband, which is your top priority. So don't you think your fashion career will affect your other responsibilities in the future?" she said, looking directly into my eyes. I paused as if someone had told me to freeze.

The food in my mouth wasn't chewable anymore, and if I made eye contact with the woman my anger would be evident.

"I am just saying, you are really pretty and may you find a handsome man, but he will be your priority then, not your career," Aunty Zara added as if this was the icing on the cake that was missing from what she had already said to me. Aunty Zara kept looking at me like she was waiting for me to agree with her, but I was so shocked by her words I didn't know how to respond. Then she continued, "What if you are not able to give time to your home? Keep that in mind while choosing a career, after all, you are a girl," she had the audacity to say to me.

My face had turned red with the anger that was burning inside me. My blood boiled hearing all those words, but what could I do? I looked at my mom, who winked at me, giving me the hint to just stay silent. What else could I have done anyway? Aunty Zara was much older than me, and she was someone my family knew, so I had to remain quiet and pretend like I understood everything that she had been saying to me.

A minute later, Aunty Zara's sister called her into the kitchen and Aunty Zara got up from the table. I took a sigh of relief. Before Aunty Zara left, she said one last thing to me. "May every girl have a great destiny," and that it was it.

I couldn't take it anymore. When Aunty Zara had gone into the kitchen, I got up and went outside to walk around a bit on the street.

I wasn't against marriage. Of course seeing Mom and Dad so deeply in love even after so many years of being together was beautiful. I believed in marriage, but I had my own views about it. Why was it that in the South Asian culture the woman was always asked or expected to sacrifice her life, her career, her dreams, her everything for the sake of starting a family? Yet men were not expected to change anything. Why is it that when a girl is getting married, she is told that now it's her responsibility to take care of her marriage and sacrifice her everything to build a home with another person. Why don't we say the same things to the man when marriage isn't a one-sided thing. Marriage is a fifty-fifty partnership; then why don't we also tell the guy that he must learn to adjust and to sacrifice for his partner too? That's the one thing I hated about my own culture. Why aren't Desi guys told to change themselves or adjust their lifestyles for a girl? If a girl is expected to change herself, the guy should be willing to change himself too. Why does our desi society put all the pressure on the girl? This phenomenon is extremely common in the South Asian culture where marriage is considered only a girl's responsibility. If you tell an American guy, they got shocked at the fact that women are treated differently in countries like Pakistan because in America the guy and the girl both take responsibility to make the marriage work. But what to do? I never found white boys attractive.

In Pakistan and in the South Asian culture, marriage is seen like the ultimate achievement that should be the goal of every girl. You can be famous or hold a PhD and doing extremely well in your career, but if you are a girl and you are not married, our society considers you of no value. It's the bitter truth. Once a girl is married, it is solely her responsibility to take care of her home. Women and men are both created by God; they complete each other. When did God say that men are superior, and women are weaker? Just because women have the power to give birth, we have formed this notion in our heads that their sole responsibility is to take care of the family. If a woman can bring life on earth, there's nothing that she can't do, and God made her so strong, so who are we as people to consider her weak just because of her gender. The Americans wanted me to sleep with every guy I went to class with. The Pakistanis wanted to marry me off to a person I had never met? Is that what being a woman in this century amounted to?

Just the way that aunty in the house was giving me marriage advice at the age of eighteen, I had heard stories of people discussing other people's marriages all the time. Whenever a marriage doesn't work in the South Asian society, people automatically started blaming the girl. "The wife must compromise. Oh, it's her fault for not paying attention to her home." What people don't realize is that marriage isn't just a compromise; it's not supposed to be a suffering or a burdening responsibility. Sure, there are ups and down in every relationship. Sure, compromise is a huge part of any relationship that involves love. Parents compromise so much for their children; that's out of love too. But in a marriage, Pakistani people think that the girl should be the only one to compromise, and the guy deserves to live his life however he pleases.

I didn't agree with how obsessed my own culture was with marriage. We think that by a certain age, like twenty-five or twenty-six, a guy and a girl should be married or else the so called "age" to get married eventually passes away. I disagreed with that. There is no age to get married, if someone is meant to be with you and wants to genuinely spend the rest of their life with you, you will find them at any age. There is no time limit on such things. It's ironic to me how we as Muslims believe that God has created us in pairs and that eventually whoever is meant for you ends up coming into your life. But at the same time, we as Pakistanis are so obsessed with the idea of marriage that as soon as we see a young guy or a girl of marriage we start matching them for potential marriage alliances. Where does our belief in God go then? Is our belief in God and his timing that weak? Or are we just hypocritical with our own values? It's just something I have always wondered. If as a believer of God, it is our faith that he has created someone for each one of us and his plan for our life unfolds little by little, why don't we just leave our trust in him and live our lives carefree? Why are both the Eastern and Western Cultures so obsessed with the idea of having a significant other in life? When it's meant to happen, it will happen, but why should you waste your time thinking about such things when you have a life to build in front of you. In Pakistan, elders and society pressure you to find a significant other. In America, the dating culture pressures you to find a partner because apparently being single is boring. I disagreed with both.

As a girl, it's not my priority to consciously choose my career according to my gender. I chose my career according to my ambitions and my dreams, nothing else. If someone is meant to be my partner in life, they will accept me the way I am and rather than asking me to compromise my life. They will respect my thinking, and if they don't, then my life won't stop for them. I didn't come this far in life only to come this far in life. If I had to sacrifice being in a relationship for my dreams, then I was more than willing to sacrifice a relationship I hadn't even made yet. Because I knew that if someone was truly made for me, he would accept me for what I am, not change me into who I am not.

There is a saying in Urdu that bothered me a lot the way desi aunties used it. "Allah har ladki ke naseeb ache karey," which means, "May God create a beautiful destiny for every girl."

Although, the literal translation of these words had a beautiful meaning, I hated the way Pakistani people and society used this phrase only when it came to marriage. The Pakistani society used this phrase to mean that may you find a husband that takes care of you and doesn't put you through misery. This annoyed me because "naseeb achhe karey" is such a pure and beautiful saying for anyone, not just a girl. May God create a beautiful destiny for all the guys out there too. Everyone deserves a beautiful destiny. It just pissed me off when this phrase was only used for a girl and never for a guy. The phrase is almost always used in the sense that the girl must leave her house and start a family, so may she find a man who takes care of her. That part didn't bother me as much as the belief in South Asian societies that once a girl is married her destiny is in her husband's hands. No, it's not. No one's destiny is in the hands of any human being. Your destiny is in God's hands and then in your hands. There were certain Pakistani values that I held extremely close to my heart. However, no way did I agree with everything in my culture. There were certain things that always went over my head, and I found them so weird because I had never seen them exist in my family.

I was standing on the porch near the black SUV van lost in my thoughts and still full of anger after what had happened inside.

Ehsan came outside to call me. "Hey, we are leaving. Come say bye to everyone," he said, standing half in and half out of the main door. I went inside to say goodbye to everyone and then came back outside to get in the car.

On our way to New York, Mom said to me, "I hope you are not thinking too much about what Aunty Zara said."

"What did she say?" Dad asked curiously, and I repeated the entire story for him.

"It's sad that people still think this way. She shouldn't have said that to you, but I am glad you didn't say anything in front of her out of respect," Dad said as we were driving into the Lincoln Tunnel.

"Hmm," I answered.

"Pakistan is a male dominant society beta, what else can I say? It's unfortunate but it's true," Dad said. He was right about that. Pakistan was a male dominated society, and all the rules in society were made according to what suited men. I was Pakistani, and I respected my own country very deeply, but I had so much resentment towards Pakistani societies and their way of treating women. It irked me that a woman's value in Pakistan always came from her relationships with others rather than herself. Your value doesn't come from your brother, your boyfriend, your husband, or from any other male in your life, but sadly that's what girls in Pakistan are taught: your value doesn't come from yourself but rather from your relationships to others. We as Pakistanis expect women to be obedient daughters, caring sisters, obedient wives, and dedicated mothers, which are all important. However, how come we don't teach her that she needs to find and love herself before being defined by her relationships? You need to be happy in your own skin before making your relatives happy. In Pakistan, a woman can't live for herself because society engraves in her mind at a young age that she needs to live her life according to others and not according to herself. I had nothing personal against the aunty that I came across at dinner, but she was the ideal example of typical Pakistani society, telling me to think about what my husband would feel or think about my career even though, ironically, I didn't even have a husband yet, nor had I ever thought of marriage either. But no, as a Pakistani girl I was expected to think about these things, but if that woman was talking to my brother, she would never say, "Oh, what is your future wife going to think of your career?" She would just let him be because in Pakistan, we don't question men, nor do we tell them to change themselves for anyone. But not in my life. I was a Pakistani girl and with all the boldness and courage in me, here I was. I was who I was and no, I was never changing myself for a man, period.

"Stop thinking about it now. Focus on New York. What you wanted is finally happening, right?" Mom said. I had only been quiet for the past few minutes, and somehow Mom knew exactly what was going on in my head.

No matter how much I thank God for choosing Mom and Dad as my parents, it will never be enough. My parents were nothing like typical Pakistani parents; they were my backbone because without them, I wouldn't be me. No wonder we don't get to choose our family. God choses them for us because he knows what we need more than we do. I could have been born in any family in Pakistan, and life could have been completely different. When I was younger, I thought everyone's family was like mine, so I used to take my parents for granted. The older I got, the more I understood the world and society. I realized that my parents were the biggest blessing and gift that God had given to me. Mom was right; my dream of coming to NYC was finally becoming a reality, and this was more important than anything else. When my parents supported me, I wasn't answerable to anyone else in the world. I had come to this city a billion times before in my life, yet this time something was different. When we got out of the Lincoln Tunnel, Dad took a left onto 9th Avenue, and we drove towards the Empire State building, which was shining brighter than ever as if it were the crown of this beautiful city. This wasn't the first time I had come to this city, but for some reason everything seemed so different, so new. Maybe because something within me was new. For the first time New York didn't feel like a distant dream anymore that only existed in my head. New York was my reality. I wasn't just here to admire Times Square and leave this time. I was finally here to live, breathe, and dream in this city. I gazed at the tall skyscrapers around. The closer we got to Times Square, the bright lights began to flash in my eyes like dreams that were coming alive. The lights, the city, everything felt like mine, as if I belonged here, and the light was representing my future. As if the city was somehow connected to my soul, it was everything I had ever taught or focused on. My eyes couldn't believe that I was living my dream. A dream that I had seen with eyes wide open stood in front of me as my life's biggest reality covered in colorful lights.

Dad pulled into the valet parking of the Westin at 42nd Street, where we were staying for the time I had come to NYU for orientation. The valet man in the black shirt took the keys from dad and all of us got out of the car. I stepped outside the car. While Dada, Dadi, Ehsan and Mom were getting their bags out of the car, I walked out onto 42nd Street to admire the Times Square area. I had come to Times Square a billion times in my life before, but the most beautiful thing about this place was that it never grew old. Every time I saw Times Square, it never felt like I had already seen this sight before. The entire world could be asleep, but the lights of Times Square never dimmed. No matter what time of the day it was, the streets around Times Square were always filled with people. People walking around, shopping, eating, talking on the phone, speaking in different languages, sitting on benches, and admiring the lights. I don't know why or how, but in this one place it felt like anything and everything was possible. I stood near Hard Rock Café on 42nd Street and just stared at the Times Square area in complete awe. The glittering lights of Times Square, the 42nd Street NYPD police station, the rush, the people, the noise, the sirens, and honks of the yellow cabs on the road. I was observing everything and taking it in. I noticed the neon red and blue "BROADWAY" sign right on top of the Forever 21 store. There were bright screens everywhere lit up with ads. Even the night seemed like daytime in Times Square. The famous red steps of Times Square were filled with people taking selfies and just sitting on the steps admiring the area. It was close to the end of summer, but it felt as if the entire world was on the streets of Times Square. Even in the rush of thousands of people, I felt so much closer and more connected to my own soul and my own purpose more than anything. People usually get lost in the crowd, and in the crowd of thousands I had found myself. I walked up the red steps and stood in the middle, staring at the people around me, then at the Times Square display, I was inhaling gratitude in each breath but also trying to believe that all this is real. Words will never be enough to describe what I felt standing in the middle of Times Square that day, but it was the most magical moment of my life. I always believed in dreams, but this was my first moment in life where I had experienced something that I had only imagined come in front of my eyes as my very own reality. My thoughts had manifested in my life as my very own reality, and I didn't know how to get over this. This was my moment, my reality. I could finally own it. This was my affirmation that what you hold in your mind is what you get to hold in your life.

I could have stood there on the steps all night, but our bags were checked in and Ehsan came to get me. "Let's go," he said, and the two of us started walking to our hotel.

The Westin @ Times Square was huge. There was a Mexican restaurant called Chui's and an AMC theater attached to the hotel. Directly across the hotel was a Starbucks, and next to the Starbucks was the Sephora store all lit up by the screens of Times Square. A block away from the hotel was the 42nd Street Subway all packed with people constantly walking in and out of the glass door station entrance. The sidewalks were packed with people constantly walking down for miles. Everything felt so full of life. The smell of sweet roasted peanuts from the "Nuts4Nuts" stand right by our hotel was probably the biggest symbol to me that I was in New York. That was my favorite smell of the city.

I got inside the hotel, and all of us took the elevator up to the fortieth floor where our rooms were. Everyone had their own rooms, and they were located right next to each other on the fortieth floor. Dada and Dadi took the first room, Mom and Dad took the second room, and Ehsan and I took the third room. After each of us had settled into our rooms, my entire family gathered in Dada and Dadi's room for dinner. Dad got the food delivered because everyone was exhausted after a long day of traveling and meeting relatives. I wasn't tired. There was a weird rush of energy within me. I felt this rush of energy in my veins telling me, "Maheen, if you can make it big here, you can make it big anywhere and everywhere."

Around midnight, after eating dinner with the family, I said goodbye to everyone. I went in my room with Ehsan, and we chatted about life for the longest time. Ehsan and I were best friends now. He was all grown up now and he understood me. We fought, but not like the way we used to like kids. After talking for an hour, Ehsan fell asleep on the other side of the room, and I laid on my bed thinking about everything.

Whatever is meant for you comes to you no matter what. It comes to you even if it's hiding under a mountain and seems impossible to attain. However, it never comes to you when you want it the most but when it's the right time for it to come to you. There is the plan that we create for our lives. Then there is the plan that God creates for our lives, and the plan we have made for ourselves does not necessarily match the plan that God has made for us. We can hope for something and work hard for it, but in the end, everything happens according to God's plan, not ours. Therefore, even when we try our best and give our all to things, sometimes things still don't work out because it's not in our hands to make things work. The only thing that's in our hands is effort; the rest is in God's hands. When things in life weren't working out for me even though I gave them my all, I started believing that maybe hard work does not always pay off. This is the wrong attitude to have because it makes you not want to put any more effort into anything. It makes you think that even when you work your hardest, things will never go your way, just like how things never went my way in high school even though I was doing everything I was supposed to be. You have to stop putting the blame on yourself or your hard work. The truth is, hard work always pays off, you just have to keep chasing what you want in life despite all the setbacks. Without constant effort, nothing works out in this world and nothing in life ever comes to you before it's time for it. There is a time and reason for everything. All the experiences in life all have a reason. You go through things to come out better.

Once you have given something your all, you need to learn to leave everything else to God. We can decide our dreams, but we don't have the power to decide the exact time of when those dreams come true in life. Everything in life has a time, and nothing happens before it's time.

My dreams of coming to New York failed a year ago, not because I didn't work hard enough for it, but because that wasn't the right time for this to happen in my life. This was the right time, and maybe if I did come to New York last year I would not have had the appreciation I had for it now. I wouldn't have realized the things I now did, and I wouldn't have had the appreciation for life that I had now. All the wait and the hard work paid off in a way I never even dreamed of. I had dreamed about it, but I never knew that when that dream will manifest into reality it would be even more beautiful than what I had imagined it to be. When you get something really easily in life, you don't really value it compared to something that you gained after working day and night for it.

The one year at VCU taught me patience and gratitude: Being grateful for what's in front of you, because without being grateful for what's in front of you, you cannot appreciate what's to come. More than anything, life is about perspective; it's only as good as the thoughts you hold in your mind. You can dwell on your failures and let them bother you or appreciate what they have taught you. You can choose to be negative in life or positive, and I had chosen positivity for myself because I had finally realized that your circumstances in life cannot bother you as much as your thoughts do. Circumstances aren't often as bad as we make them in our head, and then we start a battle in our minds with ourselves.

When you teach yourself to live through anything, you come out so much stronger. I was filled with gratitude for all the roadblocks that came in my way because they led me to growth. I was no longer the person I used to be. Learning the meaning of gratitude would never have been possible without setbacks in life. A life without struggles and challenges is boring. Without struggle, any kind of struggle, you have no story to tell the world later. So rather than feeling bad about your struggles, be grateful for them. Be grateful for every setback because it has made you the person that you are today. Without the struggle, you would have never experienced the personal growth you gained by going through what you had to go through. Life is too damn beautiful to waste it thinking negatively about the past and complaining about an experience. Life is meant to be celebrated every single day, and nothing made me happier than this very moment that I was living in this very second of my life. I couldn't believe I was finally in the city of my dreams.

The next morning when I woke up, I walked to the hotel room window and stood there for a good twenty minutes staring at the tip of the Empire State Building from the window, and right behind the Empire State Building was the view of the Chrysler building. Looking at how breathtakingly gorgeous the view in front of me was, I became lost in my own sea of thoughts. Life is only as good as your mindset, and whatever you hold in your mind is what you hold in your life. Life is what we make of it. Maybe this is what gratitude was about, and I was finally realizing it like never before. Standing there by the window, I couldn't help but think how beautiful life becomes when the true value of gratitude teaches you to be happy with whatever is already yours. When you focus on what you have instead of what you don't have, your mind comes to a state of satisfaction; you become happy with life. Your mind begins to find its happiness in the smallest things in life. If you keep telling your mind that what you are and what you already have is not enough, your mind will always want more. Real happiness lies in appreciating and being grateful for how far you have already come. In this very moment, I couldn't have wanted anything more in life. There's no end to wanting more; you could be a millionaire and still want more money. This is exactly why despite having everything, people are still unhappy with life. It's because they do not realize the power of gratitude. The same $10 bill that a billionaire can drop on the floor like it's a penny can buy a beggar a full one time meal. It's all the perspective in life. What you are doing and what you have is enough if you think it's enough. Otherwise, you can have everything, but without gratitude your mind will still urge you for more. It's great to keep running in life, after a goal, a dream, a passion. I had infinite dreams that I needed to work on still. But I realized that it's necessary to stop in life and admire the moment I was in.

We as humans tend to either live in the past or the future, but we forget that where we are is all we truly have. I didn't care about the past anymore, nor was I worried about the future. I wanted to live this moment in every breath of mine. Once a dream is achieved, it is also important to stop, look around and appreciate how far you have come. The past is gone, and no one truly knows what the future holds. But as long as you live today to the best of your abilities, your tomorrow will automatically take care of itself. When something becomes your dominant thought, it makes its way into your life. The universe realigns itself to make your vision a reality. When you make something your dominant thought, you are consciously sending energy towards it, hence, attracting it towards you. Whatever energy you send out into the universe is the energy you receive back. Even if something seems impossible in each moment, when you make it the dominant thought in your mind, you will start to see ways in which it will become possible. Don't believe anyone when they say something is impossible because they are only speaking from their perspective. The truth is, whatever you believe in will be true for you, so build your life thinking about the things you want and believe in. Don't pay attention to what the world sees as possible or impossible. If I paid attention to my failures or what people told me I am capable of or not, I would have never made it so far.

My dreams would have ended the first time I got rejected by NYU, and if I had paid attention to all the people who told me I would never get into NYU because it's too competitive or out of the league, I would have still been stuck in Richmond and never followed my heart. My path wasn't conventional, but it didn't need to be either. We live in a world where we are taught to do everything a certain, be a certain way since childhood. There are standards already set for everything in this world, and we are trained to follow those standards. But the truth is there isn't only one way in life to achieve something or get somewhere.

I had my morning coffee, got ready and took my brother out on a walk with me around Times Square, and then we were to head to NYU. As I walked from the hotel to the 42nd street Subway station with Ehsan, I couldn't help but notice how beautiful everything around me was. The rush of people crowding the streets, walking like there is no one else in the world but them, the energy, the determination to keep going and never wanting to stop in life. New Yorkers are like that. They walk with a purpose and never want to be stopped. I admired that passion of knowing exactly what you want in life and never wanting to be stopped. That's exactly what I had been wanting from my life all along. I always believed in chasing dreams more than people or anything else in life.

"You know what, let's dump the Subway and walk all the

way to the Freedom Tower," I said to Ehsan as we were walking down the Subway escalator.

He looked at me as if I were an alien who landed on earth. "You crazy? I am not doing it. We are taking the subway," he said.

I sighed. "Fine, but we are only taking it halfway," I said.

Ehsan agreed, thinking I would change my mind, but no. I had always wanted to explore New York completely on foot so I could admire even the little things about this magical city. Ehsan and I took the R train from 42nd Street and got off four stops later at "Union Square Station" since it was close to NYU. Ehsan was starving, so we stopped at Max Brenner's Chocolate Café to get lunch. The hot chocolate at Max Brenner was divine but the food was alright. We quickly finished our lunch and continued with our walk. Max Brenner was on 14th Street, and the NYU Campus began on 8th Street, so we started walking towards downtown with the view of the Empire State Building behind us and the Freedom Tower in sight ahead of us. Ehsan was least interested in looking at the campus buildings, and I had to come back to campus for orientation anyway, so we just saw the NYU buildings from a distance while walking down on Broadway. The campus was very much part of the city, so even if you didn't go inside the NYU buildings, you saw all of them while walking down Broadway towards the branded shops in Soho.

The walk to the Freedom Tower was a straight walk down Broadway, crossing all the designer shops till we got to Vesey Street. The most amazing thing about New York was that you don't need a bus or a car or taxi to go everywhere around the city. Your own two feet are all you need to get you anywhere, just got a build some enthusiasm. I was beyond excited. I didn't even care how far I had to walk. I just wanted to live every second of this. I noticed each and every building I crossed, and I couldn't stop thinking about how magical New York City was. An island that ran the world that could make any human's dreams come true. An island that had more opportunities than there are in most countries in the world, that too in every and any field that one could name. People my age thought that partying or smoking or drinking was fun, but honestly this to me was a lot more fun than a college frat party. This was an experience that made my soul feel good, rather than a frat party which would only give me superficial pleasure, and that too one that would only last a few hours. To me, this walk was fun. The feeling in my soul while walking around the city of my dreams was one that I couldn't describe in words. Life is not just about one thing or the other, life is actually about the experiences that change something inside you forever. Life is all about experiencing new things, just sitting at a house party or dancing at a club cannot give you the satisfaction experiences like this can. At least that was my thinking. It's not about what you do or how much you do of it. It's all about what moves your soul. We tend to get so caught up in doing things that are considered social norms like going to parties, etc., we barely notice what our soul craves. I had just started realizing that life does not lie in things that we think of as fun or lively. Life lies in the small things that transform our soul in a way. Somewhere in our subconscious minds, we are aware of what our soul wants versus worldly things, but what you feel or realize only comes from how deeply connected you are to the voice with in you. Often times we prioritize what the world is telling us to do, and we forget to hear our own inner voice. It's important to be aware of the voice inside you and listen to what it's calling for. One should always run after the things in life that make your soul feel good.

After a thirty-minute walk, Ehsan and I finally reached the area of One World Trade Center. The Freedom Tower was massive, shining right above us with the end of the building completely lost in the clouds somewhere. Ehsan and I stood directly underneath the massive skyscraper, admiring its height and catching our breaths. We took a selfie in which we couldn't even get the entire building in the camera because we were standing so close too. I kneeled all the way down to the ground and angled my phone upwards to get the entire building in the picture.

Then Ehsan and I walked around a bit.

"I hate you," Ehsan said.

"I love you too," I said. That's another thing about brothers: they love you but will only verbally say it once a year when it's your birthday or theirs, yet their actions tell you that they love you. On our way back to the hotel we took the Subway because Ehsan would have killed me otherwise for making him walk the entire city in one day. I don't know about Ehsan, but the adrenaline rush in my veins was surreal. I felt so alive as if life truly lie in enjoying these small moments rather than dwelling on other materialistic gains.

For the next two days, Dada, Dadi, Mom, Dad, Ehsan and Emaan all stayed in New York with me, touring the campus and just enjoying NYC because Dada and Dadi loved the city. I have never believed in showing off anything to the world. If I did something in life, it was only because I wanted to do that thing. I have always listened to my heart, and whatever I do my heart always has to be in it. I didn't come to NYU for the name, though that was one reason why my parents were proud, and I wanted to give them that moment. However, I didn't come to NYU for the name or the prestige, I came to NYU because it was the one school that made me feel like I could be anything I wanted to be here. The energy, the vibe, and the level of creativity at NYU was unmatched by any place in the world. You can ask anyone who ever went to NYU, and they would say the same thing. However, when my mom posted a picture of my parents hugging me in front of an NYU flag on Facebook, her entire Pakistani friends community on Facebook saw the pictures and began commenting beneath my mom's post about how prestigious NYU was and how well known the school was. I knew NYU's value for its name, but that's not why I went there. It's sad to me how we as a society or as a Pakistani society must make everything about status and name without counting someone's actual emotions. Yes, someone can be happy going to NYU, but someone else in the world can also be happy by going to community or a state college. Why don't we celebrate them in society equally as well?

Success has a different meaning for everyone. There is no one-fit-all definition of success. Of course I was proud of myself, but I didn't do this for people's approval or to tell anyone that I was better than them. I was here for myself. It made my parents happy, and I respected that but I wasn't about posting my accomplishments on Facebook for the world because not everyone is ever genuinely happy for you. Pakistani people are obsessed with showing off their lives to others, like, "Oh, this is the car I drive. This is the house I live in," and people do nothing but judge them. I couldn't take my parents' joy of posting this accomplishment away from them, however, I hated how suddenly people who never cared about my life before were suddenly commenting on my picture with statements like "So proud of her." My parents were proud of me. Their emotions were real because they raised me. They are my real family. They had seen my journey, but how can a random stranger who I met only once in my life be proud of me? That seemed a little fake to me. I could never stand superficiality of any kind in my life. If someone or something in life didn't feel genuine to me, I never wanted it, and it's true that your parents are the one relationship in the world that will always be sincere to you no matter what. The happiness your parents can feel for you, no other human in the world can, no matter how much they say they can.

On our third day in the city, Dada, Dadi, Ehsan, Mama, and Emaan went back to Virginia. Dad and I were the only ones left in New York, and I had to share a room with him until I could move into my dorm at NYU, which wasn't assigned to me yet. Since I was a transfer student and transfer students were not guaranteed housing on campus, I was on the waiting list. Dad and I were going to live together until my housing was going to be assigned to me.

I always had the best time when Dad and I were together. The most interesting part was that life had put us both together in the same place for two different purposes. He was in New York for his dream job and living the Corporate America life, and I was here to pursue my dreams. During the same week my dad took me to 6th Avenue and 53rd street to show me the office building where he first started off when he came to America back in 2001. It was amazing to me how life had come around full circle. But the motive behind why we were standing where we were standing had completely changed. Same city, same place, but the circumstances had completely changed. Initially, my dad came here for our family; he came here for me. Fifteen years later, I was standing in the same spot, about to start my own life.

A day later I was having lunch with dad at a Thai restaurant on Sullivan Street near NYU. I literally dug into my food without looking left or right. Soon, my phone buzzed when I received an email on my phone that my housing was approved.

The next day I took out my luggage from our hotel in Times Square, and Dad helped me move into the Affinia Hotel on 7th Avenue, directly across from Madison Square Garden and Penn Station. NYU had connections with the Affinia hotel, so whenever there weren't enough dorms to accommodate all incoming students right away, NYU made them stay at Affinia and charged us as if we were staying in a dorm. I wasn't complaining at all about the fact that I didn't get a dorm right away. Living on Fashion Avenue while going to school in downtown and having housekeeping and room service as a college student, that's every student's dream.

I moved into Affinia during the first week of September, which was also Fashion week in New York City. The day I moved into the hotel, the designer Phillip Lim had his show in the ballroom of the hotel. Unfortunately, I didn't get to see the show because I was attending Welcome Week at NYU, but I saw all the paparazzi getting ready to take pictures and all the interns who were setting up for the show.

Dad had moved me in, but I wasn't living alone. The hotel room that I was in had two twin beds and a mini lounge in the middle, so I was sharing the room with another NYU student. Her name was Carrie. She was Chinese and a junior at NYU studying psychology. Getting along with Carrie was the easiest thing in the world. The day I moved in, Carrie and I started talking right away. There was no awkwardness or fakeness. We spoke for hours, and it didn't even feel like we had just met each other. Carrie told me about how she couldn't decide whether she should stick to Psychology or change her major to Art History. The problem was that Carrie didn't know how to talk to her parents about pursuing Art because Psychology was a much more "practical field," and it would lead her to a well-paying job. That night I ended up giving Carrie an entire lecture on how she should follow her heart. There is no way you can ever be successful by doing something that your heart and soul aren't even in. Life is too short to do something you don't love doing. Every individual in this world has dreams, goals, and a passion for something different. When there is some kind of problem or struggle in life, of course anyone would do anything to get through struggle, and no job is big or small. But when you are blessed with the opportunity to be able to do something that you love, why not do it? It's a blessing to even get the opportunity to do what your heart desires, then why waste it because of the fear of society not considering your dream "realistic enough"? Chasing success doesn't really make you successful, but if you love what you do, success will always come to you, and that goes for anything and everything in life. You can't say that you are going to leave a dream because you are afraid of failing. You can't fear something just because the path is unconventional. There is no guarantee of anything in life honestly. You can be a stockbroker on Wall Street and be living the lavish life, but then one day you lose your job because the market crashed. When it comes to unconventional fields or artistic fields where a certain level of stability isn't always guaranteed, why do people start looking down upon it? If one was to look at everything through the lens of stability, then nothing in life stays the same. Then life itself is a gamble. You are not always guaranteed sunny days; you must live through the storms too. Life is unpredictable. You don't know what can or cannot work out unless you try, then why not gamble on what you like instead of what someone else chooses for you? Choose your passion. Do what you love to do because even if you fail, you will be so in love with your passion that you will get back up and try again. And until you have the courage to try again, you will never lose. Eventually even the universe falls in love with a heart that never gives up and a soul that never loses its fire despite what life throws at you.

CHAPTER TWENTY-TWO

Now that everything that I had ever wanted in life was happening all at once, I had started realizing the depth of how life works even more. The more time I spent in the city, around crowds and the hustle of New York, the more grateful I became to be here. I waited for this forever. NYU Welcome Week was still going on, and Dad had come to campus with me to attend parent orientation while I was exploring the campus club fest in the NYU Kimmel building on Washington Square South. After attending club fest, I walked out of the Kimmel building and started walking straight towards the steps outside The NYU Stern School of Business building where I was to meet Dad right after his orientation ended. I took a right from Kimmel and Stern School of Business and came on the right side directly after crossing the maroon Elmer Bobst Library building.

As I came near the steps outside Stern's entrance, I saw Dad walking towards me. He looked amazing in his grey suit and blue color shirt and the brightest smile on his face. He came right up to me and hugged me as tight as he could, kissing my forehead. I looked up at him and his eyes were slightly wet as if he had just finished crying.

"What happened?" I asked Dad, looking right at him.

"Nothing," he said, rubbing his eyes with his fingers. "They are tears of joy. I just cannot believe that I am actually here today sending you away to NYU," Dad said to me, wiping his tears off. He looked around for a second at the purple NYU letters that stood tall in front of Stern then looked back at me. "I am so proud of you, Maheen. Not just for this but for the young woman have become in life. You are my strength, and I am so proud that you were my first-born child," my dad said, smiling at me. I could see it in my father's eyes that he was so proud of me, and that made me so happy. My parents' trust in me was my pride. I could do anything in life, but I could never break the trust my parents had in me. The blind trust and absolute freedom my parents had given me never allowed me to get sidetracked in life. It inspired me to always do more and to use the freedom to make my parents proud instead of misusing it. As a Pakistani girl, I had the kind of freedom every girl in Pakistan would dream of having and I felt so grateful to God for giving me such a unique family. A family that could go to any extent for me. A family that raised me like a boy instead of a typical South Asian girl. A family who had always gone against societal norms and became the air beneath my wings to help me fly higher. I had the kind of parents that every girl in the world would dream of having. I couldn't have asked for anything more in life. Not even a man, because no man in the world would ever be able to match the endless amount of love, freedom, liberation, trust and care my family had already given me. There's a reason why God does what he does, and there's a reason why he chooses the family that we are born into and not us, because only God knows what's best for you. I wish Ehsan, Emaan, and Mom were there to experience this moment. I still couldn't believe that I was standing in the place

I had only dreamed of till now. That day I learned an extremely important lesson: what you hold in your mind is what you get in life, and if you never give up, there is no such thing as failure in life. The mind can manifest anything into reality because everything begins with a single thought.

Finally, being here after waiting so long. This had me feeling things I had never felt before. It made me realize things about this world that I had never realized before. Thoughts become reality: they actually do. If you believe in something and hold it in your mind as your dominant thought, the universe matches its energy with the frequency of your thoughts, hence attracting what you want towards you. I have experienced this myself in life, and it works with everything in life, big or small. If you want something in life and you constantly think about it all the time somewhere in the back of your head, you will surely attain it someday. When you think about something all the time and you convince yourself that in fact whatever it may be, it will come true, you are constantly filling yourself with belief that whatever you are thinking about has potential to manifest into your life. Efforts are extremely important in life. You need to make effort for everything you want, or unless how will you attain your dreams and wishes?

However, efforts not backed up by belief will always go to waste. Often in life we fail. Our efforts fail not because we were not good enough or that we didn't try enough. Those efforts failed because we didn't believe enough in what we wanted. Or maybe we forgot to believe altogether. Failure is part of life; everyone fails at something in life. However, often times we fail not because we didn't make enough effort or that our efforts were vain; we fail because we forgot to believe. We filled our minds with doubt and fear.

"Oh, will this happen?"

"Can it happen?"

"Is it realistic enough?"

So on and so forth.

Efforts are important in life in order to attain anything but efforts without believing are complete waste. You can't have doubt and fear in your mind and still attain whatever you want. Everything in this world begins with a belief. When you believe in something, you ensure the universe that yes you are capable of manifesting whatever you believe into reality. You may not know how something will happen or when it will happen, but despite that you need to believe in the fact that if you can think of it you can make it happen. The how and when isn't important. Let the universe decide that for you. Just be stubborn about holding whatever you want in your mind all the time. Unrealistic, impossible, unattainable: these are just limitations of the mind that obstruct your way to making your thoughts reality. If you believe that something is unrealistic, of course you will never see possibilities because your mind is constantly focused on all the reasons why something may be unrealistic. Reality does not have one definition that fits all. Reality is a perspective that everyone creates for his or herself through the quality of their thoughts.

Be stubborn about believing; don't be stubborn about the ways in which something comes to you. Let the universe decide how and when to make your dreams real. The power of belief is stronger than everything in the world. Whatever you want to manifest in life will come to you, even if it's hiding under a rock. It all begins with believing. Even if you fail a million times, get up and go after whatever it is that you want because it may not come to you right away. But if you never give up, one day it will. When the time is right, everything comes to you, and the truth is, effort never goes to waste. At least that's what I had learned in life. I was constantly running after this dream of being in New York, and after a year and a half my dream had come in front of me in the shape of my reality. Don't ever think that hard work doesn't pay off. It does. It may not pay off right away, but if you never give up on what you want, you will never fail. Life is all about how you get up after you fall. At this point in my life, I could no longer take anything for granted. New York City, my dreams, the atmosphere of the city, everything was so inspiring to me. When you have worked day and night just to attain something that was on your mind, you can never take it for granted because you know how much of yourself you gave to it. Maybe if I had gotten into NYU right after high school and had not struggled to get to this city, I would have never valued it the way I did now. Struggle is essential in life; it teaches you to value life. My struggles in life had shaped me into the person I was today.

Two days later, I was sitting in my very first lecture as a student at NYU when I received a text message from Sara at VCU. While I was sitting in class, I ignored her message, but when I got out of the lecture hall I checked my phone. The message read, "Hey do you want to join our sorority this semester? We are rushing again."

I replied to Sara's message right away, saying, "Sorry girl, I am actually at NYU now."

Sara seemed really shocked by my response. She replied, "What? How did this happen?"

"I transferred," I wrote back to her. She read the message instantly, but she never replied, so I closed that chapter right there and then.

I wasn't filled with pride but with unlimited gratitude that my hard work had brought me to the city of my dreams while others were still stuck on trying to fit into college social norms. Then again, I wasn't filled with pride because God doesn't like pride. I was grateful to God that he had given me the gift to be able to prioritize my goals in life above other worldly things, and my efforts were finally paying off. I was finally in the city of my dreams.

During the first week of the semester, NYU had welcome events going on that entire week for transfer students. For the first few days I went to every single event because I didn't want to miss out on even a single experience related to NYU. Going to college in New York City meant no typical college campus, but that's exactly what I had wanted all along. NYU was located right in the heart of downtown Manhattan alongside Soho and East Village. This meant that the only people one would meet were those that you wanted to meet, no unnecessary social drama in life. Everyone in New York is always on the go. People have things to do and places to be. No one had the time to sit around, smoke weed all day and waste time. I am sure there were kids at NYU who smoked and wasted their time, but overall, the vibe of NYU was full of passion. You wouldn't want to waste your time on unimportant things, and this was exactly what I was searching for all along. This was the first time that I was ever realizing that patience, what we call sabr in Urdu, pays off. Mine did. That whole year I spent at VCU, wanting the life I had now, was paying off.

Sabr (Patience) is the most powerful thing in the world. Sabr is believing that what you want will come to you. It may not come to you right away, but eventually whatever is yours will find you. Sabr is the ability to resist temptation, frustration, or anger of any kind. It's the ability to wait patiently because you know that your faith is much stronger than your fears. Sabr is the test of your faith. How much do you believe that God will grant you whatever it is that you want? Sabr is knowing you deserve the best. I love this word itself so much, and to me anything is possible with sabr. It's the key to unlocking anything in life. Sabr can make anything possible. When you show sabr for something, the blessing that's waiting for you after your test of patience ends is greater than what you can even imagine. The reward that God has for those who are patient is far bigger than anything in this world. Sabr is waiting and believing that what is yours will come to you even if it's stuck under a mountain. Sabr is believing that all is possible with God. It's become my belief that if I show sabr for anything that I want in life, when the time is right God will say yes to each one of my prayers, and what I will get will be better than my dreams. Sabr is what life is all about.

While living our lives, we as human beings start to think that everything is in our hands. But the truth is not everything in life is in our hands, and though we can write our own story, it's not necessary that what we write is approved by God. Yes, making an effort is entirely in your hands, and God only helps those who know that they must take action to help themselves. Whether those actions and efforts are successful or not is all in God's hands, not ours. When something in life isn't working out, getting angry, frustrated and giving up are the easy options out. Practicing sabr is difficult but it's also the most important thing to practice in life. When you show sabr instead of frustration or simply giving up, God takes charge and rewards you far more than what you could have ever imagined. God likes those who put their trust in him and live life freely while knowing that it is God who is the one that brings everything into your life, and without his will, nothing is possible. When you start believing in this, life becomes a lot easier. Along with sabr, you need to believe in your sabr. You need to believe that God is watching, and your reward will come from him, not from people. Sabr and faith are between you and your God, they have nothing to do with the world. If you show sabr in any aspect in life, through any situation, the reward for it will be ten fold. What God can do for you in life, no human or power can ever do for you, and my own life was the biggest example of this. From where my life journey began, there was no way I came this far and became who I am without God's hand in my life.

The idea of having patience works in all aspects of life. It's not just about getting something. My life is proof of this. After high school I was heartbroken because my dreams of going to a big-name college were crushed. I knew I wasn't a failure, but I still felt devastated for not getting what I wanted right away. I wanted to cry, and I did. It's necessary to cleanse yourself of emotions that do not serve you. But once I was done crying, I was done crying. I moved on in life and went to VCU, yet I didn't move on from my dream. I worked hard and waited for my time. I skipped nights of going out to parties with friends, and I worked for my dreams. I wanted to party too, I wanted to see the world too, but my vision was different than those around me. I wanted to explore life not waste it. I wanted to party but not for no reason, I had to have a purpose in life. I just couldn't stand wasted time. Though that may seem boring to other eighteen-year-olds, I was just mature, not lifeless. I waited. I waited very patiently. I used to tell my mom that I wanted to party when I was at VCU, but not in the way others around me partied because I could never understand the fun in drinking like crazy to the point where one doesn't even remember anything. A person does not need the support of a substance to have fun. If you want to drink, fine, but there are so many more things in life that are more fulfilling than alcohol. Going to frat parties and drinking was never my definition of fun. Though I did want to party, I just did not want to the way frat kids partied. To this my mom always said one thing: "Sabr, your time will come. And you will do everything at the right time, at the right place, and with the right people."

I still remember hearing my mom say these words, and I instantly thought to myself, "How much more patience do I need to show? Did nothing in high school, nothing in college, when was I supposed to live." I still waited, I waited because somewhere in my heart I knew I wasn't meant to live like every other person around me. Somewhere I knew I was meant to live differently because you cannot make a difference in the world if you cannot be different from the world.

A year later, everything my mom had said became true. I was in New York City, living my dream, studying in my dream college, following my passion, hanging out with people who were exactly like me, with a goal in life, and I was having fun according to my own definition of fun.

Everything I once wanted happened in my life, and it was far better than what I had ever imagined. Everything felt like it had fallen in place like the pieces of a puzzle, and this was God, not me. If I had to put the puzzle together, then reality wouldn't have been as beautiful as it was now. God only puts something in your life when you need it, not when you want it. And sometimes you receive more than what you could ever even imagine getting. You think you may know what you need, but God knows exactly what you need and when you need it.

Only after coming to New York, I realized the importance of Sabr (patience), the importance of the waiting. After my class, I was sitting in Washington Square Park where the majority of the NYU students sat and chilled during the day. I was sitting on the edge of the water fountain close to the White Washington Square Arc. Underneath the arc in front of me, I could clearly see the Empire State Building on one side of me and the Freedom Tower on the other side of me. Every time I looked back at life, I could only think to myself, "Everything had to happen the way it did. I had to go to VCU first and then come to NYU so that my experience and the waiting could teach me the lessons I had to learn through the way. Maybe, if everything had worked out initially, I wouldn't have the perspective or appreciation for life that I now had." Often when we must wait for something in life, it's super easy to get annoyed, to get frustrated and sometimes we even want to give up. But that's the test.

God tests you by making you wait for something because he wants to see how strong your faith is and this is what sabr (patience) is all about. Do you have the will to wait for exactly what you have always wanted, or will you become frustrated, give up and settle for anything? If you can wait, the win will always be yours. This is what I believe in and have learned in life.

When I came to New York, everything just fit in. My goals were in place, I had amazing friends, I was living my passion and partying at the same time. It felt like God had showered me with more than I ever even asked him for. That's the power of Sabr (patience). If you can wait for something, what you will receive will be greater than your imagination. This is the belief that is the center of my existence. This life is nothing but a test of your will, faith (Iman), and patience (sabr). Have so much sabr and determination in life that God grants you your heart's every desire, even if what you want seems impossible because in front of God, nothing is impossible. If he's pleased by your willingness to wait and stick by your beliefs, he will reward you with more than what you expected.

The older I grew, the more I started to believe that eventually everything that happens in our life happens by God's will, for he really is the ultimate planner. God knows who and what belongs in your life. Trust and let go. Whoever and whatever is meant to be in your life will come and stay. I believed this with all my heart and soul because in the end God has brought you in this world, and his plan for your life is much greater than your own. Everything that you get in life—opportunities, materialistic things, and relationships—comes to you because God put those things there. Whatever and whoever is put into your life is put there by God's will. Whoever and whatever leaves your life is also done by God's will. And whatever stays in your life stays because it's God's will. Whether it be a dream, love, opportunity, anything you ask for with a pure heart will always be yours. God up there is always listening to you, and only he knows what's inside your heart. God knows what's best for you, and he has a plan for you. You just must try your best and leave the rest to him. You don't always need to know all the answers in life, sometimes you must believe. Belief is the one thing that can make anything possible. This life is a test of your patience and will and if you pass every hurdle and never give up, your breakthrough always comes.

I didn't even know how all these realizations in life were suddenly happening to me in my subconscious mind. All I knew was that I had reached a deeper understanding of life and had gotten closer to the voice of my own soul within the past year. I realized that sometimes the most genuine people you will ever know come into your life when you least expect them to. God has everything planned for you whether you know it or not. The people that will come into your life, the people that will leave your life, the opportunities that are for you and the opportunities that aren't for you. God has it all planned, and it all unfolds as you walk through life. Therefore, whatever is meant for you will find you. You need to go out there to chase your dreams, not people. Do not chase friends; do not chase relationships. Whoever and whatever is supposed to come into your life is going to come anyway. Whatever is meant to stay in your life will stay on its own. If it's asking for too much, then maybe it's not for you.

In college everyone wants to have fun and enjoy their college experience and often in wanting to experience college life you become friends with people that are part of fraternities and sororities. However, later on you realize that you must act a certain way to maintain those friendships. You must go out with them every time they go out. You must go to parties that you may hate just because they want to go. There are a lot of things that people do just to be accepted into or by a certain social group, and that has always shocked me. You cannot lose sight of who you are just to be part of a social group. If you have to let go of who you are just to have friends, then those friends are not worth it at all. When I was in Virginia, my college friends from VCU and my extended relatives all told me the same thing: that it will be hard to make friends in New York because no one has the time to stop in the city. Everyone is running after their aspirations, and in such a fast paced city, it's easy to get lost. I had the complete opposite experience, in a city where it's so easy to get lost in the crowd, I ended up finding myself. And once I found myself, the people who were meant to be in my life came to me effortlessly. I found my best friends in college when I was least trying to find any friends at all.

One day during Welcome Week at NYU, I was at a UNICEF club interest meeting in one of the classrooms on the sixth floor of the Kimmel Student Life center at NYU. Before the meeting was about to start, the President and Vice President had set up an ice cream table in the corner of the room for students to grab some ice cream before the meeting. I got in line, and in front of me stood a girl in blue denim shorts, a grey T shirt, and her hair clipped back by a pin because it was too short to be tied. My phone was dead by now, so I decided to ask the girl the time.

"Hey, do you know what time it is?" I asked, tapping the girl slightly on her shoulder.

She turned around and looked at me. "It's 3:05 pm," she answered.

"Thanks, are you a transfer student too?" I asked, trying to be friendly. The girl seemed sweet.

"Yes, I am transfer student, studying Physics, and my name is Sophie. You?" she said smilingly.

"I am Maheen," I replied, and Sophie and I started talking nonstop to each other. We got our ice creams and sat down together, and little did I know that this random girl that I had met at a random club meeting was about to become one of the most genuine friends I would ever make. Of course, right off the bat, you don't know what will be genuine or what won't be, but sometimes you meet people in life and everything just flows as if you have known them for ages. Such connections were genuine, and I enjoyed making such friends a lot more than going into a social gathering and having to think about what I have to say to force the right impression on someone.

That night I had gone into the basement of my dorm to clean my sheets. On the basement level of my building was the laundry. Beyond the laundry was a mini study room and vending machines for snacking. While I was waiting for my laundry, I sat in the study area and decided to get some work done. It was only the first week of school, but I was already bombarded with homework. While I was on my laptop working, I heard two voices behind me talking to each other in Urdu. I looked back for a second, and there were two Pakistani boys sitting right behind me. One of the guys casually got up and walked over to the table in the corner to heat up his food in the microwave then came back and sat on his seat. The other guy sitting in front of him with an orange t-shirt and long hair began speaking. "Dude, I had four thousand dollars in the beginning of the week, and now I have one thousand left," he said.

"Didn't your parents give you four thousand dollars for the entire month? It's only been a week! What are you going to do now?" the other guy said. I was intrigued now, so I kept listening.

"I spend 400 on dinner with a girl, then I had to get my guitar fixed and we went clubbing too, nah," the guy in the orange shirt spoke again.

"You are kidding me, right? How much money did you even spend on that girl?" the other guy said. These boys reminded me of boys from high school Muslim Student Association, who used to just think about girls and spending money all the time. To be honest, I got annoyed at such behavior because it was just so immature to me. Guys who think like that clearly didn't understand what's important in life and what isn't. Those were the kind of kids who were just at NYU to spend their parents' money and have fun, not to actually make a life for themselves. When my laundry was dried, I took it back to my room.

In comparison to VCU, NYU was so different. Of course, the school had fraternities and sororities, but they were nowhere close to being a significant part of the NYU culture. Despite being in one of the largest cities in the world, NYU was not your typical party school. Students didn't come to NYU thinking how good or bad the party scene would be. Everyone at NYU was there to make a future for themselves. They knew that once they graduate from this school, the world is their playground. NYU didn't have a typical campus; it was very much spread out between Broadway and Soho in down. Unlike VCU where sorority and fraternity culture was the core of the student community and the community was so tightly knit you knew each other. Or should I say you knew of each other. At NYU, no one had the chance to just sit around and waste time doing nothing. Everyone was always constantly running after something or going about their day. I loved that; it was what I had been looking for all along. I always knew I had a purpose, and for me, chasing that purpose was far greater than chasing people, friends, and relationships. In the end, whatever must happen, happens anyway, and the people that are meant to be in your life come no matter what. I met my college best friend when I wasn't even trying to socialize or be friends with someone.

After the gym one day I went to the NYU Kimmel Student Life center to attend yoga. NYU offered meditation and yoga for students free of cost every day of the week with your NYU student ID. Technically the classes weren't free because the budget to fund them came out of the tuition we paid. But honestly, it was amazing for NYU to offer meditation and yoga for the well-being of students. The classes were held on the fourth floor in the room in front of the multi-faith prayer room, which was called "multifaith," but that was NYU's hall for namaz, and the most beautiful part of the prayer room was that it looked over the Empire State Building and the white arch of Washington Square Park. I was sitting on the bench outside the prayer room browsing Instagram while waiting for the classroom door to be unlocked so I could go inside. Meanwhile on the bench in front of me sat a girl with blonde hair, all black track suit and a yoga mat in her hands.

A few minutes later, the blonde girl asked me, "Hey, is this where yoga is usually is held? It's my first time," she said in her Irish accent.

"Yeah, you are in the right place. It's my first time as well," I said, looking at her with a smile.

The girl got up and came to sit right next to me. "What's your name?" she asked me.

"Maheen, what's yours?" I asked.

"Emily. I am an exchange student from Ireland, so I don't really know much about NYU yet," she said.

"Nice, I am a transfer student myself, but I am sure you will love New York. It's amazing," I said, looking right at Emily.

The yoga teacher was late that day, but Emily and I kept talking as if we had known each other for ages. One conversation led to another, but neither of us ever had to think about what we had to talk about. It was all so effortless, and it shocked me because growing up in the American high school culture I had always seen friendships that were super fake and required a lot of effort to maintain. Sometimes you meet people in life for the first time, but it doesn't even feel like that you are meeting them for the first time. Everything just flows organically, of course you can't tell everything about someone the first time you meet them, but you do get a feel for what flows organically and what seems forced. Through the entire yoga class, Emily and I kept talking.

Yoga ended an hour later, and after class Emily and I decided to get dinner together from the dining hall on the third floor of Kimmel. We stood in the line to get stir fry, and Emily told me about how she and her friend Mathew were the only two kids from Trinity College in Dublin to have been chosen to come to NYU for the exchange program. She had applied to fifteen different colleges as an exchange student but eventually came into NYU. I gave my stir fry order, and the two of us picked up our food and found a table towards the back of the dining hall to sit and eat.

"So did you make any friends yet here at NYU?" I asked Emily as we started eating.

"No, not really. Just the kids in my class. I don't know if it's an American culture thing, but people seem really fake here," she said to me.

"What do you mean?" I asked as I wiped the sauce off my face.

"Like, people fake smile at you when you say something to them, and it just doesn't feel real. Like I met this girl in my class, and I thought that we would get along well, so her and I planned to hang out, and I guess she didn't want to hang out, but when I saw her in class again, she kept smiling at me as if nothing had happened," she said.

I laughed at her. "I know exactly what you mean; I guess I can't stay that everyone is like that, but yes that fakeness does exist in people," I said. I took another bite of my noodles. "You know it's really rare to find people that you can just flow with. Like you don't have to think about what to talk about to carry the conversation forward. It just happens on its own. I know I just met you, but I feel like I don't need to think of things to say in front of you to keep the conversation going. You know what I mean?" I said.

"Yeah, I know exactly what you mean," Emily said. "It doesn't feel like I am meeting you for the first time," she said.

"Do you wanna hang out again soon? Like next weekend, maybe?" I asked Emily.

"Yes, definitely. Let's go out together."

We exchanged numbers and decided to meet the following Saturday and spend the day around Manhattan. I thought Emily was a really nice person, but of course I had no idea yet how far this friendship would go. Little did I know I had just met my college best friend. The people who belong in your life automatically end up coming into your life. You don't have to find them or force them into your life. Whatever belongs in your life comes into your life because it's not your plan but God's. I could have gone into a different yoga class at a different time of the day, and Emily could have gone to a different class, and we would have never come across each other. Emily had applied to fifteen other colleges, and if she had gone to any of those other colleges, she and I would have never met. But we had to become friends, and so out of everyone that I could have met on campus, I met her.

The following weekend, Emily and I decided to go to a nightclub around our campus which was hosting a nineties music night. Yes, I was okay with partying now because I had finally achieved what I wanted; this was what I had been waiting for.

The club was called Webster Hall, and it was right around the corner of 5th Avenue and East 11th Street. But before heading to the club, I had planned a dinner with Emily, and I decided to invite another girl named Chloe who I had met during my transfer student orientation. I got ready and left my dorm around 9 pm to meet the girls at Klong, which was a Thai restaurant on Sullivan, directly behind the NYU Kimmel building. I was still very much fascinated with everything about New York.

During the walk from my dorm to the restaurant, I noticed every little detail about this beautiful city. The noise on the streets of endless honks, the yellow cabs, the tip of the Empire State Building shining in red and blue lights. When I got to the arch in Washington Square Park, I stopped for a second. The view was absolutely breathtaking. To the right of me was the Washington Square Arc that sparkled under the nighttime sky with the tip of the Empire State Building visible from the middle of the arch as it spoke to the stars in the sky. To the left of me was the Freedom Tower standing tall on its own, proving that it needs nothing but its own light to be a statement, not just in New York but in the entire world. Two of New York's most iconic landmarks on both sides of me, and me directly in the middle of the two. This was a constant reminder to me to never forget my purpose in life. It was New York that always reminded me to stay focused and get my dreams, and everything else could come later.

Emily and I reached Klong around the same time. "Hey" I said, hugging Emily. We met each other and walked into the restaurant. Chloe was already sitting at the table near the register. She had grey sweatpants on, a grey hoodie, her hair messy, and a book in her hand. For a second I thought to myself, "I told her we are going to a music night, right?" but I kept the question inside and just walked over to say hi.

"Hey," I said to Chloe as Emily and I walked over to the table.

"This is my friend Emily and Emily, this is Chloe" I said.

Emily said hi, but Chloe didn't respond, and the two of us sat down in front of Chloe. Chloe looked at my outfit first. I was wearing a black tube top with jeans and my hair colored. Then, Chloe looked at Emily and noticed her outfit. Emily was wearing a black velvet crop top with black pants and a choker. "Sorry, I really didn't get the memo tonight that we had to be dressed up, plus my roommate is going to a bar with a few friends, so I think I am going to go with her tonight," Chloe said to me. My philosophy in life had become very clear. Whoever meets you genuinely in life, meet them. Don't force anything. I didn't care that Chloe wasn't bothered about going to the club with us even though she very well knew that's what I had invited her for. What bothered me was that Chloe never even bothered saying hi to Emily. When you bring a friend with you, the other person should at least acknowledge them out of respect.

The dinner was very awkward because Emily and I were the only two people talking to each other. Emily and Chloe only had one conversation that night when Emily said, "I am an exchange student from Ireland. What about you?"

And to that Chloe answered, "I am a psychology major at the College of Arts and Sciences." That's the only exchange of words Emily and Chloe had that night. The rest of the time I was the only one talking, but I felt like I had to force myself to drag on every conversation. Chloe was more interested in the book in her hands. Energy doesn't lie, nor does a person's actions. Pay attention to the energy that someone puts out.

After dinner ended, Chloe went towards her apartment, and Emily and I started walking towards Webster Hall for the Nineties DJ Night. I sighed, looking at Emily as the social awkwardness was finally over. It's weird because when you genuinely click with someone, everything just flows the way it did when Emily and I met. But when you must pretend or try to be friends with someone, it's not the same.

Emily and I walked to Webster Hall where there was a long line at the door just to get in. The line started at the end of the block and led up to the black stairs of the club. Emily and I got in line with our tickets in our hands. I was excited and nervous at the same time. Look how kind God was to me that all this time. When I was at VCU and everyone else was partying, I wasn't because I wanted to work on my life. God had put me in New York, and here I was partying in a city that is a dream to many people. The one thing that made me a little anxious was the thought that what if someone tried to approach me tonight or ask me for a drink? I wanted to have a drink with Emily, but not with a random dude. I didn't want that kind of attention. I knew people went to clubs and bars to talk to people, but meeting someone at a bar was the silliest thing to me.

Talking to strangers wasn't a problem, but when someone talks to you at a club, the intentions behind that are something else, and I wasn't okay with entertaining anyone for that attention. You don't know. For all you know, the person you just met at a bar could be a criminal. Plus, if your pastime in life is to meet people at a club, that just shows how desperate you are for attention. I wasn't desperate for attention, and underneath my breath I kept praying that tonight I wouldn't be put in any awkward situation. If I was going to be approached by a guy, I would walk away or just walk out the club. There are certain things in life that are just not who I am, and I cannot be someone's eye candy or passing time. I didn't want to attract any unhealthy attention to myself tonight. I was just going in to have a good time with my friend, not to find boys. In this case, Emily and I were very similar. She was also just there to experience New York night life. Neither of us wanted adulterated attention of any kind. Emily and I had set a code word for when things got awkward and we wanted to get away. We would just say "bathroom," and both of us would understand. It was so cool to finally have a friend whose values and mindset in life matched mine.

As Emily and I got closer to approaching the club entrance, I looked around and saw bunch of people with tattoos, piercings and pink, purple, and blue hair already for nineties rock. The gates opened at exactly 11 pm, and we went inside. The club was broken down into sections. There were three separate dancing halls upstairs and two dancing halls downstairs. The rock concert was upstairs, so Emily and I went straight into the main hall. Inside the main hall, the stage was directly in the middle, and people crowded the stage on all three sides. Emily and I found a spot in the corner where it wasn't as packed with people and started enjoying the music. To the left of me was the bar. I looked around, and people were dancing on top of each other, and I didn't want anyone dancing on top of me, so I was happy that Emily and I were in the corner, grooving to the beat in our own way. The room was dark, and the blue and red disco lights were sharp. The noise was insane. I couldn't even hear Emily, though she was right next to me. The music kept getting louder, and we kept dancing. But then a guy creeped up behind Emily and asked us if we wanted a drink. But then he asked again so then I loudly told Emily I had to go to the bathroom, and the two of us made our way out of the dance floor and went into the next dancing hall.

While dancing, I couldn't help but observe everything that was going around me. Near the bar to my left were all the old rich people who didn't really care about dancing, just drinking. They stood by the bar enjoying their drinks and looking at the crowd. Then there were the two old policemen on the side who were drinking and checking out girls much younger than them. Then there were young college kids like Emily and I who were just there on the dance floor enjoying their night and dancing away as if what came tomorrow didn't matter. I could tell who was a college kid and who wasn't. When you see young adults dancing at a club like they are at homecoming or prom, you know they are college kids right away. Last but not the least, were the people who wanted to get laid, who came to the club with the intention to find someone to go home with. I looked around, but I didn't see anyone who had intentions like that, or at least it wasn't obvious. Thirty minutes later, both Emily and I were done dancing so we decided to go downstairs.

On the lower level of the club were two other dancing halls and benches near the side of the stairs where people just sat and had drinks. Emily and I sat on one of the benches for a bit just to look around and take a break. The group of people right next to her were laughing, chatting, and having drinks. I was talking to Emily when I noticed the girl and guy sitting right behind us were both on their phones and no one was talking to each other, I just saw them take a photo together and then the two of them went back to their phones. Kind of crazy to think we were living in a time when people care more about a picture for social media than an actual interaction. There is always that one group at any public place who is always on their phones; they don't even interact with each other, but if you check their social media, they will take pictures as if they are having the time of their life. Emily and I laughed, then she started telling me about her clubbing experiences in Ireland and how her friend is the crazier one. "I don't talk to guys at bars, like you, but my friend goes all way out there," she said to me. We were having a great time and a really nice conversation when I saw the guy sitting on Emily's right staring at me and smiling. I ignored him. He did it again, and I ignored him again. The way his eyes were scanning me made me super uncomfortable, and I wasn't going to entertain such attention, so I kept talking to Emily as I leaned my back on the couch so he couldn't see me anymore. A girl can tell when a guy is just trying to flirt with her in a healthy way or when his eyes are saying something a lot more. The a lot more is what bothered me because I wasn't an object or something of desire.

That kind of attention has always made me uncomfortable inside because it's purely lust and nothing more. Nobody wants to be looked at like that. I wasn't just my face, my eyes or my skin, I was the brain and the soul that lie beneath all that. A guy you find at a club obviously isn't focusing on your soul or wanting to discuss the philosophy of life with you, he's just trying to enjoy himself, and I wasn't anyone's entertainment. There may be a lot of young girls who like such attention, but I was never that girl and nor was Emily. That's why we were both fine, sitting in the corner and talking to each other. We didn't need any other form of entertainment. Emily and I were talking about life when I noticed that the club had a full menu card and served drinks and appetizers. Emily and I ordered chips and guacamole, and I ordered a drink for myself because this was my time now to enjoy life. I wasn't going to go crazy on alcohol or at a frat party. I was in the city of my dreams, so one drink was a must to celebrate this beautiful life, where everything was finally happening my way. A drink in New York was much more exciting then weed in Monroe Park.

"What would your ideal date be like?" Emily asked me.

"Honestly, as long as I am with the person I love, anything would be a great date, but I would love to sit with my significant other on the roof top at four in the morning and talk about the meaning of life one day," I said laughingly.

"That's so cute," Emily said.

I was talking to Emily when the guy right next to her came over on our side and started talking to me. "How are you ?" he said in his hoarse voice while his breath smelt like alcohol.

I didn't even make eye contact with him, and I kept talking to Emily, who glanced over at the guy and then at me.

"How are you?" he said again.

I literally turned around and looked at him, sighed with a resting bitch face, and picked up my jacket. "Let's go," I said to Emily, and we went to the dancing hall right next to the staircase.

"You are so good at making a resting bitch face," Emily laughed. "Whatever you feel comes right to your face," she said.

I smiled. "Of course. If I don't like someone, then I don't like someone," I laughingly said. The stage in the dancing hall had two poles on it, and soon enough girls from the crowd had started pole dancing. It was girls from the public getting up on the poles and dancing while a crowd grooved with them. A lot of guys stood watching while others danced. Emily and I just stood in the corner because I did not want to get any unwanted or unnecessary attention of any kind. Emily and I both started laughing at seeing how crazy the girls got dancing around the pole. It was funny to me that this was the definition of fun to some people. Later on, the poles were removed, and the stage became a normal dance floor again. Emily and I weren't really dancing but just grooving to the beat when a shirtless guy behind Emily started screaming "I love you." I noticed it and ignored it. Then Emily noticed it and ignored it. He kept saying things for a while, and when we didn't respond, he came right beside Emily and started screaming in her ear, "I love you."

The Asian guy literally began dancing on Emily, and she kept moving towards me and I kept moving off the stage. None of us said a word. Starting a conversation would have been worse because it wouldn't end, and the guy was so drunk he wouldn't back off. Emily looked at me and we gave each other the look that it was time to get out of there, and slowly we made our way out of the hall and towards the stairs. I glanced back to see if the shirtless guy was following us, and thank God he wasn't. I guess he was too drunk to realize that we had left.

Emily and I left the club around 2 am and started walking home together. Luckily, the club was only a few blocks away from Emily's apartment and my dorm, so there was no point in taking a cab. We were together, and of course our eyes and ears were open. New York is honestly safe for the most part. There is always a crowd on the streets no matter what time of the day. If this were the Bronx, I would have never walked home alone at this time because that's just being stupid. I looked over at Emily and started laughing about the whole night. It was funny. I mean, there could have been worse things that could happen, but I didn't go there with the intention to go crazy or seek attention. Emily and I went there just for fun. I have always known where the line is and never do I ever cross it. You can go to a club and still have fun without searching for a date or a casual hook up, and I never understood club hookups. You can't find a "soulmate" at a club. Something that annoyed me about the Western clubbing culture was that people went to clubs with the intention to find a hook up or a date. I hated the idea of that. How desperate or weak are you that you have to come to a club to find a potential mate? Just the idea of that was way beyond me. Soul mates don't meet you in clubs. Only physical attraction is not enough to do anything with anyone. Whoever you are interested in, you have to be interested in them way beyond their physicality. You need to be able to respect them as a whole and be able to see them in your future. That's how you know that what you are getting into is real. Not just a random hookup at a club because you were drunk or the guy was cute. I hated the thought of that.

Emily and I both were laughing really hard on our way back to my dorm just thinking about our night. The best part was that her and I were alike and we shared the same values, so we knew when to walk out of a situation. If I had gone there with a bunch of sorority girls who wanted to get male attention, I would be putting myself in a very awkward place because that's not who I was. I couldn't seek a random guy's attention for drinks. In fact, I couldn't even flirt with anyone in that way. If I did that, then I wouldn't be respected. Rather, I would be objectified, and that was never ok with me. It is so important in life to have people around you who share the same mindset and values as you because not only does it keep you on track, but it also makes the friendship that much more fun. Emily and I may have been from two completely different cultures, but the similarities we shared were endless. She was as close to her parents as I was, and she too did not believe in casual relationships or passing time. Often times our elders think that one should find friends from the same culture because they will share our values and we will have more culturally common in them. I disagree. I don't think it's culture alone that puts value in you. It also depends on who you are inside and your upbringing.

Though Emily was Irish and I was Pakistani, I had never met someone whose core values and perspective towards life were so like mine. It was like God had sent her into my life as my best friend, like, "Here you go." Finally someone in my generation who was just like me. The point is that nothing in our life is ever an accident. The good and the bad both have a reason; we may not know what the reason behind something is right there and then, but eventually we find out why everything had to happen the way it did. God's plan is always bigger than yours, and he has written it already: what will happen in your life, who will come and who will go, what will last and what will not. We just happen to stumble upon things that lead us to where we need to be and what God has planned for us. Sometimes the most random friendships in life become the most important ones.

Later on in the semester I introduced Sophie to Emily and they got along so well that the three of us had made a pack. We called ourselves "The terrific trio." I had finally found my people, the kind of friends I always wanted. The ones that would stay real no matter what, and I never made a conscious effort to become friends with Sophie or Emily, it literally just happened because our lives crossed paths. You find who you need to find. Friends come into your life that you never expected, and those unexpected relationships turn into some of the best relationships in your life. With certain friends in your life, time passes so quickly that you don't even realize when the whole day just went by in a blink of an eye. After meeting Emily and Sophie, I felt like I had literally found the two best friends I never even knew I needed. I realized how true friendships are supposed to be effortless. The three of us never had to fake it in front of each other, we never had to pretend anything. No matter what the three of us did, whether it was a simple dinner, a party or simply just us chilling at each other's houses, everything was fun. When I met my two college best friends in life, I realized that it's not about what you do; it's all about whom you do it with. With the right company, everything becomes fun no matter what you do. I had met some of the sincerest people in life by coming to New York, a place that is actually known for people being too harsh or rude because they are too busy chasing a dream.

The older I was getting, the more I was learning to let go. Whatever was meant to be would be, and whatever wasn't could leave. So, effortlessly God brought these people into my life, made me cross paths with Sophie and Emily because he knew what I needed more than I did. This just made me realize that in every aspect in life, God knows what we need more than we do, so leave it up to him and everything begins to unfold the way he has planned it to. Through my experiences in life I learned that what God has planned for you is ten times better than how you have imagined it in your head. It's all about your faith in him. And at this point in my life, my faith in God had become unshakable. Not too long ago in life, failure scared me. Now not anymore. Failure or success were both in God's hand, and now my belief was so strong that even if I had to go through failure in life again, I had no problem with it. Because now I knew that whatever is mine will always end up coming to me, and whatever escaped me was never meant to be mine in the first place. Finally, I had found friends who were like me. I was finally around those who had the same mentality as I did. People who understood that drinking and clubbing and drugs aren't the only things in life and that following your purpose and passion in life is above parties. That's what I loved about being at NYU: though New York City is the biggest playground for partying in the world, kids at NYU were dedicated and serious about where they wanted to be in life. Even when people partied, they always showed up to their 8 am class no matter what. People enjoyed their life and followed their passions without compromising either. There's nothing bad in doing something occasionally. The problem comes when college kids don't know where to draw the line. You can party, but you don't necessarily have to do it every day of the week, but in the American culture it felt like most kids came to college to party rather than to study, as if parties were something that were highly infused in college culture, especially in college towns like Richmond.

There's nothing wrong with partying, but nothing in excess is healthy in life. We all have a purpose in life, we all came into the world to make a difference in some way or form, and the way you make a difference in the world is that you recognize what your gift is, and you use it. You make a difference in the world by being different from the world. If everyone is doing something, you do not have to do it too. You only must do what your heart feels is right. No one in this world has ever become great by following someone else. In the American college culture, partying is seen as the ultimate way of enjoying your life. I wish people looked at following your dreams the same way. It would be really cool if people saw following your passion as the new standard of cool rather than attending frat parties. At NYU, I finally felt this. Talking about dreams was more respected at this school than discussing what happened at someone's house party last night. Emily, Sophie, and I partied, but partying wasn't the only activity to do in the city. New York had endless life that had to be explored and I did it all with my terrific trio: from cafes, clubs, restaurants, movies, and museums to just sitting at home, enjoying green tea while just talking about life. The most amazing part was that talking about life in our night suits and a cup of green tea in our hands was equally as fun as exploring something new in the city, and that's how I knew that these friendships were real. It was all about the three of us being together; what we did, didn't matter.

I realized that the environment I was a part of now was what I was searching for all my life. I didn't have to compromise my values or my thinking just to fit in. Where I didn't only find myself but found my tribe that was just like me. I was finally in a place in life where I felt like I belonged, mentally, spiritually, and physically. And maybe because I had finally found who I truly was inside and embraced it with all my heart, maybe the universe was responding to my own energy and bringing things, opportunities, and people in my life that were on the same mental frequency as me. I couldn't take even the smallest details in my life for granted anymore because I knew how hard I had worked to get here. But it wasn't just my own hard work that brought me to the point where everything in my life was suddenly working out at once. It was God who had brought me thus far. It was God who knew what was in my heart. From the beginning, he took me through unconventional paths, he tested my sabr by taking me places I didn't want to go. But then he put it all together so beautifully for me in a way that I couldn't have even imagined it to be.

Every day when I walked out of my apartment on East 2nd Street and walked down Bond Street to get to the NYU Gallatin building on Broadway for my 8 am class, I used to notice every single detail around me. The morning sun shining in the cloudy New York sky, the rush of cars and yellow taxis that lined up on the traffic light on Bowery. The shops on Bond Street often reminded me of shops on the fancy streets of Paris, especially because Bond Street was full of designer shops and extremely quiet in the mornings. I would take a right on Broadway to get to the NYU Gallatin building, and the tip of the Empire State building would directly come in my view in the far distance and behind me the Freedom Tower. I couldn't help but think to myself that I was living the life which was a dream to many. So many people in this world dream to come to New York somehow, and I was lucky enough to have this city as my playground, to be at one of the most well-known universities in the world and waking up every day to work towards my dream. I had a long way to go in life, and college was just the first step. However, being in New York evoked so much gratitude in my soul. For a second, I felt like I didn't have to think about tomorrow. Instead, I wanted to live every part of what was in front of me at this very moment in life. The past is gone, and the future is yet to come, so all you really have in life is now.

Often, we spend our time either thinking about the past or thinking about the future, and we forget that this very moment that you are living in right now is actually what you truly have. I had many memories of VCU, but if anyone asked me, "What do you remember noticing while you walked the streets of Richmond?" I wouldn't be able to recall the streets of Richmond properly. Why? Because whenever I walked around VCU, my mind was always so focused on thinking about New York that I never really paid attention to any of my surroundings. Now that I was living that dream, I wanted to experience every moment of it, without thinking about what was gone or what was to come.

The NYU Gallatin Building was located on one Washington Place right across from the NYU Bookstore and McDonald's on Broadway where there was always a line of people getting coffee or breakfast in the morning. I went inside the double glass doors of the Gallatin building and waved my ID at the security guard sitting at the front desk, he nodded his head and smiled at me, and I took the silver elevators up to the fourth floor to get to class, my writing seminar classroom. Upon getting out of the elevators on the fourth floor, the large conference room with wooden doors directly across the elevators was my classroom. I went inside and sat on one of the chairs in the middle of the conference table while no one else had reached yet.

Gallatin classes were no typical classes with desk and chair. These classes were collaborative seminars consisting of ten to twelve students and a faculty member. There were still ten minutes remaining before the start of class, and I sat there on the black rolling chair in front of the conference table and stared at the purple and white NYU flag which was visible through the clear window as it waved from one side to the other from the wind. Tears started dropping from my eyes, yet I had the biggest smile on my face. My happiness had no measure. I was sitting in the place I always dreamed of in my mind. It was my moment to own. Yes, I had a long way to go ahead of me in life, but this was my American dream moment that assured me that anything in this world is yours if you never give up on your dreams and on yourself. Giving up in life is never an option. This was the moment that truly made me realize that whatever you hold in your mind, you actually attract into your life.

The universe doesn't know right from wrong or negative from positive; it's only responding to the energy you are sending out. This is why whatever happens to us in life is a reflection of what we hold in our minds. And therefore, life will only be as good as your mindset. Whatever your mind focuses on is what you end up seeing in life. This is why oftentimes when we fear something, our fear comes true because subconsciously our mind thinks about our fears, and thus energy flows in that direction, and that fear comes in front of us in the form of reality. Your mind focuses so much on your fear that it comes in front of you. Back in high school, my biggest fear in life was failing, and though I was a decent student, I gave so much energy and time to the thought of failing that when it came to college admissions, I did fail. Whatever you think about the most in life is what ends up coming in front of you in life in the form of your own reality. Therefore, think about the things you want to cultivate in life and stop giving your fears and negativity a chance to mess with the flow of your energy.

There is no such thing as "being realistic" because each person's reality is constructed by what they hold in their mind. Limitations don't exist in the world, they exist in our mind, and once we ourselves let go of the idea that "this isn't possible," we will open so much room in our brains for our minds to focus on possibility rather than limitation. This is the biggest lesson I have learned in my life. It's the smallest experiences in my life that have led me to such deep realizations. Until VCU, I never knew what it was like for something in your thoughts to become your very own reality. I had always been a hopeless dreamer, a kind of dreamer whose aims were always the skies. But none of my dreams had manifested into reality at this point in my life, yet the reason behind that was my own negative thinking. In my head I used to think of the worst possible case of everything around me, maybe because I feared failure in life. But now I knew that failure in life is not something to be feared but to be embraced with open arms because there is no great story in the world without struggle or failure. Failing is okay because as long as you are living and breathing, you can always get back up and rise higher than where you were before. It's all about the perspective you have towards life.

A year ago, I used to walk around the streets of downtown Richmond visualizing myself getting everything I have ever dreamed of. I used to visualize myself being in New York, walking down the streets of the city, reaching for my every dream. I used to imagine not visiting New York but calling it my own, and that's exactly what happened in my life. The most surprising part was that when my dreams manifested into reality, everything in front of me was a hundred times better than what I had imagined. It was perfect beyond imagination, and I just couldn't believe it that reality was far more beautiful than my dreams. Every breath of mine only filled me with more and more gratitude. Walking around New York, being at NYU, admiring the city around me, I couldn't thank God enough for making my thoughts come to life in a way where reality was far more beautiful than what I had imagined.

I was so grateful that life happened to me the way it did because it had all led me to become who I was now. If even one event in my life changed, life could have been completely different. It all made sense to me now, that God has planned everything in your life to the finest detail, and one day it all makes sense why life had to happen exactly the way it did. My life had to happen this way because I had to get here and be the person I was now. It all led me to this moment where I was sitting at the conference table, on the fourth floor of the Gallatin building with my lecture notes right in front of me and life being the inspirational force within me.

By 8:25 am, all the students walked in and then Professor Scott walked in. We called him Scott because he didn't like being called professor. Scott began writing our first assignment for the day on the board, and two of my classmates next to me, Mike and Savannah, started talking about the "hope, rope, scope method." I was all ears.

"First year of college, you enjoy your own life; second of year college you start looking around and you hope to find a potential mate for yourself," Savannah paused, and Mike looked at her like what the hell was she saying. I looked at

Savannah then at my own paper, but I was still very much intrigued with what she had to say. "Junior year is for scoping where you basically find someone and hope that they are the one with whom it all work out. Senior year is where you rope them. Ended," Savannah said, rolling her hand in front of her face as she concluded.

Mike laughed. "That's a lot of thought process," he said.

That's exactly what I was thinking, I guess you can go anywhere in the US, but the dating culture that is so engraved in America was the same everywhere. After your initial teenage years everyone becomes obsessed with finding a significant other. Why? I believed that relationships are not supposed to be things that you constantly think about or plan out in life. When it's time, it will automatically happen. Why waste your energy on hoping, scoping or roping someone? In my opinion, you are not supposed to chase people in life. God sends who you need when he has decided that you need them. That's it, period. Relationships should never be something you chase or constantly think about.

One day, after my morning class ended, one of my classmates Judith and I walked over to the The Bean Coffee Shop on 2nd Avenue to grab coffee. I got my regular white macchiato, and Judith got her green tea, and the two of us took a seat at the sofas in the middle of the coffee shop.

Judith took a sip of her tea and asked me, "What do you think about Tinder and dating culture in New York City?"

I took a sip of my coffee and answered, "I think dating apps are so stupid. They are not places where you find a soulmate. People are just on it for a good time."

"Well true, but don't you think it's hard to date in New York? Like no one has the time to commit, so you need to find people somehow," she said.

"Find people somehow?" I thought to myself. Dating was

never a game to me, let alone relationships were never a game to me. I didn't think you needed to consciously find someone. I believed that whoever is meant to be in your life ends up coming into your life anyway and fits right along. "Finding the right person isn't always about us finding them, it's about God sending the right person into your life when the time is right," I thought to myself.

"Would you ever date someone from an app?" Judith asked me.

"No, never. I know that's what everyone is on nowadays, but I would never meet anyone through a dating app because for me, if someone is on an app to find a significant other, that's a red flag that they are only looking for temporary pleasure. It's not organic anymore, you know?" I answered as I took another sip of my coffee. "You know what, Judith; people usually get excited by the idea of dating someone. I don't. I get scared. The last thing I ever want to be is someone's fling or a one-night stand. Gosh I would die if that ever happened. I have been single for so long that a relationship is the one thing in life I won't compromise on. I will not settle for anything less than an emotional, mental, spiritual connection with someone. And a spiritual connection with someone is not found through an app," I answered.

Judith smiled. "Well I think it's amazing that you know exactly what you want in life," she answered. "I was dating a guy in the summer, and it didn't really work out. Made me feel bad for not being open enough for what he wanted," Judith said.

"Why did it make you feel shitty about yourself? If you know who you are and what you believe in, then how does him leaving you change your value?" I asked curiously. "You should be proud that you didn't give in to what he wanted."

"It takes a toll on you," she said.

"To each their own, but if someone leaves you for sticking by your morals, then the problem was with them and not with you," I thought to myself.

"Think about this for a second, when we became friends, we didn't think about becoming friends; it just happened. When you are around your true friends, you don't pretend to be perfect or pretend to be anything that you are not. Then why do we live in a culture that gets so cautious around significant others? Isn't that the one most important relationship where you must be yourself? Where there shouldn't be space for pretending or doubting?" I asked.

I always wondered why every other girl around me in college used to get so conscious about herself around her boyfriend. Everyone gets butterflies in their stomach when they are around someone they like. It's normal, but that doesn't mean you change your entire behavior just to have one person in your life. Just don't try to be someone that you wouldn't be normally. If you must change yourself to be in a relationship or think about minuscule things that you wouldn't think of otherwise, don't be in that relationship. Pretending both in friendships and relationships can only go so far. I think at this point I had left it up to God to bring me the kind of man I wanted because I didn't see myself finding him in a club, on a dating app, or even at college. You shouldn't need to seek love on an app or just because others expect you to. I think if someone is meant to be in your life, you will come across them organically. It will just happen when it's meant to. I mean, I found amazing friends without even having to try. It just happened. So a significant other will happen too, when it's meant to. I need someone I can mentally connect to. In this whole dating culture generation I have never found that. It's up to God now," I said.

"You are right, but I think it's the culture we live in that encourages us to behave this way or constantly look for love on dating apps or clubs," Judith said.

"I agree, and it's sad that the dating culture that we are stuck in values temporary satisfactions over a real commit-ment. I just think our generation values things that don't mean anything, and we make fun of things that actually have value. Maybe I was born in the wrong generation; I can compromise on anything in life, but I won't compromise on love. I want something real, someone who walks through the thick and thin with you instead of just wanting to sleep with you," I laughed as I looked at the time on my phone, it was almost 12 pm, and I had to get to my economics class in Stern. "Gotta go to class girl," I said as I got up and got my things together. Judith got up too. I hugged her and went off to Stern.

CHAPTER TWENTY-THREE

Walking through life, you learn a lot of lessons. You go through attachment to dreams, to worldly things, only to realize that real meaning and value in life don't come from materialistic things or parties or clubs. Real meaning in life comes from the experiences that are soul transforming. You can go to a club and enjoy yourself, but then that time is temporary. It will end, but inside you will feel like you still didn't have enough or that you want more. You will party one week and crave it again the next because on the inside, it didn't fill you. Real meaning in life comes from inside you. It comes from your passions and the image of yourself you hold inside your head. I liked partying, but I wasn't the girl who could ever get addicted to such things because I always had my priorities lined up in life—maybe too much at times. That's why I spent my entire teenage years fighting for my dreams rather than going out and partying. I always wanted to keep hustling, but after coming to New York and seeing how full of opportunities life was around me, I learned the most important lesson in life:

to stop and look around and appreciate what you have cultivated in life so far. To appreciate how beautiful it is to simply be alive.

Appreciation and gratitude for what we have in life brings us much more abundance in life. I wish I had realized this in life before, but that's why life happens the way it does because you only learn by going through life. If you knew everything you needed to know before, what would be the point of God taking you through an experience in life? The more you appreciate everything you have, the more that you will be given to appreciate. Life will always keep going; we will always want something more, but if you don't stop and look around every once in a while, you will miss out on all that you have been blessed with. Hustle as hard as you want, but occasionally you must look around and see how beautiful your journey has been and that you have come such a far way. You have truly become successful in life when you learn that what you have is more than you will ever need, and that anything more is a blessing. Real happiness and satisfaction in life doesn't come from a job or a materialistic object; satisfaction comes from being in sync with your inner self and being content with your soul. I was content with my soul. I used to go and sit by the fountain in Washington Square Park and fill myself with gratitude. I used to notice life, people walking in and out of the park, a fashion model in a pink fur coat posing in front of the Washington Square Arc as her photographer took her photos. Students sat around the rim of the water fountain, some of them read or did homework while others chatted with friends. I don't know why, but everything suddenly inspired me.

A successful life isn't defined by money, power, or materialistic objects. It's not defined by drinking, partying, clubbing or any of those things. A successful life is defined by soul satisfaction, which is an internal experience that has been left behind by the world in which we live today. No one thinks about the soul anymore. Everyone just wants to engage in things that look fun on the outside, which is basically everything superficial. We measure success in this world through numbers: how much you earn? How big is your house? What car do you drive? What college did you get into? And so on and so forth. But no one ever asks the real question: is your soul happy? Are you internally satisfied with how life is at the moment? In my opinion, people don't bother asking these questions because society has brainwashed us into thinking that success means having more materialistically, when in reality happiness is success, and happiness comes from spirituality, not from luxury. There is no end to wanting more in life, whether that be luxury, materialistic items, or money, and wanting more in life does not necessarily mean inner fulfillment. More is merely not enough to satisfy the soul. The human mindset is the only thing that can satisfy the soul, not an object or a standard of life. If your mind is not content with what you already have, it doesn't matter how much more you attain, you will still think it's less.

There are a lot of things in the Pakistani society that I strongly disagree with, but there is one thing about the country Pakistan itself that I admire the most in the world. Every big city in Pakistan like Lahore has slums that are spread out in practically every area of the city. You have the main streets of the city with major roads and green trees, and then the inner roads lead to slums where the roads are bumpy and unfinished. There are numerous shops lined up on each side of the road, and each shop has a silver shutter that comes down at night once the shops close. Right behind these shops or next to them are people's houses, and those houses are smaller than a single car garage in a townhouse in America. Inside the slum houses, there's usually a kitchen, a bathroom if they are lucky or else the bathroom is outside the house. There are no beds, rather mattresses that lay on a single line crunched against one another. The parents in the household most likely work as housekeepers at someone's house, and the kids, if they are lucky, get education, and if they aren't lucky enough, they have to follow their parents' footsteps. Driving around the streets of Lahore's slum you will see kids playing in torn clothes, ripped shoes and some don't even have shoes. But those kids have something that is greater than anything in this world. The kids in the slums smile no matter what. For them, happiness is not as complicated as not getting your dream job or dream house or failing a test. The people of the slums don't know how to measure happiness and success with materialistic objects or gains, and that in itself is the most beautiful message in the world. It proves that happiness doesn't come from what you have, but it comes from how you think about what you have.

The rich elites in Pakistan have this attitude towards the poor that they are good for nothing, that poor people only exist to serve the rich.

When I go back to Lahore and drive around the areas of the slums, I find the meaning of life. To me, the people who live in the slums are much richer than those who live in huge houses in Lahore because the people of the slums realize that living life is an experience of the soul; it's not about your power or possessions. There is life and beauty in the kid playing in mud not caring about how his clothes look but just living the way he can. There is beauty in the smile of the rickshaw driver who knows that he will be doing the same job for the rest of his life, and yet there will be no career growth for him, but he's still happy. All the people I knew in my community who were my age and Pakistani, none of them liked Pakistan let alone enjoyed going there. Some of my friends talked about all the social issues that existed in the Pakistani society, which I agreed with.

Others talked about how they do not like going to Pakistan because the quality of life there sucks, and most of the population is poor. It's too hot there or too dirty compared to

America. I was never like that. I didn't have any issues with Pakistan itself; I just hated the societal values that people followed in Pakistan. I have always looked forward to going to Pakistan in my life because where others see a lack in quality of life, dirty filthy roads, and poverty, I saw beauty and simplicity.

Everything in life is about perspective. Living in America as a college kid, it's easy to take so much for granted. "Oh, I have so much homework. My grades are bad. This isn't working out. That isn't working out. My working hours are awful. I am not getting the raise I deserve," are all things that we as humans take for granted in our day-to-day life. But when I used to go to Lahore and look at people living in the slums, I realized that the things I so easily used to complain about were actually blessings that some of the world doesn't even have. Going to a college is a blessing because girls living in the slums of Pakistan don't even get that. Having homework is a blessing because there are kids in the slums of Pakistan who work in the fields all day long to help their fathers and then study at night on their own because it's their dream to get an education. Pakistan makes me appreciate life and makes me realize that all the little things in life are the big things. The things we as human beings tend to complain about are not even problems, rather blessings that are denied to many, and you can only realize this once you see that there are people in the world that are happy with much less than you. It gives you a deeper admiration for life and never-ending gratitude. Gratitude in life is what gives everything meaning in life. At least that's what I have learned in my own life. Having gratitude for the smallest things in life reminds you that everything is a blessing, and nothing should ever be taken for granted. More will come to you if you constantly give gratitude for what you already have. And what has been given to you by God is more than enough. I have been going to Pakistan every summer since I was a kid, but only as I got older, I realized that there is no better place that can teach you the meaning of gratitude and a fulfilling life other than the slums of Pakistan. If there is one place in the world where I would go to get away from the world and search for my own soul, it wouldn't be the woods or an exotic island in Italy. I would go to Pakistan, see life there, and be inspired by people's spirit for life and their lack of concern for all the materialistic gains in the world. I understood that materialistic gains are important. Success and money define the quality of life and how well we are doing. But in reality, you don't need materialistic objects or money to live a happy life. A fulfilling life experience comes from the soul, not from things. A young boy who has ripped clothes and torn shoes but has spent his childhood playing in mud not giving a single thought about the world or his appearance is much richer in life experience than a young boy who has spent his entire childhood on the iPad playing games. Things don't make you rich in life, experiences do. We live in a world where we focus so much on the external factors like society and its definitions of how to live a "successful life" that we have lost the inner connection to ourselves. The voice of our own souls has been lost somewhere in the noise of society, and it's the norm for us. But who sets these norms? It's normal people like us, so don't be afraid to break the norms and live a little more rather than fitting in a box that others have made for you.

Near the end of December, college was over and I was flying to Lahore on the eighteenth to see Dada and Dadi. Dada was extremely excited, so excited that I was coming to meet him that a week in advance he had started asking me about things I like to eat and the restaurants I wanted to go to. Parents love their children endlessly and selflessly, but in my life, I was blessed to have another human being who loved me the most in this entire world. He could literally do anything for me. Since childhood, he has granted my every wish and he never let a tear touch my eyes. That blessing in my life I called "Dada." His love for me has always been never ending since my childhood.

I jokingly told Aamir Chachu that I was missing my New York Christmas party with my friends just so I could come spend Christmas with him. I said it as a joke, and Chachu took my words so serious that the next day he sent his driver out and around the city just to look for a Christmas tree. He bought the Christmas tree, brought it home, and after decorating it with ornaments, he sent me a picture saying, "I did this all for you."

My heart melted. Everyone loved me so much. On the other hand, Mano khala and I spoke on the phone every day because her days weren't passing thinking about my arrival to Lahore. I loved being the center of attention. It was the day of my last final exam. My luggage was all packed and was sitting in my room to be picked up. I was out the whole day running errands, and then I took my exam. Dad was in New York, so he was going to come to my apartment. We had dinner together, and he decided to drop me to the airport. I had met Mom the weekend before, but I kept thinking about how I wanted to see her before my flight. Around 6:00 pm, Dad came over to my apartment and help me finalized the packing. Mom had sent a few gifts for Dada and Dadi that had to be added to the suitcase. I was flying Qatar Airways, and the flight was supposed to leave at nine. Dad and I dumped my luggage in his car and decided to grab a quick bite at the restaurant near my apartment at 7:45 pm. We knew we were late, but we thought there wouldn't be traffic and we would get there, but the entrance into Queens from New York City became one hell of a ride. Williamsburg bridge was packed with cars bumper to bumper.

Whenever Dad would get the space and chance he would

push the gas and fly the car to get me to the airport. He even cut a traffic light trying to get to JFK. We got to JFK by 8:45 pm thanks to Dad's car racing skills, or else we wouldn't have made it on time at all. I went inside the airport with my luggage while Dad went to go to park the car. I wasn't the only one who showed up late to the check in counter; there was an entire line of Pakistani aunties behind me wearing shalwar kameez and who were staring at me from the top of my head to the tip of my shoes as if they wanted to ask for my rishta. At first such behavior is unwanted and annoying, but the Pakistani side of me knows this so well by now that to me such behavior was amusing and intriguing. The interesting fact is that not only do Pakistani men stare at you, but the women do too. They look at you from top to bottom as if they are checking you out or rating you or something. I stared back at the aunty in the shalwar kameez, and behind her I saw Dad walking towards me.

"We finally made it," Dad said as he came and stood next to me in the check in line.

"Dad, do you see that woman staring at me?" I said as I rolled my eyes in the direction of the aunty. "She's been staring constantly."

Dad quickly glanced over. "Maybe she wants your rishta for her son," Dad laughed.

I rolled my eyes and looked away.

"Your mom and I can't believe that our daughter who we left from Pakistan with is going to Pakistan all by herself," he said.

I smiled and said, "But I have been traveling on my own for a few years now."

"It's Pakistan you are going to alone, not London. It's a different world," he said as we both laughed.

There were only two more passengers ahead of me for check in. I moved up my luggage and stepped closer to the end of the line. Dad was a bit emotional, and I still don't know why because this wasn't the first time I was travelling by myself.

"When did you grow up so fast?" he asked me smilingly.

I hugged him tightly. "Your daughter is going to make an M on the world. This is just the beginning," I said.

"Next," the lady at the check in counter called out. I pushed my luggage to the counter and gave my passport to the woman at the counter.

"The gates are closing in fifteen minutes," the woman said to me as she handed me my passport and boarding pass.

"Fifteen minutes? But there are so many passengers lined up to check in," I said as I looked at Dad.

"Let's go. You still have to go through security," he said to me.

The security line was right opposite the check in counters. Dad walked me closer to the line. I hugged him tightly again and turned around to leave. "Wait" he said, "don't you need your jacket?"

My North Face coat was still in his hands. "No, you can keep it. It's going to be hot there anyway," I said. Going from New York, Lahore is heavenly in December. It's like spring. I gave Dad a flying kiss and ran to join the security line as my flight was leaving in fifteen minutes. There were three separate security lines and none of them were moving.

"Excuse me, can I get ahead of you? I am late for my flight," I said to each person I kept crossing, and just like that I tried making it to the front of the line. But when I got to the front the line was no longer moving. "Patience," I kept telling myself.

"Be patient and everything will work your way."

A few minutes later I saw Qatar staff walking around the security area asking for who was on flight QR704 to Doha. I ran ahead of everyone and five other people who were stuck in the line behind me came running forward. The guy in the maroon Qatar vest got the six of us through security super quickly and walked us to the gate. This was such a close call, such a close call. I was one of the last passengers to board the plane. But with patience and will, everything works out in the end. Panic never helps; patience always wins.

I was in row twenty-two. I took the window seat. The plane was packed, and not a single seat around me was empty. Beside me sat two Indian men. I reached my hand over to the window and began gazing at the clouds in the sky. The plane started moving on the runaway, getting ready to take off. My mind was getting ready too, to take off to new adventures that life had to offer. Each day, each one of us makes plans for life or dwells on dreams that are still yet unfulfilled, but at the end of it all, God is the ultimate planner of life. His plan for your life will always end up outshining your plan. But through my journey in life thus far, I am at a point where I am happy with who I am and will become. I am deeply connected to my soul, and my soul serves as my guide. It always has; it always will. I have learned that the only way to get ahead in life is not by constantly running. Rather the only way to get ahead in life is appreciating where you are now and how far you have come. Dreams are life, and dreaming never ends. I will always be chasing a dream, a goal, an ambition. However, the only way you can achieve new dreams in life is by appreciating your old dreams. By appreciating and remembering the time when those dreams were nothing but a wish and then you cultivated them into reality. What you are living right now was once only a wish that you constantly wanted. Now that you have it, don't forget about it and move on. Pay gratitude for it every day. Gratitude does not only keep blessings to you, it attracts more blessings towards you. Be grateful for everything you have every day because what you have is another person's dream. Gratitude is important every step of the way in life.

Dream even if you're forty and you think that you cannot move careers around because you have gotten used to stability in your life. Find your passion. Even if you are eighty, figure out what ignites the fire in you and keep that alive.

Life isn't lived through stability, money, status, or degrees, though all those things are important. But have you actually lived at all if you didn't listen to your soul or your calling? Give your best, make every effort to attain whatever it is that you desire in life, but remember that at the end of the day we can want something, but only God knows what we need and when we needed it.

Nothing in life comes to you before it's time, and you can never attain more than what's written to be yours.

The flight from New York to Doha was twelve hours long. By the end, I could no longer feel my feet anymore. I landed in Qatar at 5 am, and the stay in Doha was three hours long, and then I had to catch my connecting flight to Lahore. The first two hours at the airport I spent at the Duty Free, and then went through the security check point for my connecting flight to Lahore. After crossing the security check point, I went towards the giant monitor in front of the yellow teddy bear in the center of Hammad International Airport and began checking for my flight number. "Gate 53," it read, which was quite a walk from the security check point. It didn't matter though because my excitement to see all my family members was at its peak. My friends often asked me why I was so connected to Pakistan, even though I was raised in America all my life, and in many ways, I was more American then Pakistani. It's because Mama and Baba often took us to Pakistan in the summer as kids, and I was spoiled rotten by Mano Khala, Aamir Chachu and all my relatives including Dada, Dadi, and Nani. Though I was an adult now, I was still the princess of the family.

After walking for twenty minutes, I saw the sign for gate "53 and 52," and it pointed towards the escalator, which was going down. I went down the escalator, and the entire scenario completely changed. Gate 53 and 52 were side by side each other, but the flight at gate 52 was going to Mumbai while the flight at Gate 53 was going to Lahore. It felt like I was suddenly not in Qatar anymore but in Pakistan. Passengers sitting on the seats at both gates were all wearing Shalwar kameez, men and women. I went and stood near the pillars between the two gates, and I and the girl in front of me were the only two people who were dressed up in western clothes. It wasn't people's attire that bothered me, but both men and women stared at me as if they had never seen a girl travelling alone before. Men in Pakistan stare at you, and it makes sense, right, because men look at women, and that is something that is unavoidable. But now the aunties stare at you too, as if they wanted your rishta for their son. Or worse, they are judging you for sure, the way their eyes scan you from head to toe. No one in America ever bothers to stare at you, but this is a South Asian culture thing: women and men in Pakistan stare at you regardless of your clothes and what you are doing. My mom used to always tell me, "The flight from America to Doha—you can wear whatever you want, but make sure you wear something that covers your hips and chest when you are getting on to the flight to Lahore."

I knew Mom was right, and I respected that. I too believed that there is a place and time for everything, and when you can wear anything you want in your daily life, then covering yourself up for a flight isn't a problem. Wherever you go in the world, you must adjust something according to the culture of the place. I was wearing a hoodie and track pants. No part of my body was visible, yet I was still getting stared at. Clothes matter. I wouldn't wear a mini skirt on my way to Lahore because God has given me a brain to think and know that that's not how I want to be looked at by others. However, clothes were not the problem here because there wasn't anything wrong with my clothes, something was wrong with the minds of those who stared.

"Passengers, please line up for boarding will began momentarily," the woman behind the desk at gate 53 announced. I got in line and boarded my plane. In my mind I kept praying to God that my seat wouldn't be with anyone creepy. When I got to my seat in the plane, there was a white man with blonde hair sitting on the window side, and I had the aisle seat. I sighed underneath my breath.

"Hi," I said to him as I got adjusted in my seat.

"Hey," he said back to me.

"You are going to Lahore?" I asked him with curiosity.

"Yeah, I actually work for the American Embassy in Islamabad and I have relatives in Lahore. So I will be going there first," he replied.

"Wow, nice," I said.

As the plane took off, I fell asleep, and three hours to Lahore went by in a blink of an eye.

The last twenty minutes of the flight when the flight attendant announced, "We will be landing Soon. Flight crew, please prepare for landing," I could feel the rush of adrenaline through my veins. I loved this part about going to Pakistan because I knew that every single member of my family, Nani, Dadi, Dada, Mano Khala, Shahrukh Mamu, his wife Bambi, Aamir Chachu and my cousins would all be standing at the airport to receive me. The excitement of meeting them all, words couldn't describe.

The plane landed at Ilama Iqbal Airport in Lahore at ten in the morning local time. I got out of my seat, grabbed my passport, phone and backpack and rushed out the plane as fast as I could.

When I crossed all the gates to get to the stairs that led down to the immigration counters, as soon as I got to the bottom of the staircase, I saw a man in grey pants and a tan shirt carrying a sign that had my name on it. I knew he was Dada's protocol because Dada had told me on the phone that Shah Saab would be there to receive me. I walked up to Shah Saab and said, "Salaam."

He said "Salaam" and took out his phone to call Dada. "She's here. Talk to her," he said and handed me the phone as he took my backpack from me so I wouldn't have to carry it.

"Hello Dada, I am here. I will meet you soon," I said and gave the phone back to Shah Saab.

"Can you give me your passport?" Shah Saab said. I handed Shah Saab my passport ,and he skipped the entire Immigration line and took me straight to one of the immigration officers. My passport was stamped without any questioning, and Shah Saab and I walked over to the baggage claim area to get my bag. Luckily, I only had one suitcase, which came out within a minute of me arriving at the baggage claim. Shah Saab took my suitcase and walked me out the front door of the airport where everyone's family was standing behind the steel railing to get their family members. As soon as I walked out, Mano Khala and Shahrukh Mamu rushed towards me. I could see everyone else standing in the crowd behind. One by one, I met everyone and hugged them.

Whenever I arrived in Pakistan, the ritual was the same. After the airport, everyone would come over to Dada's house and stay over for a while. All of us started walking towards the cars parked in the parking lot. I saw Sattar Saab (Dada's driver) and said "Salaam" as I slightly bent my head in front of him, and he put his hand over my head to bless me. Everyone of Dada's home staff was still the same. I was excited to see Azeem Saab because he was the one I had spent the most amount of time with, and he was our family member. Without Azeem Saab, Dada's house didn't feel like Dada's house. I sat with Mano Khala in Dada's car, and Shahrukh Mamu's car followed us. The world looks different when something inside you has changed. I had a different level of appreciation towards life now, so even everything about Lahore was inspiring me. The traffic, the honking, the rickshaws on the road. Even the ten people standing behind a truck on the road. The guy pushing the vegetable cart on the street. The rickshaw driver who's been driving the rickshaw all his life. People say why come to Pakistan when you can spend two thousand dollars going to any exotic country in the world? Well, family was my biggest reason for coming back to Lahore, but another was perspective. The perspective you get by looking at the common man living in Pakistan is an eye opener that you cannot get anywhere else. Looking at people in Pakistan made me realize that it's not materialistic things in life that make you happy. Happiness is truly a state of mind, not a measure of possession. People are happy with less than what you have, and yet still we complain about how difficult life is. If you are living and breathing, nothing in life is difficult. You will overcome every obstacle. And life is already a blessing. It's already beautiful the way it is in this very moment. It's the human mind that makes life complicated because it convinces you that what you have is not enough; you should chase after more. But the chasing after more never ends. Yes, if you want something in life, you yourself must go after it. No one else but you can make it yours. But the chase for more is absolutely pointless if you cannot take a moment in life to just stay still and look at how far you have made it already.

While we were on our way to the house, I was looking out the window, when Dada said, "So, you are back now?."

"Yes, I am back here now, better than I have ever been," I said with a wide smile on my face.

ABOUT ATMOSPHERE PRESS

Atmosphere Press is an independent, full-service publisher for excellent books in all genres and for all audiences. Learn more about what we do at atmospherepress.com.

We encourage you to check out some of Atmosphere's latest releases, which are available at Amazon.com and via order from your local bookstore:

The Swing: A Muse's Memoir About Keeping the Artist Alive, by Susan Dennis

Just Be Honest, by Cindy Yates

Detour: Lose Your Way, Find Your Path, by S. Mariah Rose

My Place in the Spiral, by Rebecca Beardsall

Without Her: Memoir of a Family, by Patsy Creedy

The Space Between Seconds, by NY Haynes

Geometry of Fire, by Paul Warmbier

Pandemic Aftermath: How Coronavirus Changes Global Society, by Trond Undheim

ABOUT THE AUTHOR

Maheen Mazhar was born in Lahore, Pakistan and moved to New York with her parents at the age of three. Growing up as Pakistani-American there was always a clash between both of her identities. To her she always belonged to both yet didn't belong to either at the same time as her Pakistani roots and American identity were both close to her heart and at times at odds with each other. She graduated from New York University in 2019 and currently calls New York home.

Made in the USA
Middletown, DE
02 April 2022

63518408R00257